D1521441

BOMBERS, BOLSHEVIKS, AND BOOTLEGGERS:

A Study in Constitutional Subversion

Leon F. Scully, Jr.

The *Los Angeles Times*, October 1, 1910. Los Angeles Times History Center.

BOMBERS, BOLSHEVIKS, AND BOOTLEGGERS:

A Study in Constitutional Subversion

Leon F. Scully, Jr.

Publius Books, Inc.
Houston, Texas
2001

Publius Books, Inc.
2425 West Loop South #200
Houston, TX 77027

www.publiusbooks.com

ISBN # 0-9678424-0-9
LOC # 00-111309

Library of Congress Cataloguing in Publication Data

Scully, Leon F., Jr.
    Bombers, Bolsheviks, and Bootleggers: A
Study in Constitutional Subversion. Bibliography.
Index. Footnotes.
ISBN# 0-9678424-0-9
        1. Constitutional law—Fourth Amendment
exclusionary rule. 2. American Civil Liberties Union.
3. Louis Brandeis. 4. Felix Frankfurter. 5. The Red
Scare. 6. Prohibition.

For Eileen

CONTENTS

INTRODUCTION

On January 21, 1964, the frozen body of 14-year-old Pamela Mason was discovered in a snowdrift beside an interstate highway a few miles from her home in Manchester, New Hampshire. She had been missing since the evening of January 13 when she left her house in response to a phone call from a man who had said he wanted to hire her as a babysitter. Edward Coolidge was subsequently arrested and in 1965 was tried and convicted of murdering Pamela Mason. On June 21, 1971, in *Coolidge v. New Hampshire,* the Supreme Court of the United States reversed his conviction. It did not do so because of any doubt about his guilt—the proof of which was overwhelming—but because some of the evidence against Coolidge was obtained as a result of a search which the Court's majority decided had been made in violation of the Fourth Amendment of the United States Constitution:

> The right of the people to be secure in their persons, houses, papers, and effects, against unreasonable searches and seizures, shall not be violated, and no warrants shall issue, but upon probable cause, supported by oath or affirmation, and particularly describing the place to be searched, and the persons or things to be seized.

The first point that would occur to an English-speaking person not conversant with the vagaries of our jurisprudence is that the Fourth Amendment says nothing of excluding evidence from a trial. It is excluded because of something called the *Weeks* rule as Justice

Hugo L. Black, in dissent, explains:

> It was not until 1914 . . . that the Court in *Weeks v. United States*, 232 U.S. 383, stated that the Fourth Amendment itself barred the admission of evidence seized in violation of the Fourth Amendment. The *Weeks* opinion made no express confession of a break with the past. But if it was merely a proper reading of the Fourth Amendment, it seems strange that it took this Court nearly 125 years to discover the true meaning of those words. The truth is that the source of the exclusionary rule simply cannot be found in the Fourth Amendment. That Amendment did not when adopted, and does not now, contain any constitutional rule barring the admission of illegally seized evidence.

Evidence that the murdered girl had been in an automobile belonging to Coolidge was discovered by a vacuum search of the vehicle by New Hampshire authorities. Coolidge's contention was that this evidence was obtained in violation of the Fourth Amendment and should have been excluded under the *Weeks* rule. But the Fourth Amendment prohibits only *unreasonable* searches and seizures. Was there anything unreasonable about the seizure of the car and the vacuum search which followed? Judge for yourself.

When the police seized Coolidge's car on February 19, they knew that during a blizzard Coolidge "had been absent from his home between 5 and 11 p.m. on January 13, the night of the murder. Petitioner owned a 1951 Pontiac automobile that matched the description of the car which the two witnesses reported seeing parked where the girl's body had been found." Coolidge had been questioned by the police on January 28. "They asked him, among other things, if he owned any guns, and he produced three, two shotguns and a rifle."

> [O]n February 2, two policemen went to petitioner's home to talk with his wife. They asked what firearms the petitioner owned and his wife produced two shotguns and two rifles which she voluntarily offered to the police. Upon examination the University of Rhode Island

Criminal Investigation Laboratory concluded that one of the firearms, a Mossberg .22-caliber rifle, had fired the bullet found in the murdered girl's brain.

Petitioner admitted that he was a frequent visitor to the laundromat where Pamela posted her babysitting notice and that he had been there on the night of the murder. The following day a knife belonging to petitioner, which could have inflicted the murdered girl's knife wounds, was found near that laundromat. The police also learned that petitioner had unsuccessfully contacted four different persons before the girl's body had been discovered in an attempt to fabricate an alibi for the night of January 13.

Nonetheless, the conviction of Edward Coolidge was overturned because of the 1914 *Weeks* rule. "This case illustrates graphically the monstrous price we pay for the exclusionary rule in which we seem to have imprisoned ourselves," lamented Chief Justice Warren Burger. "On the merits of the case" he found "not the slightest basis in the record to reverse this conviction."

In 1914 the Supreme Court had made clear that the exclusionary rule they created, like the Fourth Amendment itself, applied only to the federal government. The individual states, which bear most of the responsibility of protecting citizens against crime, were unaffected. But in 1961, in the case of *Mapp v. Ohio*, the Court, by a vote of five to four, applied the *Weeks* rule to the states. In 1979, in *California v. Minjares,* then Associate Justice William Rehnquist explained how *Mapp* changed our criminal jurisprudence:

> In *Weeks*, the Court held, almost casually, that evidence seized in violation of the Fourth Amendment was inadmissible against the accused at a federal criminal trial. *Weeks* was decided in 1914 when the federal Criminal Code was still a rather slim volume. The villains of the 1914 federal Code, and thus the beneficiaries of the *Weeks* rule, were smugglers, federal income tax evaders, counterfeiters, and the like. The defendant in *Weeks* itself was charged with the unlawful

use of the mails to transport lottery tickets. It is quite conceivable that society can tolerate an occasional counterfeiter or smuggler going unwhipped of justice because of what seems to the great majority of the citizens of the country to be a technical violation of the rights secured to him by the Fourth Amendment to the United States Constitution. . .

[But in 1961] *Mapp v. Ohio* brought to bear in favor of accused murderers and armed robbers a rule which had previously largely had an application to bootleggers and purveyors of stolen lottery tickets through the mail. This difference is not without force in any reasoned perception by the members of the society of how well the system of administration of criminal justice as a whole is working.

Rehnquist, joined by Chief Justice Warren Burger, thought that "a re-evaluation of the so-called 'exclusionary rule' enunciated by *Weeks* is overdue." That re-evaluation is now even more overdue. Thirty more years have passed while uncounted thousands of dangerous criminals have been set free to satisfy its rule. The law-abiding members of our society do not have to be told of how well the system of administration of criminal justice as a whole is working. There is not a major city in the country whose streets can be said to be safe.

This book is the untold history of our law of search and seizure. We shall examine the *Weeks* rule from a different perspective. Our line of inquiry shall concern itself not just with whether it is a valid interpretation of the Constitution, but whether it is the result of a series of frauds perpetrated on the Supreme Court and the American people. We shall explore a constitutional netherworld the Chief Justice and his brethren do not know exists and discover that the exclusionary rule *Mapp v. Ohio* brought to bear in favor of accused murderers and armed robbers is based entirely on bogus cases concocted to protect radicals of a bygone era from prosecution and deportation. It all began in 1910 with the "Crime of the Century."

Chapter I

THE CRIME OF THE CENTURY

In 1905 a labor dispute arose in the structural steel industry, affecting all those engaged in the enterprise of erecting buildings, bridges, and steel-framed structures. The dispute was originally between the Bridge and Structural Iron Workers Union (BSIW) on one side and the American Bridge Company on the other. The union demanded a closed shop contract under which the company would not be permitted to use nonunion labor or to use or deliver materials made by nonunion labor. The company refused, and a strike was called. Shortly thereafter there was a change in the union's leadership. Frank M. Ryan was elected president of the BSIW and John J. McNamara, a lawyer, was elected secretary-treasurer. Both men were considered to be militants.

The strike spread and by 1906 had become nationwide. The employers banded together and formed an organization called the National Erectors' Association, adopting the open shop as their fixed policy. By this they meant that workmen would be employed irrespective of membership in any organization, except that preference would be given to those who had accepted employment in defiance of the striking union.

The strike was a failure. Despite all the union could do, the construction of buildings and bridges continued unabated. In all major cities except Chicago and San Francisco the open shop prevailed. The contest was not without incident, however, and steel-framed structures erected by nonunion labor had a way of blowing up in the middle of the night. Eighty-seven such bombings were recorded between 1906 and 1911.

Nowhere was the struggle more fierce than in Los Angeles, which remained an open shop city despite the most determined efforts of organized labor. The *Los Angeles Times* and its owner and publisher, Harrison Gray Otis, were outspoken opponents of the labor movement in general and the closed shop in particular. The *Times* and its editorial policy were anathema to organized labor.

Early in the morning of October 1, 1910, a bomb placed in an area used to store inks and flammable liquids exploded at the downtown plant of the *Los Angeles Times*, killing 20 people.[1] An improvised, four-page edition appeared the next day with the headline: "Must Blame The Unions." A year later a monument was dedicated to those "who fell at their posts in the Times Building on the awful morning of October 1, 1910—victims of conspiracy, dynamite and fire: The Crime of the Century."[2]

Labor involvement in the *Times* catastrophe was denied indignantly by the unions. A panel of experts named by the California Federation of Labor, after making an investigation, attributed the explosion to a gas leak caused by faulty pipes and fixtures. Others took a different tack. Socialist Eugene Debs accused Otis of dynamiting his own newspaper, comparing him to Nero burning Rome and blaming the Christians. "The Crime of the Century" polarized American society, as the muckraker Lincoln Steffens explained:

> In order to understand this you must know that ever since the explosion in the *Times* building the class line has been drawn here and almost every one has taken a side. Moreover, almost all men have been thinking on their side. If you were for labor the building was blown

---

[1] C. Harvey Elder, Harry L. Crane, R.L. Sawyer, J. Wesley Reaves, J.C. Galliher, W.G. Tunstall, Fred Llewellyn, John Howard, Grant Moore, Edward Wasson, Elmer Frink, Eugene Caress, Don E. Johnson, Ernest Jordan, Frank Underwood, Charles Gulliver, Carl Sallada, Charles Haggerty, Howard Courdaway, and Charles Lovelace.

[2] Grace H. Stimson. *Rise of the Labor Movement in Los Angeles.* Los Angeles: University of California Press, 1955, 366.

up by gas. If you were on the capitalist side, it was blown up by dynamite put there by labor men. Out of this had developed a new principal party, the Socialist party, and with it were all kinds of workingmen and their friends and others, enough to make a number near enough to a majority to frighten everybody on the other side. And those on the other side had also united into a solid mass.[3]

On the same day as the *Times* disaster, a bomb exploded just outside a bedroom window at Otis's home, but no one was hurt. Another bomb was planted at the house of F.J. Zeehandelaar, the secretary of the Merchants and Manufacturers Association (M&M), but did not go off. It consisted of 15 sticks of dynamite attached by electric wires to an alarm clock; the clock had been wound too tightly and had stopped. The apparatus was dismantled and kept for evidence.

Rewards for the apprehension and conviction of the perpetrators were voted by the Los Angeles City Council and the California Legislature. Private organizations, including labor unions, announced sizable rewards as well. Funds were raised for the families of those who had perished on October 1. The M&M appropriated $50,000 for the single purpose of hunting down the "unionist fiends." On Christmas Day of 1910 another bombing took place: the Llewellyn Iron Works, an open shop, was wrecked by dynamite.

Since the hunt was to be nationwide and because there was no such organization as the FBI at the time, Los Angeles Mayor George Alexander decided to appoint a special investigator. He chose William J. Burns, a famous detective and head of a well-known detective agency. Burns accepted the appointment on the condition he be allowed to operate in secret.

The Erectors' Association had previously hired the Burns organization to investigate the bombings of open shop construction sites; thus Burns did not have to start from scratch. The month before the *Times* dynamiting, a bombing had taken place in Peoria,

---

[3] *LaFollette's Weekly Magazine*, December 9, 1911, 8.

Illinois; two bombs had been planted, but only one had exploded. Burns had been able to examine the undetonated bomb and trace the dynamite to its source. He knew it had been purchased by a man calling himself J.W. McGraw.

Burns had two advantages, known only to him and his closest associates. He knew that the unexploded bomb found at Zeehandelaar's house was identical to the one found in Peoria, and he had an informant within the ranks of the BSIW named Herbert Hockin. Hockin told him the men responsible for most of the bombings over the last five years were Ortie McManigal and James B. McNamara. McNamara was the younger brother of the BSIW's secretary-treasurer.

The dynamite in the unexploded bomb in Los Angeles had been purchased from the Giant Powder Works near San Francisco by three men, one of whom had given his name as J.B. Brice. The detective work is a story in itself. Suffice it to say that by April of 1911, Burns knew how and by whom the bombs had been made. He knew that J.W. McGraw was really Ortie McManigal, that J.B. Brice was in fact James B. McNamara, and that both took orders and were paid by John J. McNamara from BSIW funds. All three suspects were placed under surveillance.

On April 12 McManigal and James McNamara went by train from Toledo, Ohio, to Detroit, Michigan. A new railway station had been built in Detroit by nonunion labor, and Burns believed they intended to blow it up. Soon after their arrival they were arrested by Burns's detectives and Detroit police. Their luggage was searched and "twelve mechanical bombs such as have been used in the bomb outrages were found. These had fuses and caps attached and were ready for use."[4]

The prisoners were told they were being arrested in connection with a recent bank robbery in Chicago. Knowing they were innocent of that crime and confident of establishing an alibi, the two waived extradition and were taken by train to Chicago. On the way they realized they had been duped, and McNamara unsuccessfully tried to bribe his captors.

---

[4] "Union Leaders Arrested For Bomb Outrage," *New York Times*, April 23, 1911.

ARM OF DYNAMITER HAS BROAD SWEEP

Spreads Death and Disaster From Coast to Coast Within Half a Decade.

INDIANA HAS FULL SHARE

Series of Explosions Wreck Buildings, Bridges and Factories Throughout Country.

Members of Executive Board Photographed in Iron Workers' Headquarters.

LEFT TO RIGHT—F. M. RYAN, CHICAGO, PRESIDENT; M. J. YOUNG, BOSTON; J. T. BUTLER, BUFFALO, SECOND VICE PRESIDENT; P. A. COOLEY, NEW ORLEANS; H. W. LEGLEITNER, PITTSBURG; H. S. HOCKIN, DETROIT; EUGENE A. CLANCY, SAN FRANCISCO, FIRST VICE PRESIDENT.

AMERICAN CENTRAL LIFE BUILDING, HEADQUARTERS STRUCTURAL IRONWORKERS.

PEN PICTURE OF DETECTIVE BURNS, CRIMINAL HUNTER, AS HE REALLY IS

There Is Nothing About Him to Suggest the Nick Carter Idea—He Is Modest and Unassuming, but Possesses a Strange Personality—Giant for Work.

Hopes to Establish General Conspiracy

GOVERNOR HOLDS HIS ACTION FAIR

Denies Imputations to Contrary in Granting California Requisition for McNamara.

ASSERTS LAW WAS OBEYED

Judge Collins Says Only Question Before Him Was Identification of Man Wanted.

DOESN'T CONNECT FRENCH LICK

THOMAS TAGGART GIVES VIEWS

Says If Dynamiters Had Been After Hotel They Would Have Caused More Damage.

IRON WORKERS' UNION GROWS

REPORT SHOWS PROSPERITY

THE INDIANAPOLIS STAR, MONDAY, APRIL 24, 1911.

GOMPERS DECLARES ARREST IS OUTRAGE

Bitterly Criticises Indiana Authorities for Manner in Which McNamara Was Extradited.

HINTS AT BIG DEVELOPMENTS

Declines to Forecast Any Step Labor Organizations May Take —Talks of Habeas Corpus.

Guarding Dynamite in Indianapolis Basement.

PATROLMAN L. TYNER, GUARDING 100 POUNDS OF DYNAMITE IN BASEMENT OF AMERICAN CENTRAL LIFE BUILDING.

M'NAMARA IS NOW NEAR KANSAS CITY

Indianapolis Man Being Rushed West Eats Breakfast in St. Louis.

SILENT THROUGHOUT MEAL

Handcuffed to Detective, Attention of Crowds Distresses and Depresses Prisoner.

THINKS M'NAMARA WILL HANG

PROSECUTOR IS SURPRISED

Assistant District Attorney of Los Angeles, Cal., Declares Evidence Complete Against Union Man.

PRISONERS HIDDEN IN RUSH WESTWARD

Locked in Pullman Compartments and Under Heavy Guard, Trio Is Hurried to Coast.

SECRECY IS SAFETY MOVE

Fear of Further Dynamiting and Loss of Life Is Cause of Stealthy Trip.

LABOR MEN BITTER

THREE MEN NAMED

MARION GRAND JURY WILL INVESTIGATE DYNAMITING

Propose to Probe Local Attacks and to Seek Persons Who Stored Explosives Here.

Prosecutor Here From Los Angeles

W. J. FORD

M'Manigal Admits Dynamite Horrors

SLEUTH TELLS HOW NET WAS SPREAD ABOUT McNAMARA AND McMANIGAL

ANDERSON REALTY MAN DIES.

Milton Hersberger, Realty Agent of Home in Anderson.

PLANT WRECKING RECALLED.

The Young Business Man

The Continental National Bank

Reprinted courtesy of Indianapolis Newspapers, Inc.

Confronted with the evidence against him, and having been told by J.B. McNamara that it was every man for himself, McManigal confessed. He gave a detailed account of the bombings and of the complicity of John J. McNamara, Frank Ryan and a number of other BSIW officials. It was James B. McNamara who planted the *Los Angeles Times* bomb, said McManigal; he told how "McNamara turned open the stopcocks of the gas mains of the building when he set the bomb."[5]

On Saturday, April 22, six months after the *Times* bombing, William J. Burns and local policemen walked in on a meeting of the BSIW executive board at the union headquarters in Indianapolis with a warrant signed by the governor of Indiana for the arrest of John J. McNamara. Less than an hour later, after a snap arraignment, McNamara was on his way to Los Angeles. That night the two McNamara brothers and Ortie McManigal were in a closely guarded railway car headed for California.

The raiders also held a warrant issued by a local judge to search the BSIW offices or headquarters, a three-room suite on the fifth floor of the American Central Life Building in downtown Indianapolis. While this search was going on, one of the officers talked to the building superintendent, who told him he had given John J. McNamara permission to use a recessed area of the basement for storage space. The warrant could not have described this as a place to be searched since the police did not know of its existence until after the search was under way.

In the basement the police found a small room made of rough pine boards which had been constructed in an alcove. The door was secured by a padlock to which McNamara was said to have the only key. Breaking the lock, the police entered and found shelves on which lay "100 pounds of dynamite, several yards of fuse and twelve clocks similar to those with which bombs are discharged."[6] Also found were files and account books to which the hierarchy of the BSIW attached considerable value. According to the *Indianapolis Star,* they were evidence of a most incriminating character:

---

[5] *LaFollette's Weekly Magazine*, December 16, 1911, 8.
[6] "Dynamite Is Found Here," *Indianapolis Sunday Star*, April 23, 1911.

> Among them are receipts showing that money had been paid out by the iron workers organization to the men charged with actual part in the blowing up of the Los Angeles newspaper plant. Other receipts prove, the detectives say, that the organization paid money to men suspected of having had part in other explosions. The dates of the receipts and those of the explosions correspond, they say.[7]

On Monday morning the union sued for the return of the papers found in the basement vault. It had a rival claimant in the Marion County Grand Jury, which was investigating a local bombing at the Citizens Gas Company, suspected to be the work of the Iron Workers Union. After hearing the arguments of counsel, Judge J.T. Markey awarded the books and papers to the grand jury. Union representatives would be permitted to examine them only under court supervision, and outsiders would not be permitted to see them at all.

There is no doubt but that the documents in question were the ones found with the dynamite in the basement vault. Page 2 of the *New York Times* of April 25, 1911, states that the "books and papers demanded to-day by the grand jury were stacked indiscriminately about the four packages of dynamite fuses, explosive caps and alarm clocks discovered by the police in Saturday night's raid." The *Indianapolis News* of the same day reported: "Judge Markey's Order. It is probable the grand jury will spend the next few days going over the records taken from the basement room of the American Central Life building."[8]

The focus now changed to Los Angeles, where the McNamara brothers were to be tried for the first degree murder of Charles Haggerty, a Linotype operator killed in the *Times* explosion. The McNamaras claimed the whole thing was a capitalist plot to discredit labor. The American Federation of Labor (AFL) accepted this thesis at face value. To organized labor, the innocence of the McNamaras became an article of faith, and their cause a crusade.

---

[7] "Burns Finds New 'Plant,'" *Indianapolis Star*, April 24, 1911.
[8] "Markey Reads Order to the Grand Jury," *Indianapolis News*, April 25, 1911.

Rallies were held and supporters were asked to contribute a day's pay to a legal defense fund. "McNamara Brothers Not Guilty" buttons were sold, and union members and their families were urged to wear them.[9] A movie—*A Martyr to His Cause,* in which John McNamara was the hero—drew large crowds.

The BSIW organized a Legal Defense Committee and appealed to other unions for assistance. The AFL formed a McNamara Ways and Means Committee led by Frank Ryan and Samuel Gompers. "Advised of the arrests made in Detroit and elsewhere, President Samuel Gompers of the American Federation of Labor said that he believed they were the result of a carefully laid plot against union labor organizations."[10]

Labor Day of 1911 was declared to be "McNamara Day." On the first Monday of September, in parades throughout the United States, union men wearing McNamara buttons and carrying signs proclaiming their innocence, marched to show their solidarity with their imprisoned brethren. Later that month Gompers went to Los Angeles to visit the McNamaras. After having his picture taken with them, the AFL president expressed once again his belief that they had been framed.

As their chief counsel the Ways and Means Committee retained the famous trial lawyer, Clarence Darrow. The team of lawyers hired to assist him included the Socialist candidate for mayor of Los Angeles, Job Harriman. The McNamaras demanded separate trials, and the prosecution elected to try James B. McNamara first. His trial began on October 11, 1911, just over a year after the crime, with Ortie McManigal scheduled to be the chief witness for the prosecution.

As a general proposition a defendant may not be convicted solely on the uncorroborated testimony of an accomplice. In the case of *California v. James B. McNamara* this was not a factor. A salesman at the Giant Powder Works near San Francisco could identify McNamara as the "J.B. Brice" who purchased 500 pounds of

---

[9] Stimson, 394.
[10] *LaFollette's Weekly Magazine,* April 29, 1911, 9.

dynamite in September of 1910. Experts would prove that the dynamite found at the home of Zeehandelaar, the secretary of the M&M, came from that particular batch. The alarm clock to which that dynamite was attached—the one which was wound too tight—was identical to the clocks found in McNamara's luggage when he and McManigal were arrested in Detroit.

Moreover, the prosecution could place the younger McNamara near the scene of the explosion at the time the bomb was planted. One J.B. Brice from Chicago, Illinois, registered at the Baltimore Hotel in downtown Los Angeles on the morning of September 29, 1910. The room clerk, who happened to be from Chicago, struck up a conversation with Brice. He would testify that J.B. Brice was really James B. McNamara and that he checked out of the hotel at 7 p.m. on September 30, six hours before the *Times* blew up.[11] The circumstantial evidence the prosecution had amassed would corroborate McManigal's testimony in every detail. The case against James B. McNamara was open and shut. The case against his brother was another matter.

John J. McNamara, the secretary of the Iron Workers Union, was the director and paymaster of the dynamite conspiracy. He was also the conduit between local union officials who wanted a "job" done in their bailiwick and his brother and McManigal, who did the actual dynamiting. John McNamara would receive a request from Peoria, for example, and dispatch James or Ortie, or both of them, to take care of it.

The expenses of the dynamiting campaign were not paid directly out of union accounts, but in cash by John J. McNamara from funds provided him by the union. He kept meticulous records. After a job was completed, James McNamara and Ortie McManigal would submit what amounted to a bill for time and expenses, with outlays for travel and lodging being documented by train and hotel receipts. John would pay Jim and Ortie in cash and get a receipt from them in return. These records were kept in the vault in the basement of the Indianapolis office building.

---

[11] Geoffrey Cowan. *The People v. Clarence Darrow: The Bribery Trial of America's Greatest Lawyer.* New York: Times Books/Random House, 1993, 85-87.

Walter Drew was a lawyer who headed the National Erectors' Association. On October 6, 1911, Drew wrote Attorney General George W. Wickersham requesting that the federal government take steps to impound the evidence found in "McNamara's vault," which he described in his letter:

> In the vault constructed by McNamara's direction in the basement of his office building, were found 43 pounds of dynamite, 14 little alarm clocks such as were used in these explosions, dry-cell batteries, a fibroid case made especially to order just of the size and shape to hold a ten quart can of nitro-glycerine, and a large quantity of correspondence, photographs, records, etc . . .
>
> [A] large number of letters were found of most incriminating character,—letters from J.J. McNamara to local union officials, including members of the Executive Board, regarding explosions contemplated, and also letters from such officials to him, clearly showing that explosives were carried from Indianapolis to different sections and used in pursuance of an understanding between the officers at headquarters and those stationed in different localities. The testimony of the witness McManigal that he was assisted at different times by these local officials is fully corroborated by these letters.[12]

Drew had no doubt of the importance of this evidence. "About the only hope that the other side have in these cases is to get enough advance knowledge of the evidence to enable them to explain, evade, destroy or make [a]way with the proof in some manner."[13] He had no illusions about the other side's scruples either. "There is

---

[12] Walter Drew to George W. Wickersham, October 6, 1911, File No. 156777-26, No. 112, Straight Numerical Index, Department of Justice Archives, National Archives Building, Washington, DC. All correspondence relating to the McNamara trial bears the prefix 156777 followed by a distinguishing number. Hereinafter such a citation will be identified simply by serial number.

[13] Walter Drew to James Badorf, July 19, 1911, Box 3, Walter Drew Papers, Bentley Historical Library, University of Michigan, Ann Arbor, Michigan, hereinafter Drew Papers.

no coup they would not undertake to get these papers, once they know how important they are."[14]

Drew feared that this evidence would be handed over to the Iron Workers Union and had reason to believe that Marion County Prosecutor Frank Baker had gone over to the other side. In April Baker had successfully contested the union's suit for the return of the papers found in the basement vault. In May he had permitted two local certified public accountants, paid by the Erectors' Association, to go over the accounts of the union.[15] Since then, according to Drew, Baker had undergone a change of heart and Drew thought the prosecutor had been "bought" by the union. A detective working for the Erectors' Association had told him that "they [the union] own him [Baker] Body & soul."[16] Drew had his doubts about Marion County Judge J.T. Markey as well,[17] and he begged Wickersham to take action to protect the evidence before it was too late.

> The need for Federal action in Indianapolis is emphasized by the fact that the Prosecuting Attorney of Marion County is not only taking no steps to prosecute under State Laws, such crimes as might be within State jurisdiction, but has publicly announced that he intends to turn over to attorneys for J.J. McNamara and the Executive Board of the Iron Workers' Union the greater part of the evidence seized in the secret vault in the basement, although at the time of seizure the Executive Board disclaimed all knowledge of such vault or authority for its contents. The return of this evidence means, of course, its absolute loss to any prosecution, Federal or State, to which it might be material.[18]

A week before, when the Attorney General was in New York City, Drew had shown him a telegram from Los Angeles County Prosecutor John D. Fredericks stating that he had "full proof of the

---

[14] Drew to Badorf, July 22, 1911, Box 3, Drew Papers.

[15] Badorf to Drew, May 13, 1911, Box 3, Drew Papers.

[16] R.J. Foster to Drew, October 5, 1911, Box 7, Drew Papers.

[17] Drew to Badorf, July 19, 1911, Box 3, Drew Papers.

[18] Drew to Wickersham, October 6, 1911, File No 156777-26.

violation by McManigal, and others, of the statutes of the United States regarding transportation and shipment of dynamite."[19] At the suggestion of Wickersham, Drew phoned Assistant Attorney General William R. Harr in Washington but got little cooperation. In a letter written later that day Harr advised Wickersham against federal intervention.

> Resting, as the complaint does, entirely upon the confession of McManigal, it did not seem to me advisable, in view of the public feeling that has been excited over the proceedings against the alleged dynamiters, for the Federal Government to take any hand in the matter until we have something more substantial to proceed upon than at present. It looked to me as if the State authorities merely wished to use the Federal Government for the purpose of pulling their chestnuts out of the fire, and I did not think it good policy for the Department to allow itself to be used for such purpose.[20]

On October 18, 1911, one week after the trial of James B. McNamara began in Los Angeles, attorney Leo M. Rappaport, in the case of *Indiana v. John J. McNamara*, Marion County Criminal Court Docket No. 39889, filed a motion on behalf of the defendant praying for "an order of Court directing said Prosecuting Attorney and Grand Jury to surrender immediately to him any and all such documentary evidence belonging to said defendant."[21]

At this point fate intervened. Earlier in October, President William Howard Taft had gone to California to mend some political fences. In response to a letter from Harrison Gray Otis asking for an audience, Taft had arranged to meet with Otis at the home of Mrs. William Edwards, Taft's sister, in Los Angeles. The newspaper publisher had asked for the opportunity to persuade the President to take action against the dynamiters.

---

[19] "Transcript Of Message Repeated Over Long Distance Telephone To Mr. Harr Today, By Direction Of The Attorney General," September 28, 1911, No. 156777-24.

[20] W.R. Harr to Attorney General, No. 156777-13.

[21] A copy of the motion may be found in file No. 156777.

One would think that Taft might have been in a receptive mood the night of October 17, having escaped an attempt on his life the day before. In the early morning of October 16, shortly before the train carrying the President from San Francisco to Los Angeles was to pass over the El Capitan Bridge near Santa Barbara, a watchman discovered a bomb affixed to the bridge containing 39 sticks of dynamite.

With Otis was Oscar Lawler, a young lawyer retained by the Merchants and Manufacturers Association who had previously served with the Justice Department. "Lawler knew the facts of the case and enjoyed the president's confidence." After Lawler assured the President that there had been wholesale violations of federal law, Taft said that he would instruct the Attorney General to take appropriate action.[22] Wickersham in turn ordered Charles W. Miller, the U.S. attorney in Indianapolis, to gain control of the evidence. On November 9, 1911, Miller was able to report to the Attorney General that he had it in custody.

> We had been fighting night and day for more than a week to get certain evidence for use before the Grand Jury, which met on the 7th day of November, for the investigation of the dynamite matter, and were unable to do so, being opposed by the prosecuting attorney of Marion County, the Attorneys of the Iron Workers' Association, and the vacillation and real opposition of the Judge of the Criminal Court.
>
> We finally got the important books, papers, documents, records and writings under the order of the Judge of the [Federal] District Court, after showing was made before the Grand Jury that the parties in whose possession these papers were had failed to comply with our subpoenas duces tecum.
>
> The evidence obtained seems to be very valuable for use in this and other jurisdictions, but I have had no time to

---

[22] Geoffrey Cowan, in *The People v. Clarence Darrow*, 196-202, relates the story of the meeting between Taft and Otis, the assassination attempt on Taft, and the battle over the evidence found in the basement vault in the Indianapolis office building.

carefully examine same. I am trying to get all other matters out of the way that are to be presented to the Grand Jury this week, so that we can arrange to take up this investigation and make it a very thorough one.[23]

Meanwhile in Los Angeles, the process of selecting a jury to try James B. McNamara was proceeding at a snail's pace. In the primary election for mayor held on October 31, Darrow's assistant, Job Harriman, finished first, running well ahead of incumbent Mayor George Alexander. In the final election on December 5 it would be the Socialist slate led by Harriman against the Good Government ticket headed by Alexander. The Socialists were a strong favorite.

By late November eight jurors had been selected; the defense had seven peremptory challenges left and the prosecution five. More than 500 veniremen had been examined. Darrow had a team of investigators canvassing the prospective jurors and checking their backgrounds. His chief investigator was Bert Franklin, a former deputy U.S. marshal. On Tuesday, November 28, Franklin was arrested on the streets of Los Angeles in the act of passing $4,000 to a prospective juror. Darrow was but a short distance away.

Unbeknownst to their supporters, the McNamaras had been plea bargaining. On Thanksgiving Day, November 30, a bargain was struck. John J. McNamara agreed to plead guilty to conspiracy in the bombing of the Llewellyn Iron Works for which he was to receive a 15-year sentence. All other charges against him were to be dropped. James B. McNamara was to plead guilty to murder and receive a life sentence.

The plea bargain required the approval of Superior Court Judge Walter Bordwell. On Friday morning, December 1, 1911, when the court was called to order, Prosecutor Fredericks asked for a continuance until 2:00 p.m. "I cannot tell your honor the reasons," he said, "but must ask you to accept my word that they are of the highest importance."[24] The attorneys conferred with Judge Bordwell in his chambers and obtained his consent to the plea

---

[23] Charles W. Miller to Attorney General, November 9, 1911, No. 156777-39.

[24] "Guilty Pleas By McNamaras In Open Court In Los Angeles," *Boston Globe*, December 2, 1911.

bargain. By 2:00 p.m. the courtroom and the corridors were packed and a large crowd had gathered outside.

> The McNamara trial was a *cause célèbre*. Some sixty correspondents were in Los Angeles to report developments to all the leading United States newspapers and news services, as well as to papers in the European capitals of London, Paris, and Berlin . . . It was much more than a simple case of murder; social, industrial, and political overtones made the McNamara trial an event of unlimited significance in American labor history.[25]

The McNamaras' confessions were electrifying. "Angry men threw their McNamara buttons to the ground, spoke harsh words, and made rash threats; others wept tears of defeat over a lost ideal." Things did not bode well for the Socialist candidates; "Harriman buttons 'fell off like leaves off a tree.'"[26] The enormity of the "McNamara Affair" can only be comprehended by reading the newspapers of December 2, 1911.

Labor leaders were genuinely and profoundly shocked. "I am astounded, I am astounded," said Samuel Gompers, "my credulity has been imposed upon. It is lightning out of a clear sky."[27] The Ways and Means Committee issued a statement "To the American Public on the McNamara Case:"

> Organized labor of America has no desire to condone the crimes of the McNamaras. It joins in the satisfaction that the majesty of the law and justice has been maintained and the culprits commensurately punished for their crime . . .
>
> It is cruelly unjust to hold the men of the labor movement either legally or morally responsible for the crime of an individual member. No such moral code or legal responsibility is placed upon any other association of men in our country . . .

---

[25] Stimson, 396.

[26] Ibid., 407.

[27] "Gompers Is Astounded," *Boston Globe*, December 2, 1911 (morning ed.).

Tomorrow's Globe
Be sure to call early with your advertisements for tomorrow's Globe. Help Wanted? Use 4th Globe.

Best Results
are to have your advts in tomorrow's Globe. Houses For Sale? Use the Globe.

The Boston Daily Globe.

GUILTY PLEAS BY McNAMARAS
IN OPEN COURT AT LOS ANGELES

GOMPERS IS ASTOUNDED

Credulity Imposed Upon, Says Head of A. F. of L.

SAMUEL GOMPERS,
President of the American Federation of Labor.

No Hint, He Says, With Tears In Eyes, of the Truth.

NEW YORK, Dec 1—"I am astounded, I am astounded; my credulity has been imposed upon. It is lightning out of a clear sky."

These exclamations were those of Samuel Gompers, president of the American Federation of Labor, when advised tonight of the pleas of guilty in the McNamara case.

On Way to Washington.

Mr Gompers, who was on his way to Washington, was doing in a railway car, when he was astonished at a few lines read to by an Associated Press reporter. It reflected on the face of the train conductor as he continued to the courtroom at Los Angeles where the men to whose defense he had given and touched so strikingly assuring their guilt.

These came into his eyes and the hand that held the typed pages shook. He said nothing, however, until he had finished the story and then he broke forth with his exclamations of astonishment and indignation.

"If this is all true" he declared, "it cannot be so bad." He said, "I do not believe it; my credulity has been imposed upon," he declared, "in the gravest amazement given to us by every one connected with the trial either directly or indirectly, that these men were honest?"

No Hint of the Crimes.

Mr Gompers worried with the greatest emphasis that not the slightest that of any such charge as today's in the place of the defense of the differences had previously reached him.

Asked if he would have resorted to what he had counseled, his labor leader replied:

"No, I shall not add to their misery unnecessarily by this."

"What effect do you imagine this will have on the labor union?" was queried.

To this Mr Gompers stopped his fingers and exclaimed:

"Hum."

"When the hand that has kept up its hopes by same truth he did divined."

Continued on the Eighth Page.

☞ Books
For
☞ Boys
And
☞ Girls

See Pages 13, 14 and 15 of Today's Globe.

Another Big Juvenile Number Next Saturday.

VIEWS OF LABOR AND EMPLOYERS

Leaders Declare Unions Never Condone Criminal Acts.

Others Expected to Be Drawn in by Disclosures at Los Angeles.

FORTUNATE END OF FATEFUL CASE

George H. Ellis, president of the Boston Typothetae, and of the McNamara Conference:

"Assuming the report to be true, I am glad that the end is reached in this was rather than by trickery of the law.

"The position taken by every submitted labor unions in principle the men now so prejudiced those who blindly defend and from that it would have been re-provable to local courtroom tide of the guilt of the McNamaras. The feeling that public opinion is clarified and that bring a settlement of the new and graphic upon the verdict so decisively..."

Continued on the Eighth Page.

ONLY ASKED FOR SIMPLE JUSTICE

"Let justice be done; somewhat rises the sort of subject prevail; not a vicious criminal without with the deceasing sort into practice, the evil of the (treating party) as the fire of the lynching assembly, so far as the fact of the guilt of the McNamaras..."

Continued on the Eighth Page.

TODAY'S GLOBE CONTENTS.

THE WEATHER.

WASHINGTON, Dec 1—Forecast for New England and Eastern New York: Fair and slightly colder on Saturday except probably light snow near the coast; moderate northwest winds.

For Northern New England: Generally fair and slightly warmer on Saturday; Sunday generally fair, moderate north and west winds.

Local Forecast for Boston and vicinity—Slightly colder Saturday; fair.

The minimum temperature yesterday afternoon was 34 deg.

Republican—The Globe's forecast—Sunday settled weather slightly warmer owing to moderate westerly winds.

James Admits Murder, John Llewellyn Plant Dynamiting.

JOHN J. McNAMARA,
Who Pleads Guilty to Attempt to Wreck Llewellyn Iron Works by Dynamite.

JAMES B. McNAMARA,
Defendant Who Pleads Guilty to Times Building Murder.

Lives of Defendants Probably Saved by Sensational End Of Case--Sentences to Be Passed Tuesday.

By JOHN W. CARBERRY.

LOS ANGELES, Dec 1—Smilingly, and without even a suggestion of anxiety or concern depicted upon their amiable faces, James B. McNamara and his brother, John J. McNamara, this afternoon acknowledged that the prosecution was right in its charge that the Los Angeles Times Building was destroyed by dynamite and that members of organized labor were responsible for the appalling loss of life in that holocaust.

Standing before Judge Bordwell, James B. McNamara, the younger of the two brothers, this afternoon pleaded guilty to murder in the first degree.

"NO CHANCE TO ESCAPE," SAYS DARROW, EXPLAINING ACTION OF HIS CLIENTS

"We didn't have a chance in the world. Jim McNamara did not have a ghost of a show to escape. The evidence against him was so strong that he could not answer. He was bound to be convicted. We saw it, but were powerless to help it. It was a dead open and shut case against him. . . . We were offered a chance to save his life by pleading guilty. It was the only chance we had and we had to take it. . . . If the case had been given to the jury it would have hanged him. I'll go a great way to save a man's life, and I think I have done it in this case."

Leisurely masticating gum, "Jim" McNamara, shifting from one foot to the other, admitted that he had placed a dynamite bomb beneath the Times Building on Oct 1, 1910, and declared himself guilty of the murder of Charles J. Haggerty, a Times linotype operator, who died in the flames.

"Jim" McNamara pleaded guilty to an indictment which carries with it a sentence of death, if Judge Bordwell decides to exact the full penalty of the law. That his life will not be taken, however, his counsel have been assured by Dist Atty John D. Fredericks. But life imprisonment appears to be his inevitable fate.

John J. McNamara, the elder of the two indicted labor leaders, quickly followed his brother in presenting to the court a solemn plea of guilty to a crime for which he may be punished by imprisonment for 20 years, if Judge Bordwell imposes the extreme sentence in his discretion.

John J. McNamara, secretary-treasurer of the International Association of Bridge and Structural Steel Workers, pleaded guilty to an indictment which alleged that he exploded and attempted to explode dynamite in the Llewellyn Iron Works in Los Angeles in December, 1910.

Continued on Page 6.

Tomorrow's Globe
Be sure to call early with your advertisements for tomorrow's Globe. Help Hazzell I'm the Globe.

Best Results
Be sure to have your adverts in tomorrow's Globe. Names For Sale! The Globe.

The Boston Daily Globe.

VOL LXXX—NO 155.   BOSTON, SATURDAY EVENING, DECEMBER 2, 1911—EIGHTEEN PAGES.   PRICE TWO CENTS.

EVENING EDITION—7:30 O'CLOCK

NEGOTIATOR TELLS HOW McNAMARAS CAME TO MAKE THEIR PLEAS OF GUILTY

DARROW FEELS DISHEARTENED

CLARENCE S. DARROW.

"Organized Labor Was Not Hurt," He Asserted Today.

"Leaders Would Not Be So Bitter if They Knew the Facts."

"NO CHANCE TO ESCAPE," SAYS DARROW, EXPLAINING ACTION OF HIS CLIENTS

"We didn't have a chance in the world. Jim McNamara did not have a ghost of a show to escape. The evidence against him was so strong that he could not answer. He was bound to be convicted. We saw it, but were powerless to help it. It was a dead open and shut case against him. . . . We were offered a chance to save his life by pleading guilty. It was the only chance we had and we had to take it. . . . If the case had been given to the jury it would have hanged him. I'll go a great way to save a man's life, and I think I have done it in this case."

JOHN J. McNAMARA,
Who Pleads Guilty to Attempt to Wreck Llewellyn Iron Works by Dynamite.

JAMES B. McNAMARA,
Defendant Who Pleads guilty to Times Building murder.

Los Angeles Capitalists Made Overtures.

LINCOLN STEFFENS.

Lincoln Steffens Induced Them to Try to End Labor War.

Spirit of Revenge Buried, in Hope For Future Peace.

BOTH McNAMARAS PLEAD GUILTY IN OPEN COURT IN LOS ANGELES

James Admits Murder of Linotype Operator, John the Dynamiting Of Llewellyn Iron Works Plant.

By JOHN W. CARBERRY.

LOS ANGELES, Dec 1—Smilingly, and without even a suggestion of anxiety or concern depicted upon their amiable faces, James B. McNamara and his brother, John J. McNamara, this afternoon acknowledged that the prosecution was right in its charge that the Los Angeles Times Building was destroyed by dynamite and that members of organized labor were responsible for the appalling loss of life in that holocaust.

Standing before Judge Bordwell, James B. McNamara, the younger of the two brothers, this afternoon pleaded guilty to murder in the first degree.

Leisurely masticating gum, "Jim" McNamara, shifting from one foot to the other, admitted that he had placed a dynamite bomb beneath the Times Building on Oct 1, 1910, and declared himself guilty of the murder of Charles J. Haggerty, a Times linotype operator, who died in the flames.

"Jim" McNamara pleaded guilty to an indictment which carries with it a sentence of death, if Judge Bordwell decides to exact the full penalty of the law. That his life will not be taken, however, his counsel have assured by Dist Atty John D. Fredericks. But life imprisonment appears to be inevitable fate.

John J. McNamara, the elder of the two indicted labor leaders, quickly followed his brother in presenting to the court a solemn plea of guilty to a crime for which he may be punished by imprisonment for 20 years, if Judge Bordwell imposes the extreme sentence in his discretion.

John J. McNamara, secretary-treasurer of the International Association of Bridge and Structural Steel

Workers, pleaded guilty to an indictment which alleged that he exploded and attempted to explode dynamite in the Llewellyn Iron Works in Los Angeles in December, 1910.

Elder Brother Escapes Capital Charge.

By his plea of guilty to the indictment which alleged first degree murder, James B. McNamara assumes complete responsibility for the destruction of the Los Angeles Times Building and the death of 21 employes.

John J. McNamara was indicted for complicity in this explosion, but by agreement the indictments involving him in this homicide will be not prest'd by Dist Atty Fredericks.

The elder and more conspicuous of the two brothers avoided prosecution in connection with the Times explosion by admitting substantially that he sent Ortie E. McManigal to Los Angeles with dynamite under instructions to demolish the buildings of the Llewellyn Iron Works, whose workmen were on strike.

Men To Be Sentenced Tuesday, Dec 5.

The McNamaras will be sentenced at 10 a m Tuesday next by Judge Bordwell.

Life imprisonment is expected to be the court's decree with respect to James McNamara, while John J. doubtless will be condemned to a term in the State Penitentiary of from 10 to 20 years.

All that may lessen the severity of the sentence imposed upon the elder McNamara is the fact that Ortie

Continued on the Fourth Page.

THE WEATHER.

United States Weather Bureau forecast:

For Boston and vicinity—Probably rain or snow and colder tonight; Sunday fair, cold and moderately westerly winds.

For New England and Eastern New York—Snow in the north portion; rain or snow in south portion tonight; colder; Sunday generally fair. Moderate to brisk westerly winds.

Continued on the Twelfth Page.

LOS ANGELES, Dec 1—Fatigued and worn, his face deathly wan after the two courts closed and after Clarence S. Darrow, veteran of many a court battle in which labor has been involved, in today a disheartened man. He had read the comments of labor leaders throughout the country on the close of guilty entered yesterday by both James B. and J. J. McNamara, secretary and treasurer of the International association of Bridge and Structural Iron Workers.

So defeated chin was not the time for congratulations; the comments of both pleaders had not been filed, but that labor leaders would understand in time, came that the procedure yesterday was the only solution of a vexatious problem that had worried him for days.

"I cannot talk about it," Darrow declared, as he stood on the veranda of a business, gazing at the hills, when asked now as to how bitter if they knew the facts."

It is believed that Mr Darrow meant that the congestion offered yesterday was the only alternative that he thought he was threshing, that the State of California had to be possessed to the McNamaras that conclusion of the full...

The Temperature Today.
The thermometer at Thompson's Spa records the temperature up to 2 P M as follows:

> The books, accounts, and correspondence of the American Federation of Labor are open to any competent authority who may desire to make a study or an investigation of them.[28]

The *Boston Sunday Globe* of December 3, 1911, carried the headline: "Prosecution Hardly Begun In Dynamite Case, Declares Dist Atty Fredericks." That newspaper gives two opposing views on what should be done with the McNamaras and their co-conspirators. On the first page is the reaction of the AFL president. "Welcomes Inquiry—'Go As High As They Like', Says Gompers, 'on Men Higher Up.'" The next column to the right is entitled "Labor Bitter on McNamaras: Hanging is not too severe for the confessed crimes of [the McNamaras], according to the views bitterly expressed here today by organized labor leaders."

Typical was the reaction of Frank Duffy of the Carpenter's Union, who thought both McNamaras should receive the death penalty. They couldn't hang them up too high to suit J.W. Dougherty of the Bookbinders. "Around the various union labor headquarters today the cry was 'Hang the McNamaras.'" Labor set about getting rid of the rotten apples. "Meanwhile, union men everywhere are demanding with grim determination that their unions be purged of men of the McNamara stripe."[29]

Lincoln Steffens was a Progressive writer best remembered for his comment upon returning in 1919 from the newly formed Soviet Union: "I have been over into the future and it works." In 1911 he was covering the McNamara trial for a syndicate of 21 newspapers. Page 15 of the *Boston Sunday Globe* of December 3 carried his article "Overtures Made by Capitalists—Steffens Induced Them to Try to End Los Angeles War." In an attempt to bring about peace he called first on one of the leaders in Southern California of the Progressive Republican Party. After reminding him of what was virtually a "class war" going on in Europe, Steffens continued:

"You have it here," I said. "You have Socialists and labor

---

[28] *LaFollette's Weekly Magazine*, December 16, 1911, 8.
[29] "News Worth Remembering," *LaFollette's Weekly Magazine*, December 16, 1911, 8.

men lined up against the other class; you have hate all through your system. That's bad. It may be that the class fight is never to end, but why not try some other way than fighting it out?"

"ACT OF GENEROSITY" SUGGESTED.

And we talked about the rare opportunity he and his friends had of taking the first step in Los Angeles. They could begin with an act of generosity toward two heroes of labor who were in trouble, with all men looking on and watching. Why not let them go?

By his own account Steffens had several personal conversations with Judge Bordwell and had tried to persuade the judge to use the occasion of the sentencing to say something conciliatory as the first step toward a treaty of peace. What he had in mind appeared as the opening line of his article: "Labor and Capital both stand convicted here today, the one of direct crime, the other of inciting labor to crime."

Tuesday, December 5, 1911, was a dark day for Lincoln Steffens. Instead of taking a statesmanlike course, Judge Bordwell excoriated the McNamaras before sentencing them while a short-sighted, mean-spirited electorate, reported the muckraker, turned out in force to beat Job Harriman and his fellow Socialists. "The hate of old feuds, the rancour, personal spite and the small side generally of a small city, were all turned up here today by the utter rout of the Socialist party and the final disposition of the McNamara cases."[30]

Mark well the difference between the response of the labor leaders and that of Progressive Steffens. Punish the McNamaras, say the men of labor; our only regret is that they escaped the noose. We are hurt and humiliated that it was a few of our own who were responsible and that we let them deceive us into defending them. Go as high as you like to apprehend their collaborators; we hold no

---

[30] "Is the 'Get Together' Movement in Los Angeles to Fail?" *LaFollette's Weekly Magazine*, December 16, 1911.

brief for them. Punish the guilty and exonerate the innocent, but do not dare impute their guilt to labor collectively. We shall purge our ranks of men of the McNamara stripe and go forward, with our heads held high.

The federal government now moved against Frank Ryan and other BSIW officials suspected of aiding and abetting the McNamaras. The *Kansas City Star* of December 3, 1911, reported that "Federal Courts May Act" and that the federal grand jury in Indianapolis would meet on December 14. "Not the slightest doubt remains that the United States Grand Jury will return indictments charging conspiracy to violate the laws of the United States regarding the transportation of explosives but involving far more serious crimes."

On December 8 Attorney General Wickersham wired instructions in cipher to Oscar Lawler, newly appointed Special Assistant to the Attorney General in Los Angeles, directing that further proceedings in that city be subordinated "to investigation by Miller at Indianapolis . . . Arrange with him to have any witnesses in California, including McManigal, present at Indianapolis as he needs them."[31]

And so began the "Dynamiters" case, ultimately to go down in the books as *Ryan v. United States*, 216 Federal Reporter 13, 7th Circuit (1914). Some 50 officials of the Iron Workers Union, including president Frank Ryan, would be indicted on charges "of conspiracy to commit a crime against the United States, and of transporting, aiding and abetting the transportation of dynamite and nitroglycerin in interstate commerce in passenger trains and cars between the several states of the United States." The prosecution's case would rest on the testimony of McManigal and the evidence seized in the basement vault in Indianapolis.

The McNamara case split the Progressive constituencies and unified those of their opponents. Most Progressives, like most other Americans, agreed with Theodore Roosevelt, who, in the December 16 issue of *The Outlook*, published an editorial entitled "Murder Is Murder," which denounced the stand taken by Lincoln Steffens and

---

[31] Wickersham to Oscar Lawler, December 9, 1911, No. 156777-64.

others of his persuasion:

> Since the startling outcome of the McNamara trial
> certain apologists of these men have made themselves
> conspicuous by asserting that these depraved criminals,
> who have on their seared souls the murder of so many
> innocent persons—*all of them laboring people, by the
> way*—are "victims," or at worst "fanatics," who should
> receive sympathy because they were acting in what they
> regarded as a "war" on behalf of their class! The plea is
> monstrous in its folly and its wickedness . . .

> Murder is murder, and the foolish sentimentalists or
> sinister wrong-doers who try to apologize for it as an
> "incident of labor warfare" are not only morally culpable
> but are enemies of the American people, and, above all,
> are enemies of American wage-workers. In honorable
> contrast to these men stand the various labor leaders who
> have never asked for more than a fair trial for the
> McNamaras, whose purpose has only been to get justice,
> and who now sternly demand that murder shall be
> punished when committed in the nominal interest of
> labor precisely as under any other circumstances.

There were, however, activists within the labor movement who
condoned violence as a response to the capitalist oppressors. They
were a minority, but by far they were the most vocal. Progressive
politicians had to chart a careful course between the position of
these activists and that of the rank and file. A statesmanlike way had
to be found to appease the former without alienating the latter.
Louis D. Brandeis, a leading Progressive spokesman, was not caught
flatfooted.

> In the midst of our indignation over the unpardonable
> crimes of trade union leaders, disclosed at Los Angeles,
> should not our statesmen and thinkers seek to ascertain
> the underlying cause of this wide-spread, deliberate
> outburst of crimes of violence?

> What was it that led men like the McNamaras to really
> believe that the only recourse they had for improving the

condition of the wage-earner was to use dynamite against property and life? Certainly it was not individual depravity . . .

Is there not a causal connection between the development of these huge, indomitable trusts and the horrible crimes now under investigation?[32]

It was indeed a vexing problem. Progressives wished to establish an enlightened policy of industrial relations, enabling them to attack the "underlying cause" that "led men like the McNamaras to really believe that the only recourse they had for improving the condition of the wage-earner was to use dynamite against property and life." But this could not come about unless and until the passions aroused by the Dynamiters case had abated.

One can see how an exclusionary rule of evidence might solve their problem. The case against the union leaders rests on the documentary evidence found with the dynamite and alarm clocks in the basement vault in Indianapolis. It is this which ties the defendants together; without it the testimony of McManigal cannot be corroborated and the case against them fails. But it is unrealistic to think that the Supreme Court, in a case so politically charged, would suddenly "find" in the Fourth Amendment—120 years after its passage—an exclusionary rule not discernable from its text. There was, however, another way.

A decision by the Supreme Court on a point of law in a case before them becomes an axiom in the adjudication of future cases. Suppose an exclusionary rule were to be established in another case, one having no apparent political implications? Then, when *Ryan v. United States* arrives on the docket of the Supreme Court, as it surely will, the precedent created in the case ostensibly unrelated to that of the Dynamiters might be used to overturn their convictions.

Suppose, to take it one step further, that you are a lawyer of

---

[32] This statement, originally made by Brandeis earlier in December before a Senate committee, was repeated by him in a letter dated December 19, 1911, to Paul Underwood Kellogg. Melvin I. Urofsky and David W. Levy, editors. *Letters of Louis D. Brandeis*, 5 Vols. Albany, New York: State University of New York Press (1972), cited hereafter as *Brandeis Letters*. Since the *Brandeis Letters* are arranged chronologically, they will be identified simply by date rather than by volume and page.

Progressive bent, long on influence and short on scruple. It is December of 1911, and you wish to frame a case which can be used as a precedent to dispose of the Dynamiters case. How would you go about it? A lawyer of today would say it couldn't be done. The Dynamiters case is already underway. The evidence gleaned by the states of California and Indiana has been turned over to the federal grand jury in Indianapolis, which is expected to hand down indictments at any time. Granted, the trial of some four dozen defendants is going to take longer than most, but how can someone setup a case, have it tried, and get it all the way to the Supreme Court before the *Ryan* case gets there? Even if this could be done, what guarantee is there that the Court will hear it? The odds of success seem so slim as to make such a scheme preposterous.

In 1911 a defendant who was tried and convicted in a U.S. district court had two avenues of appellate review open to him. Then, as now, he could appeal his conviction to the U.S. circuit court of appeals and, in the event of an adverse ruling there, go on to the Supreme Court of the United States. There was also an institution known as a "writ of error."

Writs of error were finally abolished in 1928.[33] But in 1911, and at all times relevant to this discussion, a person convicted of a crime in a U.S. district court could, provided certain conditions were met, appeal directly to the Supreme Court of the United States. If the case involved the construction or application of the Constitution of the United States, and did not turn wholly on other questions, it could be appealed directly to the Supreme Court.[34]

In such a case the jurisdiction of the Supreme Court was "obligatory" rather than "discretionary."[35] If the writ of error met the specifications, the Court was obliged to entertain it. So in December of 1911, a conspiracy to suborn a precedent which could

---

[33] Payne, *The Abolition of Writs of Error in the Federal Courts*, 15 Virginia Law Review 305 (1929).

[34] Bunn, *Review in the Supreme Court of the United States of the District Court and Circuit Court of Appeals*, 35 Harvard Law Review 902 (1922).

[35] See Blair, *Federal Appellate Procedure as Affected by the Act of February 13, 1925*, 25 Columbia Law Review 393 (1925) and Taft, *The Jurisdiction of the Supreme Court under the Act of February 13, 1925*, 35 Yale Law Journal 1 (1925).

be used to reverse a conviction of the Dynamiters was far from preposterous. It was in fact quite feasible if one had the right connections.

Of necessity, a conviction of the union leaders would turn on disputed questions of fact. If convicted in Indianapolis, they would appeal to the Seventh Circuit Court of Appeals in Chicago. If the circuit court denied their appeal, a petition for certiorari[36] could be made to the Supreme Court. While all of this was going on, a case could be concocted, kept free of questions of fact, and then appealed directly to the Supreme Court. A writ of error would permit the circuit court of appeals to be circumvented and the *Ryan* case to be cut off at the pass. All that was required was the right case.

Naturally it should be a case involving the most egregious search and seizure. The search of a dwelling house at night would be the best. The searchers should not be content to seize only specific items relevant to the crime in question, but should make a clean sweep of everything in sight, particularly personal correspondence and papers. The scenario in the Iron Workers case should be replicated as closely as possible. This requires that a search be made first by state officers acting under the color of authority of state law. Afterward the evidence they have seized should be handed over to federal agents on a "silver platter," so to speak.

To present to the Court a clear-cut, uncontestable constitutional violation, an officer acting on behalf of the federal government should then conduct his own unreasonable search and seizure. There must be no question but that some of the evidence used to convict the defendant in a federal criminal case was taken by a federal officer in a search made in violation of the Fourth Amendment. The Court must be convinced that only by resort to an exclusionary rule of evidence can the high-handed excesses of overzealous law enforcement officers be deterred.

It hardly needs to be stated that the mockup requires an unreasonable search which is fruitful; one which comes up empty-handed will not do. Now finding such a case is a lot easier said than

---

[36] Certiorari. A writ used by the Supreme Court of the United States as a discretionary device to choose the cases it wishes to hear. *Blacks's Law Dictionary.*

done. Fruitful searches are usually based on probable cause, which is why they are successful, while the unreasonable searches forbidden by the Fourth Amendment are almost invariably fruitless. How about a search made on probable cause no one knows exists? If the prosecution doesn't show the probable cause on which the search was based, who will? The events which led to the search will never come to light.

Best would be a scenario in which state officers engaged in the lawful investigation of a state crime inadvertently find something that incriminates someone of violating a federal law. It should be a case where everyone will be glad to see the defendant get off, even on a technicality. It should portray him as a victim and the law as a bully. So long as the evidence is there to be found, there is no danger. The case can always be dropped, and the malefactor given a stern warning and sent on his way.

On December 21, 1911, in Kansas City, Missouri, an unsuspecting clerk named Fremont Weeks kept his rendezvous with destiny. It will be the case of *Weeks v. United States* which will establish the precedent which will permit murderers such as Edward Coolidge to escape his just deserts.

Chapter II

WEEKS v. UNITED STATES

The concept of what the Constitution required of state criminal procedure before 1961 was called "fundamental fairness." It required that justice be done in the case at hand. Its underlying purpose was the protection of the innocent against wrongful conviction. Physical evidence, such as a weapon or the fruits of the crime, was always admissible if it connected the defendant to the crime. What mattered was whether the defendant had gotten a "fair" trial. The words "fairness" and "constitutional" were interchangeable. A criminal trial in a state court was a search for the truth of the accusation and nothing more.

How we came from fundamental fairness to a jurisprudence where travesties like *Coolidge* are commonplace is a story of but a few cases, of which the first was *Weeks v. United States*. These cases are the foundation of what passes today as a system of criminal justice. Overrule them and the whole system will come tumbling down. Criminal trials once again would be a search for the truth of the accusation against the defendant—and nothing more.

Fremont Weeks was convicted of using the mails to transport lottery tickets, a felony under federal law. The evidence against him consisted of lottery tickets and certain letters and envelopes found in the drawer of a chiffonier in the bedroom he shared with his wife. In a unanimous opinion the Justices expressed their understanding of the facts in the case before them and read into the Fourth

23

amendment an exclusionary rule the framers of that amendment
had chosen to omit.

> The defendant was arrested by a police officer, so far as
> the record shows, without warrant, at the Union Station
> in Kansas City, Missouri, where he was employed by an
> express company. Other police officers had gone to the
> house of the defendant and being told by a neighbor
> where the key was kept, found it and entered the house.
> They searched the defendant's room and took possession
> of various papers and articles found there, which were
> afterwards turned over to the United States Marshal.
> Later in the same day police officers returned with the
> Marshal, who thought he might find additional
> evidence, and, being admitted by someone in the house,
> probably a boarder, in response to a rap, the Marshal
> searched the defendant's room and carried away certain
> letters and envelopes found in the drawer of a chiffonier.
> Neither the marshal nor the police officers had a search
> warrant.[1]

The invaders of the house of Fremont Weeks seem to have
executed their mission with extraordinary vigor and wantonness. A
pretrial petition filed on his behalf alleges that they "broke open the
door to plaintiff's said home and seized all of his books, letters,
money, papers, notes, evidence of indebtedness, stock, certificates,
insurance policies, deeds, abstracts, and other muniments of title,
bonds, candies, clothes and other property in said home . . ."[2]

Obviously the historic tort remedies to deter such usurpations
have not worked, not in Kansas City at any rate. If this is what
officers do in the case of a suspected lottery ticket seller, heaven only
knows what happens when they are on the trail of a real desperado.
Unless overzealous lawmen are deprived of the fruits of such
excesses, the Fourth Amendment will become a dead letter.

If letters and private documents can thus be seized and

---

[1] *Weeks v. United States*, 232 U.S. 383, 386.
[2] *Weeks*, 387.

held and used in evidence against a citizen accused of an offense, the protection of the Fourth Amendment declaring his right to be secure against such searches and seizures is of no value, and, so far as those thus placed are concerned, might as well be stricken from the Constitution.[3]

In this one paragraph is expressed the justification for the exclusionary rule. It was born of necessity. Before them the Justices saw a flagrant violation of a person's rights under the Fourth Amendment. The outrage appears to have been gratuitous, and not a word of explanation or apology was tendered. Apparently all of this is in a day's work for those charged with the duty of enforcing the law and upholding the Constitution in the Western District of Missouri. The Court picked up the gauntlet.

The decision in *Weeks* was not based upon a reading or an interpretation of the words and phrases of the Constitution. There is nothing in the Fourth Amendment, or elsewhere in the Constitution, which makes unconstitutional the admission of such evidence. In *Weeks v. United States* the Court was taunted into overruling a century and a half of Anglo-American precedent.

For 87 years the Court's restatement of the facts in this case has been assumed to be a true account. We shall challenge it with a different hypothesis. We shall entertain the possibility that *Weeks v. United States* was a sham, a fraud perpetrated on the Supreme Court of the United States in order to evoke a precedent which could be used to overturn the conviction of the Dynamiters in the event Frank Ryan and his fellow union leaders were found guilty of transporting explosives in interstate commerce.

Fremont Weeks was arrested in Kansas City on December 21, 1911, and released on bail. After he was indicted in April of 1912, he appeared with an attorney and pleaded not guilty. Shortly before his trial he withdrew his plea of not guilty and entered a plea of *nolo contendere.* The record shows this entry for November 1, 1912:

---

[3] *Weeks,* 393.

This day comes Leslie J. Lyons, United States Attorney, who prosecutes on behalf of the United States, also comes the defendant in his own proper person as well as by his attorney thereupon the defendant withdraws his plea of not guilty heretofore made herein and enters a plea of nolo contendere and prays the court to accept the same, thereupon arguments of counsel are heard and the Court being fully advised in the premises it ordered that said plea of nolo contendere be not accepted.[4]

Black's Law Dictionary defines *nolo contendere* as a "Latin phrase meaning 'I will not contest it;' a plea in a criminal case which has a similar legal effect as pleading guilty . . . a fine or sentence may be imposed pursuant to it. The principal difference between a plea of guilty and a plea of *nolo contendere,*" continues *Black's*, "is that the latter may not be used against the defendant in a civil action based on the same acts . . . A defendant may plead *nolo contendere* only with the consent of the court. Such a plea shall be accepted by the court only after due consideration of the views of the parties and the interest of the public in the effective administration of justice."

In the case of Fremont Weeks, what possible "interest of the public in the effective administration of justice" could be served by refusing to accept the plea of *nolo contendere*? The defendant would have been just as much a felon as if he were convicted by a jury. Every day to which Weeks could be sentenced to serve, every dollar he could be fined, so also could he be sentenced or fined after pleading *nolo contendere*. The usual reason for rejecting such a plea is that the conviction thereby obtained cannot be used as the basis of a civil suit brought against the defendant by his victims. This is a consideration in antitrust prosecutions, for example. But Weeks's victims, if victims they must be called, were the purchasers of a few dollars worth of lottery tickets, transactions which were gambling contracts, void and unenforceable by law.

So no third party was aided in the recovery of damages by virtue

---

[4] Transcript of Record, *Fremont Weeks, Plaintiff in Error vs. The United States,* filed in the Supreme Court of the United States February 17, 1913, Docket No. 461. The transcript has an index which makes it unnecessary to identify citations by page number.

of the subsequent trial and conviction of Fremont Weeks. Weeks could have been punished, and like-minded transporters of lottery tickets deterred, to precisely the same extent by accepting his plea as by putting him on trial and convicting him. Insofar as the interests of the public were concerned, the trial and appeal were a complete waste of time and money. Of course if the plea had been accepted there would have been no such case as *Weeks v. United States*; the case of *United States v. Weeks* would have been over there and then.

On November 6, 1912, the defendant filed a "Petition to Return Private Papers, Books and Other Property." In it is described the search of his house and the indiscriminate seizure of his private papers. The petition prayed that "the Court direct and order said District Attorney, Marshal and Clerk to return said property to said defendant."

On the following day, without the legal merits having been briefed or argued by the parties, and without any discussion of them himself, the district judge granted "said petition relative to such property as is not pertinent to this trial and denies it concerning such property as is pertinent to the trial of this cause, the court reserving the right, however, to pass upon the pertinency at a later time."

On this note the trial began. When the letters taken from defendant's chiffonier were offered in evidence, the defense objected on the same constitutional grounds set forth in the pretrial petition. The district judge overruled the objection without hearing argument or stating his reasons.

The constitutional question of whether the Fourth Amendment requires the exclusion of evidence taken in an unreasonable search and seizure never was argued in the trial court. Nor was the issue of probable cause raised; the subject was broached on two separate occasions and this is what happened:

Redirect examination by Mr. Landon:

Q. Mr. Toohey you need not answer this until the attorney objects—what was your reason for going to Mr. Weeks' room and making a search?

After a discussion at the Court bench the question was not pressed.

Witness excused.

Q. Now Mr. [U.S.Marshal] Martin you need not answer this question until the Attorney has an opportunity to object. What caused you to go to Mr. Weeks' room after you had seen this grip, the tickets and the papers I have shown you?

[Defense attorney] Mr. O'Donnell: I object to the question because it has no bearing on the question involved—does not prove or tend to prove any issue raised by the indictment—hence we object to it.

Question withdrawn.

William H. Toohey was the Kansas City police officer who made the original search. He was also present at the second search made by A.J. Martin, the United States Marshal. The question put to these two witnesses by Assistant U.S. Attorney Thaddeus B. Landon would have elicited from them whatever "probable cause" they had to make the search.

If the objections were upheld, it hardly would be fitting for the defendant, after having prevented the prosecution from eliciting the probable cause which prompted the search, to argue on appeal that he was the victim of an unreasonable search and seizure. On the other hand, if the objections were overruled and the questions answered by Officer Toohey and U.S. Marshal Martin, the trial court could then decide the issue in the light of the facts and circumstances surrounding the search and seizure, as could the Supreme Court of the United States, should the case ever come to its attention. Why then was the question to Mr. Toohey "not pressed"? Why was the question to Mr. Martin "withdrawn"? Why not at least let the court rule on the objection?

Looking at the *Kansas City Star* of December 22, 1911, we note on the front page that someone has been doing some last-minute Christmas shoplifting. In the first paragraph of this article we see that the apprehension of a shoplifter led to something else:

> Through the arrest of a woman shoplifter yesterday and
> the search of her home the police have learned of the
> extensive sale of San Domingo lottery tickets in Kansas
> City and throughout the Middle West . . .

> The disclosure of the sale of the lottery tickets in Kansas
> City came about in a peculiar way. A woman detective in
> the Jones Department Store caught Mrs. Olla Weeks,
> 1834 Penn Street, slipping several pairs of kid gloves into
> a number of bundles she was carrying. The woman was
> arrested and the gloves found in her possession. She was
> fined $25 in the South Side Municipal Court this
> morning.

Reading further we see that "other articles of woman's apparel
were found in the home, including twelve pairs of silk hose. In a
suitcase hundreds of lottery tickets were found." It also appears "the
woman sent a warning note to Fremont Weeks, her husband,"
which the police intercepted. Weeks, who was also arrested, "said he
did not know it was against the law to sell the coupons."

Now this newspaper account may not indeed prove or tend to
prove any issue raised by the indictment, but it surely casts a pall on
the official version of events. All of a sudden *Weeks v. United States*
takes on a different hue. Considering the lack of candor on the part
of the officials concerned, it would not be amiss to reconstruct a
scenario more in accord with human experience.

From the newspaper article it is clear that what began the chain
of events which culminated in *Weeks v. United States* was the arrest
of Olla Weeks by a store detective at Jones Department Store. The
police were called, and Officer Toohey arrived at the scene. Caught
in *flagrante delicto,* Mrs. Weeks made a clean breast and confessed to
other such thefts. The stolen merchandise was in her bedroom
chiffonier, she told the police. Hoping for leniency, she offered to
take them to it.

Officer Toohey testified:

> I went to his rooms, 1834 Penn Street, twice that day.
> The first time I went with John Owen; the second time
> with Officer Wolf and United States Marshal Mr.
> Martin. I searched the room when I went with John
> Owen. I found this grip in Mr. Weeks's room, 1834
> Penn Street, by the sideboard lying down.

Olla Weeks took Officers Toohey and Owen to her home at 1834 Penn Street. They entered the house with her consent, whereupon Mrs. Weeks took them to the bedroom she shared with her husband. It turned out there was more there than the 12 pairs of silk hose. The police confiscated the open grip with the lottery tickets because they were contraband, the mere possession of which was a violation of state law.

It was at the Weeks house—not the police station as the newspaper had it—where the police intercepted the warning note. Officer Joseph Wolf was dispatched to Union Station, where Fremont Weeks worked as a clerk for the Adams Express Company and, when Weeks admitted the lottery tickets were his, he was arrested.

Officer Wolf said he first saw the lottery paraphernalia at the police station when he brought Weeks in at "about 5:15 in the afternoon of December 21st, 1911." These were the items which had been seized and taken to the police station by Officers Toohey and Owen. At the trial Toohey testified that he "was at the Police Station when Officer Wolf came in with Mr. Weeks. I had been at the house once at that time."

Thus we know the first search was completed and the things seized were at the police station by 5:15 that December afternoon. According to the testimony of U.S. Marshal Martin, approximately five hours elapsed before the second search was made.

> I was called and went to the Police Station No. 4 on
> December 21st. along in the night, I suppose in the
> neighborhood of ten o'clock or half past . . .
>
> Officers Toohey and Wolf and myself went to the house
> and were admitted, I believe, by some young man, I

believe who said he roomed there. I don't know his
name. We did not break in the door—we rapped and he
admitted us. When we got to the room we went through
what seemed I think, either a dresser or a chiffonier . . .

There is a lot about this story that strikes one as odd. Officer
Toohey had already testified that it was he who called Mr. Martin
up at his residence. Toohey certainly had a lot of nerve calling up the
marshal at his home after 10:00 p.m. on a Thursday night. Getting
the goods on a suspected lottery ticket mailer somehow doesn't
seem that exigent.

But the marshal was not perturbed about this nocturnal
summons. Off he went to Police Station No. 4 and then, escorted
by Officers Toohey and Wolf, on to 1834 Penn Street to make a late
hour unconstitutional search and seizure above and beyond the call
of duty. It can not be denied that the marshal made a perfect
unreasonable search and seizure. He made a warrantless intrusion
into a dwelling house at a time of night when the occupants were or
might be expected to be asleep. Once inside he seized everything in
sight including personal papers. All of this was done in pursuit of a
criminal church mouse. This was the way the Court saw it.

> [The U.S. marshal] acted without sanction of law,
> doubtless prompted by the desire to bring further proof
> to the aid of the Government, and under color of his
> office undertook to make a seizure of private papers in
> direct violation of the constitutional prohibition against
> such action.[5]

At the trial the two policemen said nothing of Mrs. Weeks or the
shoplifting incident. Purged of probable cause, the statement of
facts presented by the record leaves a reader rightly indignant. The
blasé attitude of the prosecution adds fuel to the fire. Arbitrary
searches and seizures are so commonplace in Kansas City, it would
appear, as not to merit a word of explanation.

---

[5] *Weeks*, 393.

Fremont Weeks had an impressive array of character witnesses. His supervisor, his banker, and a circuit court judge all testified on his behalf. By their account he is a hard-working middle-aged family man, well liked and respected in the community. It is apparent that Weeks is not a common gambler but a simple clerk who made a little money on the side selling lottery tickets to people who wanted to take a chance.

For sending through the mails a piddling amount of lottery tickets, his first and only brush with the law, Fremont Weeks stands now a convicted felon. In the ordinary course of events he never would have been indicted, much less tried. Any law enforcement official with a spark of humanity or common sense would have given Fremont Weeks a stern lecture and sent him on his way. But no stone was left unturned to present to the Supreme Court a worst case scenario.

On November 16, 1912, the district judge fined Fremont Weeks $100 and sentenced him to six months in jail. On the same day he allowed the defendant a writ of error permitting him to apply directly to the Supreme Court for review and stayed the sentence pending the appeal. Three months later the transcript of record was filed in the Supreme Court. The case of *United States v. Weeks* had been handled most expeditiously in the federal district court and *Weeks v. United States* was now officially under way.

On November 11, 1913, the defendant's attorney, Martin J. O'Donnell, filed his brief. It covered 67 pages, and the table of cases and authorities cited covered four pages. There are several lines of argument which would naturally occur to any lawyer in 1913 arguing the case against the exclusionary rule. Here, however, is the brief actually filed on behalf of the United States *verbatim* and *in toto*.

IN THE SUPREME COURT
OF THE UNITED STATES
OCTOBER TERM

FREMONT WEEKS, PLAINTIFF IN ERROR,
v.
THE UNITED STATES

IN ERROR TO THE DISTRICT COURT OF
THE UNITED STATES FOR THE
WESTERN DISTRICT OF MISSOURI

STATEMENT

At the opening of the trial the defendant moved for the return of certain lottery tickets, letters, and other articles which had been taken from his house by the police without any search warrant, and were at the time in the possession of the United States attorney (Tr. 35). The court overruled the motion. Later on in the trial the court admitted the property in evidence over the objection of the defendant (Tr. 42).

The defendant having been found guilty—on a single count only (Tr. 21, 22)—comes here on writ of error, making fifteen assignments of which the only one requiring notice is in substance that the retention of this property and its admission in evidence against him violated his right to be secure from unreasonable searches and seizures and to refrain from being a witness against himself, as guaranteed by the fourth and fifth amendments.

ARGUMENT

The question is no longer open.

Adams v. N.Y., 192 U.S. 585
Hale v. Henkel, 201 U.S. 43
Amer. Tobacco Co. v. Werckmeister, 207 U.S. 284, 302
Holt v. U.S., 218 U.S. 245, 252
U.S. v. Wilson (C.C. N.Y.) 163 Fed., 338.
Hardesty v. U.S. (C.C.A., 6th C.), 164 Fed. 420, Judge (now Mr. Justice) Lurton concurring.
The *Adams* case is sought to be distinguished on the

ground that it involved a State action, whereas this involves a Federal action. The distinction does exist on the facts, but it is immaterial because the court passed that phase of the *Adams* case and based the decision on the point that, even if the amendments were applicable to State action,[1] they had not been violated.

The subsequent cases cited above have considered the question closed.

CONCLUSION

The judgment should be affirmed.

Winfred T. Denison,
November, 1913.   *Assistant Attorney General.*

---

[1] This point was subsequently decided in *Twining v. New Jersey*, 211 U.S. 78, 92. [Footnote in original brief].

On the basis of this brief, no one would accuse Winfred T. Denison of being a contentious person or an argumentative lawyer. He made no rejoinder whatever to the arguments advanced in the defendant's brief. Strip from his brief the title of the case and his statement of facts. The Court already knows these things. Note his opening and closing assertions: "The question is no longer open" and "The subsequent cases cited above have considered the question closed."

However valid they may be, self-serving assertions such as these are always better left unsaid. Judges like to make up their own minds whether the question before them is open or closed. It is always better for an advocate to lead the court to the truth by the weight of his authorities and the force of his argument. He must always remember that people like best the ideas they think they thought of themselves.

The single paragraph constituting the entire argument is complete blather. Not one of the six cases Denison cited had the remotest bearing on the case of *Weeks v. United States*, prompting the Court to remark that they were "at a loss to see the application of these cases to the one in hand."[6] They gave short shrift to *Adams v. New York*, the case Denison singled out for comment. The search in *Weeks* appeared to be a gross volation of the Fourth Amendment, whereas in *Adams* the search was perfectly legal.

> At the trial [of Adams] certain papers, which had been seized by police officers executing a search warrant for the discovery and seizure of policy slips and which had been found in addition to the policy slips, were offered in evidence over his objection . . . [I]t was held [in *Adams*] that such incriminatory documents thus discovered were not the subject of an unreasonable search and seizure . . .[7]

Martin J. O'Donnell, the attorney for Fremont Weeks, appeared and argued the case orally before the Court, whereas the United States submitted. "Submitted" means they stood on their brief believing it so persuasive as to make oral argument redundant. Always remember the 3rd of December, 1913, for it was the one time and the only time the case against the exclusionary rule was ever "argued" before the Supreme Court of the United States.

Winfred T. Denison was not just another lawyer writing briefs at the attorney general's office, but a person with a first-rate education and apparently great charm, well connected with people of considerable influence. A half century later, his closest friend, by then an old and sick man, recaptured Denison and the halcyon days of his youth.

> He was a very artistic advocate, a very good lawyer . . . He was extremely well read, a very cultivated person. A lovable character. A generous person—very charming, very successful socially. He once said of himself about going out often, perhaps too often, with a childlike innocence, "It's that damn charm of mine". . . . Denison was not a character you mention just in passing. He was

---

[6] *Weeks*, 398.
[7] *Weeks*, 394-395.

a salient personality.[8]

That Denison's brief is a sham remains an incontrovertible fact. No advocate, then or now, however brilliant or persuasive, can make the case against the exclusionary rule in 66 words, be they pearls of wisdom or drivel about the *Adams* case. That Denison forsook the oral argument, leaving the field uncontested, makes the case of treachery against him ironclad.

On November 24, 1913, President Woodrow Wilson appointed Winfred Denison to be secretary of the interior for the Philippine Islands. It was two days later, the day before Thanksgiving, that Denison filed his brief in the *Weeks* case. The oral argument took place the following Tuesday and Wednesday, December 2 and 3. In the interim Denison had left Washington for California to await his confirmation by the Senate. He was given plenty of time to cool his heels.

MISSES HIS STEAMER AGAIN
W.T. Denison, New Philippines Commissioner, Will Sail February 3.

SAN FRANCISCO. January 27. Because the United States Government was half an hour behind a press dispatch giving Winfred T. Denison the news that his appointment to be secretary of the Interior of the Philippines had been confirmed to-day by the Senate, he missed his eighth consecutive liner for the Orient.[9]

According to the reporter who talked to Denison "at the other end of a telephone line," he asked the company to hold the ship but the tide would not permit this. "He expects to sail on February 3." On the same day the *Washington Post* carried this article:

---

[8] *Felix Frankfurter Reminisces*, H.B. Phillips, ed. New York: Reynal and Company, 1961, 108, hereinafter *Reminisces*.
[9] *New York Times*, January 28, 1914.

APPEAL DYNAMITE CASE
Ironworkers Ask Supreme Court to Review Indianapolis Convictions.

Formal petition was filed in the Supreme Court yesterday for a review of the conviction of Frank M. Ryan and 23 other members of the International Association of Bridge and Structural Iron Workers, on charges of conspiracy growing out of the dynamiting of the Los Angeles Times building and other structures.

The *Weeks* decision was handed down February 24, 1914. The *Washington Post* and the *New York Times* were quick to see its significance. "Dynamite Case Affected" stated the *Post* on the morning of February 25. The *Times* explained:

The immediate result of the decision was that Fremont Weeks, an express messenger at Kansas City, Mo., will receive a new trial on a charge of using the mails to further an alleged lottery scheme. The United States Marshal entered his house and seized 600 letters, which were used against him at the trial.

The point that the Government improperly seized papers in the "Dynamiters" case against Frank M. Ryan and other Bridge Union officials in a raid in Indianapolis has been raised, and the decision today may enter into that prosecution if a new trial is granted, as sought in an application for review filed to-day with the Supreme Court. "May Not Seize Papers. Supreme Court Makes Ruling That May Affect Dynamiters' Case."[10]

---

[10] *New York Times*, February 25, 1914.

Chapter III

THE KANSAS CITY CONNECTION

The case against Fremont Weeks was in miniature a replica of that against Frank Ryan. Both men were convicted in a federal court of the interstate transportation of something illegal, after a trial in which papers said to have been taken unconstitutionally were used in evidence. In both cases the evidence in question was taken by officers acting under the aegis of state authority before being turned over to federal officials.

According to the transcript of record Weeks was found guilty of a felony in that he did "knowingly and feloniously deposit, and cause to be deposited, with the American Express Company, a common carrier of freight, express and packages between Kansas City, Missouri, and Parsons, Kansas . . . to be delivered to one J.P. Todd . . . one certain whole or dollar [lottery] ticket and one half or fifty cent ticket." In each case the documentary evidence that the defendant sought to have excluded was corroborated by an accomplice testifying under prosecutorial pressure. In the *Weeks* case, J.P. Todd, a machinist, played the role of Ortie McManigal. Fremont Weeks had sent the tickets to Todd in Kansas and Todd had mailed Weeks back the money. Under the law both were guilty. Todd refused to testify until Assistant U.S. Attorney Landon threatened him with prosecution and started to write out a complaint.

We have postulated that the *Weeks* case was suborned to obtain a precedent which could be used to dispose of the Dynamiters case. That if it came to pass that Frank Ryan and the leadership of the Iron Workers Union were convicted of the illegal interstate transportation of explosives, the precedent of *Weeks v. United States* could be used to overturn that conviction. So far the evidence seems to support our hypothesis. *Weeks* was not just a microcosm of the *Ryan* case; it was a microcosm too timely and too good to be true.

The United States district attorney is the officer charged with prosecuting those who commit federal crimes in his district. He has a great deal of latitude in deciding which cases to prosecute. Almost invariably he will try cases of serious crime if he has the evidence needed to convict; those involving lesser crimes are usually plea-bargained or dismissed. The same is true of appeals. The U.S. attorney may elect not to spend the government's time and money contesting an appeal where he feels the stakes do not warrant it.

At all times relevant to this inquiry, the United States Attorney for the Western District of Missouri was Leslie J. Lyons. If the *Weeks* case was a conspiracy Lyons had to be in on it. He could not have done it alone, nor could it have been done without him. But what militates against the complicity of Lyons is motive. As a general rule lawyers are honorable people who take seriously their oath to uphold the Constitution and the laws of the United States. It is not to be presumed they would take part in a plot to subvert them.

It must be considered also that Leslie Lyons was a young man holding high public office who might be expected to rise even higher. Absent a compelling reason to the contrary, we must be reluctant to believe Lyons would betray his public trust and dishonor the ethics of his profession. Moreover, why should he risk his career? We might start by asking who was Leslie Lyons and what kind of man was he?

The "Hon. Leslie J. Lyons, lawyer, legislator and (1908) assistant United States attorney at Kansas City, was born in Olathe, Kansas, January 30, 1872." In 1900 he received a law degree from the State University of Kansas at Lawrence and went to Kansas City, Missouri, to practice law. In 1903 he entered private practice and was elected to the Missouri Legislature. "Upon his return to Kansas City from the state legislature he was appointed assistant United States attorney by Senator William Warner . . . Politically he is a republican and socially is connected with the Knife & Fork Club of

Kansas City."[1]

Senator William Warner was the leader of the western Missouri Republicans. In 1905, at the time he was elected to the United States Senate, Warner was the incumbent U.S. attorney for the Western District of Missouri. He saw to it that his assistant, Arba S. Van Valkenburgh, succeeded him in that post. A year later Van Valkenburgh picked Leslie Lyons to be his assistant.

In June of 1910, at Senator Warner's behest, President Taft appointed Van Valkenburgh to be federal district judge and Lyons to replace him as the U.S. district attorney.[2] Lyons chose Thaddeus B. Landon to be his assistant. The U.S. district attorney's office was the ladder to political success in western Missouri, a fact which could not have eluded young Thad Landon.

Until the McNamaras confessed, the American people were unsure of the true cause of the *Los Angeles Times* disaster of October 1, 1910. Like Samuel Gompers, many believed that the brothers were being railroaded and the whole affair was a frame-up calculated to discredit the labor movement. The federal authorities, for their part, had reason to believe that the "Crime of the Century" was no accidental gas explosion, as labor claimed, but was indeed a dynamite bombing perpetrated by J.B. McNamara aided and abetted by his brother. From McManigal's confession, it seemed likely that Frank Ryan and the BSIW leadership were implicated in this and the other bombings.

But the Department of Justice had not yet had time to examine the records and books seized in the basement vault in the Indianapolis office building. It was not until November 7, 1911, that the federal district court ordered this evidence turned over to the U.S. marshal. And it remained to be seen how McManigal would stand up under cross-examination by Clarence Darrow. The

---

[1] Carrie Westlake Whitney. *Kansas City, Missouri, Its History and Its People—1800 to 1908*, Vol. III. S.J. Clark Publishing Co., 1908, 272.

[2] "Senator Warner is very anxious to have Mr. Leslie J. Lyons appointed United States Attorney for the Western District of Missouri, vice Van Valkenburgh, promoted to be a judge." George Wickersham, Attorney General, to William H. Taft, President, June 23, 1910: William Howard Taft Papers, Library of Congress, Manuscript Division. The Taft Papers have indices listing correspondents alphabetically and their correspondence chronologically.

reality was that unless and until California convicted the younger McNamara there was no federal case to be made against his co-conspirators. Like everyone else, the federal prosecutors had to bide their time and wait upon events.

The event which changed everything was the McNamaras' pleas of guilty on Friday, December 1, 1911. Before then, little thought had been given to either trying or defending the union officials, let alone the political consequences which might flow from their conviction. The federal grand jury which indicted the Dynamiters did not address the case until December 14.

There is nothing to suggest Leslie Lyons or any of his associates in Kansas City conceived the idea of setting up the *Weeks* case. Quite to the contrary, the evidence dispels any such notion. If conspiracy there was, it had to originate with Winfred Denison and his friends in Washington. If the hypothesis is to stand, Lyons had to be co-opted sometime between December 1, 1911, when the McNamara brothers confessed, and December 21, when U.S. Marshal Martin made his midnight ransack of Olla Weeks's chiffonier.

There is no evidence Denison and Lyons had ever met before December of 1911. As far as can be determined, any prior contact was through interoffice correspondence entirely unremarkable. What then would lead Winfred Denison to think that Leslie Lyons might be amenable to joining in a cabal to subvert the legal process? How could he be sure Lyons would not become indignant and report the matter to Attorney General Wickersham, either directly or through his political mentor, Senator Warner?

It so happened that Leslie Lyons was in dire trouble in December of 1911. As a result of complaints of unprofessional conduct, the Kansas City Court of Appeals was holding hearings to decide whether or not he should be disbarred. Attorney General Wickersham had dispatched Special Agent Arthur Bagley to attend the hearings in Kansas City and report back to him.

Bagley had completed his report and was about to deliver it to Wickersham, and Lyons wanted to be in Washington when he did. On November 29, 1911, two days before the McNamaras confessed, Lyons wrote the Attorney General requesting permission to come to Washington. He ended up by saying, "Unless I hear from you to the contrary, I shall leave here on Saturday night, [December 2] arriving in Washington some time Monday." Apparently the "Bagley Report" and Lyons both arrived at the Attorney General's office on Monday, December 4. Lyons was given a letter that day authorizing him to charge his travel expenses to the government. The letter was signed "For the Attorney General" by "Winfred T. Denison."[3]

One of the complaints filed against Leslie Lyons was that he had a secret law partner with whom he split fees.[4] The other lawyer was a close friend of his by the name of Davis. The gist of the charge was that if you were indicted in the Western District of Missouri you couldn't find a better lawyer to represent you than George L. Davis, Esq. Disbarment proceedings were under way against Davis as well.

December was not a good month for Leslie Lyons. The charges against him had come to the attention of President Taft. On December 7 President Taft's secretary wrote this note[5] to Wickersham:

> Dear Mr. Attorney General:
>
> The President would like to have you speak to him, when you are next at the executive office, about the charges against District Attorney Lyons of the western district of Missouri.
>
> Sincerely yours,
>
> Charles D. Hilles
> Secretary to the President

---

[3] The correspondence and other documents "In The Matter Of The Charges Against Leslie J. Lyons, United States Attorney For The Western District of Missouri" are part of the General Records of the Department of Justice, (R.G.) 60, No. 112, Straight Numerical Files, National Archives, Washington, DC, hereinafter DJA, NARA. Each document bears the prefix 158165 followed by a distinguishing number. Lyons's letter of November 29, 1911, is serial No. 158165-10 as is the letter of December 4 authorizing his expenses. Hereinafter such documents will be identified simply by serial number. The "Report of Arthur T. Bagley, Special Agent" was stamped "received" December 4, 1911, and became serial No. 158165-11.

[4] Lyons was engaged in the private practice of law in Kansas City at the same time he was the U.S. district attorney. He was permitted to do this as long as he avoided any conflict of interest. The issue was not whether Leslie Lyons practiced law on the side, but whether he did so unethically.

[5] No. 158165-13.

The *Kansas City Star* of Sunday, December 10, carried an extensive article—"Called Lyons His Partner"—on how the disbarment proceedings were going. A lawyer named McWilliams had testified that Davis had told him "he and 'Leslie' had built up a profitable practice. Davis was quoted as saying that he and Lyons had made $26,000 last year and would do better this year." An article the following day stated that a Missouri delegation headed by Governor Herbert Hadley had been to Washington to lobby for a Missouri River project. Hadley had been to see the President, and it was rumored that he had "urged that Lyons be removed for the good of the party."

> When Hadley had his conference with Taft the President asked him about the Lyons case. What Hadley told him is known only to himself and the President.

PREDICT LYONS'S REMOVAL

> The delegates found it the general belief among the Missouri Republicans in Washington that Lyons would be removed before the term of court next spring and there is a movement on foot to have John C. McKinley of Unionville appointed in his place.[6]

While in Washington Lyons conferred at least twice with "Senator" Warner,[7] and on the morning of December 13 Warner spoke to the attorney general. The upshot was that Lyons was told to go home. Before leaving that evening Lyons wrote a letter to Wickersham expressing his reservations about the Bagley Report. He requested

> [T]hat when your examination of the report was

---

[6] "'No Thanks,' Hadley Says, a Vice-Presidential Nomination with Taft Is Declined," *Kansas City Star*, December 11, 1911.

[7] By this time the title "Senator" was honorary. Warner's term had ended on March 3, 1911, and he had been succeeded by Democrat James A. Reed. See *Biographical Directory of the American Congress, 1774-1989*, U.S. Government Printing Office, 1989.

completed I would be notified in ample time to make reply . . . On account of the great number of matters gone into . . . certain inaccuracies have very naturally crept into the report of the special agent, and give an entirely erroneous impression of the matters referred to.[8]

If Leslie Lyons left on the 6:45 evening train, as he told Wickersham he planned to do, he would have been back in Kansas City on Friday, the 15th of December. Olla and Fremont Weeks came to grief the following Thursday. As one might expect, there is no documentary evidence of collusion between Lyons and Denison. The case against them depends upon what inferences can be drawn from their behavior and what we know of these two men and their friends and associates.

In the congressional elections of 1910 the Republicans had taken a drubbing which widened the rift in the party. The Progressive Republicans, whose leader had been Theodore Roosevelt, were on one side, and the political descendants of the assassinated McKinley on the other. The latter, known derisively to their opponents as the "Old Guard" or the "Stand Patters," supported President Taft.

With the exception of Grover Cleveland, the Democrats had not elected a president in more than half a century. The party had always been cleft by the Mason-Dixon Line, but a split between East and West had been more than it could bear. The chief cause of this breach had been the monetary policies of the populist wing of the party led by William Jennings Bryan. His "Cross of Gold" speech to the Democratic National Convention in 1896 catapulted him into the nomination. Campaigning on the issue of "Free and Unlimited Coinage of Silver," he had been the party's standard-bearer in 1896, 1900, and once again in 1908. Three times had Bryan led the Democrats, and three times had he led them to defeat.

As the election year of 1912 approached, Democratic prospects were on the rise. Although still influential in the party, the aging

---

[8] No. 158165-14. In this letter Lyons alludes to a conversation that morning between Warner and the Attorney General.

THE KANSAS CITY CONNECTION

"Boy Orator of the Platte" was no longer in the running. What the Democrats needed was a candidate who could heal their wounds and bring them together. The front runner was Congressman Champ Clark of the border state of Missouri, the Speaker of the House of Representatives. Next in contention was Woodrow Wilson, a transplanted Virginian who was the governor of New Jersey.

In those days dinner clubs were an important part of the American political and social scene. In each city there were clubs identified with one or the other political party, as well as clubs formed for nonpolitical purposes. At their dinners it was the custom to have men of prominence address the membership on the issues of the day. The speaker and what he had to say would then be reported in the newspapers, and criticism, debate, and discussion would go from there. For a politician, the "banquet circuit" was a way of making contacts, becoming known, and getting his message across. It was the political medium of the time.

The Knife and Fork Club of Kansas City was a dinner club of a nonpartisan nature. In 1910 and 1911 Leslie Lyons was its president and, so it appears, the person in charge of recruiting speakers for its monthly dinners.[9] On August 24, 1910, Lyons wrote the attorney general requesting a 10-day leave of absence.

> I make this request for the purpose of enabling me to make a trip to Washington, New York and other Eastern points on behalf of the Knife and Fork Club of this city, of which I am President. This is a literary and social club which gives monthly dinners, at which public men are invited to make addresses, and it is for the purpose of securing speakers for the coming season that the Club has requested me to make this trip.[10]

By autumn of 1911 the political consensus was that President William Howard Taft could not be reelected. It had come to be

---

[9] See letter from Lyons to Wickersham, January 13, 1911, requesting a leave of absence for Knife and Fork Club business. R.G. 60, No. 119—Judicial District Administration—DJA—NARA—26N22, 148088-5.

[10] Lyons to Attorney General, August 24, 1910, Id. No. 148088-3.

accepted as a political truth that if the Republicans renominated him in 1912, they would be backing a sure loser. In October of 1911 the National Progressive Republican Conference met in Chicago and endorsed Senator Robert Marion LaFollette of Wisconsin.

LaFollette could not have had a better man in his corner than Louis D. Brandeis. Intelligent and articulate, Brandeis was particularly effective in addressing these dinner clubs. "Fighting Bob" and the "People's Lawyer," to use their respective sobriquets, were both friends and political confidants. When Fighting Bob announced his candidacy, Louis Brandeis, a Progressive Republican himself, became one of his most ardent supporters. On the LaFollette bandwagon from the very beginning, raising money and rallying support for the Progressive candidate, Brandeis will campaign for Senator LaFollette by making the banquet circuit.

There were two leading issues of the day. One was how to deal with monopolistic combinations in restraint of trade—the "trusts." After waffling, Taft took the position that the Sherman Anti-Trust Act, if vigorously enforced, was adequate to ensure competition. Brandeis, on the other hand, had championed the need for new legislation and had written a significant part of the proposed LaFollette-Stanley Anti-Trust Act. In *LaFollette's Weekly Magazine* of September 30, 1911, Brandeis wrote an article pointing out the defects in the Sherman Act which would be remedied by LaFollette's bill: "Far-Famed Lawyer Points Out Defects in the Anti-Trust Law that Will Be Remedied By The LaFollette Bill."

The other was the issue of industrial relations. Brandeis and LaFollette, as most other Progressives, were fervent supporters of a national labor relations act under which the federal government would intervene to settle disputes between management and labor. The biggest impediment to a rational discussion and resolution of this question was something Progressives called "labor unrest." Most people, and most Republicans, called it "labor union violence," the most egregious example of which was the Los Angeles bombing.

LaFollette's strategy was to demonstrate Taft's unpopularity by trouncing him in the 1912 Republican primaries. He was given a better than even chance of getting the Republican nomination provided a certain "Roughrider" remained in political retirement.

The McNamaras' confessions on December 1, 1911, ushered in a month of political ferment. Ominous rumblings were heard from the direction of Oyster Bay in late December after Theodore Roosevelt's article "Murder Is Murder" was published in *The Outlook*.

At LaFollette's request, Brandeis had undertaken a speaking tour through the Midwest. New Year's Day of 1912 found him campaigning in Ohio. He made his keynote speech in Canton that night.

> [T]he people of this country should not be surprised because the McNamaras and their allies resorted to violence to gain their ends, Attorney Louis D. Brandeis of Boston [declared] in an address here tonight . . . "Only the revolutionary and civil wars have surpassed in importance the progressive movement now before the people," Brandeis said. "The struggle for industrial liberty is on."[11]

He made the circuit through Wisconsin, Minnesota, and Illinois that week with engagements in Madison, Minneapolis, and Chicago. Returning east, he arrived in Washington at noon on Saturday, January 6, 1912. Brandeis recounted his trip in a letter written that afternoon to his brother, Alfred, who had written him earlier that week. He did not respond to his brother's criticism of his statements on the campaign trail. "I am afraid you are too radical for me to follow. I do not believe that I can subscribe to any justification of the Los Angeles dynamiting, or in any way excuse what the McNamaras or their friends have done. I am afraid it is too much of an arraying of labor against capital, for me to follow in your footsteps."[12]

A month later the People's Lawyer was back on the circuit plumping for LaFollette. His theme was to take the two pressing issues of the day—the trusts and labor union violence—and counterpoise them as moral equivalents causally connected. On the night of Monday, February 5, he addressed the Knife and Fork Club in Kansas City,[13] an engagement, one would think, that

---

[11] "Sees Socialism Grow," *Cleveland Plain Dealer*, January 2, 1912.

[12] Louis D. Brandeis to Alfred Brandeis, January 6, 1912, together with commentary, *Brandeis Letters*.

[13] *Kansas City Star*, February 5, 1912.

was arranged by Leslie Lyons.

Brandeis could have saved himself a lot of trouble. In the *Kansas City Star* of that day, in between a cartoon showing "Louis Brandeis, the People's Lawyer," pointing his finger, and an article captioned "Lyons Case Called February 19—Court of Appeals Sets a Time for the Disbarment Proceedings," is another article entitled "LaFollette Is Out Of It."

The previous Friday night Senator LaFollette had been the featured speaker at the Periodical Publishers banquet in Philadelphia. During his address he experienced some sort of a breakdown. His symptoms were not unlike those found in lesser men suffering from inebriation. He raved and ranted and rambled on incoherently for an inordinate length of time about how badly the press had been treating him. Fighting Bob stayed in seclusion for some time thereafter. According to the *Star,* the damage was irreparable.

CHANGED THE POLITICAL SITUATION.

> Regardless of anything that may be said to the contrary, Senator LaFollette's breakdown has utterly changed the situation politically . . . That necessarily increases the demand for the candidacy of Theodore Roosevelt and means almost to a certainty that in the event of Senator LaFollette's enforced withdrawal the Progressive strength will all go to Roosevelt.

The stumping came to an abrupt end. Brandeis made his speech in Kansas City that night and headed east, stopping only in St. Louis to speak at a luncheon the next day at the City Club, a club founded by his young friend Roger Baldwin.[14] The only entry in Brandeis's "Pocket Notebook" for February 6, 1912, reads: "City Club St. Louis, Roger N. Baldwin, 911 Locust." *The St. Louis Republic* of the following day reported his speech under a headline titled "Louis

---

[14] "The St. Louis City Club, which I organized in 1910. . . was a luncheon forum for all sides of public questions." Roger N. Baldwin. *Recollections of a Life in Civil Liberties*—I, Columbia Oral History, 1972, 48.

Brandeis Likens Industrial Struggle to Contest for Liberty."

From there on out LDB's efforts on behalf of LaFollette were purely medicinal. On Wednesday, on the train from St. Louis to New York, he advised Mrs. LaFollette to "make Bob take the rest he needs." At the same time he wrote to his brother Alfred telling him that for his own part "it may be all for the best to have him completely out of the Presidential race."[15] Meanwhile, back in the Western District of Missouri, events had taken a nasty turn for the beleaguered U.S. attorney.

Lyons's chief accuser was another lawyer named Ernest D. Martin, who had been indicted for fraud in connection with the sale of stock in the bankrupt Interstate Railway Company. Martin claimed that the charges were without foundation and that Lyons had engineered his indictment to extort money from him. Shortly after he was indicted, Martin said, he had received a visit from George Davis, Lyons's alleged partner, in which Davis offered his services in seeing to a satisfactory resolution of the matter. In March Martin was brought to trial in the U.S. district court. The prosecution so failed to make its case that the court directed the jury, as a matter of law, to acquit Martin and a co-defendant named Avery.[16]

On March 12 the U.S. House of Representatives adopted a resolution directing the Attorney General "to transmit forthwith to the House of Representatives a copy of the charges filed against Leslie J. Lyons... together with the report of Arthur T. Bagley... and a statement of the action of the Department of Justice, if any, upon said charges and said report." The next day Wickersham wrote Speaker of the House Champ Clark "that justice to Mr. Lyons requires that no action be taken" while the disbarment proceedings were pending. He declined to comply with the request, stating "it is not compatible with the public interest" to do so.[17]

On April 1 the Kansas City Court of Appeals dismissed the

---

[15] Louis D. Brandeis to Belle Case LaFollette, February 7, 1912, *Brandeis Letters* together with commentary.

[16] Francis Wilson, U.S. Attorney, to James C. McReynolds, Attorney General, December 31, 1913, No. 158165-37.

[17] George Wickersham, Attorney General, to Champ Clark, Speaker of the House of Representatives, March 13, 1912, No. 158165-20. The House resolution bears the same serial number.

disbarment proceedings against Lyons.[18] The tribunal did not pursue the charges against him which, if true, constituted malfeasance in his office as a United States attorney. Lyons had argued, and they agreed, that this was a matter best left to federal authorities. On April 5 Attorney General Wickersham forwarded to the Speaker of the House a copy of the Appeals Court's decision: "This decision deals with substantially all of the charges filed against Mr. Lyons with this Department, and acquits him of any improper conduct in connection with any of them."[19]

This did not satisfy Congressman William P. Borland, Democrat of Missouri, who had introduced House Resolution 488 to direct the Attorney General to produce the requested information. "The fact is," stated Borland, "that the disbarment proceedings . . . wholly failed to reach the most serious charges against the conduct of Mr. Lyons." If these allegations were true, he concluded, Lyons "should not be permitted to resign, but should be instantly dismissed from employment by the United States Government."

According to Borland, Lyons, during his tenure as U.S. district attorney, had been involved in land swindles in both Florida and Oregon operated by companies based in Kansas City. One of them, the Oregon Valley Land Company, had used the mails to defraud. "If the investigation was made with the ample facilities at the command of the Department of Justice," continued Borland, "it would disclose that Lyons had been attorney for one of the meanest swindles ever devised or conducted in this country, resulting in the victimizing of about 25,000 poor people."

> It might be contended that the connection of Lyons with the company was merely in a professional character and that he is not responsible for the sins of his client . . .
>
> In the minds of the people, however, and in the minds of the members of the bar there is a plain distinction between representing a client in litigation and acting as counsel and confidential advisor of a crooked scheme. If

---

[18] "Lyons Exonerated by Appeals Court," *Kansas City Journal,* April 2, 1912.
[19] George Wickersham to Champ Clark, April 5, 1912, No. 158165-25.

Lyons is guilty of the latter, he has no right to occupy an official position as the law officer of the United States Government.[20]

The House passed the Borland Resolution on May 25, 1912, and sent it to the Attorney General:

> RESOLVED, That the Attorney General of the United States be, and he is hereby, directed, if not incompatible with public interest, to transmit forthwith to the House of Representatives a copy of the charges filed against Leslie J. Lyons, United States district attorney for the western district of Missouri, together with the report of Arthur T. Bagley, special agent detailed by the Department of Justice to investigate said charges, and a statement of the action of the Department of Justice, if any, upon said charges and report.[21]

The Attorney General again declined to comply. "In my opinion," he said, "it would be most unfair to Mr. Lyons to give publicity or currency to the report of the special agent referred to [Bagley], which was a confidential report for the information of this Department, or to the papers accompanying the report . . . [I]t is not compatible with the public interest, to make them public."[22]

In his letter of April 5, Attorney General Wickersham had informed Speaker of the House Champ Clark that the Kansas City Court's decision dealt "with substantially all of the charges filed against Mr. Lyons with this Department, and acquits him of any improper conduct in connection with any of them." Not only was this statement false, the Attorney General knew it to be false.

Wickersham had instructed A. Bruce Bielaski, Acting Chief, Bureau of Investigation, to examine the opinion of the Kansas City Court of Appeals and to advise him "whether or not the charges

---

[20] Quotations are from "Hearings before the Committee on the Judiciary" (Special Subcommittee No. 7) Sixty Second Congress, Second Session, on House Resolution 488, April 22, 1912. LESLIE J. LYONS.

[21] House Resolution 488.

[22] George Wickersham to Champ Clark, May 28, 1912, No. 158165-27.

before the Department are all covered by that opinion." Bielaski concluded that there were two charges which were not. These were the two charges made by Congressman Borland. One was "the matter of Mr. Lyons' employment as Attorney for the Oregon Valley Land Company" of Kansas City and the second "was his alleged partnership with George L. Davis." Bielaski's report did not rebut the charges Borland had made; it bore them out.

> Evidence is found in Agent Bagley's report concerning Mr. Lyons relations with [George] Davis, which was not brought out in the disbarment proceedings. It seems to me clear that regardless of any provisions of the state law which do not seem to be applicable, no attorney as closely associated with Mr. Lyons as Mr. Davis appears to have been, should defend criminal cases which are prosecuted by Mr. Lyons . . .

> The report of Agent Bagley also contains much data with reference to the Oregon Valley Land Company matter which was not before the Kansas City Court of Appeals. It seems clear that the concerns promoted and operated by Mr. Lyons' clients may well be termed "shady" and that they have been under investigation by the Post Office Department at different times which is apparently known by Mr. Lyons. An investigation of the company is now in progress and should be completed within the next two months. It seems highly probable that this investigation will develop facts calling for a criminal prosecution. Mr. Lyons' connection with this company, as shown by Agent Bagley's report, seems to me to be one which subjects him to severe criticism and one which ought not to continue.[23]

Nor was that the end of the matter. On July 17, 1912, Wickersham wrote a letter to President Taft. "Word comes from your Secretary's office, asking that a copy of the charges against United States Attorney Lyons, at Kansas City, shall be sent over to you."[24] This was done and on August 5 Taft returned the papers

---

[23] "Memorandum for the Attorney General," A. Bruce Bielaski, April 5, 1912, No. 158165-24.
[24] George W. Wickersham to William H. Taft, July 17, 1912, No. 158165-29.

along with a letter concurring with Wickersham's recommendation. "Deferring to that judgment, in which I concur, notify Mr. Lyons that he is acquitted of any charges made against him."[25]

A synopsis of this letter, now among the Taft Papers, was made for the President's own records. Entitled "The White House Files— Memorandum,"[26] it listed the papers Taft reviewed and returned to Wickersham. Significantly the Bielaski Report is not among them. One doubts that William Howard Taft would have "acquitted" Leslie Lyons had he been aware of Bielaski's conclusions.

The President had his hands full at the time. After LaFollette's breakdown in Philadelphia, Colonel Theodore Roosevelt threw his hat in the ring and, to the surprise of no one, thrashed both Taft and LaFollette in the Republican primaries. But Taft controlled the party machinery, and when the Republican Convention met in June, he was renominated.

When the Democratic Convention met in Baltimore shortly thereafter, the front runner was House Speaker Champ Clark. However, the Missourian was never quite able to muster the then-required two-thirds majority, and on July 2, on the 46th ballot, the nomination went to Woodrow Wilson. In Chicago Progressive Republicans organized the Bull Moose Party and held their own convention. Everyone knew who the Bull Moose was, and on August 6, 1912, Theodore Roosevelt accepted their nomination.

Having sat on the sidelines since February, Brandeis declared for Wilson in July. On August 28 he met the New Jersey governor at Sea Girt and agreed to campaign for him. And campaign he did. In October he spoke in 15 different cities in 23 days urging Progressive Republicans to support the Democratic candidate. His message was heard and heeded. On November 5 Thomas Woodrow Wilson was elected the 28th President of the United States by a plurality of the popular vote. His victory was due in no small measure to the support of Louis Brandeis.

Two days later the trial of Fremont Weeks began. Arrested in December and indicted in April, Weeks, as we have seen, was not

---

[25] William H. Taft to George W. Wickersham, August 5, 1912, No. 158165-31.

[26] Taft Papers.

brought to trial until November. The delay was due to the fact that the federal court for the Western District of Missouri in 1912 was in a sense a circuit court dividing its time among six cities.[27] It sat in Kansas City only in April and November.

Fremont Weeks was convicted on November 9, 1912, and sentenced one week later. No one can accuse the judge or the lawyers of foot-dragging. The writ of error and the accompanying transcript were filed in the Supreme Court on February 17, 1913. On the 4th of March came the changing of the guard.

The new President chose as his Attorney General James C. McReynolds, a noted anti-trust lawyer and former professor at Vanderbilt University Law School in Nashville, Tennessee. A self-styled "old-time Cleveland Democrat," McReynolds had gone to Washington to serve in the administration of Theodore Roosevelt.

> In 1903 Philander C. Knox, Republican Attorney General, was looking for a $30,000-a-year lawyer who would work for $5,000. A friend gave him the name of James Clark McReynolds but warned that he was a Democrat. Mr. Knox said that he wanted a lawyer, not a politician, and he made the young Tennessee lawyer Assistant Attorney General and put him in charge of antitrust prosecutions. In this position McReynolds remained from 1903 to 1907 and successfully prosecuted many important cases. Thereafter he practiced for several years in New York City.

In 1910 McReynolds "came back to the Department of Justice as Special Assistant to the Attorney General and successfully prosecuted and argued in the Supreme Court the celebrated *American Tobacco Company* case."[28] He resigned in protest in 1911

---

[27] Kansas City, St. Joseph, Springfield, Jefferson City, Joplin, and Chillecothe. The two terms allotted Kansas City commenced on the fourth Monday in April and the first Monday in November. The cities and the terms were printed on the stationery of the U.S. attorney as well as the district judge.

[28] The quotes with reference to McReynolds are taken from *In Memory of Mr. Justice McReynolds*, 334 U.S. v-xxiv, March 31, 1948.

when Wickersham "approved a dissolution decree that left control of the reorganized tobacco industry in the hands of the former owners of the so-called 'Tobacco Trust.'"[29]

On June 9, 1913, the Justice Department petitioned the Supreme Court to advance the *Weeks* case and to "place it on the summary docket for hearing at the beginning of the next term" in October. This motion was made over the signatures of both McReynolds and Denison. Martin J. O'Donnell, Weeks's attorney, had no objection, and the motion was granted on June 16.[30] Thereafter nothing remained to be done in Kansas City. The case would be briefed and argued in Washington by Winfred T. Denison.

McReynolds, a man not known as long-suffering, had shown a remarkable tolerance of Leslie Lyons and the problems his continuing presence was causing the administration of justice in the Western District of Missouri. This came to an end on July 1 when the Attorney General wrote his Republican holdover a letter asking for his resignation. On July 5 Lyons complied by tendering his resignation "to take effect at such time as the president may designate."[31]

After Weeks's conviction in 1912 Leslie Lyons had written a letter to Wickersham[32] setting forth the facts and circumstances surrounding the arrest of Weeks and the search of his house. Anyone thereafter reviewing the case file in Washington or in Kansas City would have this understanding of the sequence of events:

> The police officers at Kansas City discovered lottery tickets and other evidence of a lottery enterprise in Weeks' possession when they arrested him at the union depot in this city, on some state charge. The police thereupon went to his residence, and found a grip full of lottery tickets and other paraphernalia connected with

[29] Arthur S. Link. *Wilson, The New Freedom*. Princeton: Princeton University Press, 1956, 116.

[30] Solicitor General John W. Davis to Martin J. O'Donnell, September 23, 1913, No. 160003-10, #112, Straight Numerical Files, 1904-37, DJA, NARA. All correspondence relating to *Weeks v. United States* bears the prefix 160003. Henceforward they will be identified simply by serial number.

[31] Leslie Lyons to James C. McReynolds, July 5, 1913, No. 160003. A copy of the letter to Lyons requesting his resignation is missing, but reference is made to it in Lyons's letter of resignation.

[32] Leslie Lyons to George W. Wickersham, December 2, 1912, No. 160003-2.

the lottery enterprise; took it to the police station, and called United States Marshal Martin. He went to the police station, examined the tickets, and went with one or more police officers to the residence of Weeks, and procured a large number of letters and other evidence pertaining to the lottery.

The Supreme Court eventually held that the search by Marshal Martin was made in violation of the Fourth Amendment. They reversed the conviction of Fremont Weeks and ordered the return of the evidence seized by the marshal. Since, however, the Fourth Amendment does not apply to the states, said the Court, the U.S. attorney, should he elect to try the defendant again, was free to use "the papers and property seized by the [Kansas City] policemen."[33] This established what became known as the "silver platter" doctrine.

Assistant Attorney General Ernest Knaebel inquired into the possibility of trying Weeks a second time using only the evidence seized by the Kansas City policemen. The inquiry ended up being referred to Post Office Inspector Frank F. Sharon in Kansas City, who had prepared the original case against Fremont Weeks. Compare his statement of the facts to that of Leslie Lyons, the testimony of the U.S. marshal, and the Court's opinion:

> You will recall that all the evidence in this case was secured by the Police Department of Kansas City, Missouri, from the residence of Mr. Weeks which had been entered for the purpose of securing evidence against his wife on a charge of shoplifting. This evidence consisting of lottery tickets and correspondence from persons who were purchasing from him lottery tickets was turned over to the United States Marshal by the Police Officers who discovered it. The case was made up of the evidence thus secured, there being absolutely no evidence obtainable of

---

[33] "As to the papers and property seized by the [Kansas City] policemen, it does not appear that they acted under any claim of Federal authority such as would make the [Fourth] Amendment applicable to such unauthorized seizures." *Weeks*, 398.

the promotion of this lottery scheme except through the papers secured as stated above.[34]

But Fremont Weeks was never tried again. Having played his brief role on the stage of American legal history, he fell back into the obscurity whence he had been plucked. Nothing is known of what happened to Weeks; he simply disappeared.

Arba S. Van Valkenburgh was elevated to the United States Circuit Court of Appeals for the Eighth Circuit. He retired in 1932 and died November 4, 1944, at the age of 82.[35] Thaddeus B. Landon was 36 years old when he tried the *Weeks* case in 1912. He served as a municipal court judge in Kansas City from 1920 to 1926 and died January 11, 1944, at the age of 67.[36]

Leslie Lyons went on to live a long and pious life. According to his obituary[37] he "taught a Sunday school class 60 years." His longevity was perhaps due to his abstemiousness. An ardent "Dry," Lyons lamented the repeal of Prohibition. "Churchmen," he said, "should have played a greater part in the elimination of liquor and should have continued the crusade." Undaunted he carried on. "In the early 30's, Lyons headed the Anti-Saloon League here in its drive to strengthen the law against the use of liquor in Missouri." Leslie J. Lyons died on Thursday, November 21, 1963. His obituary was published the next day, a good day to disappear into history.

---

[34] F.S. Sharon to F.M. Wilson, April 29, 1914; File No. 160003.

[35] "Van Valkenburgh Dies," *Kansas City Star*, November 5, 1944.

[36] "Thad B. Landon" obituary, *Kansas City Times*, January 12, 1944.

[37] "Leslie J. Lyons Dies," *Kansas City Times*, November 22, 1963.

Chapter IV

THE HOUSE OF TRUTH

Henry Lewis Stimson (1867-1950) served in the cabinets of four Presidents. He is perhaps best known for serving as Secretary of War during World War II under Presidents Franklin Roosevelt and Harry Truman. He had held the same post in the Taft Administration before the First World War, and in between times he was Secretary of State in the administration of Herbert Hoover. In 1920 he wrote this eulogy to the memory of the man who wrote the brief for the United States in the case that established the exclusionary rule.

> Winfred Thaxter Denison was born of New England parents at Portland, Maine, on the 30th day of June, 1873. He was educated at Phillips Exeter Academy and Harvard University, graduating in 1896. During his course at Harvard he attained distinction in English, being made Editor-in-Chief of the Harvard Monthly during his school [senior] year, the highest recognition obtainable by an undergraduate in that field. After a year's travel abroad, he entered the Harvard Law School, graduating with an LL.B. degree in 1900. He then came to New York and joined the office of Stetson, Jennings & Russell, remaining with them until he became Assistant United States Attorney for the Southern District of New York in 1906.[1]

---

[1] *Memorial of Winfred T. Denison*, 1921 New York City Bar 180, Law Library, Association of the Bar of the City of New York.

In 1906 President Theodore Roosevelt appointed Stimson to be the United States Attorney for the Southern District of New York with the understanding that he would reorganize that office and undertake a vigorous prosecution of the Sherman Anti-Trust Act. To assist him, Stimson recruited some young and able lawyers, including Winfred Denison. The youngest and probably the most able was 24-year-old Felix Frankfurter. Denison and Frankfurter became fast friends.

Felix Frankfurter was born in Vienna, Austria, of Jewish parents in 1882 and, when brought to the United States at the age of 12, spoke no English. In 1902 Frankfurter graduated from City College in New York the third highest in his class. He then entered Harvard Law School and graduated first in the class of 1906. Before the year was out Frankfurter was one of Stimson's bright young men.

At the expiration of Theodore Roosevelt's second term Stimson resigned and, by the spring of 1909, had resumed the practice of law in New York City. The following year he was the Republican candidate for governor of New York, and Frankfurter his personal secretary and speech writer. Colonel Roosevelt campaigned for him unstintingly, but to no avail. The political tides were running against the Republicans, and 1910 was a Democratic year. John A. Dix beat Stimson handily while Woodrow Wilson, the president of Princeton University, was elected governor of New Jersey.

As we have seen, the 1910 debacle widened the breach between the Progressive Republicans led by Theodore Roosevelt and the "Old Guard" who supported President William Howard Taft. In 1911, as a gesture of conciliation, Taft invited Stimson to be his Secretary of War and, with Roosevelt's blessing, he accepted. When Stimson went to Washington, he took Felix Frankfurter with him.

Denison, meanwhile, had already moved to Washington to become assistant to Attorney General George W. Wickersham. He and a college classmate shared bachelor quarters at a townhouse near Dupont Circle, where they did a lot of entertaining of some very important people. A half-century later Mr. Justice Frankfurter reminisced that "almost everyone who was interesting in

Washington sooner or later passed through that house."[2] It was Justice Oliver Wendell Holmes Jr. who dubbed it the "House of Truth,"[3] and the name stuck. Another frequent visitor was the man who will shape the life of Felix Frankfurter, Louis Dembitz Brandeis.

While a law student, Frankfurter had attended a lecture by Brandeis and had since corresponded with the older man. But the first time they met socially, so it seems, was at a luncheon with Winfred Denison on October 20, 1911. That night Frankfurter began keeping a diary in which he noted the luncheon and his appraisal of Brandeis. "Brandeis is a very big man, one of the most penetrating minds I know; I should like to see him Attorney General of the United States."[4]

It must have been a heady experience for such a young man to be on familiar terms with the notables of the day. On his "morning ride" on the "crisp" autumn day of October 24 Frankfurter ran "into the Attorney General and rode with him. He was exceeding cordial and genuinely friendly . . . Wickersham has a vivid, fresh, agile, prehensile mind." From Frankfurter's description of the encounter, "Wick" gave him his opinion on just about everything and everybody.[5] Frankfurter had a fine evening as well.

> Delightful evening with Dobbin Denison and his sister. Had a good talk—he is a generous spirit, with plenty of self assurance for the good of others. Worries whether to become a judge or not—really thinks himself more fitted for higher secular leadership and I am not sure but that he is right . . . I'll top off the night by reading LaFollette's autobiography in the November *American*. As [with] Denison, LaFollette's stock is going up with us.[6]

---

[2] *Felix Frankfurter Reminisces*, 106.

[3] Bruce Allen Murphy. *The Brandeis/Frankfurter Connection: The Secret Political Activities of Two Supreme Court Justices*. Garden City, New York: Anchor Press/Doubleday & Company, 1983. "The conversation there was so lively that Oliver Wendell Holmes soon dubbed it 'The House of Truth,'" 36, 37.

[4] *From the Diaries of Felix Frankfurter*, Joseph P. Lash, editor. New York: W.W. Norton, 1975, 104, hereinafter *Diaries*.

[5] *Diaries*, 107, 108.

[6] *Diaries*, 109.

On October 29 Frankfurter had "a good, cozy evening with Denisons."[7] He had not as yet moved into the House of Truth, but on November 21 was there as a guest. "Had a fine evening with Ray Stannard Baker at Denison's. Baker talked LaFollette to whom I am 'cottoning' more and more."[8] The next day the diary breaks off.

It is a pity for posterity that Frankfurter did not continue the diary so that, to use his own words, "events out of the ordinary . . . should be preserved . . . in whatever amber of permanence this halting pen of mine can give them."[9] He did it so beautifully and so well. That he did not continue makes our task the more difficult but nevertheless possible. As we shall see, much can be gleaned from the *Papers of Louis D. Brandeis* and from *Felix Frankfurter Reminisces* as well as from the correspondence between Denison, Frankfurter and Stimson which has been preserved. Chapter 12 of *Felix Frankfurter Reminisces* is entitled "The House of Truth." It begins:

> When I first came down to Washington I lived in an apartment house for bachelors, but shortly thereafter I moved into what became known as the House of Truth. The house was at 1727 Nineteenth Street and was owned by Robert G. Valentine who was at that time Commissioner of Indian Affairs. He was a gifted, imaginative, poetical thinker. Indeed, he wrote a lot of poetry. I came to know him because he was a classmate of Winfred T. Denison . . . Anyway, Valentine asked us to join him in his house when his wife and his child moved north. The child, a daughter, had an illness which made the climate of Washington unsalubrious for her . . .
>
> That was the original group that lived in the House of Truth—Valentine, Winfred Denison, Eustace Percy, Loring Christie, and myself. The house continued as bachelors' quarters, and we lived an easy and gay life.[10]

---

[7] *Diaries*, 114. Denison's sister was visiting him.

[8] *Diaries*, 120, 121. Ray Stannard Baker later became Woodrow Wilson's official biographer.

[9] *Diaries*, 102.

[10] *Reminisces*, 105, 106. Mrs. Valentine and her daughter moved to her parents' home in South Braintree, Massachusetts.

In December of 1911, five young men dwelt in the House of Truth. Three of them were Americans, one an Englishman and the other a Canadian. Of the Americans only Felix Frankfurter will live a full life and rise to prominence; Valentine and Denison will die young. The Canadian was Loring C. Christie, a graduate of the Harvard Law School and an assistant to Denison in the Attorney General's Office. In later life a Canadian diplomat, Christie died in New York City in 1941.

The Englishman was "Lord Eustace Percy who was the seventh son of the seventh Duke of Northumberland, one of the great magnates of the United Kingdom. Percy himself was much more of a dreamer and a mystic than the son of a great landowner."[11] Shortly before his death in 1958, his autobiography, *Some Memories,* was published by Eyre & Spottiswoode of London. It is a book which gives an insight into both the author and the House of Truth. Chapter II—"Before 1914: Washington, 1910-14"—begins:

> The American scene bulks very large in my memories. For one thing, it was the scene where I began my working life, and of such scenes it is written!
>
> "We've only one virginity to lose
> And where we lost it, there our hearts will be."

In 1914 Percy returned to the U.K. and, after a career in the Foreign Office, became rector of Kings College, Newcastle.[12] Eustace Sutherland Campbell Percy died April 3, 1958, at the age of 71 as Lord Percy of Newcastle. His lifelong friend, Sir Harold Nicolson, attended his funeral. In a letter that day to his wife, Vita Sackville-West, Nicolson recalled: "And I thought back on the days when Eustace was young and regarded as among the most gifted and promising of my generation."[13]

---

[11] *Reminisces,* 105.

[12] Harold Nicolson. *The Later Years, 1945-1962,* Vol. 3, Nigel Nicholson, editor. New York: Athenaeum, 1968, 235.

[13] *Vita and Harold, The Letters of Vita Sackville-West and Harold Nicolson.* Nigel Nicholson, editor. New York: G.P. Putnam's Sons, 1992, 424-425.

Since the arrest of the McNamara brothers in April of 1911, the case had been front-page news throughout the United States, and word of their confessions hit the East Coast like a bombshell shortly after 5:00 p.m. on Friday, December 1. From the headlines and commentary in the newspapers we can be sure that the drawing rooms of Washington were abuzz with talk about the confessions and how this development might affect the 1912 presidential election. At no place would the discussion have been more animated than at the House of Truth, and most likely it was there, over the weekend of December 2 and 3, that the *Weeks* conspiracy had its genesis.

The dynamiting of the *Los Angeles Times* had generated enormous publicity and Progressives in both major parties had gone out on a limb for the two brothers. Their confessions—in open court—were a devastating blow. And more was yet to come. There will be a protracted trial in 1912—an election year for which Progressives had great hopes—and in the end the union leaders involved are bound to be convicted. There could be no innocent explanation for the dynamite and alarm clocks stashed in the basement vault, and this evidence, taken along with the papers and receipts found amongst them, was more than sufficient to condemn them.

Men like Frank Ryan and the McNamaras by no means considered themselves to be criminals. In their own minds they were revolutionaries not bound by the statute books in their war against capitalist oppression. That blood had to be shed was regrettable but also inevitable; they were but soldiers fighting on behalf of the working class. This posture was condoned if not tacitly endorsed by some Progressives including Louis Brandeis.

Louis Brandeis never mentioned the Los Angeles bombing without coupling it to the trust issue. The idea was to make big business the moral equivalent and underlying cause of labor union violence. He usually began with a reference to the "unpardonable crimes of trade union leaders" and then proceeded, rhetorically at least, to pardon the "unpardonable" and absolve the perpetrators of "individual depravity." And "pardons" were a word very much on the minds of Progressive politicians.

The dynamiting of the *Times* was constantly being compared to another bombing 25 years earlier—the Chicago Haymarket Riot of

1886. The analogy was certainly apt. Each was a *cause célèbre* in which the loss of life was severe—seven policemen were killed at Haymarket Square—and in each case the defendants sought to make their trial a contest between capital and labor. The defendants in the Chicago case, *Spies v. Illinois,*[14] were members of the International Workingmen's Association (IWA), an organization founded by Karl Marx. August Spies was the leader of the Chicago organization. Seven members, including Spies, were convicted of the murder of Mathias Degan, one of the policemen, and sentenced to hang. But Spies, so he claimed, was the victim of an unlawful search and seizure.

On the morning after the bombing, Chicago police had conducted a search, without a warrant, of the office of the IWA, and, on the desk of August Spies, found two dynamite bombs encased in round iron shells. Inside a desk drawer was a letter to Spies from a comrade named Johann Most outlining in the minutest detail the ingredients and the procedure to be used in constructing these "czar bombs." The letter, and the cross-examination in which it was used, discredited Spies's testimony as to the provenance of the bombs.[15]

Spies, who had taken the witness stand in his own defense, apparently had forgotten about the letter. His lawyers appear to have been taken by surprise as well. At any rate no attempt was made to exclude it at the trial. Later, on appeal to the Illinois Supreme Court, his lawyers contended that the use of the letter against Spies violated his rights under both the Illinois and United States Constitutions. That court refused to pass on this objection.

> The objection, that the letter was obtained from the defendants by an unlawful seizure, is made for the first time in this court. It was not made on the trial in the court below. Such an objection as this, which is not suggested by the nature of the offered evidence, but depends upon the proof of an outside fact, should have been made on the trial. The defence should have proved that the [Johann] Most letter was one of the letters

---

[14] 122 Ill. 1, 12 N.E. 865 (1887).
[15] 122 Ill. 233, 234.

illegally seized by the police and should then have moved to exclude it, or opposed its admission, on the ground that it was obtained by such illegal seizure. This was not done, and, therefore, we can not consider the constitutional question supposed to be involved.[16]

The conviction of the Haymarket defendants precipitated a propaganda campaign the intensity of which had never been seen in American politics before. A defense committee was formed and the defendant's supporters pressured prominent citizens into making statements proclaiming the unfairness of the trial and the innocence of the defendants. Progressive politicians found themselves put to a test of fealty. It was a time "when every individual, especially every individual of prominence, had to choose between the path of shame and the path of glory."[17] "In Chicago stand convicted, Seven of nature's noblest men," began a poem which ended "Noble men who lived for others, Cannot, will not, must not die."[18] However, the largest union in the country, with a membership of more than 700,000, had a different opinion.

Let it be understood by all the world that the Knights of Labor have no affiliation, association, sympathy or respect for the band of cowardly murderers, cut-throats and robbers, known as anarchists, who sneak through the county like midnight assassins, stirring up the passions of ignorant foreigners, unfurling the red flag of anarchy and causing riot and bloodshed. Parsons, Spies, Fielding, [sic] Most and all their followers, sympathizers, aiders and abettors should be summarily dealt with. They are entitled to no more consideration than wild beasts. The leaders are cowards and their followers are fools.[19]

Spies and his comrades took their appeal to the Supreme Court of the United States. The use of the letter found in Spies's desk in

---

[16] Ibid., 233.
[17] Paul Avrich. *The Haymarket Tragedy.* Princeton: Princeton University Press, 1984, 301.
[18] Ibid., 306, 307.
[19] Ibid., 220.

cross-examining him, he alleged, not only violated the Fourth Amendment's guaranty against unreasonable search and seizure, it compelled Spies, in a criminal case, to be a witness against himself in violation of that provision of the Fifth Amendment. On November 2, 1887, addressing a packed courtroom, Chief Justice Morrison R. Waite delivered the opinion of a unanimous Court stating once again that the Fourth and Fifth Amendments, like the rest of the Bill of Rights, apply only to the federal government and not to the individual states:

> That the first ten Articles of Amendment were not intended to limit the powers of the state governments in respect to their own people, but to operate on the National Government alone, was decided more than a half century ago, and that decision has been steadily adhered to since.[20]

These words sounded the death knell. Two of the condemned men were spared when Governor Richard Oglesby commuted their sentences to life imprisonment. One, Louis Lingg, committed suicide on the eve of the execution by lighting a dynamite-laden cigar. On November 11, 1887, in the Cook County Jail, amid a crescendo of protest by their sympathizers outside, from a specially constructed gallows for four, August Spies and three of his comrades were hung. After an effusion of funeral corteges and graveside eulogies they were laid to rest and the Defense Committee began a campaign to free those serving prison sentences. The tactics remained the same.

In 1892 John Peter Altgeld was elected governor of Illinois. A Progressive Democrat, Altgeld was known for having written a book, *"Our Penal Machinery and Its Victims*, a powerful plea for society to focus its energies on eliminating the causes of crime rather than on punishing wrongdoers."[21] In 1893 Governor Altgeld pardoned the remaining Haymarket defendants on the grounds that they had not been given a fair trial. In 1896 he ran for re-

---

[20] *Spies v. Illinois*, 123 U.S. 131, 166 (1887).
[21] Cowan, 27.

election and was defeated decisively in a campaign in which the pardons were the overriding issue.

Altgeld's defeat was viewed from different perspectives. To Clarence Darrow, who had influenced the governor's decision to issue the pardons, "a flood of vituperation and gall was poured upon Altgeld's head."[22] New York City Police Commissioner Theodore Roosevelt, on the other hand, charged Altgeld with justifying "wholesale murder . . . by elaborate and cunning sophistry for reasons known only to his tortuous soul."[23]

"The election was a fiasco." Shortly before election day, a number of Chicago Democratic ward leaders defected "and the whole organization disrupted."[24] John Peter Altgeld never recovered from his defeat and died at the age of 54, a broken man.[25] The lessons to be learned from the Haymarket Riot and its aftermath, you can be sure, were not lost on Progressive leaders a quarter of a century later.

In one way the McNamaras' perfidy had worked in favor of the Progressives. To most men of labor the name McNamara now ranked with Iscariot; martyrdom would not be their lot. As far as Progressive politicians were concerned, the brothers could rot in San Quentin forever. But the prosecution of a large number of labor leaders with varying degrees of culpability was a different matter. So far as could be foreseen, the BSIW's leadership was going to be indicted and most likely convicted. When the law has run its course they will come looking for pardons. And when they come, they will come singing "Solidarity Forever." All kinds of pressure will be brought to bear to free the convicted unionists.

A Progressive President, should Americans choose to elect one in the 1912 contest that was fast approaching, would have to make a choice. If he refuses the pardons he incurs the wrath of the Socialist constituency of the Progressive coalition. If he grants the pardons he offends those working class voters who, in the vernacular of today's

---

[22] Ibid., 31.
[23] Ibid., 37.
[24] Ibid., 37.
[25] Ibid., 46, 47.

politics, would be called "cultural conservatives," as well as the vast majority of the people who, like Theodore Roosevelt, believe that "murder is murder." It would be the "Altgeld dilemma" all over again.

It is clear how an exclusionary rule—established in a case with no apparent connection with that of the Dynamiters—would have served Progressive interests at this time. Bear in mind that "labor unrest" was not an issue between the major parties. Those who thought as did Louis Brandeis were every bit as influential in the Republican Party as they were in the Democratic Party. And had LaFollette prevailed in 1912 they would have been in ascendancy.

The fate of Frank Ryan and his fellow union leaders depended upon the evidence found in the basement vault; without it the testimony of McManigal could not be corroborated and the case against them would fail. But suppose, on the basis of a precedent decided in an intervening case—a nonpolitical, innocuous, nondescript case—*Jones v. United States*, to give it a name—the Supreme Court reversed the Dynamiters' convictions on the ground that evidence used to convict them was taken in a search and seizure forbidden by the Fourth Amendment? *Jones*, the case on which they posit their decision, established the principle that such tainted evidence must be excluded in a federal criminal trial. It was error—reversible error—for the trial court in Indianapolis to have admitted it and the defendants must be granted a new trial in which, of course, the unlawfully obtained evidence must be excluded under the *Jones* rule.

This would mean, would it not, that a newly elected Progressive President—a Fighting Bob LaFollette, for example—would never have to face the divisive question of whether to pardon union men who, in their own minds, and in the minds of their supporters, were nothing more than combatants in the struggle for industrial liberty? An Attorney General in a LaFollette administration—Louis Brandeis being the most likely—could simply announce that the prosecution no longer had the evidence—the constitutionally admissible evidence—necessary for a conviction, so that the case against the Dynamiters must be dismissed.

There would be protests, of course, but nothing Progressives couldn't deal with. The Fourth Amendment, after all, protects the security of the homes and persons of us all against unjustified intrusions by federal officers, and if as a result some criminals go free, that then is the price we pay for freedom. They would urge Americans to unite and put this ugly incident behind them. They would say the country should move forward and establish an enlightened policy of industrial relations so as to remove, as Louis Brandeis had put it, "the underlying cause . . . that led men like the McNamaras to really believe that the only recourse they had for improving the condition of the wage-earner was to use dynamite against property and life."

We never can really know, of course, what was discussed at the House of Truth that December weekend so long ago. But we do know that its residents were highly politicized Progressive Republicans— mostly lawyers—who would have seen the political implications of the McNamaras' confessions and the inevitability of the trial and conviction of the union leaders which was sure to follow. They would have made the analogy to Altgeld and Haymarket in a flash.

Necessarily we must speculate to some degree, but it will be well-informed speculation. Subsequent events will lead to the conclusion that Felix Frankfurter and Winfred Denison, guided by the invisible hand of Louis Brandeis, conspired to set up what became the *Weeks* case. That they had the propensity to do so will become clear. Opportunity the conspirators had in the person of Winfred Denison. But Assistant Attorney General Denison could not play his role until a case—the right case—made its way to the Supreme Court. And how was this to be accomplished?

When Leslie Lyons appears in the Attorney General's Office on Monday, it is *Kismet*. Here is a United States district attorney in desperate need of help—someone who will do anything for a favor. The Republicans out there in Missouri want to get rid of him for the good of the party. It falls to Winfred Denison to handle this political headache from Kansas City. At some time during his 10-day stay in Washington, Lyons is plumbed and found receptive. The microcosm is discussed in the abstract. Leslie Lyons has plenty of time for reflection on the train ride back to Kansas City. By the time he gets there he knows what he must do as a favor for his friend Winfred Denison. Six days later Olla Weeks went shoplifting for some gloves.

The federal district court sat in Kansas City only in April and November. The docket was congested, and all criminal matters had been put over to the April term.[26] From the very beginning Lyons knew that Fremont Weeks, arrested in December, could not be indicted until April nor tried until November. The fall term commenced on the first Monday in November, which in 1912 was the day before election day.

This meant *United States v. Weeks* was always an expendable case. If the election results were not to their liking, or for some reason the case against the Dynamiters did not jell,[27] the conspirators could simply drop it. Weeks could be given a break. There would be no complaints from a grateful and chastened Fremont Weeks. He would simply vanish into the obscurity whence he came and that would be that.

The campaign of 1912 and the split in the Republican Party brought change to the House of Truth. None of the Americans was for Taft, in whose administration they served. In September Valentine resigned as Commissioner of Indian Affairs to campaign for Roosevelt. Henry L. Stimson was torn between his Progressive principles and his friendship with Theodore Roosevelt on one hand, and the loyalty he owed the Republican Party and the President he served on the other. In the end party and President prevailed and Stimson and Roosevelt became estranged.

There was one Republican, however, who foresaw that the election of Woodrow Wilson could bring about a party realignment much to the advantage of Progressives. And Louis Brandeis ran his own campaign to see that this came to fruition. In a letter to Progressive Republican Gifford Pinchot he pointed out that while the "reactionary forces in that party [the Democrats] are of course strong, stronger perhaps even than in the Republican party," it was "in the power of the Progressives today to make complete their

---

[26] Van Valkenburgh to Lyons, December 28, 1911; Lyons to Wickersham, December 28, 1911, No. 158165-15.

[27] The trial of Frank Ryan et al. began in Indianapolis on October 1, 1912, and was in progress when Fremont Weeks was tried. The Dynamiters were convicted in December of 1912.

control of the Democratic organization."[28] Later that week he wrote Felix Frankfurter that the "duty of Progressives was clearly to support Wilson and practically capture the Democratic party."[29] And this is what came to pass.

Frankfurter had intended to return to New York with Stimson when the Wilson administration took over in 1913. Much to his surprise, he was asked to stay by the new Secretary of War, Lindley M. Garrison. Happily, Democratic Attorney General McReynolds let Denison hold over as well. This meant that but for Valentine, their group remained intact, and Frankfurter and Denison could ponder their future for another year in the congenial confines of the House of Truth.

On June 12, 1913, ostensibly on his own initiative, Winfred Denison wrote his classmate Professor Edward H. Warren of Harvard Law School to see whether there might be an opening on the faculty for Felix Frankfurter. Four days later Warren replied that there "is no vacancy existing or in sight, but [?] an endowment could be raised sufficient for a new professorship the work of which F would be peculiarly fitted to do." Before proceeding further, said Warren, "I think F ought to tell us what his state of mind is." He asked that Denison pose to Frankfurter the following question:[30]

> Suppose a professorship were established for work on criminology or other or further topics in the selection of which [Professor Roscoe] Pound would have a good deal to do. Suppose this professorship became available at the opening of the academic year 1914-15, and was offered to you. Would you accept it?

Thirty-year-old Felix Frankfurter realized he had reached a crossroads in his career. On July 5, 1913, he wrote himself a memorandum listing the alternatives as he saw them.[31] Number (1)

---

[28] LDB to Gifford Pinchot, July 8, 1912, *Brandeis Letters.*

[29] LDB to FF, July 12, 1912, *Brandeis Letters.*

[30] WTD to E.H. Warren, June 12, 1913; E.H. Warren to WTD, June 16, 1913. The Papers of Felix Frankfurter, Library of Congress Manuscript Division, hereinafter Frankfurter Papers.

[31] *Reminisces*, 83.

was "The Valentine thing. [Industrial Relations]" which he rejected because he ought not to "give up the tools of the law." Number (2) was "Stay on here" with the Wilson Administration. He rejected that because Wilson "lacks the very robustness of equipment on those social-economic questions that I want so much to get. Then too, the atmosphere is Southern-Democrat."

What remained was (3) "practice in New York" or teaching at Harvard. Frankfurter knew he must choose between going back to New York City and practicing law and Progressive Republican politics under the tutelage of Henry L. Stimson, or accepting the professorship. He took the road which would lead to Cambridge and beyond as the *alter ego* of Louis D. Brandeis. Two days later he wrote to Stimson to advise him he had opted for Harvard. He closed by telling Stimson about how his two proteges were getting on that summer in Washington. "It's hot here—rather—but Denison & I are conjugally happy."[32]

October of 1913 ended a long, hot summer and began a new term of the Supreme Court. It was a year of decision at the House of Truth. As a result of the chain of events set in motion by the *Weeks* case, two friends would soon part. Felix Frankfurter will take the road to prestige and influence while Winfred Denison's lot will be misery and an early grave.

Senator James A. O'Gorman, Democrat of New York, was very much concerned with the future of the Philippine Islands, whose emancipation was a plank in the Democratic Platform of 1912. A Democratic President now had been in the White House for more than three months, yet no steps had been taken in the right direction. Senator O'Gorman, Chairman of the Committee on Naval Affairs, had no reticence in telling Joseph P. Tumulty, Woodrow Wilson's personal secretary of long standing, exactly what those steps were.

> But while the actual job of emancipating the Filipinos must be the work of Congress, President Wilson, it seems to me ought to remove the Republicans Taft

---

[32] FF to HLS, July 7, 1913, Frankfurter Papers.

appointed as Commissioners, and put Democrats in
their places, especially as they are known to be working
against independence.[33]

Felix Frankfurter was employed by the War Department as the
law officer for the Bureau of Insular Affairs, the same post he had held
under Henry L. Stimson. Insular Affairs, as the name implies, had
jurisdiction over the island possessions of the United States including
those taken from Spain in the 1898 war. In October of 1913, three
Republicans resigned as commissioners of the Philippine Islands,
giving President Wilson the opportunity, as Senator O'Gorman had
hoped, to put Democrats in their places. No one would have learned
of this fact any sooner than Felix Frankfurter.

Henry L. Stimson got the first inkling of what was to happen to
his remaining protégé on October 22 when Frankfurter telephoned
to say Denison had been offered an appointment in the Philippines.
Stimson was horrified; he thought "that Denison is disqualified by
physique and temperament. I think it would be probably the worst
place in the world for him to go to. I don't think you ought to
suggest it to him."[34] The problem was that Denison had previously
contracted typhoid fever.[35]

Frankfurter had arranged to spend the first weekend of
November at Highhold, the Stimson family home at Huntington,
Long Island. On October 28 FF wrote his erstwhile mentor that he
would be bringing along his friend Herbert Croly. With reference
to the "Philippine business," he said, "The thing is in a curious
situation and I'll tell you the story when I see you this week-end."[36]
On the same day Denison wrote this note to presidential secretary
Joseph Tumulty:

---

[33] James A. O'Gorman to J.P. Tumulty, June 12, 1913, Woodrow Wilson Papers, Library of
Congress, Manuscript Division. The Wilson Papers have an index listing correspondents
alphabetically and their correspondence chronologically so that further identification is
unnecessary.
[34] HLS to FF, October 22 and 23, 1913, Henry L. Stimson Papers, Manuscripts and Archives,
Yale University Library, hereinafter Stimson Papers.
[35] WTD to HLS, November 11, 1913, Stimson Papers.
[36] FF to HLS, October 28, 1913, Frankfurter Papers. In 1914 Croly founded *The New Republic*.

Confirming our conversation this morning:—

Before action is taken upon the [War] Secretary's
suggestion of my name, may I have an opportunity to say
yes or no finally?

The idea is very sudden to me and would
revolutionize my whole long-settled course, and so I do
not wish to act hastily or without the advice of several
people who can enlighten me.[37]

The moment of truth came the following Tuesday, November
4, when the Court "entered an order assigning all the cases on the
summary docket [including *Weeks*] for argument on December first
next."[38] December 1, 1913, fell on a Monday, which being the first
Monday in December, was, before the passage of the 20th
Amendment, the date for Congress to convene. On November 4
Winfred Denison sent his patron a long letter which opened:[39]

Dear Mr. Stimson

On that Philippine question I should have written
you except that I was swamped by a bunch of cases here
and I thought it would be better to have Felix give you
the whole situation and my point of view *viva voce*.

The decision had not been easy and "for 4 or 5 days after he
[Felix] put it to me," Denison agonized, and then decided to take
the job if it were offered to him. There were considerations, he
wrote, of which Stimson had been unaware. "I told Felix to give you
the story fully, and I assume from his note he's done so. Of my
health and physique, I have no fears. My doctor advises me to go;
and I'm in far different condition (medically different) from the
days we used to be together."

---
[37] WTD to Joseph Tumulty, October 28, 1913, Wilson Papers.
[38] J.D. Maher, Clerk of Sup. Ct. to Sol. Gen., November 4, 1913, No. 160003-12, #112,
Straight Numerical Files, 1904-37, DJA, NARA.
[39] WTD to HLS, November 4, 1913, Stimson Papers.

While going to the Philippines would be an adventure, what weighed most heavily in this decision was the money. The annual salary was the then princely sum of "$15,500[40] and traveling expenses and they say I can live suitably on less than half of it which would mean a savings of $22,000 in the 3 years." Denison had hoped to visit Stimson in New York to talk it over, but this was not to be.[41] On November 25 he sent Stimson a letter[42] bidding him *au revoir*.

On Saturday, November 22, Secretary of War Garrison wrote President Wilson that "I have just seen Senator O'Gorman, and he is satisfied to have Denison's name go in."[43] On Monday, November 24, 1913, President Woodrow Wilson nominated Winfred T. Denison as the Secretary of the Interior of the Philippine Islands.[44] On Wednesday Denison filed his brief in the *Weeks* case and on Thursday, Thanksgiving Day, wrote Frankfurter this handwritten note.[45]

Dear Felix

What can I say to you?

I suppose you have no real conception of what you have done for me these years and how your unwavering patience has filled me with astonishment and your wonderful wisdom and ideas with inspiration and a glimmering hope which your final magic touch in these last few weeks has changed to a final confidence.

You were There at the Crossing of my Rubicon, and built in a good many of the [Embers of my Forge?]. More anon but this immediately.

Faithfully yours,
W.

[40] On January 5, 1914, the Ford Motor Company made history when it raised basic wage rates from $2.40 for a 9 hour day to $5.00 for an 8 hour day, or about $1,300 a year. "U.S. History by year"—*The World Almanac*.

[41] WTD to HLS, November 13, 1913, HLS to WTD, November 14, 1913, Stimson Papers.

[42] WTD to HLS, November 25, 1913, Stimson Papers.

[43] L.M. Garrison to WW, November 22, 1913, Wilson Papers.

[44] "Named For Filipino Board," *New York Times*, November 25, 1913.

[45] WTD to FF, November 27, 1913, Reel 31, Frankfurter Papers.

When the *Weeks* case was argued in Washington the following Tuesday, the advocate for the United States was in San Francisco. On the same day, December 2, 1913, Frankfurter wrote Stimson that Denison had left. "Denison has gone to the Coast—and it is a big 'gone' for me. But he went in such high spirits and was so eager for the adventure, that I am happy about it."[46] However, there was a snag in the Senate.

> There is a temporary slip up in Denison's confirmation, due to O'Gorman's absence. Senator [James A.] Reed [D-Mo.], who is acting Chairman of the Committee, is a bit unwilling to let what someone has called the "noble salary" of the Philippine secretaryship be withdrawn from Democratic consumption. O'Gorman had been seen, however, before the name was sent in and I anticipate no trouble. The President is especially interested in the appointment and will see it through.

Denison's problems in the Senate came not from the Democrats who controlled it but from members of his own party. In the course of his duties he had been involved in an investigation into the Board of United States General Appraisers. A "Committee of Inquiry," including Denison, concluded that a Republican named Starretts "should be removed forthwith"[47] for malfeasance in office. Starretts had friends in high places, of whom one was Senator Reed Smoot, Republican of Utah. It was Smoot who was holding up the confirmation.

On December 21, 1913, we find Winfred Denison headed north on the Shasta Limited De Luxe train en route from San Francisco to Seattle typing a letter to Mr. Stimson. In it he tells how "one after another, four of them [steamers] has sailed away into the Pacific with empty rooms in my name." With respect to the holdup of his confirmation by the Senate Denison had this to say:

---

[46] FF to HLS, December 2, 1913, Frankfurter Papers.

[47] "Report of the President's Committee of Inquiry on the Procedure, Practice, Administrative Methods and Personnel of the Board of United States General Appraisers etc.," February 15, 1913. Frankfurter Papers, Container No. 51—Reel 31, Denison Correspondence.

Indeed I particularly would prefer that neither you nor anyone else should do anything at all. I am afraid that Felix has been making some moves by way of a quiet campaign. I am wiring him not to lift a finger because I have not sought this position and I would rather not, directly or indirectly, bring any influence to bear to put it through . . . If you see Felix, I wish you would make sure the busy generous fire-fly is keeping his universal hands off.[48]

A pair of "universal hands" was indeed hard at work undoing the mischief caused by Starretts. In January "the generous fire-fly" had "a long talk with Smoot" and emerged confident that "it is only a question of time before Denison will be confirmed."[49] Stimson had enlisted the aid of Senator Elihu Root, Republican of New York, who said that he would "do whatever I can toward the confirmation of Denison."[50]

On January 19, 1914, Denison dropped Stimson a line from San Francisco to say he had just returned from "a most gorgeous visit into Alaska." He had "got as far up as Juneau and Sitka and found myself amazed every few minutes." He "hoped to get off on the 'Siberia' next Thursday, the 22nd."[51] As it turned out he was confirmed on January 27, 1914, but, because the news was delayed in transmission "he missed his eighth consecutive liner for the Orient."[52]

On January 31, 1914, a Saturday, Winfred Denison, who was staying at the Fairmont Hotel, had General John J. Pershing to tea. Pershing had returned to San Francisco earlier that month after an extended tour of duty in the Philippines.[53] In a letter to his grandmother, Denison described the man who will command the American Expeditionary Force in the coming World War as having

---

[48] WTD to HLS, December 21, 1913, Stimson Papers. The letter is typed on the stationery of the Shasta Limited De Luxe, Southern Pacific R.R.

[49] FF to HLS, January 16, 1914, Stimson Papers.

[50] Elihu Root to HLS, January 10, 1914, Stimson Papers.

[51] WTD to HLS, January 19, 1914, Stimson Papers.

[52] "Misses His Steamer Again," *New York Times*, January 28, 1914.

[53] Gene Smith. *Until the Last Trumpet Sounds: The Life of General of the Armies John J. Pershing.* New York: John Wiley & Sons, Inc., 1998, 118.

"honest blue eyes, and a most friendly and charming manner."[54] On the following Tuesday, February 3rd, Denison sailed "at one o'clock on the S.S. China for Manila."[55]

There were at least three good and sufficient reasons for Winfred Denison to be in Washington the week beginning December 1, 1913. One, of course, was to argue the *Weeks* case. No lawyer, however successful and eminent he might be, would give up the opportunity to argue a case before the Supreme Court of the United States unless he had to. Denison's appearances before the Court were not that frequent.[56] There had to be a reason, a compelling reason, for him to forgo oral argument.

Secondly, civility and ethics demanded he stay long enough to turn over the cases he was "swamped with" to someone else. It has never been considered good form at any time or in any place to walk away from a job without briefing your successor on the matters you have been handling. That Denison was nominated on a Monday, filed the *Weeks* brief on Wednesday, and left for California on the eve of the oral argument is most suspicious. He did not tender his resignation to Attorney General McReynolds before he left, but resigned by telegram from California three weeks later.[57]

It is not expected of a person tapped by the President for foreign service that he pack his bags and proceed forthwith to a seaport proximate to his new post to await the outcome of his confirmation hearings at the quay. The normal thing for anyone in Denison's shoes would have been to wind up his affairs in Washington while keeping himself available to the Senate in case anything cropped up.

The original idea had been to have Leslie Lyons set up a case— a cameo of *Ryan v. United States*—and cosset it through to the

---

[54] WTD to "Na," January 31, 1914, *Gignoux Collection*. Thanks is extended to Mrs. Edward T. Gignoux and Margaret G. Hay of Falmouth, Maine, who made their private collection of letters and memorabilia relating to Winfred T. Denison available.

[55] WTD to "Na," February 3, 1914, Ibid.

[56] Denison argued, so it appears, two cases that term. Both were fully briefed and orally argued. These were *Cameron v. United States* 231 U.S. 710, argued October 21, 1913, and *Kansas City Southern Railway v. United States*, 231 U.S. 423, argued October 29 and 30, 1913. He lost the first and won the second.

[57] WTD to HLS, December 21, 1913, Stimson Papers.

Supreme Court on a writ of error. Denison would write the brief and argue the case ineffectually before the Supreme Court which, it was hoped, would come to the conclusion that without an exclusionary rule the Fourth Amendment rights of people like Fremont Weeks might as well be stricken from the Constitution. The first beneficiary of this precedent would be Frank Ryan and his fellow union leaders, whose case was right on schedule before the Seventh Circuit Court of Appeals in Chicago.

It was not until Denison got around to writing a brief that he realized that he could not take the risk of participating in the oral argument. In the give and take of oral argument, questions would be put to Denison which he dared not answer. "I see, Mr. Assistant Attorney General, that the defendant here entered a plea of *nolo contendere*. I am mystified sir; for what possible reason was this plea refused? And another thing, Mr. Denison, why *did* the police go to Mr. Weeks's house and make a search in the first place? Did they have probable cause to believe lottery tickets would be found?"

The Dynamiters case had been front-page news for more than two years. Had the plan succeeded their convictions would have been reversed on the basis of a precedent created a few short months before in the case of a lottery-ticket peddler who never harmed a soul. This would have precipitated a public outcry and calls for an investigation. The *Weeks* case could never have withstood scrutiny. But if Denison stayed in Washington, what possible excuse could he have for not going to oral argument? The only thing to do was to leave town under cover of a more pressing duty.

The appointment got Denison as far away as possible from the *locus delecti* and investigators with troublesome questions. Efforts to reach Secretary Denison in Manila would be unsuccessful. His duties in the Islands would always be too urgent to permit his return. Denison could expect help from above in the event of trouble. If the going got tough, the tough would cover for him. The conspirators would be safe even if the Court caused an inquiry to be made of the Justice Department to see just who had slipped up.

The Supreme Court "Minutes" suggest this is what actually happened. For Wednesday, December 3, 1913, appears the following entry on page 222: "Fremont Weeks. The argument of this case was concluded by Mr. Martin O'Donnell of counsel for the plaintiff in error, and the cause was submitted on a printed argument by Mr. Solicitor General Davis[58] and the Assistant A.G. Denison, of counsel for the defendant in error." Either the Court cut off Weeks's attorney in mid-argument on December 2 or it continued the case to the following morning to give the United States a second chance. The latter seems more likely.

What the conspirators did not reckon on was trouble from the Republican side of the aisle. This is certainly understandable. Here is Denison, a Republican in good standing with friends well placed in the party, being awarded a plum by a Democratic administration. Why should Republican Senators object to this splendid example of bipartisanship? "The best laid schemes o'mice and men" went astray when the vindictive Starretts threw a monkey wrench into them.

According to the *Washington Post* of January 28, 1914—"Appeal Dynamite Case"—on the same day that Denison was confirmed by the Senate, a "Formal Petition was filed in the Supreme Court . . . for a review of the conviction of Frank M. Ryan and 23 other members of the International Association of Bridge and Structural Iron Workers, on charges of conspiracy growing out of the dynamiting of the Los Angeles Times building and other structures." The coup failed four weeks later on February 24, 1914, when the Court handed down its decision in *Weeks*. It was this paragraph at the end of the opinion that established the silver platter rule and slammed the door on the Dynamiters.

> As to the papers and property seized by the policemen, it does not appear that they acted under any claim of Federal authority such as would make the [Fourth] Amendment applicable to such unauthorized seizures . . .

---

[58] The only "printed argument" submitted on behalf of the United States was the brief which appears on pages 32-34. The sole name on that brief is Winfred T. Denison. The reference in the "Minutes" to John W. Davis, the illustrious advocate who had become Solicitor General the month before, was strictly *pro forma* in accordance with the vexing habit of court reporters and clerks of inserting the name of the incumbent solicitor (or attorney) general as being on the brief when in fact he was not.

> What remedies the defendant may have against them we
> need not inquire, as the Fourth Amendment is not
> directed to individual misconduct of such officials. Its
> limitations reach the Federal Government and its
> agencies. *Boyd Case*, 116 U.S., *supra*, and see *Twining v.
> New Jersey*, 211 U.S. 78.[59]

This meant that the documentary evidence found in the
basement vault in the Indianapolis office building by the city policemen was admissible and was properly used against the Dynamiters.
On March 9, 1914, the Supreme Court denied the petition of Frank
M. Ryan et al. for certiorari.[60] As is customary, no opinion or explanation was given.

Meanwhile their adherents were active on other fronts. On May
16 the Seventh Circuit Court of Appeals ordered the defendants to
surrender to the warden of the federal prison at Leavenworth,
Kansas, on the 6th of June. Their attorney presented President
Wilson with a petition carrying nearly 500,000 signatures urging
that he pardon the Dynamiters.[61] A delegation of congressmen
requested Wilson to obtain a stay from the Seventh Circuit so that
he would have an opportunity to review all the proceedings and
applications for pardon.[62]

On June 1, at the request of the federal prosecutor, the Circuit
Court extended the surrender date to June 25 because President
Wilson needed more time to study petitions for pardons.[63] On
Wednesday, June 24, Wilson commuted the sentences of four of
the defendants.[64] On Thursday, the remaining Dynamiters were
given a send-off by their brethren in Kansas City and escorted to the
nearby federal penitentiary on the Kansas side of the Missouri

---

[59] *Weeks*, 398.

[60] 232 U.S. 726.

[61] "Order Dynamiters To Prison June 6 . . . Pardon Their Only Hope,"*New York Times*, May
17, 1914.

[62] "Appeal for Dynamiters, Congress Members Ask Wilson to Have Sentences Stayed,"*New York
Times*, April 17, 1914.

[63] "Dynamiters Get Respite. President Needs Time In Which to Read Pardon Appeal,"*New York
Times*, June 2, 1914.

[64] "President Frees Four Dynamiters," *New York Times*, June 25, 1914.

River.[65] On Sunday the shots were fired at Sarajevo which ignited the conflagration which would soon sweep through Europe. Whether the United States would become involved became the question which eclipsed all others.

But even if the world had been spared the calamity of the 1914-1918 war, the case of the Dynamiters would never have aroused the passions which swirled around the Haymarket Riot. The duplicity of Frank Ryan, like that of the McNamaras, disqualified him from the liberal Pantheon. The next to be enshrined will be Tom Mooney in 1916, followed in the 1920s by Sacco and Vanzetti. In the world of Progressive folklore, the Dynamiters case turned out to be a dud.

And so our Philippine secretary went to Luzon and the Dynamiters to Leavenworth. The denial by the Supreme Court of their petition for certiorari came one week after Denison's arrival in Manila. No doubt he was relieved. It meant a lot of questions would never be asked and no one would link the case of Fremont Weeks with that of Frank Ryan.

---

[65] "Dynamiters Enter Prison, Kansas City Union Men Console Them With Brass Bands and Dinner," *New York Times*, June 26, 1914.

Chapter V

THE CRIMSON TIDE

The election of Woodrow Wilson in 1912 established Louis Brandeis as a most influential man. The Boston lawyer was the idol of Progressives, regardless of party affiliation, and a man to whom Woodrow Wilson was in the deepest of political debt. Not only had Brandeis stumped for him all over the country, his position papers and published articles furnished much of the fodder for Wilson's campaign speeches. In the mind of Wilsonian expert Arthur S. Link, Louis Brandeis was the "chief architect of Wilson's New Freedom."[1]

Brandeis was also Wilson's first choice for Attorney General. Fighting Bob LaFollette, who had unofficially supported Wilson in the three-way race, left no doubt that had there been a LaFollette administration, the People's Lawyer would have been its Attorney General. LDB had the support of not only the Progressives but the agrarian populists as well. Williams Jennings Bryan, who became Wilson's Secretary of State, gave Brandeis his endorsement.

> "I do not know that a better man can be found," Bryan advised. "He has a standing among reformers and I am quite sure that all progressives would be pleased."

---

[1] *Wilson, The Road to the White House.* Princeton: Princeton University Press, 1947, 489.

Senator Robert M. LaFollette of Wisconsin sent word that Brandeis, more than anyone else in Washington, could "pull together the progressives—whether LaFollette, Democratic, or Bull Mooser—and harmonize progressive legislation."[2]

What nowadays would be called a trial balloon for "Attorney General Brandeis" evoked not only a flood of commendatory letters from his admirers but a storm of protest from his detractors. The charges against him related not just to political radicalism but to his integrity and professional behavior as well. In the end Woodrow Wilson yielded to the counsel of Edward Mandell House, his confidant and personal advisor. "Colonel" House—the title was honorary—kept a diary[3] which today gives entree to the inner circles of the Wilson administration. The following entries tell us of his conversations with the President-elect with respect to the consideration and rejection of Louis Brandeis as Attorney General.

> *November 16, 1912*
> We talked again of (Jas.) C. McReynolds as Attorney General. We practically eliminated Brandeis for this position because he was not thought to be entirely above suspicion and it would not do to put him in such a place.

> *December 18, 1912*
> We discussed again the Attorney Generalship and he asked about Brandeis. I told him that it was with much regret that I had to advise against him, that I liked him personally but he was not fit for that place.

> *January 17, 1913*
> We discussed the Attorney Generalship and we practically eliminated Brandeis from any cabinet post.

The balloon went up again when "the *Boston Post* announced

---

[2] Id., Vol. II, *The New Freedom* (1956), 11.
[3] *House Diary*, Manuscripts and Archives, Yale University Library.

authoritatively on February 18, 1913, that Brandeis would be the next Secretary of Commerce and Labor." Business organizations and practically the entire Democratic leadership in Massachusetts, with Mayor John F. Fitzgerald of Boston in the van, opposed him.[4] The posts remained unfilled until virtually the eve of the inauguration when Wilson named Congressman William C. Redfield of New York as Commerce Secretary and James C. McReynolds as Attorney General.

A southern Democrat, McReynolds had served as a Special Assistant Attorney General under both the Roosevelt and the Taft administrations and had gained recognition as a trust-buster through his successful prosecution of an antitrust suit against the tobacco companies.[5] He and Brandeis became acquainted during this time and were allies in the battle against the trusts.

The day after the inauguration, Brandeis sent McReynolds a generous letter of congratulations[6] and praised the new Attorney General in letters to at least two of his own supporters. He told one he had "the highest opinion of his [McReynolds's] ability and character"[7] and another that "McReynolds will be a first rate Attorney General. His record in the trust prosecutions is excellent, and if Wickersham had not turned him down in the tobacco trust case, we should have had a real disintegration."[8] Both McReynolds and Brandeis believed in the vigorous enforcement of the Sherman Act and the need for new antitrust legislation.

In the first week of the new administration, Brandeis had "a good private talk with the President this evening for an hour," following an earlier meeting with McReynolds and other members of the Cabinet.[9] Thereafter, Brandeis was consulted by McReynolds on judicial and Department of Justice appointments for the New

[4] *The New Freedom,* 14.
[5] *United States v. American Tobacco Company,* 221 U.S. 106 (1911).
[6] LDB to JCM, March 5, 1913, *Brandeis Letters.*
[7] LDB to Maurice Leon, February 28, 1913, *Brandeis Letters.*
[8] LDB to Gilson Gardner, March 5, 1913, *Brandeis Letters.*
[9] LDB to Alfred Brandeis, March 10, 1913, *Brandeis Letters.*

England area. Later that month, Brandeis, in response to an inquiry by the Attorney General, recommended two men as candidates for a vacancy on the First Circuit Court of Appeals. One of them, Judge George Bingham of New Hampshire, received the appointment.[10]

In August Brandeis and the Attorney General met in New York, and McReynolds asked Brandeis his opinion "as to a proper man for United States Attorney for Massachusetts." Massachusetts Public Service Commissioner George W. Anderson, a political kinsman of LDB, was eventually chosen.[11] Congress was at the time debating the abolition of the Commerce Court, one of the judges on which was Julian W. Mack, another Brandeis crony. In September LDB wrote the Attorney General expressing the hope "that there is some vacancy to which Judge Mack can be appointed. It would be a calamity to lose him from the public service."[12] Shortly thereafter, Mack was appointed to the Seventh Circuit Court of Appeals.

McReynolds was not the only Cabinet member to consult the Massachusetts sachem on patronage. William Gibbs McAdoo, soon to be Woodrow Wilson's son-in-law, was Secretary of the Treasury. During the first five months of the Wilson Administration, he cleared many appointments with Brandeis,[13] including the one most coveted by the leader of Boston Democracy, Mayor John Francis Fitzgerald.

The Boston mayor, grandfather of President John Fitzgerald Kennedy, bitterly opposed the awarding of the plum-laden post of Collector of the Customs for the Port of Boston to one Edmund Billings. In a telegram to the President, Fitzgerald stated that the appointment of Billings, "a commercial Democrat, *if a Democrat* at all," would be "an insult to the rank and file of the party."[14] In recomending Billings to the President, McAdoo listed Louis Brandeis as his leading

---

[10] LDB to JCM, March 28, 1913, *Brandeis Letters*.

[11] LDB to JCM, August 13, 1913, *Brandeis Letters*, see footnote 2 in commentary. LDB to Thomas W. Gregory, September 18, 1914, *Brandeis Letters*.

[12] LDB to JCM, September 25, 1913, *Brandeis Letters*.

[13] LDB to Wm. G. McAdoo, April 14, 1913, July 15, 1913, July 17, 1913, July 23, 1913, July 30, 1913, *Brandeis Letters*.

[14] J.F. Fitzgerald to WW, September 10, 1913, *Wilson Letters*.

backer.[15] Despite the considerable pressure brought to bear by Mayor Fitzgerald,[16] the appointment went to Billings. "Wilson appointed Edmund Billings, LDB's old friend from the Good Government Association, to the collectorship of Boston on 8 October 1913. He served until 1 July 1921."[17]

Another plum eluded Fitzgerald when the President picked Henry J. Skeffington to be New England Immigration Commissioner. A friend of Brandeis, Skeffington, like Billings, served throughout Wilson's two terms. As we shall see, Immigration Commissioner Skeffington will show his gratitude by coming through for his benefactor at a critical moment.

In 1913 aging veterans of the Civil War sat together in Congress and on the Supreme Court. Those who had fought for the Union were mostly Republicans while the Confederates were Democrats to a man. The nation over which they had fought had since been transformed by immigration and an Industrial Revolution. In the cities of the North the Democratic Party was controlled by immigrants and the children of immigrants, notably the Irish. It was their ascendancy that Louis Brandeis and his fellow Reformers were challenging.

In the South the sons of Confederate soldiers held sway.[18] Cast in a coalition they did not forge, northern and southern Democrats were as different in culture and political outlook as night and day. When Charles Dudley Warner said that "politics makes strange bedfellows," he must have had Democrats in mind. What bound them together was self-interest, which to politicians means patronage and "access." Access is the ability of a lawyer or lobbyist to penetrate the walls of officialdom so as to state his case directly to those on high. This right of audience, its practitioners aver, does not

---

[15] WGM to WW, September 10, 1913, Wilson Letters.

[16] E.M. House to WW, September 11, 1913, Wilson Letters, in which Colonel House told the President that the "Congressmen are being told by him, that if they permit Billings to go through that he, Fitzgerald, will hold them accountable."

[17] Commentary following letter from LDB to Wm. G. McAdoo, September 13, 1913, Brandeis Letters.

[18] After the Civil War, courthouse posts in the South were unofficially reserved for crippled Confederate veterans. It was their sons in particular who entered politics.

mean the official will necessarily go along. No doubt this has happened more than once or twice. But a politician who will open the door to what is metaphorically the boudoir, only to become recalcitrant, does not make much of a bedfellow.

In 1913 James McReynolds and Louis Brandeis were the best of political bedfellows. With respect to patronage, McReynolds saw to it that Brandeis got his share. Brandeis did not get his way all the time, but then again McReynolds had the mayor of Boston to consider. McReynolds did not have an easy time of it since Brandeis and "Honey Fitz," you might say, did not gee and haw.

The Louis Dembitz Brandeis Papers archived at the University of Louisville include diaries LDB kept during these years which provide a day-by-day account of his appointments. The author has used them to establish the whereabouts of Louis Brandeis at various times during the years 1912, 1913 and 1914. Hereinafter, whenever LDB is placed in a city other than Boston, the reader may assume, without further citation, that his diary is the source.

During the first year of the Wilson administration Louis Brandeis had virtually unlimited access to the Attorney General. His diary for Friday, March 21, 1913, shows that he talked with McReynolds twice that day before leaving Washington on the 4:00 p.m. train. On Monday in Boston LDB had a full day at the office.

Monday, March 24, 1913.

> United Shoe Machinery Co. Gregg in. Advised him to con. with McReynolds before Wed. Arranged to go with him Teleg to Pullman Office. Con. with McC. Left for N.Y. and Washington on 5:00 train. 6 3/4

These notes, if I read them correctly, mean that a client named Gregg came to Brandeis's office in Boston on Monday morning, and they talked about a case involving the United Shoe Machinery Company. LDB advised Gregg to go consult with McReynolds in Washington before Wednesday, and then arranged to go with him himself. All of this consumed 6 3/4 hours of chargeable time, after which both attorney and client took the night train to Washington.

Brandeis and Gregg spent the following morning consulting with McReynolds and his assistant, James A. Fowler, about the Shoe Manufacturers Alliance,[19] and Brandeis spent the afternoon consulting with McReynolds, Fowler, and Assistant Attorney General Jesse Atkins about a merger.[20] Louis Brandeis appears to have had the run of the office as well as the ear of the Attorney General.

Back in October of 1911, Louis Brandeis, together with Winfred Denison, had lunch with the young man destined to become his "half brother, half son." Felix Frankfurter was at the time very much the protege of Henry L. Stimson. As Frankfurter himself was aware, he was being accorded a status beyond his years and station by prominent figures because, as he put it, he was "Stimson's man."[21] After the Democratic victory in 1912, Frankfurter was preparing to go home "with the guy what brung him" until "fate" intervened.

The official version of how Felix Frankfurter became a professor of law at Harvard was narrated in the previous chapter. It has been told and retold by nearly every historian who has written of the two jurists. Denison started the ball rolling with a letter to his classmate Professor E. H. Warren.[22] Warren replied that while there was no vacancy at the moment, a new one might be created under Professor Roscoe Pound but only if an endowment could be raised. Before funds were solicited however, he thought that Frankfurter ought to

---

[19] The diary entry for "Tuesday, March 25, 1913," reads: "L.D.B. in Washington. Shoe Manufacturers Alliance. Con. with McReynolds in Washington; with Gregg and Fowler. See Memo. 1/2 day."

[20] "Merger. Con. with Attorney General, with Fowler and Atkins. Later saw Comm. Harlow and Brown. See memo 1/2 day." Ibid.

[21] Of a certain major general FF met at a dinner party he noted: "Very nice to me and helpfully friendly—regards me as 'Stimson's man' and treats me as if I had status. This has more or less filtrated through and I enjoy the pleasantest feelings and relations with the War Department officials—other generals, service chiefs, etc." Diaries, October 25, 1911.

[22] According to his obituary Professor Edward H. Warren was, as was Denison, a member of the Harvard Law School Class of 1900. New York Times, July 26, 1945. There is nothing to indicate that they were particularly good friends.

tell us whether he would accept. Denison put the hypothetical question to Frankfurter, who thereupon reviewed his options and narrowed them down to two. He then decided not to go back to New York and practice law and Progressive Republican politics as the protégé of Henry L. Stimson but rather to become a law professor at Harvard and a disciple of Louis D. Brandeis.

"There is a tide in the affairs of men, which, taken at the flood, leads on to fortune."[23] In the life of Felix Frankfurter that tide flowed in his 31st year. In the beginning of 1913 it flowed distinctly in the direction of New York City.

> There isn't any doubt that in the normal course of affairs I would have left with Mr. Stimson when he left the Taft Administration . . . I was with Mr. Stimson, came down to Washington with him, and I suppose in the ordinary course of affairs, if I hadn't been mid-stream working on questions of the regulation of water power, I would have gone back to New York and practiced law with him.[24]

But then the tide turned in response to a strange magnetic force which has never been properly explained. Young Felix was swept past Manhattan and up Long Island Sound. The irresistible current carried him past Highhold at Huntington, where the lunar influence of Henry L. Stimson was at its zenith, northeasterly into Massachusetts Bay. From there he ineluctably was sucked right up the Charles River and deposited at Cambridge swathed in a cap and gown.

The tide which Felix Frankfurter took at its flood in 1913 led him to fame if not to fortune. He described that year and the decisions he made in two chapters of his *Reminisces* which he titled "Holdover with Wilson" and "The Call to Harvard." Fate had nothing to do with either; there was an invisible hand charting his course at every turn.

> The reason why I stayed over after Mr. Stimson left and there was a change of administration was that they asked

---

[23] Shakespeare, *Julius Caesar*.
[24] *Reminisces*, 78.

> me to stay. Garrison [the new Secretary of War] said the
> President wanted me to stay, instead of going to New
> York and practicing law with Mr. Stimson.

There is no reason to think the former New Jersey governor and Princeton professor had ever even heard of the 30-year-old Republican lawyer or his work on water power regulations,[25] much less that he would concern himself with the young man's future plans. Whatever Woodrow Wilson said to War Secretary Lindley Garrison about keeping Frankfurter, he said to accommodate Louis Brandeis. Frankfurter's reaction to Garrison's invitation was to ask Stimson what he should do. His unsuspecting mentor then made his first mistake. "I think you ought to stay," he replied.[26]

The "Pound" referred to by Professor Warren, in his letter to Denison, was Roscoe Pound (1870-1964). He was a most unlikely professor of law in that he had never obtained a law degree. His undergraduate work was in botany, and his legal education consisted of a year at Harvard Law School. Nonetheless, he was admitted to practice law in his native Nebraska and went on to become dean of the University of Nebraska Law School.

In 1910, after spending the previous year at the University of Chicago Law School, Pound became the Joseph Story Professor of Law at Harvard.[27] He became the dean of the Harvard Law School in 1916 and held that post until 1936. According to one observer, Pound at Cambridge became the "titan among titans." Apparently what distinguished him from lesser Crimson titans was not the green eyeshade he was never seen without, but his "new approach to the law called sociological jurisprudence."[28] Pound was an exponent of socializing the law and had delivered an address in April of 1912 entitled "Social Justice and Legal Justice" with which Louis Brandeis was greatly impressed.[29]

---

[25] One must wonder how water power regulations came under the purview of the War Department.
[26] *Reminisces*, 78.
[27] LDB to Roscoe Pound, December 6, 1909, *Brandeis Letters*, and commentary following.
[28] Liva Baker. *Felix Frankfurter*. New York: Coward-McCann, Inc., 1969, 45.
[29] LDB to Norman Hapgood, July 30, 1912, *Brandeis Letters*. The phrase "socializing the law" is LDB's.

Pound and Brandeis agreed that the education of lawyers in general, and at Harvard in particular, was sadly lacking in this area and that something must be done to correct the deficiency. Brandeis had approached Pound about introducing into the curriculum a course propagating the "sociological jurisprudence" both men espoused.

On July 17, 1912, the professor informed Brandeis that the press of his duties had made it "utterly impossible for me to call upon you as I promised," but that "in any event it would not be possible to make any change in the program for the ensuing year." Pound said he was obliged to leave immediately for Chicago to deliver a summer lecture series, but that:

> As soon as I return I shall call you up by telephone and endeavor to make some arrangement whereby we may talk over the matters in which you are interested. I have had some conversation with Mr. [Dean] Thayer about your propositions and I am satisfied he will concur in anything upon which you and I may agree.[30]

Brandeis replied on July 31. He understood the professor's reference to the "ensuing year" to mean the academic year 1913-14. He said he hoped that Pound "will be able to take up early in the Fall the preparation of the work for the following year [1914-15]."[31] On August 10, 1912, Pound sent Louis Brandeis a handwritten letter from Chicago which tells us something of his "sociological jurisprudence."

> Mr. Thayer and I have been writing to each other this summer about the work in which you are interested . . .
>
> Criminal law is and must be our chief reliance in securing purely social interests. We neglect it shamefully at Cambridge. We have absolutely no library on criminalistic. I suppose a first class one might be had for not much more than $5,000. I wish someone might be

---

[30] Roscoe Pound to LDB, July 17, 1912, Reel 31, Frame 5, #423-425: "Papers of Louis Dembitz Brandeis at the University of Louisville" (cited hereafter as Brandeis Papers).
[31] Brandeis Papers, Reel 31, Frame 5, #429.

> induced to give the money for it! We ought also to have
> or to develop a specialist for this and for the teaching
> work in criminal law. For the two must go together . . .
>
> Before long someone else ought to take over the criminal
> side. Of itself it is one man's work. But I know of no one
> [illegible]. Probably I may have to train such a man.[32]

On November 7 Brandeis told Pound that if "no individual is found ready to provide funds for the Criminal Law Library, I think it would be well to have the Dean take up the matter with the Harvard Law School Association . . . It probably has funds on hand which could be applied in part to this purpose, and, if required, could readily raise additional funds."[33]

Now if anyone could speak with authority in this regard, it was Louis D. Brandeis. Not only was he a friend of Ezra Ripley Thayer, the incumbent dean, he had been a friend of James Bradley Thayer, Ezra's father and a professor of law at Harvard before him. LDB had graduated from the law school in 1877 at the age of 20. In 1882-83 the first Professor Thayer took a sabbatical during which his former pupil taught his course on "Evidence." Thereafter, Brandeis was offered a professorship. He declined, as he preferred practicing law to teaching it.

The younger Thayer graduated from Harvard Law School in 1891 and, after serving a year's clerkship with Supreme Court Justice Horace Gray, began the practice of law in Boston with the firm of Warren and Brandeis.[34] After Warren's suicide in 1910,[35] Ezra Thayer became a partner in the successor firm of Brandeis, Dunbar and Nutter. Later that year Thayer became dean of Harvard

---

[32] Ibid., # 430 *et seq.*

[33] LDB to RP, November 7, 1912, *Brandeis Letters.*

[34] "He [Brandeis] made a place in his office for Professor Thayer's son, Ezra, and in a short time put him on a ten percent basis plus one hundred and fifty dollars monthly salary." Alfred Lief. *Brandeis, The Personal History of an American Ideal.* New York: Stackpole Sons, 1936, 53.

[35] See Martin Green, *The Mount Vernon Street Warrens: A Boston Story, 1860-1910.* New York: Charles Scribner's Sons (1989), which begins: "On the night of February 18, 1910, in his country home at Dedham, Massachusetts, Samuel Dennis Warren II took a gun and killed himself."

Law School, in which post he served until his suicide in 1915.[36] Roscoe Pound succeeded him as dean.

"The formation of the Harvard Law School Association was Brandeis's greatest accomplishment for the school."[37] It came about as a result of a form letter LDB sent out to former members of the law school.[38] "As secretary of the Harvard Law School Association, Brandeis was again its fount of energy. His office at 50 Devonshire Street was its headquarters . . . [and] he was mainly responsible for its activities." In 1913 Louis D. Brandeis was "the Association's Vice-President, a position he held even after he became an Associate Justice of the Supreme Court." It is fair to say of Louis Brandeis in 1913 that he was the association's guiding spirit and leading money raiser.

In January of 1913 Pound learned that a library on what he called "criminalistic" was being put on the market. "I fear very much that we shall lose the opportunity unless something can be done at once," he wrote LDB.[39] On Friday, January 31, Pound reported back to Brandeis that he had gotten the money.

> After receiving your telephone communication Tuesday, I went at once to see Dean Thayer and the matter was brought up at a meeting of the faculty a few hours later . . .

> Accordingly I went in with Mr. Thayer [before the council of the Law School Association] and as it turned out it did not become necessary for me to say anything as the money was voted at once on Mr. Thayer's stating what the faculty desired . . .

> I return Mr. Frankfurter's letter herein.[40]

---

[36] "On September 14, 1915, at the age of forty-nine, in the fullness of his powers, and at the beginning almost of what promised to be a most distinguished and useful career in the field of education, he died." *Ezra Ripley Thayer*, 29 Harvard Law Review 1 (1915), a memorial to Dean Thayer written by William H. Dunbar, the law partner of Louis Brandeis. See also "Dean Thayer A Suicide," *New York Times*, September 17, 1915.

[37] All quotes in this paragraph are from James M. Landis, *Mr. Justice Brandeis And the Harvard Law School*, 55 Harvard Law Review 184, written in tribute to the Justice shortly after his death on October 5, 1941.

[38] LDB to The Alumni of the Harvard Law School, August 9, 1886, *Brandeis Letters*.

[39] RP to LDB, January 14, 1913, Reel 31, #465, Brandeis Papers.

[40] RP to LDB, January 31, 1913, Reel 31, #480-81, Brandeis Papers.

The letter to which Pound referred was one written by Frankfurter in response to this letter from Brandeis:

> You have probably heard of the progressive law work which the Harvard Law School is undertaking, and in which Professor Pound is particularly interested.
>
> Professor Pound thinks there is an unusual opportunity to obtain what is perhaps the best criminal law library in the world, for about $5,000, and I want to help him raise that amount . . .
>
> It occurred to me that you might know of some New York (or other) lawyers, who would be glad to join in making this gift.[41]

Three days later Frankfurter replied that he had "written to several New York lawyers of the opportunity to ease their swollen fortunes." He had sent U.S. Circuit Court Judge Julian W. Mack a copy of their correspondence. "Judge Mack," he said, "is in touch with people who want to spend some of their money wisely."[42] To complete the circle, shortly before the meeting with the Law School Association was to take place, Brandeis had transmitted Frankfurter's letter to Pound along with this note:[43]

> My dear Pound:
>
> I hope the meeting of the Law School Association will solve the criminal law library problem; but I know you, and possibly the Dean and [Professor] Beale will be glad to see the letter of the 27th from Felix Frankfurter which I enclose. I sent him a copy of Beale's letter in connection with an effort to raise the necessary money.
>
> Most cordially,

---

[41] LDB to FF, January 24, 1913, *Brandeis Letters.*

[42] FF to LDB, January 27, 1913, Reel 31, #474, Brandeis Papers.

[43] LDB to RP, January 29, 1913, Reel 31, #477, Brandeis Papers.

And so with the invaluable assistance of Louis Brandeis, Professor Roscoe Pound got his library on "criminalistic." All that remained was to find or develop a specialist, for as we know, "the two must go together." Presuming the right man can be found, Pound's course will begin on schedule at Harvard in September of 1914. With this background let us now take another look at Denison's shot-in-the-dark letter to Professor Warren, the official version of how Felix Frankfurter got "the Call to Harvard."

Warren had been a member of the law school faculty since 1904 and a full professor since 1908.[44] At this time the faculty consisted of Dean Ezra Thayer, 10 professors, and two or three lecturers. Professors Beale and Wambaugh had been working with Thayer and Pound to change the curriculum, and their proposals had been submitted to Brandeis.[45] Whether or not Warren was present at the meeting when the faculty discussed the library and decided to ask the association for the money, he would have known about it. It was certainly no secret.

On January 23, 1913, five months before the Denison-Warren exchange, Brandeis wrote Beale asking him to announce the change in curriculum to students so that they could plan accordingly. The commentary in the *Brandeis Letters* adds that:

> In a conversation with Roscoe Pound, LDB had suggested that the Law School should offer a course in criminal procedure and reform as part of its fourth-year graduate program. Beale was preparing to offer this course in the fall, and he wrote to inform LDB about some of the details as well as about some of the problems involving a library.

Warren would have known of the ongoing efforts to establish this new area of study in the law school and of how the library necessary for its pursuit became endowed. He would know of Louis

---

[44] Warren obituary, *supra* 89.
[45] These were referred to as "Mr. Beale's Scheme" and "Mr. Wambaugh's Scheme." See Reel 31, #442 *et seq.*, Brandeis Papers.

Brandeis, of his relationship with the Thayer family and the Harvard Law School Association, and of the extraordinary interest the school's leading benefactor had taken in the project.

According to Denison's letter, Warren was acquainted with Frankfurter and his reputation. The professor therefore would have known that even if there had been any current vacancies on the faculty, Felix Frankfurter was not the man for the job. The 1913-14 curriculum consisted of "Contracts," "Torts," "Bills and Notes" and the other bread and butter courses which are standard fare at any law school. Warren's field of expertise was "Corporations" and "Property," on which he had published casebooks.

There was but one opening which suited Frankfurter's style, and that was to teach the proposed course on "sociological jurisprudence" slated for September of 1914. Anyone who knew Frankfurter and Pound, and Warren knew them both, would have known immediately that they were a perfect combination. It was almost as if the job had been tailor-made for Felix Frankfurter by an invisible hand. He would be the ideal apprentice to "the titan among titans," soon prepared to train the evangelists needed to spread the gospel of "sociological jurisprudence." For as Pound told Brandeis, the "[t]raining of a new generation of law-teachers must be almost the first item. Happily Harvard, directly or indirectly, trains nearly all law-teachers today. Hence our opportunity here is assured."[46]

According to Denison's letter he and Warren had had a "fine little visit" shortly before it was written.[47] Why then did not Warren tell Denison the story of Pound's program and Brandeis's interest in it? There are several possible answers to this question, the most obvious of which is that the subject never came up. This is not the only possible answer, but it is the only one which does not lead inevitably to the conclusion that the letter was a put-up job. For if Denison and Warren had discussed the possibility of "F" teaching at Harvard Law School, Warren would not have failed to tell Denison that there was no man who could be of more help than Louis D. Brandeis.

---

[46] RP to LDB, August 10, 1912, Reel 31, #430-433, Brandeis Papers.
[47] WTD to E.H. Warren, June 12, 1913, Frankfurter Papers.

The *dramatis personae* in this tale were all lawyers whose stock in trade was the spoken and written word. They attached great value to a certain elegance of expression and the ability to use precisely the right words for a given situation. The inarticulate would never have felt at home in the House of Truth.

The medium of exchange in the circles in which Denison and his friends traveled was not money but favors. We may assume that they were sensitive to all the nuances of "networking." Careful consideration would be given to the best person to see about getting a job for a friend. It would be a grave *faux pas* to pick the wrong one, particularly if you knew the right one. People like Denison and Frankfurter also prided themselves on being *au courant*. Their correspondence is filled with gossip.

It is out of character for Frankfurter not to mention to Denison his exchange of letters with Brandeis about Pound's "library on criminalistic," particularly after Frankfurter had taken it upon himself to send their correspondence to Judge Mack in Chicago. It is out of character for Denison to write such a clumsy and uninspired letter in the first place, or any such letter without the approval of the friend with whom he lived at the House of Truth.

How could Winfred Denison be sure that he would not be setting awry some well-laid plans, playing the fool who rushes in where angels fear to tread? Why would he not seek the sage advice of an older and wiser man who just happened to be in town? Denison must have known Brandeis was in Washington. LDB spent three and a half hours at the Justice Department talking to Denison's fellow Assistant Attorneys General Thomas W. Gregory and Jesse C. Atkins shortly before Denison wrote his letter.[48] While Felix Frankfurter's own version of the "Call to Harvard" is possible, it is surely improbable, considering what we know of the people involved. Let us entertain a competing hypothesis and see how it measures up.

Louis Brandeis arrived in Washington from New York early on the morning of Monday, June 9, and stayed until Wednesday, the

---

[48] His diary for Tuesday, June 10, 1913, notes "L.D.B. in Washington . . . Merger. con. with Gregory and Atkins in Washington 3 1/2." The diary did not say what he did that evening.

day before Denison wrote his letter, when he left on the noon train to "speak in Baltimore and be back in Boston Thursday or Friday."[49] Let us suppose the letter was written at the instigation of Brandeis, who, for reasons of which we are not yet aware, wanted it to appear that the overture came from a source other than himself.

According to Frankfurter, the letter from Warren came "out of a clear sky—a completely clear sky."[50] In 1960 he reminisced that "when this offer from Harvard came, after I slept with it, worried about it, thought about it, I disregarded all my advisors except one and went up there."[51] The advice he took was that of Louis Brandeis; the advice he got from Henry L. Stimson he put aside. However, a lot went on behind the scenes which FF apparently had forgotten by the time he reminisced.

> Mr. Stimson, I understand, engaged in a correspondence on the subject with the then dean of the law school, Ezra Thayer, who was a great friend of his and classmate at the Harvard Law School. I've always wished I could have seen their exchange of views.[52]

This is an odd thing to say because a significant part of their exchange of views is among the papers Justice Frankfurter deeded to the Library of Congress in 1955, where they now repose in the Manuscript Division open to public inspection. As you follow the exchange try to imagine a bullfight in which the erstwhile Secretary of War is the bull and Dean Thayer the picador who torments him. Off in the shadows of the arena is the matador, confident of the outcome but watching every move. It was from Thayer that Stimson first heard of his protege's new opportunity. You might say that it came "out of a clear sky—a completely clear sky."[53]

---

[49] LDB to Alfred Brandeis, June 8, 1913, *Brandeis Letters*. In this letter to his brother Brandeis gave the above as his itinerary. His diaries confirm that he adhered to it. He arrived back in Boston on Thursday, the 12th of June, early enough to log four and a quarter hours at his office.

[50] *Reminisces*, 78.

[51] *Reminisces*, 86.

[52] *Reminisces*, 79.

[53] LBD's diary for Thursday, June 19, 1913, five days before Thayer wrote his letter, notes "Harvard Law. Pound in about Frankfurter. 1/4 [hour]."

Dear Harry:

It has just come to my ears that Frankfurter might be persuaded to take up academic work. This interests Pound and me tremendously. Pound is a wonderful creature, and his advanced work is something from which I expect great results sometime, but he particularly needs to get the right sort of man with him, and I cannot think of anyone who would fit the place better than Frankfurter.[54]

What stood in the way, explained Thayer, was the "financial question," as to which "Mr. Brandeis suggested you might be able to help." Stimson was not overly pleased with this turn of events and evidently wrote a discouraging letter in answer. This is a fair assumption because Stimson soon wrote Thayer a second letter which began: "My Dear Ezra: I was afraid after I wrote my [first] letter that it did not sound sufficiently sympathetic."[55]

On June 26 Frankfurter, ostensibly unaware of Thayer's letter, wrote his mentor to be the first to give him the good news.[56] Stimson advised his protégé against going to Harvard. "To me you seem a man whose place is at the center of the great liberal movement which is now going on in national and industrial life . . . The law school will be a side track . . . Pretty soon you will have to be thinking of getting back to New York." The letter ended: "With love to all members of the 'House of Truth.'"[57]

Meanwhile Brandeis had suggested to Pound that he too approach Stimson about raising the money to endow the new professorship. Pound must have been rebuffed because on July 12 Brandeis wrote Winfred Denison:

As to Frankfurter: in suggesting to Pound that he call on Stimson I had no thought of what Stimson personally would give, but rather what Stimson could do in bringing

---

[54] ERT to HLS, June 24, 1913, Stimson Papers.

[55] HLS to ERT, July 11, 1913, Stimson Papers.

[56] FF to HLS, June 26, 1913, Stimson Papers.

[57] HLS to FF, June 28, 1913, Stimson Papers.

the matter to the attention of men in New York, who would recognize the great opportunity for public service that was offered. My own recent clashes with the capitalistic world seem to disqualify me for that task.[58]

The same day he urged Pound to persist in his efforts with Stimson telling him he thought that now "you will have no difficulty in securing Stimson's co-operation."[59] Thayer, as well as Pound, apparently proceeded on this assumption. However, Stimson's response to Thayer's next letter must have been something less than a paradigm of "co-operation" because he again thought the better of it. His second letter opened: "Dear Ezra: I was tired the other day, and am afraid I wrote a rather snappy letter."[60]

This letter of apology crossed in the mail with Thayer's response to the "rather snappy letter" in which he let Stimson know that part of the problem had been solved "when Brandeis yesterday agreed to pay $1,000 a year for five years toward his salary."[61] Brandeis must have thought the matter was settled since he wrote Pound that "[w]ith you, Thayer and Frankfurter there, the school ought to do great things."[62]

In any event, Frankfurter's professorship was assured the following month when Professor Bruce Wyman suddenly resigned from the Harvard Law School faculty. Wyman, it seems, had been speaking and writing in favor of the interests of the New Haven Railroad, with whom Brandeis had been feuding.[63] When the *Boston Journal* of December 22 broke the story that Professor Wyman had been receiving a monthly retainer of $833 from the

[58] LDB to WTD, July 12, 1913, *Brandeis Letters*.

[59] LDB to RP, July 12, 1913, *Brandeis Letters*.

[60] HLS to ERT, November 5, 1913, Stimson Papers.

[61] ERT to HLS, November 4, 1913, Stimson Papers.

[62] LDB to Roscoe Pound, November 5, 1913, *Brandeis Letters*.

[63] On September 26, 1913, LDB had written to the Massachusetts Public Service Commission to ask that they press their investigation of the New Haven, particularly with respect to "publicity, legislative and other expenses." He also urged Attorney General McReynolds to take action against the railroad, which McReynolds did the following year. LDB to Charles Marshall Cox, June 5, 1914, *Brandeis Letters*.

New Haven, "his resignation was tendered and immediately accepted"[64] by the law school.

Louis Brandeis was sufficiently incensed by this breach of ethics to send his friend Norman Hapgood, the editor of *Harper's Weekly* magazine, "a clipping from today's *Boston Journal*, containing the sensational resignation of Bruce Wyman of Harvard." He suggested that it would be an appropriate subject for an editorial deploring the railroad's improper use of money to obtain what he called "tainted news."[65] Previously Hapgood had been the editor of *Collier's Weekly* but had been sacked after the 1912 election for publishing pro-Wilson editorials which some people claimed were ghost written by Louis D. Brandeis.[66] This had been the subject of some acrimonious correspondence between the publisher and Brandeis.

On November 14, 1912, LDB wrote Robert J. Collier, the publisher of *Collier's*, a letter which opened: "My Dear Mr. Collier:— Yours of the 12th is at hand and I am very glad to learn that you have concluded to 'consider the incident with Norman closed.'" This was on a somewhat less ominous note than Brandeis's previous letter, which began: "My Dear Mr. Collier:—Yours of the 4th has come. I hope you will, upon further consideration, conclude that the character of Collier's can be sustained without an attack on Norman personally. Such an attack would, of course, be answered; and from controversies of this nature both parties usually emerge as losers."[67]

In his December 22 letter to Hapgood, along with the clipping about Wyman's resignation, Brandeis enclosed his "check to the order of *Harper's Weekly*, for $822, being payment for the 274 yearly subscriptions to Massachusetts libraries." He asked "Norman" to provide him with "the number of libraries in Maine, New Hampshire and Vermont not now subscribers to the Weekly." Earlier that year Brandeis had arranged for another friend of his, Charles R. Crane, to

---

[64] LDB to Alexander Galt Barret, January 31, 1914, *Brandeis Letters*.

[65] LDB to Norman Hapgood, December 22, 1913, *Brandeis Letters*.

[66] LDB to Alfred Brandeis, September 15, 1912, *Brandeis Letters*. *"Entre Nous* I have Norman supplied with editorials—through the October 19th number & shall probably add two more to make the full measure."

[67] LDB to RJC, November 14, 1912, and November 7, 1912, *Brandeis Letters*.

raise the $100,000 Hapgood needed to purchase *Harper's*.[68] LDB was a frequent contributor to the magazine.

And so it became unnecessary to endow the professorship. While Winfred Denison was enjoying a most gorgeous visit to Alaska, the "matter was settled, and Felix Frankfurter was appointed January 12, 1914, as Professor of Law, to begin serving September 1, 1914."[69]

> When he went to Harvard, he was only across the Charles River from Louis Brandeis in Boston, and the relationship of the two men changed, from role model and admirer to friends . . . This, however, did not cement their blossoming friendship into the "half-brother, half-son" relationship it became. For that, Zionism was needed.[70]

In the coming years Louis Brandeis would become a leader in the Zionist movement. But the interest of Brandeis in Zionism came late in life and contemporaneously with his interest in the sociological jurisprudence of Roscoe Pound. According to biographer Leonard Baker, a "joke at the time had it that Louis Brandeis 'became a Bar Mitzvah at the age of sixty'."[71]

Before 1912 Louis Brandeis was a paragon of Theodore Roosevelt's "unhyphenated American." He had little interest in Jewish affairs. His law partners, and most of his friends, were Anglo-Saxon Protestants of a caste his biographers uniformly refer to as "Brahmans." To one of his friends, Charles Culp Burlingham, this indifference to his kinsmen was Brandeis's "one great fault. 'He was a Jew but he never took any interest in the Jews.'"[72] Brandeis biographer Philippa Strum made these observations:

---

[68] See *Brandeis Letters*, LDB to NH, January 28, 1913, and commentary, as well as LDB to NH April 28, 1913, in which LDB stated that he did not have "any great objection" to other investors "provided we retain control." "We" meant Brandeis, Crane and Hapgood.

[69] Leonard Baker. *Brandeis and Frankfurter: A Dual Biography*. New York: Harper & Row, 1984, 70.

[70] Ibid.

[71] *A Dual Biography*, 75.

[72] *A Dual Biography*, 71.

How and why did Brandeis become a Zionist? Although his family never denied its Jewishness, it did not seem to consider being Jewish particularly important. Neither Brandeis nor his parents practiced any religion. Brandeis's donations to Jewish charities were minimal, well below his contributions to other causes: up to 1912 he had given less than $1,500 to Jewish organizations; between 1912 and 1939, in contrast, he donated over $600,000 to Jewish organizations . . . [73]

One Brahman friend of LDB was Massachusetts Public Service Commissioner George Weston Anderson. In 1913 a vacancy occurred on the Interstate Commerce Commission and Anderson and Brandeis wanted it filled by a friend of theirs named Ives. Anderson cautioned Brandeis that their support for Ives should be covert.

I have said to the people who are active in this matter that I thought your name and mine should be mentioned as little as possible; that our activities should be quiet—subterranean. Subterranean activities, you know, befit a Public Service Commissioner in Massachusetts.[74]

As it turned out, the efforts of Louis Brandeis on behalf of Ives were quite open and aboveboard. He wrote both the President and the Secretary of the Interior urging Ives be appointed to the ICC.[75] But the "sage of Devonshire Street" did not need George Anderson to tell him the value of secrecy. LDB was a past master at staying behind the scenes and letting others do his bidding. On October 9, the day before he sent his letter to Woodrow Wilson supporting Ives, Brandeis had written his friend Norman Hapgood:

My Dear Norman: Possibly you may care to give the Boston Journal a boost for the fight that it is making for

---

[73] Philippa Strum. *Louis D. Brandeis: Justice for the People*. New York: Schocken Books, 1984, 224,225.

[74] Alpheus T. Mason. *Brandeis, A Free Man's Life*. New York: Viking Press, 1946, 405.

[75] LDB to WW, October 10, 1913, and LDB to F.K. Lane, October 15, 1913, *Brandeis Letters*.

free journalism; and incidentally, also to George W. Anderson, our new Public Service Commissioner.[76]

The November 8 issue of *Harper's Weekly Magazine* carried an editorial entitled "Freedom in Massachusetts," the opening paragraph of which should serve as a lesson to those skeptics who think writing a letter to the editor is a waste of time.

> The *Boston Journal* deserves a good boost for the fight it is making for free journalism, and, at the same time, a great, strong boost ought to be given to George W. Anderson, the new Public Service Commissioner.

The *Boston Journal*, you will recall, was the newspaper whose scoop on December 22 would soon break the Wyman scandal and thus bring about a vacancy on the faculty of the Harvard Law School. George W. Anderson was the Public Service Commissioner investigating the affairs of the New Haven Railroad. It is a small world.

---

[76] LDB to Norman Hapgood, October 9, 1913, *Brandeis Letters*.

Chapter VI

THE INVISIBLE HAND

L et us return to the Constitution from which we have wandered so far afield. What does all of this have to do with the Fourth Amendment, the exclusionary rule and Edward Coolidge, the murderer of 14-year-old Pamela Mason of Manchester, New Hampshire? Let us hark back to the words of Justice Black's dissent in *Coolidge v. New Hampshire* (1971).

> It was not until 1914 . . . that the Court in *Weeks v. United States*, 232 U.S. 383, stated that the Fourth Amendment itself barred the admission of evidence seized in violation of the Fourth Amendment. The *Weeks* opinion made no express confession of a break with the past. But if it was merely a proper reading of the Fourth Amendment, it seems strange that it took this Court nearly 125 years to discover the true meaning of those words. The truth is that the source of the exclusionary rule simply cannot be found in the Fourth Amendment. That Amendment did not when adopted, and does not now, contain any constitutional rule barring the admission of illegally seized evidence.

That Winfred Denison "took a dive" in the *Weeks* case must be regarded as an incontrovertible fact; no other explanation of events accounts for his behavior. But why he did what he did is another matter. Somehow, derailing the case against the Dynamiters does not seem to tip the scales of motivation. Like the McNamaras, Frank Ryan and his cohorts betrayed their fellow unionists. They were not worthy of so great a risk.

We must consider also the character of the conspirators. Denison was too timid to have done what he did alone. Frankfurter was made of sterner stuff but he was too young, having just turned 29 two weeks before the McNamaras confessed. Denison and Frankfurter "crossed the Rubicon" together, but they had to have help from ashore. They could never have succeeded without James Clark McReynolds. It did not take the new Wilson Administration's Attorney General long to know that he had a headache in the Western District of Missouri. On April 28, 1913, he sent the following wire to Judge Van Valkenburgh.

> It is represented to me that, because of personal enmity, the District Attorney is about to institute grand jury investigation with the purpose of indicting Ernest Martin. Will you be good enough to inquire, so far as you properly can, into the circumstances and advise what course ought to be pursued by this Department.
> McREYNOLDS[1]

The answer came not from Judge Van Valkenburgh but from Leslie Lyons.

> Referring your wire this day to court here have to advise that no such prosecution as referred to in your telegram is contemplated at this grand jury. Wrote you fully relative to this matter last Tuesday. Court is writing today.
> Lyons,
> U.S. Attorney.[2]

McReynolds had discussed the situation with United States

---

[1] McReynolds to Van Valkenburgh, April 28, 1913, No. 165917-5, #112, Straight Numerical Files, 1904-37; DJA, R.G. 60, NARA.

[2] Leslie Lyons to James McReynolds, April 29, 1913, No. 165917-4 1/2, Ibid.

Senator James A. Reed by telephone. Reed, the head of a Kansas City law firm, was the former prosecuting attorney and a two-term mayor of Kansas City.[3] A Democrat, he had succeeded to the seat of Republican Senator William Warner. Reed wired McReynolds from Kansas City to say that "[i]n accordance with our conversation" he had seen Judge Van Valkenburgh, who told him essentially that the problem was the Attorney General's and not his. Senator Reed closed by saying he had "been detained here beyond my expectations otherwise would have seen you personally before this expect to be in Washington friday."[4] On Thursday, while Senator Reed was presumably en route to Washington, McReynolds received a message from Postmaster General A.S. Burleson. This apprised him that Lyons's conflicts of interest came not just from one, but from two sources.

> I am advised by the Chief Inspector that an investigation conducted by post office inspectors has developed evidence of gross misuse of the mails by the promoters of the bankrupt American Union Trust Company of Kansas City, Missouri, and that they are ready to submit conclusive evidence of guilt to the United States Attorney for the Western District of Missouri. It happens, however, that [Ernest D. Martin] one of the parties implicated has had serious difficulty with the United States Attorney and another [George L. Davis] is an intimate friend.[5]

Albert Sidney Burleson, a former congressman from Texas, was the Postmaster General. An "intimate friend" of Colonel E.M. House, the President's confidant, he was the Wilson administration's "chief dispenser of patronage."[6] Burleson was something of a character, effecting an eccentric mode of dress and demeanor.

---

[3] *The Official Manual of the State of Missouri, 1913-14.* Jefferson City, Missouri: Hugh Stephens Printing Co., 37.

[4] Reed to McReynolds, April 28, 1913, No. 165917, #112, Straight Numerical Files, 1904-37, DJA, R.G. 60, NARA.

[5] Postmaster General to McReynolds, May 1, 1913, No. 165917, #112, Straight Numerical Files, 1904-37, DJA, R.G. 60, NARA.

[6] Link. *Wilson: The New Freedom*, 135.

"Burleson acted the part he spoke, complete with black coat, wing collar, rolled umbrella, and a calculated pomposity that provoked Woodrow Wilson to call him 'the Cardinal.'"[7] The "Cardinal" was a good man to know if you had political aspirations—like becoming a Justice of the Supreme Court, for example.

While the Civil Service Act covered some federal jobs in 1913, many were still appointive and filled by the political party in power through the patronage system. The Postal Service was rich in such jobs, and the first order of business for the Democrats when they took over in March of that year was to see to it that the local Republican postmasters resigned and were replaced by worthy Democrats. It was for this reason Burleson gave up his congressional seat and became Postmaster General. March 4, 1913, was a banner day indeed for many faithful and hardworking Democrats who had not tasted so much as a drop of patronage from the federal spigot in 16 years. Their time had come.

McReynolds had a lot on his agenda during his first 60 days in office, and one of the top items was patronage. In so far as possible, he was expected to fill the top offices of the Justice Department with deserving Democrats acceptable to their local party leaders. As we have seen, he consulted Louis Brandeis on some Massachusetts appointments, and no doubt he consulted Boston Mayor Fitzgerald as well. His job was to placate the rival factions in the party or, failing in that herculean task, to make as few enemies as possible.

The Attorney General would be aware of the prevailing customs regarding patronage and of the President's choice to abide by them.[8] He would know without asking that Senator Reed had more on his

---

[7] *Dictionary of American Biography* (Supplement Two), New York: Charles Scribner's Sons, 1958.

[8] "In speaking of patronage I asked him [Woodrow Wilson] what his attitude would be regarding consulting Senators and Representatives. The practice was to consult Senators regarding district attorneys, marshals and collectors, and Congressmen as to postmasters." January 25, 1913, *House Diary*. This assumes the senator or representative is of the same political party as the President. There were two Democratic senators from Missouri in 1913: Reed from Kansas City on its western border and William J. Stone from St. Louis on its eastern border. It seems logical to assume Reed would have the say on the appointment of the United States Attorney for the Western District of Missouri and Stone the Eastern District.

mind than the proper enforcement of the law in Western District of Missouri. To throw the rascals out and replace them with some of his own supporters would be high on Reed's list of priorities.

The scandals surrounding Leslie Lyons were no small matter to Congressman William P. Borland, the sponsor of the House resolution Wickersham had defied. Reed and Borland, both Kansas City lawyers, would be hard put to explain the continued presence of the Republican incumbent to those eager party workers who felt their time had come. From the tone of Reed's wire we may judge he would have wasted little time in finding out from the Attorney General exactly what he was going to do about the mess the Republicans had left in Kansas City.

McReynolds spent that weekend in New York City. The *House Diary* for May 3 and 4 shows that the Colonel and the Attorney General had lunch and supper together on Sunday. Louis Brandeis arrived in Washington on Monday of the week Senator Reed most likely would have met with McReynolds. LDB's diary shows that on Tuesday, May 6, he "called on Atty. General"—for how long is not specified. On Thursday he "talked with McReynolds in Washington" about the "Shoe Mfrs. Alliance" for a quarter of an hour, and later about a "merger" for a half hour. He had a busy afternoon and evening.

> *Insurgency.*[9] LDB in Washington; talked with [Treasury Secretary] McAdoo. Called on President about commission. saw Secy. [of Commerce] Redfield, Secy. [of Labor William B.] Wilson, Miss Julia Lathrop. Atty. Gen. in P.M. and then McAdoo; Kent in evening.

Some politicians will do what is in the public interest most of the time, whether or not it is politically expedient, and some politicians will do what is politically expedient most of the time whether or not it is in the public interest. But when something in the public interest is also politically expedient, every politician will

---

[9] LDB appears to have used "insurgency" as a code word for his personal political activities. When adding up his chargeable hours, his secretary would know, one would conjecture, that time spent on "insurgency" was not to be billed to a particular client or case.

do it every time, and when one seemingly does not, something is wrong. There must be something, you say to yourself, that I don't know about. What could it be?

It was in the public interest that Lyons resign, and the sooner he did, the better that interest would be served. It would have been politically expedient for McReynolds to force Lyons to resign. The Missouri Democrats, in particular Senator Reed, would be obliged. The word would go forth that James Clark McReynolds was a man of decision, an Attorney General who saw his duty and did not falter. People would say he was a solid party man as well. Democrats who thought the less of him for having served in two Republican administrations would be reassured.

McReynolds would have been justified in following Borland's advice that Leslie Lyons "should not be permitted to resign, but should be instantly dismissed from employment by the United States Government." He even could have gone further and have had Lyons prosecuted for malfeasance in office. That he did not, however, may be related to facts and circumstances having nothing to do with the *Weeks* case and of which we are unaware. It is unwarranted, therefore, to attach too much significance to McReynolds's failure to pursue this course.

Whatever grounds he had for asking Lyons to resign on the 1st of July, McReynolds had in the first week in May. Yet he waited until after the *Weeks* case was safely on the Court's summary docket and nothing more remained to be done in Kansas City. But two months is not a long time in the life of a new attorney general, harried and beset from all quarters. So while this may be evidence, it is not conclusive evidence, that one had anything to do with the other.

McReynolds would have reviewed the evidence against Leslie Lyons both for his own information and to be prepared for Senator Reed. He would have read the Bagley Report and the Borland Resolution with which Wickersham had refused to comply. Without being asked, McReynolds would review, in the light of the circumstances now prevailing, whether it was not now "compatible with the public interest to make them public." The new Attorney General would have read the letter his predecessor had sent the Speaker of the House and the Memorandum for the Attorney

General that A. Bruce Bielaski prepared for Wickersham. And when he was finished, James Clark McReynolds would have realized there had been a cover-up, a Republican cover-up, and a scandal of enormous significance.

I cannot honor your request, George Wickersham told the Speaker of the House of Representatives, because these reports are confidential and their release would be most unfair to Mr. Lyons. But you may have my word on it that the gentleman from Missouri was mistaken when he said that the disbarment proceedings wholly failed to reach the most serious charges against the conduct of Mr. Lyons. The fact of the matter is, sir, that the Kansas City court's decision dealt with substantially all of the charges filed against Mr. Lyons with this department and acquits him of any improper conduct with any of them.

Now this is not just a case of a Republican Attorney General telling an out-and-out lie to a Democratic Speaker of the House to cover up for a crooked Republican United States Attorney; it is a case where his Democratic sucessor has him dead to rights. The papers before McReynolds proved beyond a doubt that at the time Wickersham made this statement he knew it to be false. Bielaski had just shown him that Borland was right. The most serious charges against Leslie Lyons never were before the Kansas City Court of Appeals. They had never examined his connection with the "Oregon Valley Land Company" and "his alleged partnership with George L. Davis." Lyons had argued, and the state court had agreed, that these were matters best left to federal authorities.

McReynolds didn't like Wickersham; he considered him responsible for undoing by a consent decree most of what he himself had accomplished in the prosecution of the tobacco trust. Nor would this have been a case of accusations and denials being traded back and forth, with the public wondering where the truth lay and inevitably concluding it was "just politics." All McReynolds had to do was to make public the Bielaski memorandum and Wickersham's letter of the same day, and the newspapers would have taken care of the rest.

James C. McReynolds and Louis D. Brandeis will be chosen by Woodrow Wilson to fill the next two vacancies on the Supreme

Court of the United States. While in 1913 this lay in the future, the future was by no means opaque. Being an attorney general was a leg-up to a seat on the Court, particularly if one happened to be the first attorney general chosen by an incoming President. In the race for the Supreme Court in 1913 McReynolds had tradition on his side.

His premier rival was Louis Brandeis, who, since LaFollette's downfall and the defeat of the Bull Moose, had become the leader of the Progressive movement. While McReynolds had supported Wilson, he was somewhat of an unknown and had no particular following. Brandeis, on the other hand, was the "Pied Piper" of Progressives.

But as Louis Brandeis had passionate friends, so had he foes, and his appointment to the Court would be by far the more controversial. Any nomination of Louis Brandeis was bound to be resisted in the Senate. Wilson would not name Brandeis unless and until he was ready for a fight. Brandeis and McReynolds represented two distinct and disparate constituencies in the Democratic coalition—northern Progressive and southern Conservative. But successful Democrats, when it is in their interest to do so, have always been able to accommodate one another, and there is no reason to think Brandeis and McReynolds were any different.

Should a vacancy occur, the President naturally would take into consideration the political realities of the moment. There were factors beyond anyone's control that would work in the favor of one contender or the other. One would be the particular Justice who was to be replaced. Mr. Justice Horace Lurton, a Tennessean who had been a sergeant major in the Confederate Army, was known to be in poor health. Lurton and McReynolds had served together on the faculty of Vanderbilt Law School in Nashville.[10] His death or retirement would tend to favor McReynolds.

The Attorney General was a man thought to be incorruptible,[11] yet McReynolds protected Wickersham and Lyons when simply

<hr />

[10] See *Horace Harmon Lurton*, 237 U.S. vii, viii, and *In Memory of Mr. Justice McReynolds*, 334 U.S. v-xxiv.

[11] At about this time Colonel House had lunch in London with Samuel Untermeyer, a famous American lawyer of the day. "One of the interesting things he told me was the fight being made upon McReynolds. He said they were trying to bring about his undoing because he was fearless and independent, and he could not be reached in an improper way." *House Diary*, July 4, 1913.

doing his duty was in his obvious interest. If ever "the path of duty was the way to glory,"[12] it was then and there for James McReynolds. Not only had Wickersham lied to the House of Representatives, he had deceived President Taft as well. Here was a cold case of obstruction of justice. "McReynolds the Trustbuster" could have covered himself with glory in his first 60 days in office. There must be something, you say to yourself, that I don't know about. What could it be?

Let us hypothesize that sometime in 1913, probably in the beginning of May, McReynolds and Brandeis came to a gentlemen's agreement. McReynolds would expose neither Lyons nor the Republican cover-up and would give Denison free rein in handling the *Weeks* appeal. For his part Brandeis would stand aside when the first vacancy on the Supreme Court occurred, or at least he would stand aside if it was Justice Lurton's seat which became vacant. So long as the attorney general was in the running, LDB would not urge the appointment of a Progressive or do anything which might damage McReynolds's chances.

What Brandeis lent the conspiracy was his influence. When Stimson and the Taft administration left Washington in March of 1913, they left Felix Frankfurter and Winfred Denison political orphans. All their friends were Republicans. The only person they knew who had access to the Democratic Attorney General was Louis Brandeis. It could only have been Brandeis who got McReynolds to do his part. His final contribution was to provide Denison with an alibi for missing the oral argument and a safe haven in the Philippines. Here Louis Brandeis left his tracks.

As Law Officer in the Bureau of Insular Affairs, Felix Frankfurter was in a position to learn of the opening for the Philippine secretaryship before it could be appropriated by a covetous Democratic Senator as a reward for a faithful constituent. But Frankfurter could have done nothing on his own to get the post for Denison.

The departure of Henry L. Stimson left Frankfurter with little

---

[12] Alfred Lord Tennyson, *Ode on the Death of the Duke of Wellington.*

influence in the War Department. That summer, when Secretary of War Lindley M. Garrison was preparing to make an inspection tour of the Philippines, Felix Frankfurter thought there were some social and economic facts which should be called to his attention. Apparently unable to do this himself, Frankfurter tried to get Brandeis to go over Garrison's head by speaking to the President. Brandeis demurred; it would not be "wise for me to make any [such] suggestion to the President," he replied.[13]

In 1913 the legal residence of Winfred Denison, his sojourn in Washington notwithstanding, was the state of New York. James A. O'Gorman was at the time the lone Democratic Senator from the Empire State. The traditions of the Senate, for that reason alone, required that the appointment of Denison by a Democratic President be acceptable to O'Gorman. Therefore, not only was Senator O'Gorman to chair the committee which would pass on Denison's nomination, the institution known as "senatorial courtesy" gave him a veto power over it. This is the same Senator O'Gorman who in June had gone on record saying that President Wilson should remove the Republican appointees in the Philippines and put Democrats in their place.

Louis Brandeis spent a considerable amount of time in the nation's capital in 1913 and kept a suite at the Gordon Hotel, which had become his second home. He made three trips that November,[14] the third of which was for 10 days. His "access" was truly remarkable; it was a rare day that he did not visit or receive a visit from a congressman or cabinet member. His diary shows that on Thursday, November 20, a week before Thanksgiving, LDB saw the Secretary of the Interior and then spent an hour conferring with Attorney General McReynolds.

On the next day, Friday, November 21, President Wilson sent Republican Senator Elihu Root of New York the courtesy letter due a Senator of the opposite party inquiring whether he knew of any

---

[13] LDB to FF, July 19, 1913, *Brandeis Letters.*

[14] LDB was also in Washington on October 30 and "talked to [Presidential Secretary Joseph] Tumulty" that afternoon or evening. This would have been two days after Denison sent Tumulty his temporizing letter.

fact which would make Denison's appointment inadvisable. The Senator replied that he did not.[15] On Saturday, November 22, Secretary of War Garrison reported to the President that "I have just seen Senator O'Gorman, and he is satisfied to have Denison's name go in."[16]

Senator O'Gorman had a special reason to do the President a favor, and on Monday he told him what it was. O'Gorman "had recommended a German Lutheran" for the postmastership in Buffalo, President Wilson explained in a letter to Postmaster General Burleson,[17] and through a misunderstanding had "permitted it to be announced in Buffalo that his candidate would be appointed, whereupon the said candidate was serenaded, etc., by several Lutheran societies and his not being appointed had caused him considerable mortification." Wilson asked Burleson to see what he could do to rectify the situation.

There is nothing to indicate that Woodrow Wilson, Lindley Garrison or James O'Gorman had ever heard of, much less met, Winfred Denison. Garrison did not see O'Gorman on his own initiative, nor was he working on the weekend as a favor for Frankfurter. He had to have been acting on instructions from the President of the United States. The only reason O'Gorman was "satisfied to have Denison's name go in" was that he wished to do Woodrow Wilson a favor and get one in return.

The President knew who and what Garrison was talking about, because on Monday, November 24, he nominated Winfred T. Denison to the Philippine secretaryship.[18] The day before had been a busy day for Louis Brandeis, as his diary attests.

---

[15] WW to Elihu Root, November 21, 1913; Elihu Root to WW, November 25, 1913, Wilson Papers.

[16] L.M. Garrison to WW, November 22, 1913, Wilson Papers.

[17] WW to Albert Sidney Burleson, November 25, 1913, Wilson Papers. O'Gorman also had other patronage appointments pending the President's approval. See J.A. O'Gorman to WW, November 12, 1913.

[18] "Named For Filipino Board," New York Times, November 25, 1913.

Sunday, November 23, 1913
LDB in Washington

Shoe Mfrs. Alliance. Discussed situation fully
with McReynolds, and agreed to take up
matter further with him.   1 1/4

Merger. Discussed situation with McReynolds. 1/2

Trusts, Discussed with McReynolds shoe matters,
sugar trust, met H. Ward Leonard at Willard.

Insurgency. Con with Denison on Philippine Matters 1/2
Con. with Ives on I.C.C. matters. 1 1/2

Louis Brandeis spent all week in Washington. On Wednesday
he met with McReynolds at the latter's home at the Shoreham. On
Thursday he logged only three billable hours; one might conjecture
that he was invited over to the House of Truth for Thanksgiving
dinner or to a going away party for the new Philippine
commissioner. It was also an eventful week for Winfred Denison.
Nominated on Monday, he filed the *Weeks* brief on Wednesday.
On Thursday, Thanksgiving Day, he wrote his "Rubicon" letter to
"Dear Felix," and by Friday he was on his way to the Pacific Coast.
The case of *Weeks v. United States* was argued before the Supreme
Court the following Tuesday and Wednesday, December 2 and 3,
1913, by the attorney for Plaintiff in Error Fremont Weeks. The
United States submitted.

Louis Brandeis left Washington for Boston at 5:35 Saturday
afternoon, November 29. The night before, Woodrow Wilson had
dined with Colonel House at the latter's apartment in New York
City. It was at this dinner, the night after Thanksgiving, that the
President decided to appoint McReynolds to Justice Lurton's seat
should it become vacant. According to House, the Attorney General
was being kicked upstairs. "The only reason for transferring
McReynolds from the Department of Justice is on account of his
lack of political acumen. He is a great lawyer and will probably bring

to successful conclusions the various suits in which his department is now engaged."[19]

A grueling schedule appears to have taken its toll on the Attorney General. On December 18, 1913, Louis Brandeis wrote his wife a letter which opened: "Dearest: Had 1 1/2 hours with McR[eynolds] & [Thomas W.] Gregory last evening. The former is very tired and I think must look back longingly to the days of obscurity."[20]

Louis Brandeis was in Washington when the *Weeks* decision was handed down on Tuesday, February 24, 1914. He had spent the preceding two days at the Gordon Hotel composing a lengthy letter to McReynolds giving him, as the Attorney General had requested, his "suggestions" on "the so-called 'Trust Bills.'" "Although," Brandeis wrote, "I shall want to work over the details further before I have a talk with you." The letter ends in mid-paragraph, indicating the last page or pages have been lost or destroyed.[21]

On Thursday LDB talked with the Attorney General on the same matter for over an hour and spent the evening in the company of "McReynolds et al."[22] His diary shows that on Sunday, March 1, 1914, Brandeis and McReynolds spent three and a half hours working over the details of what eventually became the Clayton Antitrust Act of 1914. In a letter to his wife Brandeis again alluded to McReynolds's fatigue. "The Conference with Atty Genl. was not exciting. He is weary & I think almost wishes he was out of the job."[23]

Up until this time the relationship between LDB and the Attorney General had been quite amicable and collegial. There is no evidence of friction between them. Whenever Louis Brandeis was in Washington they met on business and on occasion socially. But in

---

[19] *House Diary*, November 28, 1913.

[20] LDB to AGB, December 18, 1913, *Brandeis Letters*.

[21] LDB to JCM, February 22, 1914, *Brandeis Letters*. Although it is dated Sunday, February 22, LDB's diary indicates he worked 6 1/2 hours on the letter on Monday, which, being Washington's Birthday, was a holiday.

[22] "Thursday, February 26, 1914. L.D.B. in Washington" "Trusts. On letter to McReynolds. Talked with and appointment for Monday. Lr. to G.R. 1 1/4 . . . Con. with McReynolds et al in evening."

[23] LDB to AGB, February 27, 1914, *Brandeis Letters*.

the spring of 1914 something happened between Louis Brandeis and James McReynolds and things between them were never the same. According to LDB's diary, they talked on March 17, after which they no longer met, and correspondence between them ceased. The People's Lawyer no longer had "access"—in fact the Attorney General wouldn't see him at all. An entry on May 18 indicates that Secretary of Commerce Redfield offered to intervene: "Price Maintenance. Tele. fr. Redfield: asking me to call. Discussed Kellogg case. He said he would see McReynolds; also bring matter up at Cabinet meeting if necessary."

Felix Frankfurter resigned from the War Department and "left Washington in early summer of 1914 and spent the summer in the stacks [Harvard Law Library] trying to find out what had happened to the law generally since [he] left the school in 1906."[24] He was at Cambridge when Justice Lurton died on July 12, 1914.

Roscoe Pound was also at Harvard when, five days later, he wrote LDB asking if it would be proper for him, Pound, to write President Wilson to urge the appointment of U.S. Circuit Court Judge Julian W. Mack to the Supreme Court. Brandeis responded on July 20 that "I can see no possible impropriety in your writing the President your opinion of Mack."[25]

This is curious. The leading candidates for the Court were thought to be McReynolds and Brandeis. But Pound wouldn't consider supporting Julian Mack or anyone else so long as Louis Brandeis was in the running. According to his diary LDB had not been home for a month, yet Pound, with Lurton hardly in his grave, knew Brandeis was not in contention. Bear in mind the "titan among titans" had his new apprentice at his elbow when he wrote this letter.

We have postulated that Louis D. Brandeis and James C. McReynolds, probably in May of 1913, entered into a gentlemen's agreement. The Attorney General agreed to cover up Wickersham's coverup of Leslie Lyons and to permit Denison to stay on and handle the *Weeks* appeal. Brandeis, for his part, would stand aside

[24] *Reminisces*, 86.
[25] LDB to RP, July 20, 1914, and commentary, *Brandeis Letters*.

when the next vacancy on the Court came about, or at least he would stand aside if it were Lurton's seat which became vacant. LDB would not oppose McReynolds or endorse another candidate so long as McReynolds was under consideration.

The known facts are not only consistent with this hypothesis, they are supportive of it. The decision to appoint McReynolds to the Court was made November 28, the day after Thanksgiving, after a week in which McReynolds and Brandeis were in constant communication. And Woodrow Wilson never would have made this commitment without talking to LDB; Brandeis would have been deeply offended had he been presented with a *fait accompli*. As it turned out, McReynolds got the first seat and Brandeis the second. Perhaps this was agreed to as well.

Woodrow Wilson got to make a third appointment when Justice Charles Evans Hughes resigned from the Court to accept the Republican nomination in the 1916 presidental election. As we shall see, Louis Brandeis, as a sitting Justice, no less, took active measures to influence the selection of Hughes's successor. Yet, with respect to the appointment of McReynolds in 1914, when he was not bound by the constraints of judicial propriety, he did nothing. Despite the fact that he and McReynolds had become estranged, Brandeis did not oppose him, nor did he endorse or promote anyone else. Aside from telling Roscoe Pound that he saw "no possible impropriety in your writing to the president your opinion on Mack," Louis Brandeis was as quiet as a mouse. This, as we shall also see, was quite unlike him.

On Saturday, July 11, 1914, the day before Lurton died, Colonel House had been in London talking to American Ambassador Walter Hines Page about the storm clouds gathering over Europe. British Foreign Minister Sir Edward Grey, Page informed him, "was much disturbed about the Russia-Austria-Serbia complication, and was afraid something serious might grow out of it."[26]

On Monday House made this entry in his diary. "I have a cable this morning from Gregory announcing the death of Justice Lurton.

---

[26] *House Diary*, July 11, 1914.

120

I seriously hope the President will 'stay put' and give McReynolds the vacancy and make Gregory the Attorney General as planned before I left."[27] Two days later he wrote Wilson that he was returning home and gave him a piece of advice. "I am sorry to hear of Justice Lurton's death. I hope you may not change your decision as to McReynolds and Gregory, for that seems to be the wise solution."[28]

Alas, what grew out of "the Russia-Austria-Serbia complication" was a cataclysm. By the 4th of August all attempts at conciliation had failed and Europe was at war. That day Woodrow Wilson proclaimed the neutrality of the United States. Two days later the President suffered his own personal tragedy when his wife of almost 30 years, Ellen Louise Axson Wilson, died at the age of 54.

The German strategy was to deal the French a decisive blow while fending off the Russians on the Eastern front. Time was of the essence. The Germans had the advantage of interior lines of communication and the ability to mobilize and deploy their forces faster than their enemies. Expediency and geography required the Germans to invade France through Belgium; honor and what German Chancellor Bethmann-Hollweg called "a scrap of paper" required the British to go to war if they did.

The month of August brought the Germans a massive victory in East Prussia when they trapped and annihilated the invading Russians at Tannenberg. On the Western Front they had taken most of Belgium and a wide swath of France from what the Kaiser called a "contemptible little army"—the British Expeditionary Force—and a French Army in full retreat. As August drew to a close it appeared the Germans would envelop Paris and win a war as short and decisive as the Franco-Prussian War of 1870-71.

August 30 found Colonel House with Woodrow Wilson at his retreat at Harlekendon, New Hampshire. The day before Wilson had "[a]ppointed James Clark McReynolds Associate Justice of the Supreme Court."[29] Wilson and House "discussed the appointments

---

[27] *House Diary*, July 13, 1914.

[28] EMH to WW, July 15, 1914, Wilson Papers.

[29] *Woodrow Wilson 1856-1924, Chronology—Documents—Bibliographical Aids.* R.V. Vexler and H.F. Bremer, editors. Dobbs Ferry, New York: Oceana Publications Inc., 1969, 12.

of Gregory and McReynolds, news of their confirmation having just reached us." But Woodrow Wilson was bereft, a broken man who did not think he could go on. "The death of his wife had left him in despair, as he looked forward to the next two years and a half with dread. He did not see how he could go through with it."[30]

James Clark McReynolds "took his seat on the bench on the opening of the October Term 1914."[31] The next vacancy came 15 months later when Justice Joseph R. Lamar of Georgia died early in January of 1916. Woodrow Wilson named Louis Brandeis to replace him. As expected, the confirmation was fiercely opposed:

> [S]ixty-one prominent persons, many of them leading lawyers and citizens of Boston and vicinity, [protested] urging that Brandeis did not have the confidence of the bar or the public and that he was not fit for the position . . . They accused Brandeis of mismanaging the affairs of clients . . . Trickery of various sorts was charged or implied. Fundamentally, the opposition boiled down to the charge that he was guilty of unprofessional conduct, and that, being an advocate in social causes and a crusader, he lacked judicial temperament."[32]

Six former presidents of the American Bar Association— William Howard Taft, Elihu Root, Joseph H. Choate, Simeon E. Baldwin, Francis Rawle and Moorfield Storey—sent a letter to the Senate Committee on the Judiciary stating their opinion that Louis Brandeis was "not a fit person to be a member of the Supreme Court of the United States."[33] The contest ended on June 1, 1916, when the nominee was confirmed by a vote of 47 to 22.

The following November marked the beginning of a long-term financial arrangement whereby LDB—now Mr. Justice Brandeis— agreed to underwrite expenses that his protégé might incur in his

---

[30] *House Diary*, August 30, 1914.

[31] 234 U.S. front.

[32] Carl Brent Swisher. *American Constitutional Development*. Boston: Houghton Mifflin Company, 1943, 593.

[33] *Nomination of Louis D. Brandeis*, Hearings, Senate Committee on the Judiciary, Senate Doc. No. 409, 64th Congress, 1st session 1226, cited by Swisher at 593.

endeavors for the "public interest." "I ought to feel free," said he to FF, "to make suggestions to you, although they involve some incidental expense. And you should feel free to incur expense in the public interest."[34] Subsidized by this allowance, Professor Frankfurter picked up where the People's Lawyer left off.

No two men were more kindred in spirit than Louis Brandeis and Felix Frankfurter; they were as twins born a generation apart. As the younger man modeled himself after the older and followed in his footsteps, the older man molded the younger into his image and likeness. They had no secrets from each other. "Frankfurter would often migrate to Chatham, where Brandeis kept a home on Cape Cod. He sometimes stayed there for weeks at a time, as he did during the summer of 1924 while [his wife] Marion was in California." In a letter to her that summer he described their relationship:

> He feels as one continually bottled up and as he puts it "When I talk to you I feel I'm talking to myself" so out come the innermost judicial secrets . . . LDB and I have the best kind of professional time together, even better than Holmesy would be these days, for L.D.B. nowadays tells me more. You see how much on the make I am professionally.[35]

Being a professor at Harvard gave Frankfurter the chance to select young men of promise to serve as clerks to both Justice Holmes and Justice Brandeis. There is no greater honor for a law graduate than to be chosen to clerk for a Justice of the Supreme Court, and there is nothing more certain to advance his career. This power of appointment enabled FF to build a network of young Progressive lawyers whose influence will proliferate in the years to come.

As two of the *Weeks* conspirators became the closest of friends, two became the bitterest of enemies. James C. McReynolds and Louis D. Brandeis sat together on the Supreme Court as anything but brethren. From 1916 to 1939 Justice McReynolds carried on a

---

[34] LDB to FF, November 25, 1916, *Brandeis Letters.*

[35] H.N. Hirsch. *The Enigma of Felix Frankfurter.* New York: Basic Books, 1981, 86.

campaign of aloof discourtesy against Justice Brandeis to which the other members of the Court were held hostage.

Whatever the cause of the rift between them, McReynolds was unforgiving to the end. On February 17, 1939, four days after Justice Brandeis retired, the other Justices sent him a farewell letter praising his service, regretting his departure, and extending their "best wishes and the assurance of our affection and profound esteem." McReynolds refused to sign it. One of the signatories was the newly seated Justice Felix Frankfurter.[36] In his *Reminisces*, published in 1961, FF described McReynolds and this incident.

> Mr. Justice McReynolds was a strange creature . . . He
> had a very good head. He was also primitive . . . He had
> primitive anti-Semitism. A tough-skinned fellow like me
> could deal with him because I could be just as rude as he
> could be. Rude isn't the exact word. He was not rude
> really, but indifferent which is worse than being rude.
> He was handsome, able, and honest. I sort of respected
> him . . . There was the usual letter of farewell to a
> colleague, and he wouldn't sign it. I respected that,
> because he did not remotely feel what the letter
> expressed, and I despise hypocrites even more than
> barbarians. [37]

In 1965 Dean Acheson—Secretary of State 1947-49—published *Morning and Noon*, an autobiography of his younger days when he was an observer rather than a shaper of events. In 1919 Acheson—then 26—had been a clerk for Mr. Justice Brandeis, having been recommended for that post by Harvard Law School Professor Felix Frankfurter. Acheson explains the purpose—and hence the title of the book—in the introduction. It was to:

> Bring to those who never knew those . . . people living
> pictures of them . . . I have tried to make them live as
> parts of the vanished time in which they were once so

---

[36] 306 U.S. v, vi.
[37] *Reminisces*, 101.

much alive. Some of the people will bear familiar names; but time and biography will have made them mythical characters, figures modeled out of virtues or faults. I have tried to bring back something of the living persons who once inhabited these shadows, to help us see their times as they saw them, breathe the air they breathed, share their passions, their hopes, their follies, their disappointments.[38]

In a chapter entitled *"Our Court"* Acheson discusses the members of the Supreme Court as it was constituted in 1919-20. This was what he had to say of McReynolds:

Mr. Justice James Clark McReynolds of Tennessee was a different kettle of fish. The ogre of the liberals, a deplorable judge, an outrageous old curmudgeon, or, to put it in another's supreme understatement, "a man of numerous and abrasive personal idiosyncrasies," he remained my friend until death . . .

Before my arrival on the scene, McReynolds had ceased speaking to his brethren Brandeis and Clarke because of some imagined slight on their part. This bothered Justice Holmes, who was most sensitive to personal friction near him and rendered acutely unhappy by rudeness. He struggled to mend matters, but McReynolds would neither explain nor forget.[39]

In 1922 the members of the Supreme Court were asked to attend a ceremony at Constitution Hall in Philadelphia. They were to sail from Washington to Philadelphia. This did not sit well with McReynolds who sent Chief Justice William Howard Taft this scrawled undated note—in part unreadable—which now reposes in the Taft Papers in the Manuscript Division of the Library of Congress:[40]

---

[38] Dean Acheson. *Morning and Noon.* Boston: Houghton Mifflin Company, 1965, xi-xii.
[39] Ibid., 70, 71.
[40] JCM to WHT, *ca* February 1922.

THE ROCHAMBEAU
Washington, D.C.

Dear Chief Justice—
    I [vote with you concerning?] the Philadelphia trip.
As you are aware, I not am always to be found when there
is a Hebrew aboard. Therefore my "inability" to attend
must not surprise you.

Sincerely,
J.C. McReynolds

It seems to have become a fact, well known to all who have
written of Louis Brandeis, that James Clark McReynolds was a
virulent anti-Semite. They rest their case on the icy indifference
with which McReynolds treated Brandeis when they sat on the
Court together with his note to the Chief Justice regarding the
Philadelphia boat trip. But they never take into account, if indeed
they are aware of, the relationship that existed between the two men
before the spring of 1914.

Nor have they considered Acheson's appraisal of Justice
McReynolds and what it implies. Dean Acheson was the devoted
disciple, protégé, and friend until death of both Louis Brandeis and
Felix Frankfurter. *Morning and Noon*, written a quarter-century
after the death of LDB, was dedicated to "FF." If Acheson thought
for a moment that the reason McReynolds did not speak to Brandeis
was because Brandeis was a Jew, he would never have written that
McReynolds "remained my friend until death." Acheson would
have shunned him.

Nor would Justice Oliver Wendell Holmes have "struggled to
mend matters." Anti-Semitism, after all, is hardly a subject for
mediation. It appears that all concerned knew that the root of the
problem was a personal matter which "McReynolds would neither
explain nor forget." Nor did Brandeis offer any explanation
although he must have known what was behind McReynolds's
behavior.

Associate Justices James C. McReynolds, Willis Van Devanter,
George Sutherland and Pierce Butler were known as the "Four

Horsemen" of the "Nine Old Men" who struck down as unconstitutional legislation deemed essential to Franklin D. Roosevelt's "New Deal." In 1937 FDR attempted to remedy the situation by increasing the number of Supreme Court Justices— "packing the Court," it was called—but was rebuffed by Congress. Eventually, age and attrition solved Roosevelt's problem. By 1939, the only "Horseman" left was McReynolds, the seats of the other three having been filled by loyal New Dealers of whom one was Felix Frankfurter. James Clark McReynolds retired in 1941 and died in 1946.

McReynolds is never mentioned by the biographers of Louis Brandeis without being characterized as both a "reactionary" and an "anti-Semite." Charges relating to the former focus on his Supreme Court decisions to the exclusion of McReynolds's earlier career when he won acclaim as a "trust-buster." From LDB's diary it appears that virtually all of the conferences he had with Attorney General McReynolds concerned antitrust matters. If there were any differences between the two men with regard to the enforcement of the antitrust laws, or any of the other political issues of the day, they never emerged in LDB's diary or the copious correspondence he had with his friends and his wife. The same can be said with respect to the charge of anti-Semitism.

The purpose of this discussion, however, is not the posthumous rehabilitation of James Clark McReynolds. Believe what you will of the "primitive anti-Semitism" Mr. Justice Frankfurter imputed to Mr. Justice McReynolds 15 years after the latter's death. And whatever connotation one wishes to put on McReynolds's note regarding the Philadelphia boat trip is irrelevant as well. Whether it evinced an amimosity towards Jews in general or was just another gaucherie by a man Acheson thought "an outrageous old curmudgeon" is also beside the point.

The point is that this anti-Semitism—if indeed he was an anti-Semite—did not manifest itself or rise to such a level in the persona of Attorney General James McReynolds so as to interfere with his having an amicable and reciprocal working relationship with Louis Brandeis during the first year of the Wilson administration. And reciprocity had to be part of the gentlemen's agreement we have postulated.

Attorney General James C. McReynolds was an essential participant in the *Weeks* conspiracy; it could never have been carried off without him. Why did not the Attorney General follow the clear path of duty, expose Republican corruption and deceit, and cover himself with glory? The answer is that he got something in return for his forbearance. The *quid pro quo* could only have been an unobstructed path to the seat on the Supreme Court McReynolds took in 1914. It is doubtful Woodrow Wilson would have appointed JCM had LDB decided to oppose him.

And what did Louis Brandeis get out of it? For one thing, the appointment of McReynolds—a southern Democrat of conservative bent—virtually ensured that President Wilson's next nominee to the Court would be a Progressive from outside the South. The Wilson Administration had a decided Southern tilt, a fact which had not gone unnoticed by Democrats from north of the Mason-Dixon line.

Given the ages of the justices, there was a better than even chance in 1913 that Wilson would get the opportunity to make a second appointment to the Supreme Court. Were he to choose Louis Brandeis, there was sure to be resistance in the Senate. The appointment of McReynolds meant that this opposition would not focus on regional or ideological grounds. For if a Brandeis nomination failed, Wilson's next choice perforce would be another northern Democrat with Progressive credentials. There is yet another consideration which cannot be overlooked.

When the *Weeks* conspiracy began, Felix Frankfurter was the protégé of Henry L. Stimson, "conjugally happy" with Winfred Denison at the House of Truth. But for an invisible hand both Frankfurter and Denison would have returned to New York with Stimson in the beginning of 1913. But when the story ended, FF was Harvard Law Professor Felix Frankfurter, the "half-brother, half-son" of Louis Brandeis, the two impediments to this relationship having been dissolved.

And Winfred Denison, whatever happened to him? In the Frankfurter Papers in the Library of Congress, there is a "Denison" file which tells us how the Philippine adventure turned out. In it is a clipping from the *Manila Daily Bulletin* circa September 1915 with the leading story captioned: "Denison Sails For U.S. On Mongolia Wednesday—Gets Indefinite Leave of Absence—Secretary of Interior Ill and Must Consult Specialists in Homeland—Return Depends Upon Advice of Doctors."

> Secretary Denison arrived in Manila on March 2, 1914, and immediately took up the duties of his office. A little more than a month after his arrival he set out for a trip of inspection through the Mountain province, and early in May was taken ill in the mountain country. It is from the effects of this illness that the doctors now believe that he has never fully recovered.

Winfred Denison returned to New York City and to Stetson, Jennings & Russell, the law firm he left in 1910. Like many Wall Street lawyers he became a commuter, taking up residence at Roslyn, a suburban town on the north shore of Long Island not far from Huntington, the home of Henry L. Stimson. Denison and Stimson were prominent in New York City Republican circles, and, in 1919, were promoting the candidacy of Progressive Republican Fiorello LaGuardia for President of the Board of Aldermen, the leading office at stake in the municipal elections that year.

We will never know the state of mind of Winfred Denison when he arrived at his office the morning of Wednesday, November 5, 1919. Certainly the political news was to his liking. The lead article in that day's *New York Times* tells how in a see-saw battle decided in the wee hours of the morning LaGuardia eeked out a victory over Democratic incumbent Robert L. Moran. "LaGuardia Wins By 1,530: Beats Moran for President of Board of Alderman in a Close Contest."

But if Winfred Denison was happy that morning, his spirits took a terrible turn for the worse. Leaving his office in the early afternoon Denison took the subway uptown to Pennsylvania Station, whence he could take the Long Island Railroad back to Roslyn. But he never did. The next day's *Times* tells us how it all came to an end.

WINFRED T. DENISON COMMITS SUICIDE
Former United States Assistant Attorney
General Jumps in Front of Subway Train

Despondent because of ill health, Winfred Thaxter Denison, formerly Assistant Attorney General of the United States, threw himself in front of a downtown local subway train at the Pennsylvania Station early yesterday afternoon and was killed instantly.

Although the station platform was crowded, none of the people standing there saw Mr. Denison jump in front of the approaching train, as he was standing at the northern end of the station, apart from the others. Before jumping, he threw his overcoat over his head, according to the motorman of the train, Thomas Marion of 250 West Twenty-first Street. Marion quickly stopped his train, but not until one of Mr. Denison's legs had been severed from his body, which was badly crushed. A surgeon of the New York Hospital staff, who arrived shortly after the accident, stated that Mr. Denison had been killed instantly . . .

The body was taken from the Thirty-seventh Street Precinct Station to the Campbell Funeral Church, where the funeral will be held on Saturday. A brother and a sister in Portland were notified of his death. Mr. Denison was unmarried.[41]

Henry L. Stimson attended Denison's funeral but Felix Frankfurter did not. On November 4, the day before the suicide, Frankfurter had sent Stimson an announcement of his engagement to marry Miss Marion Denman.[42] One would think he sent an announcement to Denison as well. On Saturday, November 8, after returning from the funeral, Stimson sent Frankfurter his congratulations. He would have responded sooner, Stimson told his

---

[41] *New York Times*, November 6, 1919.
[42] FF to HLS, November 4, 1919, Frankfurter Papers.

former protégé, but "I thought that possibly I should see you at poor Denison's funeral and be able to tell to you in person how glad I am that you are going to have such a happiness."[43]

[43] HLS to FF, November 8, 1919, Frankfurter Papers.

Chapter VII

THE ROAD TO *MAPP v. OHIO*

P otter Stewart (1914-1985) sat on the Supreme Court of the
United States from 1958 to 1981 and was considered an
expert on the exclusionary rule. He was the author of the
Court's opinion in *Coolidge v. New Hampshire*, the case with which
we began. After his retirement Justice Stewart wrote a treatise which
he delivered as a series of lectures at Columbia Law School entitled
*The Road to Mapp v. Ohio and Beyond: The Origins, Development
and Future of the Exclusionary Rule in Search and Seizure Cases.*[1] He
began with a description of the events leading to the American
Revolution and the "Formulation and Adoption of the Fourth
Amendment."

> Historians who have analyzed the framers' reasons for
> adopting the fourth amendment have consistently
> reached the same conclusion. The framers sought to
> ensure that the newly formed federal government could
> not employ the two devices used by the British Crown
> that they believed jeopardized the liberty of every citizen:
> the general warrant and the writ of assistance.[2]

Central to British policy was the form of economic oppression

---

[1] Delivered as the Harlan Fiske Stone Lectures in April of 1983, and published in 83 Columbia
Law Review 1365.
[2] Ibid., 1369.

known as mercantilism. Colonial manufacturing was discouraged and high tariffs inhibited trade with other countries. To buy or sell Americans had to deal with the mother country at a considerable disadvantage. The result was predictable; smuggling became not only a profitable occupation but an honorable one as well. Many of our Founding Fathers were smugglers, John Hancock chief among them.

George III took the throne in 1760. The 15 years between his succession and the outbreak of the Revolutionary War was a period of ever-increasing hostility between the Americans and the British. There were constant incidents in this contest between smuggler and tax collector. The weapon of the latter was a form of search warrant known as a writ of assistance. If untaxed goods were thought to be about, British customs officials armed with a writ of assistance would search every house in the vicinity.

> The Crown felt the need for the writs because the colonists had responded to its restrictions and taxes on trade by practicing the age old craft of smuggling. The task of curbing such smuggling fell upon the customs officials in each colonial port city. In an effort to assist these officials, the Crown armed the customs inspectors with writs of assistance. The writ permitted its bearer, the customs official, to search with unlimited discretion for the duration of the life of the reigning monarch.[3]

During the War of the American Revolution, British troops and their American allies, the Tories, used general warrants to search at will and arrest those they considered disloyal. As the Redcoats held the populated areas for most of these six years, virtually every American family of patriotic sympathy had personal knowledge of arbitrary searches and arrests. It was a matter familiar to the First Congress, whose number included many the British had sought the most. It was with this in their memories that they drafted the Fourth Amendment to the Constitution, which together with the rest of the first ten amendments, became law on December 15, 1791.

---

[3] Ibid., 1370.

> The right of the people to be secure in their persons, houses, papers, and effects, against unreasonable searches and seizures, shall not be violated, and no warrants shall issue, but upon probable cause, supported by oath or affirmation, and particularly describing the place to be searched, and the persons or things to be seized.

The understanding of those who proposed and ratified the first eight amendments was that they were restraints against the newly created federal government and it alone. It is an indisputable historical fact that those who made the Bill of Rights law did not intend that its prohibitions should apply to the individual states. This was affirmed by the Supreme Court in 1833,[4] and the Fourth Amendment itself was specifically held inapplicable to the states in 1855.

> If rested on that clause in the constitution of the United States which prohibits the issuing of a warrant but on probable cause supported by oath, the answer is, that this restrains the issue of warrants only under the laws of the United States, and has no application to state process.[5]

Let us look at our pristine Fourth Amendment through crystal waters as yet unclouded by case law. That it says nothing of excluding evidence is plain to see. Note that the amendment outlaws only *unreasonable* searches and seizures. Nothing in its text evinces an intent on the part of the Framers that searches and seizures should be deemed the more reasonable if made pursuant to a warrant; nothing suggests that the lack of a warrant should make an otherwise reasonable search unreasonable. In fact it was warrants—broad and sweeping warrants—that were the bane of our colonial ancestors as a recent text explains.

> The history of the amendment suggests that the drafters weren't worried about limiting searches in general. What

---

4 *Barron v. Baltimore*, 32 U.S. 243.
5 *Smith v. Maryland*, 59 U.S. 71, 76.

they wanted to limit were *search warrants*. This is curious to the modern sensibility because today we regard warrants as a check upon police power. That's not how the Founders saw it. In their time, warrants shielded the king's officials from civil actions by the victims of unjust searches; only warrantless searches could result in the award of damages against the offending officials.[6]

A warrant is a writ issued in the name of the sovereign authorizing an officer of the law to make a search, a seizure or an arrest. A warrant confers immunity upon an officer who executes it so that in the event the facts thought to constitute probable cause turn out to be false, he is not liable for the indignities the victim may have suffered. This is why it is essential that warrants be narrow in scope and verified under oath. If a warrant does not specify who or what is sought and no one vouches for the probable cause which prompts the search, there is no accountability. What the British had done was to create warrants which gave agents authority to search at will with impunity. A victim of an arbitrary search or seizure had no recourse.

Under the Fourth Amendment, a warrant must be narrow and specific, "particularly describing the place to be searched, and the persons or things to be seized." An application for a warrant must be made under oath and state the reasons which give rise to "probable cause." Anyone attesting to the facts does so at his peril. A false statement would be grounds for both a criminal prosecution for perjury and a lawsuit by the party against whom the warrant is directed.

An officer of the law who makes an unreasonable search or seizure has committed a trespass, and an unreasonable arrest may constitute an assault. It is the law throughout the United States that a police officer is liable for those torts in a civil suit brought against him by the aggrieved party. Depending on the intent of the officer and the circumstances of the case, a search, seizure or arrest without probable cause may also be a violation of the criminal law. Illegal searches and seizures are deterred by the same sanctions used by the law to deter any other type of tortious or criminal behavior. The perpetrators are subject to civil liability and criminal punishment.

---

[6]   Max Boot. *Out of Order*. New York: Basic Books, 1998, 66.

It is where an unlawful search or seizure turns up probative and otherwise admissible evidence of a person's complicity in a crime that the controversy begins. One school of thought says that to permit the prosecution to use evidence unlawfully obtained is to ratify the illegal act and make the government a lawbreaker. The law, they maintain, must take affirmative steps to deter official invasions of privacy. This school would therefore exclude such evidence from being used against a defendant at his trial.

The opposite view holds that the exclusion of evidence does nothing for the person in whose home, or on whose person, nothing incriminating was found. By its nature it protects only the guilty. That one wrong has been committed by an officer of the law is no reason to let another lawbreaker go unpunished. The law we inherited on our independence was the common law rule that the "admissibility of evidence is not affected by the illegality of the means by which it was obtained." At common law, courts would "not take notice how they were obtained, whether lawfully or unlawfully."[7]

For almost a century the common law rule prevailed in this country without challenge. The Fourth Amendment by its terms does not require the suppression of evidence obtained through its violation, and no one thought it did so by implication. We will let Potter Stewart take it from here:

> The actual birth of the exclusionary rule was not the product of a spirited debate over the various alternative doctrinal bases for such a rule. The famous cases cited as the roots of the rule are not in themselves works of constitutional brilliance—they have become legendary only through the ability of subsequent cases, articles, classroom discussions, and speeches to find the seeds of constitutional genius between the lines of the opinions. None of the three Supreme Court cases credited with producing the rule [citing *Boyd v. United States, Adams v. New York* and *Weeks v. United States*] focused on whether the exclusionary rule, as we know it, should

---

[7] *Olmstead v. United States*, 277 U.S. 438, 467 (1928).

exist—yet somehow, in 1914, after all three cases had been decided, the rule was established.

The first case associated with the development of the exclusionary rule is *Boyd v. United States.* Yet the *Boyd* case was a civil case not a criminal case, no police were involved, and no search and seizure ever took place.[8]

It was *Boyd v. United States* that planted the seed for the rule which 28 years later prevailed in *Weeks.* All discussions of the exclusionary rule start in 1886 with *Boyd.* Its centennial was duly observed by those who are fond of citing *Boyd* to show what a truly time-tested, good old American institution is the exclusionary rule. Let us check its credentials and see how they stand up.

Edward A. Boyd & Son were New York City glass merchants who were the successful bidders on a contract to supply the foreign plate glass required for the federal building then under construction in Philadelphia, Pennsylvania. The Boyds submitted two bids, the higher of which was based on the glass being imported with the duty paid, and the lower on its being imported duty free. The Treasury Department accepted the lower bid of $4,181 and the Boyds supplied the glass out of their existing stock with the understanding they would be permitted to replenish it by importing a like amount of plate glass duty free.

On April 2, 1884, Boyd & Son requested a permit to enter free of duty 29 cases of plate glass en route to the Port of New York on the steamer *Baltic.* "This glass is intended to replace, in part, glass supplied by us from stock, for the construction of the U.S. courthouse and post-office building at Philadelphia, Pa."[9] The permit was granted and the glass cleared customs duty free and presumably found its way into the Boyd inventory.

The Boyds had informed the Treasury Department that 81 cases of plate glass had been shipped to the Philadelphia post office

---

[8] Stewart, 1372, citing *Boyd v. United States,* 116 U.S. 616 (1886).

[9] Transcript of Record, *Edward A. Boyd and George H. Boyd, Claimants of Thirty-Five Cases of Plate Glass, Plaintiffs in Error, vs. The United States,* Docket No. 983. The transcript has an index which makes it unnecessary to identify citations by page number.

and on April 11 instructed their representative in Washington to reconfirm this fact to the Treasury Department. On May 29 they requested a second permit, to import free of duty another 35 cases due to arrive in New York on the steamer *Alaska*. "This importation and the 29 cases heretofore admitted makes 64 of the 81 cases furnished to said building, leaving a balance of 17 cases yet to be imported."

When the *Alaska* arrived, the 35 cases were seized by the Collector of Customs and the second permit revoked. An action *in rem* was then commenced by the United States asking that the 35 cases be forfeited on the ground they were imported with intent to defraud the government of the lawful duty "by means of false statements, written and verbal." Boyd & Son, appearing through counsel, intervened and filed a claim stating they were the true owners of the 35 cases of glass.

As permitted by federal statute in such cases, the U.S. Attorney petitioned and obtained from the court an order directing the claimants to produce the invoice for the first shipment of 29 cases. The Boyds objected on the ground "that the statute, so far as it compels production of evidence to be used against the claimants, is unconstitutional and void." The judge overruled the objection, and the invoice was produced and admitted into evidence. The case against the *Thirty-Five Cases of Polished Plate Glass* was a matter of simple arithmetic.

There was never a question as to how much glass was installed in the Philadelphia federal building. The bid that Boyd & Son submitted contained a schedule including diagrams that described the windows and doors to be glassed down to the square inch, floor by floor. The specified amount was 9,222 square feet plus an allowance for breakage which brought it to 9,454. "[A]n additional number of 1,228 square feet, or thereabouts, were cut upon a subsequently countermanded order. So that about 10,700 square feet were actually furnished." The invoices for the two shipments, less breakage, completed the government's case.

> [T]he whole quantity of glass, if unbroken, which was contained in the twenty-nine cases and the thirty-five

cases was at least 50,000 square feet of the value of
$35,000, and dutiable at least at $13,000, perhaps more,
whereas the glass furnished and cut under the contract
was under 12,000 square feet, of the value of perhaps
$5,000, duty free, and that the duties on these 12,000
square feet would have been about $2,500; and that no
attempt is made to show that E.A. Boyd & Sons were not
aware of the nature of the statements which they made.

That, gentlemen, is the claim of the government.

The only disputed figures were for wastage and breakage. The
Boyds claimed that "some 22,500 feet were used up in supplying the
orders of the government for the building. The government says
this is a ridiculously large statement for wastage, and so large that it
shows on its face that it is an untruthful statement." The claimants
also said "that two-thirds of the twenty-nine cases were broken and
worthless when they arrived." The government pointed out "that
no mention of breakage in these twenty-nine cases was ever made to
the [Treasury] architect as a reason for wanting other cases to be
admitted free of duty."

It was further in evidence that the cases imported by the
Baltic and the Alaska each contained from 800 to 1000
square feet of plate glass. It was also in evidence that the
cases sent by the claimants to Philadelphia contained
from 100 to 250 square feet of plate glass.

What the Boyds did was not only grounds for a forfeiture; it was
a felony. Contrary to Potter Stewart's understanding, there *was* a
criminal case. In *United States v. Boyd*, the Boyds were convicted of
"the fraudulent entry of 35 cases of imported plate-glass as free, by
means of a false and fraudulent letter."[10] The criminal case against
them rested on exactly the same evidence as did the forfeiture
proceeding.

At the time they intervened, the Boyds and their lawyers had all
of the facts before them. They had the invoices for both shipments

---

[10] *United States v. Boyd*, 24 F. 692 (1885).

and knew that they totaled more than 50,000 square feet. They knew that the story about the first shipment arriving "broken and worthless" would not wash. They knew that less than 11,000 square feet was installed and that only a reasonable amount of "wastage" would be credible. They knew of the misrepresentations the Boyds had made to the Treasury Department in writing.

In the criminal case the government could not have compelled the production of the invoice for the first shipment of 29 cases. The invoice was demanded in the forfeiture case under a statute that applied only in " a suit or proceeding *other than criminal,* arising under the customs revenue laws of the United States."[11] The name "Boyd" was nowhere mentioned in the noncriminal forfeiture proceeding. Not contesting the forfeiture—simply staying out of it—would have created no legal presumption or anything else which could be used against them in the criminal case. And this should have been their only concern.

It was madness for the Boyds to appeal the civil case to the Supreme Court of the United States. Their attorney's fees alone would be more than the merchandise was worth, and the chances of getting it back were nil. And by the time the writ of error was filed in the Supreme Court Edward A. Boyd and George H. Boyd were convicted felons.[12] Appealing the forfeiture of the glass was hardly a declaration of remorse. The Boyds were defiant at a time when it behooved them to be prostrate in penitence.

Nor was an appeal worthwhile to the government. All the Supreme Court was being asked to do in the writ of error was to grant a new trial in which title to the 35 cases of plate glass would be acertained without reference to the invoice for the first 29 cases delivered to our shores. Why not just *give* the Boyds the new trial they are asking for?

Trying the case over again would have involved little time and effort. It certainly would have been easier than briefing and arguing

---

[11] *Boyd,* 116 U.S. 619 [emphasis added].

[12] The Boyds' convictions were upheld June 12, 1885, whereas the transcript of record and writ of error in the forfeiture case were not filed in the Supreme Court of the United States until September 29, 1885.

an appeal before the Supreme Court. The government could have made its case without the invoice for the first shipment. The bid itself, the correspondence and the 35 cases in their possession was more than sufficient evidence. Given the unusual circumstances of the case, and the remote chance of their replication, any precedent the government stood to gain was of little value.

Anyone importing goods into the U.S. is required to declare their value and attach an invoice. If customs officials do not like your declaration or supporting papers, they will make their own appraisal and fix the duty themselves. If you decide to contest their appraisal the burden of proof is on you to prove them wrong. Try doing this standing on your rights under the Fourth Amendment. Any precedent arising out of the *Boyd* case would be meaningful only in customs cases where an importer had already gotten something through without paying the proper duty.

Whether the Boyds ever paid a fine or served a jail sentence is buried in the past. The files in their criminal cases contain only their indictments and recognizance bonds along with a rather pitiable doctor's certificate to the effect that Edward A. Boyd was physically unable to stand trial. The forfeiture case was settled by a compromise agreement dated March 18, 1887, by which time the elder Boyd was dead. The family paid the United States $15,000 and was given the plate glass.[13]

Had counsel for both parties acted as one would expect ordinary prudent lawyers to act under the circumstances that prevailed, there would be no such case as *Boyd v. United States*. The only relic of this incident would be a file captioned *Thirty Five Cases Polished Plate Glass* gathering dust in the archives at Bayonne, New Jersey, no different in appearance or significance from the 100,000 or so others that molder along with it.

Like all federal courts, the Supreme Court is limited in its jurisdiction to deciding "cases" or "controversies" arising under the

---

[13] *U.S. v. Boyd*, U.S. Circuit Court, SDNY,1884, Criminal, Box 24, File # B-1043, 1044, Box 25—1067, 1068, 1076, Record Group 21, Records of the District Court of the States, National Archives—Northeast Region, New York, New York, hereinafter referred to as NANER. The doctor's certificates are in case file B-1067.

Constitution or laws of the United States. The Court may not initiate action, but only may decide cases brought before it by litigants. It may not render advisory opinions at the behest of private parties or the other branches of government. A decision by the Supreme Court on a point of law necessary to the determination of a case properly before it becomes an axiom in the adjudication of future cases. This is called the doctrine of *stare decisis*.

The doctrine rests on the implicit assumption that a case on which a precedent is based was a genuine "case" or "controversy" honestly arrived at. To put it another way, our jurisprudence will be subverted if precedents can be created by means of bogus cases argued by lawyers masquerading as adversaries when they are really allied in achieving the same end.

The validity of *stare decisis* therefore depends on both sides of a legal argument being fairly represented by counsel. Anything less than the most skilled and dedicated advocacy before the nation's highest court is inadequate. Anything short of arm's length dealing, in the utmost good faith, is unfair. To suborn the selection, or to collude or connive in the prosecution of a case, strikes at the very heart of our jurisprudence. This has always been recognized by the Court:

> And any attempt, by a mere colorable dispute, to obtain the opinion of the court upon a question of law which a party desires to know for his own interest or his own purposes, when there is no real and substantial controversy between those who appear as adverse parties to the suit, is an abuse which courts of justice have always reprehended, and treated as a punishable contempt of court. *Little v. Bowers*, 134 U.S. 547, 557 (1890)

We shall travel with Potter Stewart down the *Road to Mapp v. Ohio* somewhat more cautiously and a little less credulously than our guide. We shall examine his milestones from a different perspective. The principles of law they enunciated—their logic or their wisdom—shall not be the sole issue. Our line of inquiry shall concern itself not only with whether they were "cases" or "controversies" correctly decided, but whether they were "cases" or "controversies" at all. In each instance the question shall be whether the clash of opinions the Court perceived as genuine, were—like *Weeks v. United States*—a sham.

Whether *Boyd* was genuine cannot be proved or disproved conclusively. It is suspicious in that both parties acted against their apparent interest. But since *Boyd* cannot be connected with any other case, we shall release him on his own recognizance. The docket is backlogged and we must move on to Justice Stewart's next case. "The second of the three cases identified as the source of the exclusionary rule, *Adams v. New York*, was a criminal case."[14]

"Policy"—sometimes called the "numbers game," or more pejoratively the "numbers racket"—was a privately run gambling enterprise which in days of yore got the "action" that now goes to the state-run lotteries. It would be more accurate to say, in New York City at least, that policy was a quasi-public enterprise, since the payroll was heavily laden with public officials paid to overlook the existence of a game of which everyone knew, and knew was illegal. This arrangement did not jar the sensibilities of most citizens of that city, experience and revelation having conditioned them to expect things of this sort. There was a generally recognized distinction, as Tammany leader George Washington Plunkitt once explained, between "honest graft" and the other kind. In the eyes of most New Yorkers, getting paid off to let the numbers game operate came under the heading of "honest graft." At least, it was nothing to get excited about.

Nevertheless, to keep up appearances, every few years the police would raid the betting parlours and the miscreants would be rounded up and brought to book. Thereafter they would be fined and sometimes sentenced to serve a short time under benevolent supervision. All of this would be duly reported by the press and the cycle would begin anew.

To most policy operators this was part of the cost of doing business. They pleaded guilty, paid their fines and suffered the attendant indignities in silence. One of them, however, for some peculiar reason, did the opposite. He pleaded not guilty, was tried,

---

[14] Stewart, 1374.

and to the surprise of no one was convicted. Thereafter he appealed all the way to the Supreme Court of the United States, where his case is now enshrined in our jurisprudence. His name was Albert J. Adams, at the turn of the century New York's "King of Policy."

Adams was convicted of being a "common gambler," a misdemeanor under New York law. Some 3,500 policy slips had been seized by police searching his office under a search warrant for "gambling paraphernalia." In the course of the search they came across some letters signed by the defendant and in his handwriting. While unrelated to gambling, the letters could be used to show that the handwriting on some policy slips was that of Adams, so the police seized the letters as well. At his trial the handwritten letters were used for that purpose and Adams was convicted.

When the letters were offered in evidence, the defendant objected on the grounds that their use would be in violation of his constitutional rights. Since the letters were beyond the scope of the warrant, contended Adams, their seizure was a violation of the Fourth Amendment. Not only that, he continued, the use of these letters at his trial compelled him in a criminal case to be a witness against himself in violation of that clause of the Fifth Amendment. That this is a state and not a federal case does not matter, Adams maintained, because the Fourth and the Fifth Amendments were made applicable to the states by the Fourteenth.

But it was not necessary for the prosecution to prove that the policy slips were in Adams's handwriting. More often than not, such slips would be in the handwriting of a subordinate. All they had to do was show that Adams had the slips under his control, and knew that they were policy slips and not something else—innocent pieces of paper like candy wrappers, for example.[15] The circumstances surrounding the arrest of Al Adams and the seizure of the betting slips make it clear that possession could have been proved without using the letters.

---

[15] See *People v. Adams*, 85 App. Div. 390, 392.

Among the papers seized in the defendant's office were thirty-five hundred of these "manifold sheets," upon some of which were endorsements and entries in his handwriting.[16]

We also think it quite clear that the evidence was sufficient to sustain a finding that these manifold sheets were in the defendant's possession. They were found in a trunk in his private office, which the defendant had directed should be placed in his office . . .

It had been occupied by the defendant for several weeks as his private office and had his name upon the door.[17]

The sole issue in the *Adams* appeal was whether it was constitutionally permissible to use the specimens of his handwriting incidentally found by the officers in the course of the execution of a valid warrant to search for "gambling paraphernalia." Had the Supreme Court of the United States decided in Adams's favor, New York would still have been free to try him over again. The prosecution would have been able to use all the evidence it had against him except the letters.

With this in mind, if you were the lawyer representing Adams, would you advise him to appeal his conviction all the way to the Supreme Court of the United States? Or would you tell your client that the fruits of victory would be but a new trial in which the issue of possession would be decided on the fact that 3,500 policy slips were found in an office having his name on the door and in which he was personally present? Would you tell him that, in your professional opinion, this is more than sufficient evidence of possession to convict him of being a "common gambler"?

By the same token, if you were the District Attorney of New York County, would you go through the travail of briefing and arguing this case all the way to the nation's highest tribunal? Or would you just forget about using the handwritten letters and let the

---

[16] *People v. Adams*, 176 N.Y. 351, 356 (1903).

[17] 85 App. Div. 396.

issue of possession stand or fall on the fact that 3,500 policy tickets were found along with the defendant in his office. This is not the only peculiar aspect of this case.

For some reason the King of Policy was tried before a jury in the Supreme Court of New York. New York's Supreme Court is a trial court[18] of "general jurisdiction," which means it can try any kind of case. Seldom, however, was its criminal jurisdiction exercised. For the Supreme Court in New York County to try a felony case was rare, and to try a misdemeanor case was unheard of. Cases of "common gamblers," "petty larceny" and the like were customarily tried by a magistrate without a jury. Trying Adams in the Supreme Court rather than in Magistrate's Court eliminated at least one tier of appellate review. It is fair to infer from the forum that the attorneys for both Adams and New York knew from the beginning that this was going to be a very uncommon gambler's case.

Adams v. New York was a milestone in our Fourth Amendment jurisprudence. It was the case Winfred Denison relied on in his brief in *Weeks*. *Adams* stands for the proposition that evidence incidentally found by the police while executing an otherwise valid search warrant is constitutionally admissible. In the case of Al Adams it was a completely bogus issue, part of the scenery so to speak. The lawyers on both sides had to know this. What they were looking for was an affirmative answer to a question the Court did "not feel called upon to discuss."

> We do not feel called upon to discuss the contention that the Fourteenth Amendment has made the provisions of the Fourth and Fifth Amendments to the Constitution of the United States, so far as they relate to the right of the people to be secure against unreasonable searches and seizures and protect them against being compelled to testify in a criminal case against themselves, privileges and immunities of citizens of the United States of which they may not be deprived by the action of the States.[19]

---

[18] The Court of Appeals is the highest appellate tribunal in New York.
[19] *Adams v. New York*, 192 U.S. 585, 594 (1904).

Potter Stewart put *Adams* in perspective. "Ten years later," he said, "it became clear that the *Adams* case was just a wild turn in the exclusionary rule roller coaster track. In the third case, *Weeks v. United States*, the defendant Weeks, like Adams, was tried for and convicted of illegal gambling."[20] We shall not devote much space to Justice Stewart's analysis of the *Weeks* case except to say that it never occurred to him that *Weeks*, like *Adams*, was a long shot, and that the odds against two "illegal gambling" cases coming down "the exclusionary rule roller coaster track" to finish up in the Supreme Court are pretty stiff. It's a cinch Potter Stewart never played a parlay.

Adams v. New York was an attempt, by a mere colorable dispute, to obtain the opinion of the Court upon a question of law which certain parties wanted for their own purposes, when there was no real and substantial controversy between those who appeared as adverse parties. Had it succeeded, the travesties of justice it will take *Weeks* and *Mapp* another 60 years to foist upon us would have been inflicted on an unsuspecting public in 1904. *Adams v. New York* was a fraud that failed.

William Travers Jerome was the District Attorney of New York County at the time. A famous trial lawyer in his own right, he was also the first cousin and close friend of Jennie Jerome, the American mother of an up-and-coming Englishman named Winston Churchill. It is hard to believe Jerome did not know what was going on. Nor could the case have reached the appellate level without the collusion of L. Laflin Kellogg, who represented Adams throughout.

Howard S. Gans (1872-1946) was the "assistant District Attorney in charge of the appeals bureau"[21] of the New York County District Attorney's Office who briefed and argued the case at all levels. If not the composer, the 32-year-old Gans was certainly the conductor of this charade. We have not seen the last of Howard Gans.

Potter Stewart's next stop on the *Road to Mapp v. Ohio* is *Silverthorne Lumber Co. v. United States*, 251 U.S. 385 (1920), in

---

[20] Stewart, 1374.

[21] According to his obituary in the *New York Times* of December 13, 1946, Howard Gans "graduated from Harvard College in 1892 and the New York Law School two years later."

which "agents of the federal government had illegally raided the offices of a lumber company and had seized books and papers."[22] To read between the lines of *Silverthorne* to find the seeds of the constitutional genius who sired it, we must first understand another case which did not make Potter Stewart's list. That case is *Schenck v. United States*. But *Schenck* as well as *Silverthorne* must be viewed against the backdrop of war and revolution.

At the outbreak of hostilities in 1914 President Wilson declared this nation's neutrality. "The United States must be neutral in fact as well as in name," he told the Senate on August 19. Many Americans were for neutrality and many for intervention. Most, including Woodrow Wilson, were for preparedness. Should the day ever come, as sadly it will, when "God helping her, she can do no other"[23] than fight, America must be prepared. There was in this country, however, a small but well-knit minority to whom the war was a golden opportunity to foment trouble and promote revolution.

On Saturday, July 22, 1916, "Preparedness Day" parades were held in the major cities throughout the United States. In San Francisco a bomb planted along the parade route exploded, killing 10 people and wounding many more. Tom Mooney and Warren Billings were later tried and convicted of this atrocity. Mooney, an organizer for the International Workers of the World, was sentenced to death.

The IWW was an association of migratory anarchists who moved about the country insinuating themselves into other people's labor disputes. They denounced the slogan of the American Federation of Labor—"a fair day's wages for a fair day's work"—as a palliative, and were considered by the AFL to be an enemy of the American labor movement. To the "Wobblies," as they were called, "[e]very strike is a small revolution and a dress rehearsal for the big one."[24] Their weapons were the general strike,

---

[22] Stewart, 1375.

[23] Quote is from the last sentence of what would be President Wilson's address to Congress on April 2, 1917, asking for a declaration of war.

[24] This IWW slogan appears on the masthead of their newspaper, *The Labor Defender*, circa 1918.

sabotage, beatings and murder. The international secretary and leader of the IWW in 1916 was William Dudley ("Big Bill") Haywood.

Big Bill was no stranger to dynamite. In 1905, the ex-governor of Idaho, Frank Steunenberg, was killed by a bomb attached to the front gate of his home in Caldwell, Idaho. As governor of that state in 1899, Steunenberg, a Democrat, had declared the Coeur d'Alene mining district "in a state of insurrection and asked for federal troops to suppress the riots. After a lengthy military occupation, quiet returned to the Coeur d'Alenes, and the union responsible for the trouble, the Western Federation of Miners (WFM), lost not only the strike but its influence within the state as well."[25]

Suspicion for Steunenberg's murder fell on a stranger posing as a sheep buyer who was later identified as Harry Orchard, a minor functionary of the WFM. Confronted with evidence that inextricably tied him to the bomb that killed Steunenberg, Orchard confessed. He confessed to other murders as well, including a heinous bombing which took the lives of 14 miners in the Colorado "labor war" of 1903-04. All of these murders, so Orchard averred, he committed on the orders of the secretary-treasurer of the WFM, William D. Haywood.

In the summer of 1907 Haywood was tried for the murder of Steunenberg. "Boise for the moment became the news capital of the world. Fifty correspondents of newspapers, wire services, and `muckraking' magazines gathered for the trial."[26] After having plea-bargained for his life, Harry Orchard was the leading witness for the prosecution. Of the two prospective witnesses who were to corroborate his story, one recanted and one disappeared. Clarence Darrow represented Haywood. His impassioned summation lasted 11 hours and carried the day. The defendant was acquitted, and the names Darrow and Haywood became household words.

Professor Felix Frankfurter shared with his mentor, Louis

---

[25] David H. Grover. *Debaters and Dynamiters: The Story of the Haywood Trial.* Corvallis, Oregon: Oregon State University Press, 1964, 2. Charles Moyer and George Pettibone, two other officers of the WFN, were tried along with Haywood for the murder of Steunenberg and acquitted as well.
[26] Ibid, 4.

Brandeis, an abiding interest in "labor unrest" and a proclivity for taking the side of union leaders accused of violence. In 1917 President Wilson established a Mediation Commission to settle labor disputes harmful to the war effort and named Frankfurter its secretary and counsel. The visiting professor's first stop was the copper mining town of Bisbee, Arizona, where there had been a strike which had become violent after the IWW arrived in force. The copper production resumed and the violence ceased after the Wobblies were rounded up by vigilantes and "deported" by train to New Mexico.[27] Frankfurter condemned the deportation in a report which some people, including Theodore Roosevelt, thought was one-sided. Roosevelt wrote an open letter to Frankfurter:

> No official, writing on behalf of the President, is to be excused for failure to know and clearly to set forth that the I.W.W. is a criminal organization . . .
>
> No human being in his senses doubts that the men deported from Bisbee were bent on destruction and murder . . .
>
> When no efficient means are employed to guard honest, upright, and well-behaved citizens from the most brutal kind of lawlessness, it is inevitable that these citizens shall try to protect themselves . . .
>
> In times of danger nothing is more common and nothing more dangerous to the Republic than for men— often ordinarily well-meaning men—to avoid con- demning the criminals who really are public enemies by making their entire assault on the shortcomings of the good citizens who have been the victims or opponents of the criminals.[28]

The roving commission moved on to San Francisco, where it

---

[27] The lobby of the Copper Queen Hotel in Bisbee has a number of photographs which recall the "deportation" of the Wobblies in 1917.

[28] Theodore Roosevelt to Felix Frankfurter, December 19, 1917. This letter and Professor Frankfurter's response to it appear on pages 12-16 in the "Hearings before a Subcommittee on the Committee on the Judiciary, United States Senate . . . on the Nomination of Felix Frankfurter to be an Associate Justice of the Supreme Court" on January 7, 10, 11 and 12, 1939. Roosevelt's letter had previously been published in the *Congressional Record* in 1930.

investigated the conviction of Tom Mooney for the bombing murder of the Preparedness Day paraders the year before. (One might be permitted the observation that this hardly comes under the category of "labor mediation.") On behalf of the commission, Frankfurter wrote another report which urged the President to intercede on behalf of Mooney with California Governor William B. Stephens. This led Theodore Roosevelt to admonish Frankfurter once more.

In May of 1918 Felix Frankfurter was named chairman of the newly created War Labor Policies Board in the Labor Department. One would suspect Professor Frankfurter's appointments were due to the influence of Louis Brandeis. The same can be said for former Massachusetts Public Service Commissioner George W. Anderson, who, after then Attorney General McReynolds consulted Brandeis "as to a proper man for United States Attorney for Massachusetts," was appointed to that office.[29]

The nomination of Louis Brandeis to the Supreme Court had been confirmed by the Senate on June 1, 1916. Nine days later, Woodrow Wilson got his third appointment to the Court when Associate Justice Charles Evans Hughes resigned to accept the Republican nomination to run for President. As we shall see, Mr. Justice Brandeis did not let his robes get in the way of his politics. In the idiom of the gridiron, it did not take long for "Coach" Brandeis to start calling the plays from the bench and sending them in through his protégés. The diary of Colonel House contains this entry for June 19, 1916: "I had a telephone message from District Attorney [George W.] Anderson, who was in Justice Brandeis' office in Boston and was speaking for the Justice as well as for himself." They urged House to use his influence to have Gregory appointed as a Justice of the Supreme Court.[30]

Justice Brandeis cultivated a vast network of contacts on all levels of government. According to one of his biographers the influence of LDB was "like many invisible wires into many

---

[29] LDB to JCM, August 13, 1913, *Brandeis Letters*; see also footnote 2 in commentary.
[30] *House Diary*, June 19, 1916.

government bureaus."[31] He and Frankfurter were assiduous in seeding a growing bureaucracy with friends and allies.

For at least 17 years from the time Brandeis took his seat in 1916, Justice Brandeis provided Professor Frankfurter with a substantial annual allowance for "expenses in public matters undertaken at my request." Brandeis made clear that he wanted to "feel free to make suggestions to you, although they involve some incidental expense."[32] His letters show that LDB constantly assigned FF political tasks which would have been undertaken by the "People's Lawyer" but for the shackles imposed by judicial circumspection. For most of the 22 years Mr. Justice Louis D. Brandeis sat on the Supreme Court, Professor Felix Frankfurter was his subsidized surrogate.[33]

Justice Brandeis was involved in other politics as well. In July of 1916, the month after he took his seat on the Supreme Court, he attended a convention of nearly 40 separate groups held at the Hotel Astor in New York City, the purpose of which was to promote a national congress of Jews in the United States. There were some sharp exchanges between Brandeis and other Jewish leaders, some of whom challenged the propriety of his participation in such matters, as did the *New York Times* on July 18, 1916 in the following editorial:

Out Of Place

It has been the custom, faithfully honored by observance, for the Justices of the Supreme Court of the United States, upon taking office, to withdraw from

---

[31] Alfred Lief. *Brandeis, The Personal History of an American Ideal.* New York: Stackpole Sons, 1936, 407.

[32] Louis D. Brandeis. *"Half Brother, Half Son:" The Letters of Louis D. Brandeis to Felix Frankfurter,* ed. by Melvin I. Urofsky and David W. Levy. Norman, Oklahoma: University of Oklahoma Presss, 1991. LDB to FF, November 19, 1916 and November 25, 1916.

[33] For an exposition of the financial arrangements between Brandeis and Frankfurter, see Levy and Murphy—*Preserving the Progressive Spirit in a Conservative Time; The Joint Reform Efforts of Justice Brandeis and Professor Felix Frankfurter, 1916-1933,* 78 Michigan Law Review 1252 (1986).

many activities of a political or social nature, in which as private citizens they were free to engage, in order, not only that they might give their whole time and attention to official duty, but further to avoid all controversies or commitments which might seem in any degree to affect their judicial impartiality of mind.

The *Brandeis Letters* show that this rebuke accomplished its purpose. Three days later in five separate letters dated July 21, 1916, Louis Brandeis resigned the offices he held in five Jewish organizations to which he belonged. The first of these letters began thusly:

> My dear Judge Pam: The occurrences at the Hotel Astor on July 16th at the conference called by the American Jewish Committee and others, together with the reports and comment in the press, compel me to resign as Temporary Chairman of the Executive Organization Committee for the American Jewish Congress, and as its Honorary President. Please present my resignations at the next meetings of the Committee.

Justice Brandeis had converted an apartment directly above his living quarters in Washington as an office and law library for himself and his clerks. There was a constant stream of visitors. As one commentator put it:

> While judicial precedent was being forged above, political strategy was being planned below.
>
> Thus did Brandeis make the transition from the People's Attorney to a Supreme Court justice. By employing Frankfurter and developing a style that satisfied the appearance of proper judicial temperament, he set forth, behind the scenes, to attempt to mold American society and government to his liking.[34]

---

[34] Bruce Allen Murphy. *The Brandeis/Frankfurter Connection: The Secret Political Activities of Two Supreme Court Justices.* Garden City, N.Y.: Doubleday, 1983, 45.

It is hard to mold society and government to your liking without friends in high places. One friend of LDB was Secretary of the Treasury William Gibbs McAdoo, who had married Woodrow Wilson's daughter, Eleanor, in 1914. When the government seized the railroads after our declaration of war, Wilson wanted McAdoo to become the Railroad Administrator while retaining his Treasury portfolio; however, the President was concerned that this would lead to charges of nepotism. It was Louis Brandeis who persuaded Wilson to appoint him never-theless.[35] "This, in turn, resulted in the justice's advisory role with McAdoo's subordinates following the appointment."[36] McAdoo chose as his second-in-command Walker D. Hines, a Kentuckian whose friendship with Louis Brandeis dated back to their hometown of Louisville.

Soon after war was declared, Congress passed a conscription act requiring men of military age to register. The Selective Service Draft Law of May 18, 1917, made the wilful failure to register for the draft a felony. Inciting or abetting others to disobey the law was likewise a felony. The following month Congress passed the Espionage Act of June 15, 1917, which among other things proscribed acts of sabotage which might hamper the war effort.

On September 5, 1917, by order of "the Attorney General, Mr. Gregory, United States Marshals in more than one hundred cities and towns descended on the local IWW headquarters at exactly two o'clock in the afternoon, central time. The federal agents seized books, cheques, correspondence and other documents in every instance." In Chicago, the IWW national headquarters, "William D. Haywood, national secretary of the organization, was taken into custody, but released later.[37]

---

[35] According to Murphy, McAdoo's appointment was decided by the President while at Brandeis's apartment. "Wilson explained to Brandeis that, 'I could not request for you to come to me, and I have therefore come to ask your advice.'" 47.

[36] Murphy, 54.

[37] "Government Checks I.W.W. Activities By Unexpected Raids on 100 Headquarters," *New York Herald*, September 6, 1917.

The search warrants under which the raids were made were signed by Evan A. Evans who was appointed to act as Judge of the Federal Circuit Court during the September term. The warrant used was a special form drawn under the terms of the recently enacted espionage act.[38]

And so began the case of *Haywood v. United States*,[39] the great Chicago trial of the IWW leadership. On September 28, 1917, after examining the documentary evidence seized in the raids, a federal grand jury indicted William D. Haywood and more than 100 other IWW leaders for violation of the Espionage Act. "In February, 1918, defendants petitioned the court for an order to return the property, and the government moved for an impounding order. In March, 1918, the defendants moved to quash the indictment on the ground that evidence illegally obtained had been used before the grand jury."[40] These motions were denied. After a trial which "lasted from the middle of April to the middle of August, 1918,"[41] Big Bill and most of his comrades were convicted.

On August 30, 1918, Federal Judge Kennesaw Mountain Landis pronounced sentence, giving most of the defendants jail terms. Haywood he sentenced to 20 years in prison. The Wobblies appealed, one of the grounds being that their rights under the Fourth Amendment had been violated by the use of the documentary evidence taken in the raids. The search warrants under which the seizures were made were invalid, so they contended, because the supporting affidavits did not state facts sufficient to establish probable cause nor state with sufficient specificity the things which were to be seized.

The defendants sought to be freed on bail pending the appeal, but to no avail. While "[p]rior to a verdict of guilty, [a] defendant is presumed innocent," held the Seventh Circuit Court of Appeals on December 21, 1918, the "defendant stands in a different position

[38] "Government Raids 8 Places in Chicago," *New York Herald*, September 6, 1917.
[39] 268 F. 795, Seventh Circuit (1920).
[40] 268 F. 801.
[41] 268 F. 802.

after conviction . . . After conviction and sentence, the burden is upon the convicted party to show error in the conviction."[42] This was a burden Big Bill Haywood and the Wobblies had not sustained, and so they went to Leavenworth to keep Frank Ryan and the Dynamiters company.

To understand the cases we will delve into and the characters who will play a part, it is necessary to place them in the context of 1917-1920. It is the World War and the Russian Civil War which followed from which all else will flow. To comprehend the political passions that raged in the United States, it is essential to know of the events in Europe which inspired them. Accordingly, from time to time, we will digress from our synthesis of American constitutional law to look at the larger picture.

For the Russians the World War was a series of disasters, beginning with their defeat at Tannenberg in August of 1914. By early 1917 the Russian Army, ill-equipped and poorly led, was in a state of utter demoralization and mutiny. On the 15th of March Nicholas II abdicated and Czarist rule was replaced by a provisional government headed by moderate socialists who undertook to carry on the war against Germany as a member of the Triple Entente.

In November of 1917, in the so-called "October Revolution,"[43] the provisional government was overthrown by Bolsheviks led by V.I. Lenin. A civil war ensued. In March of 1918, and in violation of Russia's treaty obligations to France and Britain, the Bolsheviks signed a separate peace treaty with the Central Powers. The Treaty of Brest-Litovsk gave both the Bolsheviks and the Germans a free hand with which to smite their enemies.

The Germans and their allies knew their only chance for victory in the west lay in dealing the British and the French a knockout blow before the Americans arrived in full strength. On March 21, 1918, reinforced by troops shifted from the East, they attacked the

---

[42] *United States v. St. John*, 254 F. 794, 795-796. Vincent St. John was an IWW organizer who in earlier days had been a lieutenant of Haywood in the WFM.

[43] That the "October Revolution" took place in November and the "February Revolution" in March was due to Russia's failure to adopt the calendar change accepted by the Western world in 1752. They were behind the times in more ways than one.

British on a 50-mile front in what was to prove in terms of total casualties to be the bloodiest day on the Western Front. By April 5 they had overrun the British lines and advanced beyond the Somme battlefield of 1916, by now the graveyard of more than 100,000 members of the British Expeditionary Force.

The final German offensive began on the 27th of May in the French sector, where they broke the line on a 30-mile front. Driving the disheartened *poilus* before them, the Germans advanced rapidly through the province of Champagne to the River Marne. Thrown into the breach in the vicinity of Chateau-Thierry, a city on the Marne some 40 miles east of Paris, the Americans for the first time fought in significant numbers.

They held their ground against the Germans in the Second Battle of the Marne. It was there in June and July of 1918 that the mettle of the "doughboy" was tested. On the 15th of July the Germans launched a full-scale attack along the entire Marne front and were repulsed after suffering heavy losses. That night the German high command came to the realization that they could no longer win the war. They would continue to fight, but only for a stalemate and a negotiated peace treaty which would restore the *status quo ante bellum.*

From that day forward the Germans did what they had learned to do best. Retreating in stages back through Champagne that summer of 1918, they traded French real estate for American blood. By September of 1918 the adversaries on the Western Front faced each other once again over what were essentially the lines of March 21. Inferior in number, the Germans in most cases had the advantage of being entrenched in positions they had held for years. Nowhere were their defenses better prepared than in the Meuse-Argonne sector on the German left and the Allied right flank of the Western Front.

What in March had been a trickle of Americans had by September become a torrent. Unlike their allies and enemies, sadder and wiser by experience, the Yanks looked forward to the fray. What many were afraid of most was that it would be "over" by the time they got "over there." The bulk of the American Expeditionary Force, more than a million strong, were assigned to the Meuse-

Argonne. On September 12 they attacked and drove the Germans out of the St. Mihiel Salient between Verdun and Metz, a heavily fortified area the enemy had held since 1915. That accomplished, they wheeled and attacked on a sector to the west of Verdun, through the center of which ran the hills and ravines of the Argonne Forest. Here, from September 26 to the Armistice, outnumbered Germans in carefully prepared positions sold ground dearly to Americans willing to pay the price with a passionate prodigality.

When it was over, the Americans stood on the Meuse from Verdun to Sedan. Behind them lay the graves of 30,000 of their comrades. It is one of the terrible ironies of that terrible war that more than two-thirds of the American casualties were sustained in its last two months. But when the end came, it came quickly.

On September 29 three divisions, one British and two American, "cracked" the Hindenburg line at Bellicourt in the Somme. According to the eminent British historian B.H. Liddell Hart, the Hindenburg line wasn't the only thing that "cracked" that day.

> The issue of the war had been finally decided on the 29th September—decided in the mind of the German Command. Ludendorff and his associates had then "cracked," and the sound went echoing backwards until it had resounded throughout the whole of Germany. Nothing could catch it or stop it. The Command might recover its nerve, the actual military position might improve, but the moral impression—as ever in war— was decisive.[44]

By November 3 both Turkey and Austria-Hungry had accepted the Allied terms and Germany was isolated. The German Navy mutinied and seized control of warships and ports. On November 7 Bolsheviks under the leadership of Kurt Eisner proclaimed a dictatorship of the proletariat in the Free State of Bavaria. On November 9 Kaiser Wilhelm abdicated and fled to Holland; Fredrich Ebert, a Socialist, was installed as president. Two

---

[44] B.H. Liddell-Hart. *Strategy*. New York: Frederich A. Praeger, 1954, 218.

days later German plenipotentiaries signed the Armistice in the railroad car at Compiegne. On the 11th hour of the 11th day of the 11th month of 1918 the World War was over. Alas for humanity, the end of the "War to end all Wars" did not bring peace.

Chapter VIII

THE RED SCARE

R oger Nash Baldwin was born in 1884 "in Wellesley, an outlying middle-class suburb of Boston." His father was "a prosperous shoe manufacturer" and his mother "an agnostic and something of a feminist"; both "were Unitarians, liberal for those times, and non-conformist."[1] After attending Wellesley public schools Baldwin matriculated at Harvard College and graduated in 1905. Many years later he described the turning point in his life:

> After graduating, I had a year of fun and adventure traveling in Europe with my family, then was advised by my father's lawyer, Louis D. Brandeis, to choose social work rather than a business career. I had received an offer to run a neighborhood house in St. Louis, Missouri, and also to teach courses in sociology at Washington University. Brandeis sensed my interest in people and social problems, and realized that Boston held too many ties and relationships for me to be my own man there.[2]

In 1906 Baldwin went to St. Louis and established a settlement house for delinquent boys. He became a volunteer officer of the juvenile court and later its chief probation officer. He took a

---

[1] Roger Baldwin. *Recollections of a Life in Civil Liberties—I*. New York: Oral History Collection of Columbia University, 1972, 1 (cited hereafter as *Recollections*).
[2] Ibid., 40.

personal interest in his wards.

> I carried my own caseload of boys to supervise personally
> ... For two neglected little boys, both sons of prostitutes,
> I became legal guardian during their minority and
> assumed their care and expense until they were of
> working age. One of them lived in my apartment; the
> other joined me in it when he was of working age, after
> leaving his foster mother, a reformed prostitute. Both
> boys remained my intimate companions through young
> manhood.[3]

When war was declared in April of 1917, Roger Baldwin moved to New York City where he became the director of an organization called the National Civil Liberties Bureau (NCLB). The following month he and Harry Weinberger, a lawyer with his own antiwar organization, formed an alliance to protect the civil rights of those opposed to the war.[4]

After the raids on the IWW in September of 1917 "Baldwin sprang to the IWW's defense, writing to President Wilson, Secretary of Labor William B. Wilson, and Frankfurter to demand the indictments be dropped. In private meetings he suggested to Justice Department attorney John Lord O'Brian and presidential advisor Joseph Tumulty that 'wholesale prosecutions were about the most unfortunate methods which could be devised of dealing with radical organizations in America.'"[5]

John Graham Brooks was a Unitarian minister and Harvard lecturer who shared Roger Baldwin's views on civil liberties. In 1972 Baldwin recollected a luncheon meeting he and Brooks arranged with Secretary of Agriculture David F. Houston. Previously Houston had been chancellor of Washington University in St.

---

[3] Ibid., 42.

[4] "Memorandum of Conference between Roger Baldwin and Harry Weinberger," May 11, 1917, Reel 5, Vol. 35, #194. American Civil Liberties Union Papers, Seeley G. Mudd Manuscript Library, Princeton University, Princeton, New Jersey. Used by permission of the Princeton University Library. Hereafter cited as ACLUP.

[5] Samuel Walker. *In Defense of American Liberties: A History of the ACLU.* New York: Oxford University Press, 1990, 25.

Louis, where Baldwin had taught sociology.

> "[I]t was at the Century Club in New York, and our
> purpose was to try to get to the President through
> Houston and tell him to lay off prosecuting the IWW if
> they wanted the war industry to prosper. Again I didn't
> say much. Mr. Brooks carried the conversation, but I
> spoke up once as a civil libertarian, pointing out the
> rights of the IWW people and suggesting what would
> happen if they were suppressed and what kind of strike
> they might pull."

> "No success?"

> "None. Houston was cold—very cold to me. He was a
> cold man anyhow. And [U.S. district attorney] Caffrey
> just said that the IWW people had to be suppressed and
> so nothing came of the meeting and the policy continued
> and the IWW men—a hundred and sixty-three of
> them—were indicted and the great Chicago trial took
> place."[6]

In the company of Clarence Darrow, Roger Baldwin called on
Postmaster General Albert Sidney Burleson, only to be given
another chilly reception.[7] For a time Baldwin had entrée to the War
Department, but then Secretary of War Newton Baker, in response
to mounting pressure from military intelligence, "caved in" and
closed the door.[8]

In early 1918 Louis Brandeis waged an underground campaign
to replace the "caved in" Newton Baker with a Secretary of War
more to his liking. Justice Brandeis tried to get Colonel House to
use his influence, but House refused and Baker stayed. On February
23, 1918, the Colonel confided his distaste for this impropriety in
his diary. "I cannot understand why a Justice of the Supreme Court

---

[6] Peggy Lamson. *Roger Baldwin—Founder of the American Civil Liberties Union—A Portrait.*
Boston: Houghton Mifflin Company, 1976, 80.
[7] Lamson, 79.
[8] Lamson, 75,77. See also Walker, 37, 38.

should bother about other people's business as Brandeis does."

The least satisfactory member of the Wilson Cabinet, in the opinion of Roger Baldwin, was Attorney General Thomas W. Gregory. Instead of controlling such matters from Washington, Gregory was permitting offenses arising under the Draft Law and Espionage Act to be prosecuted the same as any other felony—by the United States attorney for the judicial district in which it occurred. Eventually Baldwin and his friends were able to ameliorate the situation.

> It was a terrible time. Every district attorney enforced the Espionage Act as he wished. It wasn't until toward the end of the war that the Department of Justice established a central control, which was a step we had long urged. Then they appointed two assistant attorneys general who were in a sense friends of ours—John Lord O'Brian and Alfred Bettman—and those two men put the lid on most of the free-speech prosecutions.[9]

We can approximate the date this central control was established by a letter written by Justice Brandeis to his wife in October of 1917—the month following the IWW raids—telling her that "Gregory selected John Lord O'Brien [sic]."[10] No other reference to either Gregory or O'Brian is made in the letter nor is there a word of clarification to this terse message. It is apparent that Justice and Mrs. Brandeis had discussed the matter previously and that Mrs. Brandeis knew exactly who her husband was talking about and the position for which O'Brian had been selected.

John Lord O'Brian was born and raised in Buffalo, New York. After his graduation from Harvard College in 1896, he obtained his law degree from the University of Buffalo Law School. He practiced law in Buffalo and was active in Republican politics. In 1909, on the recommendation of New York Governor Charles Evans Hughes

---

[9] Lamson, 78.

[10] LDB to AGB, October 16, 1917, *Brandeis Letters.*

and with the endorsement of Senator Elihu Root,[11] outgoing President Theodore Roosevelt appointed O'Brian to be the United States Attorney for the Western District of New York, a post he held until 1914.

In October of 1917, after his selection by Gregory, O'Brian went to Washington to become head of the War Emergency Division of the Attorney General's Office. He lived to be 98 and spent his life alternately in Buffalo and Washington, practicing law and Progressive Republican politics. In 1938 he was the unsuccessful Republican candidate for the U.S. Senate seat held by Democrat Robert Wagner of New York City. He is an icon venerated by the legal profession in Buffalo, and the law school from which he graduated is now housed in John Lord O'Brian Hall.[12]

John Lord O'Brian and Winfred Denison, members of the Harvard Class of '96, were fraternity brothers and personal friends.[13] Alfred Bettman, O'Brian's assistant in the War Emergency Division, was Class of '94 and a contemporary of Denison's at Harvard Law School. Besides being close friends themselves, Denison, O'Brian and Bettman were friends and correspondents of Felix Frankfurter and each of them had more than a nodding acquaintance with Louis Brandeis.

As we shall see, O'Brian and Bettman did not view their appointment as a mandate for the vigorous prosecution of those who violated the war emergency acts. To the contrary, they did what they could to thwart such prosecutions and, as Roger Baldwin later recollected, did much to dissipate the "hysteria" which then prevailed.

---

[11] "Chronological Outline of Professional Career and Other Activities," *Papers of John Lord O'Brian*, Charles B. Sears Law Library, University at Buffalo, State University of New York, Buffalo, New York, File 47-2, 12. This document is a 57-page typescript with handwritten emendations prepared by John Lord O'Brian and will be cited hereafter as *O'Brian Chronology*. Other papers from the collection will be cited as *O'Brian Papers*.

[12] The biographical information on O'Brian is taken from his obituary in the *New York Times* of April 11, 1973, *Who Was Who in America*, and the *John Lord O'Brian Commemorative Issue* of the Buffalo Law Review published in 1974.

[13] Denison and O'Brian were members of the Harvard chapter of Delta Upsilon Fraternity, *O'Brian Chronology*, 2.

The attorney general, Thomas Watt Gregory, was unapproachable and unsympathetic, but he had two assistants of a different view, John Lord O'Brien of Buffalo, a real friend of civil liberties, and Alfred Bettman of Cincinnati, even more committed. They tried against odds to restrain the fervor of prosecution of district attorneys, but they made an impression on the hysteria only toward the end of the war when all prosecutions had to be cleared first in the Justice Department.[14]

O'Brian often stayed with Winfred Denison when visiting Washington before the war. An undated entry in his Chronology for 1913 reads, "Washington House of Truth. Spent weekend there with Win Denison, Frankfurter, Louis Bissell, Lord Eustace Percy and Alan [?] Campbell."[15] It was there that O'Brian met Louis Brandeis.

I had met him [Brandeis] at the "House of Truth" here in Washington. The "House of Truth" was the home in the latter part of the Taft administration and the early years of the Wilson administration of Felix Frankfurter . . . Sir Eustace Percy [and] Winfred T. Denison, a classmate of mine at Harvard who died many years ago. They had a house up on Nineteenth Street which came to be dubbed the "House of Truth." They were extraordinarily brilliant individuals. I first met Brandeis at dinner there. Afterward this ripened into a very close friendship and in after years I saw a great deal of him.[16]

This would have been about the same time O'Brian and Felix Frankfurter became acquainted. Almost a half century later Mr. Justice Frankfurter himself reminisced about how they met through Winfred Denison.

---

[14] *Recollections*, 55.

[15] *O'Brian Chronology*, 15.

[16] *The Reminiscences of John Lord O'Brian*. New York: Columbia University Oral History Research Office, 1953, a copy of which may be found in the O'Brian Papers. The statement quoted above appears in Volume I at page 213 (cited hereafter as *O'Brian Reminiscences*).

> I pause because he evokes very sad reflections . . . He
> ended his life by throwing himself in front of a subway
> engine in New York, but Denison was a very
> considerable personality. It was through him that I
> became intimately acquainted with John Lord O'Brian,
> one of the really, absolutely, first-class characters in
> Washington . . .[17]

Along with its efforts to induce the Wilson administration "to lay off prosecuting the IWW," the Civil Liberties Bureau mounted a campaign to raise funds for their legal defense in Chicago. Volumes of correspondence between officials of the NCLB and the IWW are archived in the Seeley G. Mudd Library at Princeton. Roger Baldwin was in constant communication with George Vanderveer, the IWW lawyer. During February and March of 1918 no fewer than 27 written communications passed between them. Big Bill Haywood and his lieutenant Vincent St. John sent Roger Baldwin at least seven letters and telegrams in 1918 and received no fewer than five in return.

On January 5, 1918, Baldwin addressed a letter to "Mr. Felix Frankfurter, Judge Advocate General's Office, War Department, Washington, D.C." asking Frankfurter to meet with him and a group of sympathizers to discuss the pending IWW trial.[18] Frankfurter responded in a telegram asking him to "please get in touch with me when you reach Washington."[19] On January 31, 1918, Roger Baldwin and George Vanderveer met Frankfurter in Washington.[20]

In early February the IWW lawyer sent Roger Baldwin a copy of a letter he had just written to Secretary of War Newton Baker. In it Vanderveer expressed his understanding "that the President is entirely out of sympathy with this prosecution." Among others "sharing the same view" Vanderveer named "Mr. Justice Brandeis; all the members of the Mediation Commission, particularly the

---

[17] *Reminisces*, 108.
[18] RNB to FF, January 5, 1918, Reel 4, Vol. 27, #1995, ACLUP.
[19] FF to RNB, January 7, 1918, Reel 4, Vol. 27, #1997, ACLUP.
[20] RNB to E.F. Doree, January 31, 1918, Reel 4, Vol. 27, #2009, ACLUP.

secretary, Mr. Frankfurter."[21]

The following week Baldwin sent money and securities to Chicago so that Haywood could make bail.[22] In March he asked Vanderveer to send John Graham Brooks, c/o Cosmos Club, Washington, a set of defense bulletins and to let him know to what extent a dismissal of the IWW cases would tend to "check labor unrest."[23]

In the meanwhile the National Civil Liberties Bureau was monitoring the case of *United States v. Charles T. Schenck et al,* Docket No. 111, June Sessions 1917, in the U.S. District Court for the Eastern District of Pennsylvania. The United States Attorney for that district was Francis Fisher Kane, a Philadelphia lawyer who, according to his obituary, "was often identified with the defense of left wing sympathizers."[24] On September 21, 1917, 16 days after the IWW raids, Kane advised the NCLB that "these defendants will very likely be tried . . . during the next week or two."[25] There is a newspaper clipping in the NCLB file which shows that four of the defendants were arrested on September 19.[26]

U.S. Attorney Kane lost no time in getting the trial under way. By January defense counsel for Charles Schenck was able to report to the NCLB that he expected to appeal before the month was out. "Inasmuch as a Constitutional question is involved in this case, we may be allowed to appeal directly to the Supreme Court."[27] Shortly thereafter Schenck did appeal his conviction, and did so directly to the Supreme Court on a writ of error.

Schenck's offense was to mail pamphlets to men who were being inducted into the armed forces, the intent of which was to cause insubordination and to disrupt enlistment programs. *Schenck*

---

[21] George Vanderveer to Secretary of War Newton D. Baker, February 6, 1918; GNV to RNB, February 6, 1918, Reel 4, Vol. 27, #1881-1885, ACLUP.

[22] RNB to GV, February 11, 1918, Reel 4, Vol. 27, ACLUP.

[23] RNB to GV, March 16, 1918, Reel 4, Vol. 27, ACLUP.

[24] "Francis Kane, 88, Lawyer, is Dead, Philadelphian was leader in Liberal causes and a former U.S. Attorney," *New York Times,* May 28, 1958.

[25] Reel 5, Vol. 36, #229, ACLUP.

[26] Reel 5, Vol. 36, #230. ACLUP. The newspaper appears to be *The Call,* and the byline is Philadelphia, September 19. "4 Socialists Seized in Phila."

[27] Henry J. Gibbons to Walter Nelles, January 18, 1918, Reel 5. Vol. 36, #235-236, ACLUP.

v. United States is remembered as a First Amendment case. Even if the purpose of the circulars was to interfere with the war effort, Schenck contended, it was nonetheless "free speech" protected by the First Amendment.

But this was not the only issue in *Schenck*. Although the case did not make Potter Stewart's list, there was a search and seizure question as well. The evidence against Charles Schenck had been gleaned from books and papers seized at Socialist Party headquarters under a warrant that he maintained was invalid under the Fourth Amendment. But who is Schenck to question the validity of such a warrant?

Both Schenck and Haywood, we must take note, were convicted of a violation of the Espionage Act for uttering or publishing statements they each contended were constitutionally protected. In Schenck's case, as in Haywood's, papers seized by federal agents under search warrants said to be defective were used in evidence to obtain a conviction. But neither Haywood nor Schenck can claim the benefit of the Fourth Amendment or the *Weeks* rule, so it would appear, because the search in question was not of *their* premises and the things seized had never belonged to *them*. No constitutional right guaranteed either defendant under the Fourth Amendment could be said to have been violated.

We must consider the hypothesis that *Schenck v. United States* was a "ringer" for *Haywood v. United States*. *Schenck* has all the indicia of a vehicle that was used to transport to the Supreme Court the very same questions it would have had to decide in the *Haywood* case, had that case come before the Court first. The attorneys for both sides in the *Schenck* case saw to it that the two issues of constitutional law—free speech and search and seizure—remained unbeclouded by factual issues so that *Schenck* could go directly to the Supreme Court on a writ of error while *Haywood* took the long way around through the circuit court of appeals. In this scenario Charles Schenck was to Big Bill Haywood what Fremont Weeks was to Frank Ryan.

From the defendant's standpoint *Schenck* presented the case in the most favorable light and *Haywood* the least. Schenck, as far as the record shows, was nonviolent. Essentially what he was advocating was passive resistance to the draft. No one got hurt because of anything Schenck said or did. This was anything but true of the IWW. Their leaders made speeches about "direct action" and violence followed in their wake. In an interview with Peggy Lamson, 50 years later, octogenarian Roger Baldwin maintained that the IWW "didn't use violence," but somehow his recollections of their activities do not seem very reassuring.

> *Lamson*: "But if they [the IWW] weren't violent why was everyone so afraid of them?"

> *Baldwin*: "Well there were three or four reasons. For one thing they were highly mobile. They didn't have wives and children so they could summon men from all over the country—thousands of them would come together very quickly to hold a huge meeting on freedom of speech for example. And a lot of angry unemployed men, all massed together in one place, scared people to death."[28]

You do not have to be a legal giant to see that the case against the harmless Schenck is but an exsanguinated microcosm of the case against the IWW leaders, and once you know the *modus operandi* of *Weeks,* the presumption in favor of *Schenck's* legitimacy rapidly fades. Francis Fisher Kane stood in for Leslie Lyons at the trial level, and O'Brian and Bettman played the role of Winfred Denison in briefing and arguing the appeal. *Schenck* brought directly to the Supreme Court on a writ of error the identical questions shortly to be argued in *Haywood* before the Seventh Circuit Court of Appeals.

A decision for Schenck on either the free speech or the search and seizure issue could have been used by the lawyers for the IWW to obtain a reversal of the convictions by the circuit court of appeals. Most likely an appeal would not have been necessary. Those "friends of civil liberties" who ran the War Emergency Division of the Attorney General's Office simply would have announced that the *Schenck* holding obliged them to drop the case against the IWW. Ever so regretfully they would have been constrained to dismiss the

---

[28] Lamson, 81.

case against Haywood and quash any other "free-speech prosecutions" they had theretofore been unable "to put the lid on."

The oral argument in *Schenck v. United States* was concluded January 10, 1919, but the decision was not handed down until the 3rd of March. Apparently the suspense was more than some could bear. On February 4 acting NCLB director Albert DeSilver (in the place of Roger Baldwin, then serving a one-year prison term as a conscientious objector)[29] sent a one-paragraph note to John Graham Brooks. It was Brooks, you will recall, who had accompanied Roger Baldwin to the "unsatisfactory" luncheon with the "cold" Cabinet member David Houston.

> Thank you very much for your note.
>
> I know that you have been doing all that is in your power. Do you suppose that there is any step that we can take at Washington that will be of any assistance in getting the IWW cases dropped. If there is, I wish you would tell me about it.
>
> Sincerely yours,[30]

Brooks indeed had been doing all in his power to get the IWW cases dropped. To use an idiom of the day, no one could accuse him of being a "slacker." Previously he had sent RNB this letter which later fell into the wrong hands.

> My dear Mr. Baldwin,
>
> [Chist?] got off. Now if you have important facts that would help Judge Anderson (<u>Don't tell his name to anyone</u>) send them (few as possible or so arranged at least that he can get at their significance easily) at once to Judge Geo. A. Anderson. Cosmos Club, Wash. D.C.

---

[29] Baldwin entered prison on November 11, 1918, which turned out to be Armistice Day, and was released July 19, 1919. Walker 41, 42. He was released "three months early because of a clerical error in computing his time served." Walker, 45.

[30] Reel 11, Vol. 86, #253, ACLUP.

> You can count on him to do all that can be done in
> ways of which we spoke. I shall send you some more
> questions from him to me in a day or two.[31]

Each volume of the Federal Reporter series lists by circuit the entire federal judiciary as it existed at the time of publication. According to the volumes for the years in question, the only federal judges named Anderson (or Andersen) were George W. Anderson of Boston and Albert B. Anderson of Indianapolis. The latter presided over the trial of the Dynamiters, and was the judge who sentenced Frank Ryan and the leadership of the Ironworkers to Leavenworth. George W. Anderson—"subterranean George"—the former Massachusetts Public Service Commissioner—was appointed to be a federal judge on October 24, 1918.

Meanwhile, all was not quiet on the Eastern Front. In March of 1918, when Russia left the war, the British landed forces at Archangel and Murmansk. With the straits leading out of the Baltic and Black Seas controlled by the Central Powers, these two northern seaports were Russia's only access to the Atlantic. Britain had been supplying Russia with arms to fight Germans and did not want them to fall into the hands of the "Reds"—the generic name applied to the Bolsheviks and their partisans throughout the world. The "White Russians," who recognized neither the Bolshevik regime nor the Treaty of Brest-Litovsk, still were fighting the Germans.

In early August of 1918, 4,500 American troops equipped with skis and snowshoes landed at Archangel and in a few days were in combat against the Bolsheviks fighting side by side with the British, the French and the White Russians.[32] In September an American Expeditionary Force of 9,000 men under General William S.

---

[31] This letter from Brooks to Baldwin may be found between pages 1056 and 1057 of the report titled *"In the Senate of the State of New York, Part I, Revolutionary and Seditious Movements Abroad and at Home."* 4 Vols. (Albany, New York:) J.B. Lyon Company, 1920), hereinafter referred to as the Lusk Report after its chairman, State Senator Clayton R. Lusk.

[32] John Toland. *No Man's Land: 1918, The Last Year of the Great War.* Garden City, New York: Doubleday & Company, 1980, 401.

Graves landed at Vladivostok.[33] That port city, Russia's main outlet to the Pacific Ocean, had been occupied since April by Japanese marines and a small British contingent.

Uppermost in the minds of the new masters of the Kremlin was the danger to the revolution posed by this intervention. To paraphrase Winston Churchill, never in the history of human conflict could so few have done so much for so many. The world would have been spared incalculable grief had the Allies intervened in sufficient strength and strangled Bolshevism in its cradle. The Reds mustered all the forces at their command to see that they did not. Their comrades in the United States answered the call with strikes, demonstrations, arson and bombings.

The month after the "October Revolution," the home of California Governor William B. Stephens was dynamited. Stephens had refused to commute the death sentence of Tom Mooney.[34] Members of the IWW were arrested and ultimately 46 of them were convicted in federal court of violating the Espionage Act "by threats, assaults, injuries, intimidations and murders of persons . . . The case [was] similar in many respects to the Chicago I.W.W. conspiracy case which resulted in the conviction of William D. Haywood, Secretary-Treasurer of the organization, and about ninety other men."[35]

The authorities, both state and federal, had raided offices of the IWW and the Communist Party and seized manifestos and membership lists. In comparing the lists with immigration records they established that most of the Reds were aliens. In September and October of 1918, at the same time American boys were dying in the Argonne Forest at the rate of 500 a day, the Congress of the United States debated how best to deal with those in our midst whose only allegiance was to the red flag.

Congress took the position that whatever right of revolution citizens may have, aliens are in this country by our sufferance, and

[33] Ibid., 402-403.
[34] Governor Stephens did commute Mooney's death sentence but only after the Armistice and at President Wilson's request.
[35] "Find 46 I.W.W.S Guilty Of Plot," *New York Times*, January 17, 1919. According to this article Stephens's home was bombed December 17, 1917.

we need not suffer any whose purpose it was to overthrow our government. On October 16, 1918, Congress passed a law ordering the deportation of any alien who was a member of any organization advocating the overthrow of the government by force or violence.

To deport an alien under the 1918 Act the United States did not have to prove that he or she personally had advocated the overthrow of the government by force or violence, only that the person belonged to an organization which did. With respect to an alien member who took care not to carry a party card, the best evidence lay in the confiscated manifestos and membership rolls. If they can be used as evidence it will be *bon voyage* for many a comrade.

If the deportation of alien revolutionaries was to be thwarted,these records had to be suppressed, and the only hope of accomplishing this lay in the *Weeks* rule. While the rule applied only in criminal cases, and deportation is not a criminal case, certain analogies could be made. A Russian national being held for deportation, for example, cannot be repatriated until he can be put aboard ship. In the meanwhile he is a person being held in custody, the validity of whose detention may be tested in a habeas corpus proceeding.

When the alien is produced in court immigration officials will have to show that the detention is lawful. They will have to prove that the detainee is not only an alien, but that he is an alien who belongs to an organization advocating the overthrow of the government. In most cases the immigration authorities will not be able to meet this burden without using the literature and the membership records seized from party headquarters or information that has been adduced therefrom. When this evidence is offered a motion can be made to exclude it on the grounds that it was obtained in a search forbidden by the Fourth Amendment.

But here the precedent of *Weeks* falls short. In the case of a Communist deportee it will not be *his* house or office which was searched nor *his* papers and effects which were seized. No Fourth Amendment right of his was violated. He cannot ask that the documents be restored to him because they do not belong to him. They are the property of the party.

Suppose the membership lists and the other materials are

restored to the party? What is to prevent the government from issuing a new subpoena on what is now the best of probable cause? What is to prevent immigration officials from photographing the material or using knowledge they have gained from examining it which they otherwise would not have had? In a deportation case, what standing would a deportee have to object to the use of records seized from the party?

While these questions were being pondered the world was being ravaged by the horsemen of the apocalypse. The winter of 1918-19 was dreadful. The influenza epidemic took an even greater toll than did the World War, killing an estimated 20 million people worldwide and more than half a million in the United States. In the erstwhile Central Powers hunger, disease and riots were endemic. One pictures Germany as a nation of sick and half -starved people with limbless veterans begging on street corners.

Bolsheviks led by Bela Kun took over Hungary and began the systematic elimination of their enemies. In Germany the Communist Party went by the name of the Spartacus Union. Two days before Christmas in 1918, the Spartacists paraded around the Reich Chancellery in Berlin in such a manner as to hold the Ebert Government captive. The demonstrations were escalated daily until January 5, 1919, when 200,000 of their supporters, carrying red flags and weapons, were mobilized around government buildings.[36]

That night armed Spartacists took over Berlin in a coup. After the Socialist militia, whose duty it was to defend the government, surrendered without firing a shot, a "Free Corps" of ex-soldiers was formed to fight the Reds. On January 15 some three thousand of them retook Berlin and captured the ringleaders. The two leading Spartacists, Karl Liebknecht and Rosa Luxemburg, were shot out of hand. The following month Kurt Eisner, the dictator of the proletariat of Bavaria, was shot dead in Munich.

This was the harbinger of Germany's downfall. In time the Free Corps will give way to the brown-shirted battalions of Adolf Hitler's National Socialist German Workers Party, whose acronym in

---

[36] Gordon A. Craig. *Germany: 1866-1945*. New York: Oxford University Press, 1978, 406,407.

German was the NSDAP or derisively NAZI. The Nazis and the Reds, although they will battle each other in the nation's streets and beer halls, had a symbiosis both exploited to the hilt. The best argument each side had to offer those caught in the middle was that it was only their side that could save them from the other.

Early in 1919 Thomas Watt Gregory resigned as Attorney General. His successor, Alexander Mitchell Palmer, of Stroudsburg, Pennsylvania, was no ordinary politician. A life-long Quaker, A. Mitchell Palmer had been a child prodigy. In 1891, shortly after his 19th birthday, he graduated *summa cum laude* from Swarthmore College, and two years later, after reading law under a local judge, was admitted to the Pennsylvania bar. Palmer was a progressive Democrat and "a leader of insurgent forces within the party determined to overthrow the 'old guard.'" In 1908 A. Mitchell Palmer was elected to Congress as a reformer. "Reelected in 1910 and 1912, he received considerable attention on Capitol Hill because of his able debating and his staunch support of progressive measures."[37] At the 1912 Democratic National Convention, Palmer had been New Jersey Governor Wilson's floor manager and was instrumental in his getting the nomination.

> As national committeeman from Pennsylvania he controlled that state's delegation to the Democratic National Convention at Baltimore, a control which proved vitally important in the ultimate nomination of Woodrow Wilson for president. Even more important was Palmer's dogged work as floor manager for the Wilson forces and his refusal to be swayed or bought, although offered the vice-presidential nomination at one point by the supporters of Champ Clark.[38]

As a Congressman, Palmer was best known for his advocacy of the National Child Labor Act of 1914, which prohibited the shipment in interstate commerce of goods manufactured in

---

[37] These quotations and the biographical data relating to Palmer are taken from the *Dictionary of American Biography*, Volume XI, Supplement Two, New York: Charles Scribner's Sons (1958).
[38] Ibid.

violation of the standards it prescribed. The use of the Commerce Clause to permit the federal government to impose its will on matters otherwise constitutionally beyond its authority was considered by many to be a radical and dangerous precedent. While Palmer's bill passed in the House of Representatives by a vote of 233-43, it failed in the Senate after the President refused to support it. In Woodrow Wilson's opinion "the measure was unconstitutional and would open the door to virtually unlimited national economic regulation" over matters which historically had been considered the province of the several states.[39] Mitchell Palmer was a New Dealer before Franklin Roosevelt invented the term.

The appointment of Palmer was welcome news indeed to Progressives tired of dealing with the intractable Gregory. Albert DeSilver, filling in for the imprisoned Roger Baldwin, was granted an interview by Mitchell Palmer soon after he became Attorney General. Palmer talked "very fully and frankly," reported DeSilver, who found him to be a "different type of man from Gregory." Mitchell Palmer "takes a larger view of things" and in DeSilver's opinion was "the kind of man who is susceptible of being convinced."[40]

The decision in the *Schenck* case was handed down on March 3, 1919, two days before Palmer took his oath of office. The decision, written by Justice Holmes, contains this famous passage:

> The most stringent protection of free speech would not protect a man in falsely shouting fire in a theatre and causing a panic. It does not even protect a man from an injunction against uttering words that may have all the effect of force. *Gompers v. Bucks Stove & Range Co.,* 221 U.S. 418, 439. The question in every case is whether the words used are used in such circumstances and are of such a nature as to create a clear and present danger that they will bring about the substantive evils that Congress has a right to prevent. It is a question of proximity and degree. When a nation is at war many things that might

---

[39] Link, 256-257.

[40] Albert DeSilver to Fred H. Moore, Reel 111, Vol. 86, April 21, 1919, #270, ACLUP.

> be said in time of peace are such a hindrance to its effort
> that their utterance will not be endured so long as men
> fight and that no Court could regard them as protected
> by any constitutional right. *Schenck v. United States*, 249
> U.S. 47, 52.

It is the "clear and present danger" doctrine for which the case is remembered today. But at the time it was not the First Amendment holding which really mattered. By the time *Schenck* was decided, the issue was no longer whether anyone should be prosecuted for what might be "free speech," but whether the sentences of those so convicted should be commuted. What alien revolutionaries feared most in 1919 was deportation, and the Fourth Amendment holding of *Schenck* appeared to have sealed their fate. Since the search warrant issued against the Socialist Party headquarters, Schenck, said the Court, had no standing to contest its validity, and thus had no recourse under the *Weeks* rule.

The *Schenck* decision came as a bombshell to the Reds to which they responded in kind. Shortly before May 1, 1919, 34 packages were mailed to the Americans most hated by the Reds. Each contained a bomb rigged to explode when it was opened. Among the addressees were Justice Holmes, Postmaster General Albert Sidney Burleson, Federal Judge Kennesaw Mountain Landis, Secretary of Labor William Wilson and Attorney General Palmer.[41]

Fortunately the plot was discovered and most of the bombs intercepted. The only casualty, so it seems, was a maid in the home of Senator Thomas W. Hardwick of Georgia who had her hands blown off. On May 1 death threats to the enemies of the revolution appeared in the newspapers, and throughout the country May Day parades turned into bloody riots. The public was outraged but "Palmer stood firm against the clamor."

> The Administration came under intense pressure from
> the public, the press and Congress, but the recently
> appointed attorney general, A. Mitchell Palmer, refused

---

[41] Mark Sullivan. *Our Times: The Twenties.* New York: Charles Scribner's Sons, 1935, 170.

to be panicked. Palmer was a genuine Wilsonian Progressive. His Quaker beliefs made him refuse appointment as secretary of war. He had proved to be a zealous and popular alien property custodian. It had been a rapid rise since his election to Congress from Pennsylvania in 1908. Palmer was able, incorruptible, and hard-working. He had consistently favored organized labor, votes for women, and the abolition of child labor.

One of his first actions as attorney general was to secure presidential clemency for nearly half of the 239 people still in prison under Espionage Act convictions. He resisted efforts to force his department to use its wide powers of investigation and arrest to round up aliens and radicals. He dropped scores of pending Espionage Act prosecutions. Palmer stood firm against the clamor.[42]

Despite the political pressure the Attorney General refused to take action. Then, on the night of June 2, 1919, as Palmer and his wife prepared for bed, a bomb exploded under the front steps of their house at 2132 R Street, NW. The bomb had apparently been carried in a suitcase and had exploded as the bomber was placing it under the stairs. The head of the dead man was blown entirely across the street from the house.

He [Palmer] would venture no opinion as to what individuals or organization might be responsible for the outrage. The Attorney General and his wife left the wrecked house and went to the home of Assistant Secretary of the Treasury [sic] Franklin D. Roosevelt in the neighborhood a short time after the explosion. The Roosevelt home was shaken by the bomb.[43]

Forty years later James Roosevelt recalled the bombing and his father's description of Palmer's reaction. "I never knew before that Mitchell Palmer was a Quaker," said FDR. "He was 'theeing' and

---

[42] Geoffrey Perrett. *America in the Twenties: A History*. New York: Simon and Schuster, 1982, 54.

[43] "Red Bombs Palmer's House; Dies Himself; Family Is Not Injured," *Washington Post*, June 3, 1919.

178

'thouing' me all over the place—'thank thee, Franklin!' and all that."[44] But the bombing had a profound effect on the Attorney General and what an editorial in the *New York Times* of May 4 had criticized as his "policy of tolerance" toward the "Bolshevik movement."

> The May Day riots, the bomb outrages and preceding occurrences in different parts of the country have convinced members of the House that the policy of tolerance which has marked the attitude of the Department of Justice . . . must be dropped for one of vigorous prosecution if the Bolshevist movement is to be held in check.

Albert DeSilver was correct in his assessment that Mitchell Palmer was "the kind of man who is susceptible of being convinced." These years will become what some will call the "Red Scare," a dark age in which the rights of hapless aliens and American citizens alike were violated wholesale. Woodrow Wilson's third and last Attorney General will earn the undying enmity of the Reds. A. Mitchell Palmer will become the *bete noire* of the American left.

The decision in *Schenck v. United States*, as we have seen, triggered many events. But if *Schenck* was a fraud, it was like *Adams*, a fraud that failed, and we shall lay it aside for the time being. In the meanwhile we must be vigilant—be on the lookout for another search and seizure case coming up to the Court on a writ of error. *Voila!*

> Mr. Justice Holmes delivered the opinion of the court.
>
> This is a writ of error brought to reverse a judgment of the District Court fining the Silverthorne Lumber Company two hundred and fifty dollars for contempt of court and ordering Frederick W. Silverthorne to be imprisoned until he should purge himself of a similar contempt. *Silverthorne Lumber Co. v. United States*, 251 U.S. 385, 390 (1920).

---

[44] *Affectionately, F.D.R.: A Son's Story of a Lonely Man*. New York: Harcourt, Brace & Company, 1959, 60.

The gravamen of the charge against the Silverthornes was that they shorted the Lehigh Valley Railroad of something called "grain door boards." Like all railroads in the country, the Lehigh Valley had been taken over by the federal government which made such a fraud a federal crime. The defendants were "railroaded" in more ways than one. Sixty days from the date the case began, *Silverthorne v. United States* was before the Supreme Court on a writ of error.

The arrests and the search and seizure took place on February 25, 1919. On March 1 the Silverthorne Lumber Company moved to recover their records.[45] On March 3 U.S. District Judge John R. Hazel ordered the books and papers surrendered to the court.[46] Three days later he returned the original documents to counsel for the lumber company and impounded the photographic copies the prosecution had made.[47]

On March 10 the Silverthornes were indicted on a charge of conspiracy to defraud the United States.[48] The following day they entered a plea of "not guilty" and the court fixed an onerous bail.[49] Six new subpoenas were then issued for the returned records which counsel for the lumber company argued "were too sweeping and violated the Fourth and Fifth Amendments."[50] Judge Hazel upheld the subpoenas and ordered the defendants to produce the books and papers. They refused and were found in contempt.

On March 31 the United States commenced a civil suit against the Silverthornes and their lumber company. Simultaneously they obtained from Judge Hazel a writ of attachment and attached the bank accounts of the Silverthornes and their company. They also seized the lumber, saws and equipment used in the operations of the Silverthorne Lumber Company and served garnishees on those with whom the Silverthornes traded. All of this was done *ex parte*, that is without a hearing.

---

[45] "Takes Steps to Recover Records." *Buffalo Courier*, March 2, 1919.

[46] "Judge Impounds Seized Books of Silverthorne Co." *Buffalo Courier*, March 4, 1919.

[47] "Silverthorne Papers Returned to Counsel; Bonds Still Lost." *Buffalo Courier*, March 7, 1919.

[48] "One Indictment is Reported by Federal Jurors." *Buffalo Courier*, March 11, 1919.

[49] "Silverthornes Plead Not Guilty, Court fixes Bail—$10,000 amount Required for Father, $5,000 for Son." *Buffalo Courier*, March 12, 1919.

[50] "Silverthorne Co. Fights for Books," *Buffalo Courier*, March 23, 1919.

On April 1 the corporation was fined $250 and Frederick Silverthorne incarcerated in the "Bastille," as the federal prison in Buffalo was known. He applied for a writ of error to the Supreme Court and filed a petition to be released on bail pending the outcome of the case. On April 2 Judge Hazel granted the writ of error but denied the petition for bail.[51]

While young Silverthorne was in prison the "domestic tranquillity" our Constitution was meant to "insure" was under grievous assault. Attorney General Palmer was not the only one to have his house dynamited on the night of June 2, 1919. The front page of the *New York Times* of June 3, 1919, was topped by this four-deck banner headline:

Midnight Bombs For Officials In 8 Cities;

Bombers Die At Attorney General's House;

Two Victims At Judge Nott's House Here;

Bombs In Boston, Cleveland, Pittsburgh.

Nor were the Reds idle elsewhere. Another headline tells us that there was violence in Toledo, Ohio, where a "Mob Attacked Employees of the Willy's Overland Plant with Sticks and Stones . . . Two are dead, another is dying, and five are seriously injured at St. Vincent's Hospital" in that city. Mayor Cornell Schrieber was under seige at City Hall after being driven from his home by a mob. He wired Ohio Governor James M. Cox that he was "unable to cope with the situation" and asked him to "send troops immediately."

On June 13 we see that counter revolutionary forces have reacted. "New York Office Of The Bolsheviki Raided By State," blares the front page of the *New York Times*. The New York State Senate had established a committee chaired by Senator Clayton R. Lusk to investigate revolutionary radicalism. On June 21 agents of the Lusk Committee raided the Rand School of Social Science in lower Manhattan and seized records and papers. According to a manifesto

---

[51] The information in these two paragraphs is taken from *United States v. Silverthorne*, Law Case No. 1836, Box 53, NANER.

issued by the National Civil Liberties Bureau dated July 18, 1919, the Rand School was a somewhat esoteric institution of learning.

> The Rand School of Social Science last year had 5,000 students. Rand students, when they finish their training, go out to be lecturers, street speakers, teachers and organizers in the labor movement. They become leading spirits among their fellows, for they have supplemented their toil-won knowledge of present social and industrial evils with an intelligent, constructive idealism that builds in a new and better way where the present system fails and collapses.

On July 16 the Rand School obtained a temporary writ of prohibition to prevent the use of all papers seized in the raid from being used by the Lusk Committee.[52] But on July 31 the writ was dissolved and the papers were handed over to the Committee.[53] "On Saturday morning, August 31, federal agents broke into the office [of the NCLB]. Leading the raid was Archibald Stevenson, a wealthy attorney and full-time radical hunter . . . Stevenson's men began carting off the NCLB files, many of which the Lusk Committee used in its report entitled *Revolutionary Radicalism*."[54]

On November 25 Mitchell Palmer's men hit paydirt at 133 East 15th Street in New York City, the headquarters of the Union of Russian Workers: "Red Bomb Laboratory Found Here; Hid In Secret Room In Russians' House" is the headline of the next day's *Times*. It seems to be quite a find—"Deadly TNT Discovered . . . Material For 100 Bombs." Most of the members of the Union of Russian Workers, according to one source, "were vunerable to deportation under the Immigration Act"[55] as aliens who were members of an organization which advocated the overthrow by

---

[52] "Rand School Wins Temporary Writ," *New York Times,* July 17, 1919.
[53] "Rand School Loses Plea For Papers," *New York Times,* August 1, 1919.
[54] Walker, 38.
[55] Walker, 43. Professor Samuel Walker, who characterized the URW raid as "one of the worst violations of civil liberties in American history," makes no mention of the discovery of the bomb laboratory in the concealed room. He managed, however, to find out that "Agents broke into the Russian People's House in New York, smashing furniture and beating everyone in sight," an outrage which eluded the reporters for the *New York Times* who covered the story. Mr. Walker, according to its "Report of Activities—1986-87," is a national director of the ACLU.

force or violence of the Government of the United States.

The case against the Silverthornes presented a scenario which was a microcosm of the predicament faced by alien revolutionaries in 1919-20. In the case of the individual Red, the evidence against him had been obtained by a search not of his home or office, but of Communist Party headquarters. The books and papers seized were not his; they belonged to the party. In the case of either Silverthorne the evidence against him was obtained by a search of the headquarters of the capitalist lumber company. The books and papers seized were not his; they were the property of the corporation. In the cameo Frederick and Asa Silverthorne were cast in the role of the beleagered Reds while the Silverthorne Lumber Company stood in the stead of an entity called the Communist Party of America.

It was not only the documents seized from the party that made the case against the Reds, but the leads they provided the investigators. Working from the information found in the party's books and papers enabled the government to build a case against a Red they could not have done otherwise. The same was true of the microcosm, in the opinion of Federal District Judge Hazel in *United States v. Silverthorne*, 265 F. 859, 862:

> But certainly it is positively asserted that the books and documents were worked over by the United States attorney and his assistants, and from sources, clues, and leads information of the business affairs of the defendants was obtained, which enabled them to adduce the evidence before the grand jury. It is manifestly impossible for the defendants to be more specific or definite as to the nature of the clues and leads, but that the illegally seized books and papers were worked over, and information gleaned therefrom upon which the present indictment was found, is an unmistakable assertion of fact.

If in the beginning of 1919 you were a Communist facing deportation, you would be looking for a precedent which could be used to exclude evidence seized at the party's headquarters. The precedent must hold that not only is the documentary evidence seized inadmissible, but that any evidence it led the government to find is inadmissible as well. In 1939 this doctrine will be encapsulated in the metaphor of "a fruit of the poisonous tree."[56] But this is 1919 and the man who minted that metaphor did not become a Supreme Court Justice until 1939. In 1919 he was a professor at Harvard Law School.

---

[56] *Nardone v. United States*, 308 U.S. 338, 341 (1939), Frankfurter J.

Chapter IX

SILVERTHORNE v. UNITED STATES

The judicial power vested in the Supreme Court of the United States by Article III of the Constitution is limited to "cases" and "controversies" arising under the Constitution and the laws of the United States. The object of this inquiry is to determine whether *Silverthorne Lumber Co. v. United States* was in fact a genuine "case" or "controversy" or whether it was a fraud perpetuated on the Court for the sole purpose of obtaining a precedent to be used in frustrating the will of Congress and the Executive Branch expressed in the Deportation Act of 1918, the constitutionality of which was never in question.

The immediate objection to Silverthorne's being a setup is that the raid took place on February 25, six days *before* the Supreme Court announced its decision in *Schenck* on March 3, 1919. A favorable decision in *Schenck* on the Fourth Amendment question would have obviated the necessity of conniving *Silverthorne*; hence, if the hypothesis is to stand, the conspirators had to have advance knowledge on how the Court would decide the *Schenck* case. It would make no sense to go to the trouble of setting up *Silverthorne* without first finding out whether *Schenck* would solve the problem.

To posit a conspiracy, we must posit conspirators. The only people who would have known in advance how *Schenck* would be decided were the Justices of the Supreme Court. The only Justice we are considering under this hypothesis is Louis Brandeis. If he is not the mastermind of this conspiracy, the hypothesis fails. *Silverthorne*

185

just happened, and it was a coincidence that it just happened to help the Reds in their hour of need.

Schenck v. United States was argued on the 9th and 10th of January, 1919. On February 3, as a consequence of the influenza epidemic that was ravaging the nation, the Court recessed and did not sit again until Monday, March 3,[1] the date on which the decision in *Schenck* was announced. Sometime during this period, most likely before the recess, the Justices met in conference and voted to affirm the conviction of Charles Schenck for espionage.

While *Schenck* was pending, two other events took place which have a bearing on this story. The first was the replacement of Thomas W. Gregory as Attorney General by A. Mitchell Palmer. Gregory announced his resignation on January 9, 1919, as *Schenck* was being argued. The resignation was to become effective on the 4th of March, which turned out to be the day after the decision was handed down. A. Mitchell Palmer became Attorney General on March 5, 1919,[2] one day later.

Silverthorne was set up during the changing of the guard when one would suspect no one was really in command of the Justice Department. On February 26, the day after the Silverthorne raid, not even the President of the United States knew who the next Attorney General would be. From Paris Wilson wrote Gregory, "I have been thinking, and thinking hard and in many directions, about the appointment of your successor, and each time my mind comes back to Mitchell Palmer. I think that on the whole he is my most available man."[3]

The second event was the replacement of William Gibbs McAdoo as Director General of Railroads by Justice Brandeis's fellow Kentuckian, Walker D. Hines. Hines, who had been the

---

[1] Letter dated July 22, 1998, from the Office of Public Information of the Supreme Court of the United States.

[2] Thomas Watt Gregory "Resigned January 9, 1919, to take effect March 4, 1919. On March 5, 1919, A. Mitchell Palmer, of Pennsylvania, took the oath of office as Attorney General, under a recess appointment." 249 U.S. front. He was confirmed by the Senate August 29, 1919. 250 U.S. front.

[3] WW to TWG, February 26, 1919, Wilson Papers.

Assistant Director, took over on January 10, 1919,[4] the day the argument in *Schenck* was concluded. The new Director of Railroads was a "frequent visitor"[5] to the Justice's apartment and a friend of his brother Alfred as well.[6]

In the coming year Walker Downer Hines will receive a sinecure which will establish him as an international lawyer. According to his obituary, when the railroads were returned "to private hands in May 1920," the former Railroad Director was sent "to Paris as arbitrator of the disputes arising over the allocation of shipping on the international rivers of Europe as between our allies and former enemy countries."[7]

Let us test the hypothesis that sometime between January 10 and February 25, 1919, the case of *Silverthorne v. United States* was concocted in the Washington apartment of Louis Brandeis, on the metaphorical mezzanine between the floor upon which judicial precedent was being forged above and that on which political strategy was being planned below. The sole purpose of this case would have been to create a precedent which under the doctrine of *stare decisis* could be used to forestall the impending deportation of alien revolutionaries. Joining Justice Brandeis in this cabal were Railroad Director Walker Hines and John Lord O'Brian, Special Assistant to the Attorney General.

The microcosm had to present a search and seizure unarguably unconstitutional, a matter apparently not within the competence of the local U.S. marshal. The chief security officer of the Railroad Commission was dispatched to Buffalo to see that a proper job was done. "The arrests were supervised by William J. Flynn, former chief of the United States Secret Service and now chief of the Secret Service bureau of the United States railroad administration ... Chiefs Flynn and Booth, accompanied by three marshals from the federal building ... went to the Silverthorne residence [877 Delaware Avenue] at 7

---

[4] WW to J.P. Tumulty, January 10, 1919, Wilson Papers.

[5] Murphy, 50.

[6] LDB to Alfred Brandeis, May 2, 1926, *Brandeis Letters*.

[7] "Walker D. Hines is Dead in Italy," *New York Times*, January 15, 1934. See also *Louisville Courier Journal*, January 15, 1934.

o'clock in the morning to make the arrests."[8]

Half measures were not in order. With the villains safely behind bars, an expeditionary force of "seven or eight or more, men in four taxicabs" sortied to the Tonawanda office of the Silverthorne Lumber Company, Inc. to complete their mission. "Everything in the way of books, papers, memoranda and documents in the office was seized and taken away." *All* employees were arrested and "taken to the United States District Attorney's office" in a commandeered trolley car. The office door was left "wide open and various papers and documents scattered on the floor, along the highway in front of the office and in the yard."[9] A good day's work, if your aim is to conduct as egregious an unconstitutional search and seizure as possible.

Dan B. Leonard of the Division of Law of the U.S. Railroad Commission had been in Buffalo the week before laying the groundwork. The day after the raid, he reported to his boss: "I was engaged in the Silverthorne case Friday and have been constantly working on it ever since then. We made arrangements to arrest the defendants on the morning of Tuesday, Feb. 25. Mr. Flynn and Inspectors McCarthy and Willets arrived here on Monday, Feb. 24th."[10] On the 5th of March, "Edward E. Gann, Special Assistant to the Attorney General, of Washington arrived . . . to assist in preparing indictments."[11]

While this was going on, Felix Frankfurter was in Paris representing Louis Brandeis at a Zionist conference. With him was Howard Gans, the relentless prosecutor of Al Adams, New York's King of Policy back in 1904. In January the War Labor Policy Board had been abolished and Frankfurter, its chairman, and Gans,[12] his

---

[8] "Two Silverthornes and J.M. M'Conkey Federal Prisoners," *Buffalo Courier*, February 26, 1919.

[9] Affidavits and Rule to Show Cause, filed February 4, 1920, *USA v. Silverthorne Lumber Co.*, Criminal Case No. 1809-1919, Box 51, USDC—WDNY, NANER.

[10] Dan B. Leonard to Philip J. Doherty, February 26, 1919, File 1627, #44, General File of the Counsel General, 1918-37; U.S. Railroad Administration, Record Group 14, National Archives, Washington, D.C., cited hereafter as Railroad Adm.

[11] Leonard to Doherty, March 5, 1919, Ibid.

[12] LDB to Emma Winter Frankfurter, May 16, 1918, *Brandeis Letters*. This was a letter to FF's mother congratulating her on her son's "new appointment." The employment of Gans is discussed in the commentary following a letter from LDB to Jacob deHaas on February 3, 1919.

assistant, became available for what Justice Brandeis once called "joint endeavors for the public good." At Brandeis's instructions the two had sailed for Europe on February 15.[13]

On March 5, 1919, Justice Brandeis wrote Zionist leader Charles A. Cowen: "As you know I am anxious to have Howard Gans go to Palestine . . . to stay as long as necessary—even if it runs far into the autumn. He thought when he left that his family affairs would require his return in 8 weeks."[14] In any event, Howard Gans did not go to Palestine. In a cable to Frankfurter on June 5, Brandeis expressed reservations about making the Palestine trip himself, one of them being that Gans had not gone ahead to survey the situation.[15] There is a tantalizing trail of clues suggesting that Howard Gans had been dispatched on another mission instead.

By the time the Silverthornes went to trial in the autumn of 1920, John W. Ryan, a lawyer in private practice, had been appointed a Special Assistant Attorney General to take charge of the case. Ryan may not have been the only private practitioner to be pressed into service. A reporter covering the trial who needed a filler inserted this irrelevant exchange which took place during the examination of witness F.W. Silverthorne:

> "When the court here imposed a jail sentence on you in March 1919, for contempt of court in refusing to turn papers over to the government, what did Howard Hans [sic] say?" Gans is an assistant to the federal attorney general.

> Mr. Ryan objected to the question and was sustained by the court.[16]

Two days later the United States Attorney for the Western

---

[13] LDB to Jacob deHaas, February 10, 1919, Brandeis Papers, Reel 84, 0381, "Felix and Gans sailing on Baltic due to leave February fifteenth." Jacob deHaas to LDB, February 17, 1919, Brandeis Papers, Reel 84, 0408, "Expect Felix and Gans on the Baltic stop."

[14] LDB to CAC, March 5, 1919, *Brandeis Letters*.

[15] *Half Brother, Half Son*, No. 18.

[16] "Silverthornes' Lawyers Right On Job For Him," *Buffalo Express*, December 1, 1920.

District of New York took the witness stand.

> Stephen T. Lockwood, United States district attorney, testified that Edward E. Gans has been an assistant to the attorney general for years.
>
> Having failed in their attempt to have Fred Silverthorne tell what Gans was reported to have said in court when Judge Hazel ordered that the defendant be confined in jail for contempt of court, the defense yesterday recalled James O. Moore, Silverthorne's counsel.
>
> Gans said: "that damned crook got what was coming to him, and I hope he stays in jail until he rots," Moore testified.[17]

Now, as we have seen, there was an Edward E. *Gann*, Assistant to the Attorney General, who was in Buffalo at various times in March and April of 1919, working on the case. According to the reports sent by U.S. Railroad Administration Attorney D.B. Leonard to P.J. Doherty on March 5, March 11, and May 1, Gann was in Buffalo on those dates. Whether he was in Buffalo on the day in question cannot be proved or disproved.

The same is true of Howard Gans. A letter from Frankfurter places Gans with him in Paris on March 7.[18] The February 1919 edition of *The Macabees* on page 51 lists Howard Gans as a delegate to the conference of Zionists. According to *The Zionist Review* of April 1919, the conference sat from February 23 to March 12. The whereabouts of Howard Gans during the remainder of March and the beginning of April cannot be ascertained. It was certainly possible for him to return to the United States—as he had planned to do anyway to take care of family affairs—and be in Buffalo on April 2, the day F.W. Silverthorne was led off to the Bastille.

Howard Gans was a New York lawyer who would have known what had to be done and how to do it. The possibility that he was

---

[17] "Silverthorne's Fate Will Be Up To Jury Tuesday," *Buffalo Express*, December 3, 1920.
[18] FF to LDB, March 7, 1919, Reel 84, Brandeis Papers.

dispatched to Buffalo cannot be proven, but it cannot be dismissed either. One question that must be asked is whether the name Edward E. Gann was so similar to Howard Gans as to evoke a slip of the tongue. Another is, why did the United States Attorney for the Western District of New York deem it of sufficient importance to take the witness stand to clarify the identity of a person whose statement, aside from being irrelevant, was never admitted into evidence in the first place?

By April 2 the Silverthornes and their lumber company were out of business, and Frederick W. Silverthorne was in jail. U.S. District Judge Hazel denied bail but issued a writ of error. The next step was to compile the transcript of record and file it in the Supreme Court praying that the Court review the action of the district court. This was done on April 26, 1919, and *United States v. Silverthorne Lumber Co. et al* became *Silverthorne Lumber Co. et al v. United States,* No. 358 on the docket of the Supreme Court of the United States.

In 1919 the federal court system was divided geographically into nine circuits. Each circuit had a number of district courts—trial courts in which criminal and civil cases originated—and a circuit court of appeals which had appellate jurisdiction over the district courts in that circuit. But as we have seen, one convicted of a crime in a district court could, provided certain conditions were met, bypass the circuit court of appeals by filing a writ of error in the Supreme Court.

The nine circuits were allotted among the nine Justices of the Supreme Court so that each Justice presided over a circuit. In 1919 the Second Circuit had six judicial districts. The entire state of Vermont comprised one district and the state of Connecticut another. New York was divided into four districts—Southern, Eastern, Northern, and Western.[19] Buffalo, New York, was the perfect venue for the microcosm. Not only was it in the Second Circuit, over which Justice Brandeis presided, it was in the Western District of New York, where John Lord O'Brian had been the United States Attorney.

---

[19] Volume 255 of the Federal Reporter (v) *et seq.* gives the array of federal judges circa 1919.

There is no reason for the Solicitor General of the United States or a Justice of the Supreme Court presiding over his circuit to make inquiries as to the business which may be coming his way from the hinterlands. Invariably they wait until the appellate jurisdiction of the Supreme Court is invoked by the filing of an appeal or writ of error and thereafter respond in due course after due deliberation. Consider, in this light, the following letter of May 9, 1919, from Mr. Justice Brandeis to Solicitor General Alexander C. King:

> My dear Mr. Solicitor General:
>
> I had delayed from day to day replying to your letter of April eighteenth in reference to the case of United States v. Silverthorne Lumber Co., et al., expecting that an application would be made to me. In view of the petition filed for Silverthorne on May fifth and your memorandum in opposition filed on May seventh, I assume that the likelihood to which you referred no longer exists.[20]

Here is the response from King four days later:

> My dear Mr. Justice Brandeis:
>
> Please accept my thanks for your favor of the 9th instant in reply to my letter regarding the case of the United States v. Silverthorne Lumber Co. et al. I understand that the petition filed on May 5 in the matter of bail in the Silverthorne case was in place of the proposed application to you as Circuit Justice. With high regard,[21]

The first question is how, on "April eighteenth" or at any time prior to April 26, the date upon which the transcript of record was

---

[20] Brandeis to King, May 9, 1919, No. 199768-23, Straight Numerical Files, 1904-1937, DJA, NARA. All Department of Justice correspondence regarding *Silverthorne v. United States* bears the prefix "199768" followed by a distinguishing number. Hereinafter such a citation will be identified simply by serial number.

[21] Ibid., No. 199768-23.

filed with the Supreme Court, did either the Solicitor General or Justice Brandeis know that among the thousands of cases pending in the district courts of the Second Circuit there was a case denominated "United States v. Silverthorne Lumber Co., et al."? The second question is why should either of them have concerned themselves until the Court was asked to review it? This letter, written the following October, tells us what was going on behind the scenes.

October 8, 1919

Mr. Stephen T. Lockwood,
United States Attorney,
Buffalo, N.Y.

Dear Sir:

Your favor of October 4 was received yesterday but engagements in the Supreme Court have prevented an earlier reply. As heretofore written you, the Silverthorne case did not reach the Supreme Court in time to be advanced at the last term. The record was not actually filed until the 26th of April, and prior to that time the Supreme Court had announced that the docket would be closed for argument on Friday, May 2nd . . . Under the rules a case must be moved to be advanced and the motion is not passed on until the Monday following the time it is made; also the record must be printed before the case is heard; so that this case only reaching the court in unprinted form on April 26, could not be heard upon the merits on oral argument last term. It was for this reason that this office endeavored to get it decided by making the motion to dismiss or affirm upon the ground that the constitutional question raised had been settled by previous decisions of the Supreme Court; and that even if the Court considered them not settled so as to dismiss the writ of error for want of jurisdiction, they were so unfounded that the court ought to affirm the case on motion. This motion was duly submitted but the court refused to decide it, but after holding it until nearly the end of the term, passed an order that it be heard in connection with the main case.

I will move to advance the case at this term so that it can be heard. I do not think, however, from what I can learn from the court, that any cases set down on motion to advance will be heard earlier than the first Monday in December.

> Very truly,
> (Signed) Alex C. King
> Solicitor General[22]

In other words, when the Solicitor General wrote his missing letter to Justice Brandeis on Friday, April 18, he knew that if *Silverthorne* was to be advanced so that it might be decided before the term ended in June, the transcript of record and a motion to advance had to be filed no later than the following Friday, April 25. As it turned out, the transcript was filed on April 26, a Saturday. Had the transcript been filed one day earlier, a motion to advance could have been filed along with it and argued on April 28, the following Monday. Had this been done, *Silverthorne* might well have been decided in June of 1919 instead of January of 1920. This, as we shall see, would have made a difference.

On Monday, May 5, the "Petition of Frederick W. Silverthorne to be Enlarged on Bail" together with a supporting brief was submitted to Circuit Justice Brandeis. On the same day the Solicitor General filed a "Motion by the United States to Dismiss or Affirm and Brief in Support" and two days later a "Memorandum in Opposition to Petition of Frederick W. Silverthorne to be Enlarged on Bail." All of these documents were in printed form. After additional briefs and motions the Court, on June 9, 1919, entered an order postponing further consideration of the case until October and releasing Frederick W. Silverthorne on bail.

Courts and judges usually act with celerity when an appeal is

---

[22] Ibid., No. 199768-61.

Supreme Court of the United States.
Washington, D.C.

May 9, 1919.

My dear Mr. Solicitor General:

I had delayed from day to day replying
to your letter of April eighteenth in reference to the case of United
States v. Silverthorne Lumber Co., et al., expecting that an application would be made to me. In view of the petition filed for Silverthorne on May fifth and your memorandum in opposition filed on May
seventh, I assume that the likelihood to which you referred no longer
exists.

Cordially,

Associate Justice of the Supreme Court
of the United States.

Hon. Alex. C. King,
Solicitor General,
United States.

May 13, 1919.

My dear Mr. Justice Brandeis:

Please accept my thanks for your favor of the 9th instant in reply to my letter regarding the case of United States v. Silverthorne Lumber Co. et al. I understand that the petition filed on May 5 in the matter of bail in the Silverthorne case was in place of the proposed application to you as Circuit Justice. With high regard,

Very respectfully,

(Signed) Alex C. King
Solicitor General.

Hon. L.D.Brandeis,
Associate Justice,
Supreme Court of United States.

199768 - 61

October 8, 1919.

Mr. Stephen T. Lockwood,
United States Attorney,
Buffalo, N. Y.

Dear Sir:

Your favor of October 4 was received yesterday but engagements in the Supreme Court have prevented an earlier reply. As heretofore written you, the Silverthorne case did not reach the Supreme Court in time to be advanced at the last term. The record was not actually filed until the 26th of April, and prior to that time the Supreme Court had announced that the docket would be closed for argument on Friday, May 2nd, except as to the cases against the Post-master General, involving telegraph and telephone intrastate rates, which had previously been specially set to be heard on May 5. Under the rules a case must be moved to be ad-vanced and the motion is not passed on until the Monday fol-lowing the time it is made; also the record must be printed before the case is heard; so that this case only reaching the court in unprinted form on April 26, could not be heard upon the merits on oral argument last term. It was for this reason that this office endeavored to get it decided by making the motion to dismiss or affirm upon the ground that the consti-tutional question raised had been settled by previous decision

STL 2

of the Supreme Court; and that even if the court considered
them not settled so as to dismiss the writ of error for want
of jurisdiction, they were so unfounded that the court ought
to affirm the case on motion. This motion was duly submitted
but the court refused to decide it, but after holding it until
nearly the end of the term, passed an order that it be heard
in connection with the main case.

I will move to advance the case at this term so that it
can be heard. I do not think, however, from what I can learn
from the court, that any cases set down on motion to advance
will be heard earlier than the first Monday in December.

Very truly,

(signed) Alex C. King

Solicitor General.

made to them on behalf of a man imprisoned without benefit of trial. If there appears to be any merit to his contention, and he is not likely to flee, he should be released on bond pending the outcome of the appeal. Of course, appellants out on bond are not nearly as apt to spur on their lawyers as are those cooling their heels in jail.

When the case of *United States v. Silverthorne Lumber Co., et al* has run its course, neither of the Silverthornes, father or son, nor the Silverthorne Lumber Co. or anyone else, will be convicted of any wrongdoing. Yet Frederick W. Silverthorne was imprisoned from April 2 to June 9, 1919, on an order from District Judge Hazel that the Supreme Court will later reverse. The callous indifference to his plight evinced by the correspondence between the Solicitor General and Justice Brandeis was unconscionable. The letters themselves are downright unethical.

With limited exceptions not here germane, it is a breach of ethics for a judge presiding over a case to discuss that case with counsel for one side without counsel for the other side being present. This applies to government lawyers as well. The letters between Circuit Justice Brandeis and Solicitor General King concerning the tactics to be pursued in the Silverthorne case are beyond the pale.

There is yet another curiosity. Had the usual protocols been followed, the originals of King's letters of April 18 and May 13 and a carbon copy of LDB's reply of May 9 would be among the Brandeis Papers. The author is advised by the archivists of the University of Louisville and Harvard Law School, the sole repositories of the Brandeis Papers, that no copy of LDB's letter or the original of either of King's letters is to be found. The reverse would be true of the Solicitor General's papers. Yet no copy of the April 18 letter can be found in the Department of Justice Archives where the letter from Mr. Justice Brandeis and the copy of King's reply now repose.

While the Solicitor General and Justice Brandeis were planning their strategy in *Silverthorne*, the new Attorney General and his Special Assistant were not getting along. A chronology of his career prepared by John Lord O'Brian provides evidence of friction with Palmer. Entries for 1918-19 refer to "[s]trained relations with

Mitchell Palmer"[23] and later to "[f]ears of hysteria affects [?]" and "[d]isbanding of staff of J.L. O'B. being promoted [by] Mitchell Palmer."[24] On May 30, 1919, John Lord O'Brian resigned and returned to Buffalo.[25]

No doubt he was glad to see his old friends. Among them would be James O. Moore, one of the lawyers representing the Silverthornes. When O'Brian was the United States Attorney for the Western District of New York, Moore had been his assistant.[26] In 1920 O'Brian will be the candidate of New York Progressive Republicans opposing the renomination of incumbent Republican Governor Nathan Miller. It will be Moore who will place O'Brian's name in nomination in a speech before the Republican State Convention.[27]

U.S. District Judge for the Western District of New York John R. Hazel was a patron of John Lord O'Brian and before his elevation to the bench was one of "the leading [Republican] political bosses" in Buffalo. O'Brian had "made his first acquaintance with" the judge back in 1904-05.[28] It was Hazel, with Secretary of War Elihu Root looking on, who had administered the oath of office to Theodore Roosevelt after President McKinley's assassination in Buffalo in 1901.[29]

Meanwhile, over at Harvard, Roscoe Pound was debating whether or not he should resign as dean of the law school, a fact which gave Louis Brandeis great concern. "I trust you will not decide definitely in regard to your future without first giving me the opportunity of discussing matters with you. To lose you as a teacher of law and of lawyers would be a calamity,"[30] he told Pound. A few

---

[23] *O'Brian Chronology,* 19.

[24] *O'Brian Chronology,* 20.

[25] *O'Brian Chronology,* 20.

[26] *O'Brian Chronology,* 12.

[27] *O'Brian Chronology,* 21.

[28] *O'Brian Chronology,* 8.

[29] Walter Lord. *The Good Years: From 1900 to the First World War.* New York: Harper & Brothers, 1960, 61.

[30] LDB to RP, May 28, 1919, Brandeis Papers.

weeks later, when Louis Brandeis sailed for England, Roscoe Pound was in New York to see him off. LDB gave Pound a pep talk which he felt "did some good." They "are gunning hard for Felix" as well, he wrote his wife grimly. "Apparently Felix's attitude on the Mooney case is being much discussed."[31]

On June 20 Brandeis arrived at Southampton, where he was met by a delegation including Felix Frankfurter.[32] After a weekend in London, Brandeis and Frankfurter went to Paris, where they met Eustace Percy and Arthur Balfour.[33] On June 25 Justice Brandeis left Paris en route to Palestine. His only companions appear to have been Jacob deHaas and Alfred Zimmern. After a tour of Palestine, Brandeis returned to England via Paris, and, after a three-week stay, he and Frankfurter returned to the United States in early September.

September of 1919 was an eventful month in the history of the United States. The overriding question facing the nation was the health of its President. Miffed at being presented with a *fait accompli,* Republican Senators had expressed reservations about the Versailles Treaty. Woodrow Wilson thereupon decided to take his case to the people and undertook a "whistle stop" tour around the country. After speaking at Pueblo, Colorado, on the 25th of September, the President suffered a stroke which would incapacitate him for the rest of his second term. Many, if not all, of his official duties were thereafter transacted through his second wife as an intermediary. In the opinion of many, if anyone was at the helm of the ship of state, it was Edith Bolling Galt Wilson, whom the President had married in 1915. A recent book lends support to this belief.

After reaching an impasse with Senate Republicans over the ratification of the Versailles Treaty, Gilbert Hitchcock of Nebraska, on behalf of himself and other Senate Democrats, wrote a letter to the President urging compromise. He received a "flat no" from Mrs. Wilson. "On November 17 Hitchcock, still hoping for compromise,

---

[31] LDB to AGB, June 13, 14, 1919, *Brandeis Letters.*

[32] LDB to AGB, June 22, 1919, *Brandeis Letters.*

[33] LDB to AGB, June 25, 1919, *Brandeis Letters* and commentary.

visited the White House. Wilson was wheeled out unto the lawn. 'I beheld an emaciated old man with a thin white beard,' Hitchcock recalled." The answer came in the form of a letter in which Wilson refused to budge. It "did not bear the President's signature . . . the words 'Woodrow Wilson' were affixed thereto by a rubber stamp . . . in purple ink."[34] The Versailles Treaty was never ratified.

On October 4, 1919, the roving Felix Frankfurter, having resumed his professorial duties at Harvard, wrote a letter to Howard Gans in New York. "Dear Howard," he said, "I have had not so much need for your counsel as for your companionship . . . Come up and look at Cambridge. It is really surprisingly lovely."[35] Most likely the invitation was accepted and Gans spent a fall weekend at his alma mater, for the two friends had a lot to talk about.

There would be good news and bad that autumn. Soon Felix Frankfurter would announce his engagement to Marion Denman and two days later, on November 4, Winfred Denison would commit suicide in New York City. But casting a pall over Cambridge were the antagonisms engendered by the Red Scare. The previous term, Roscoe Pound had tried to get three young men appointed to the law school faculty only to be told by the Brahmans who controlled the Harvard Corporation that he was "recommending three Bolsheviks." "All over the country a vigorous attempt is making to push out from our universities everybody suspected of liberal ideas," Pound reported.[36] A month later he wrote Frankfurter that it "seems likely that I shall be made to take a leave of absence." Things had gotten so bad, he added, that the son of one of the members of the Harvard Corporation had had the effrontery to tell Professor Zechariah Chafee "that if he had his way you [FF] would be deported."[37]

The Red baiters then started hounding Harold Laski, the brilliant young Socialist theoretician who had come to Harvard at

---

[34] August Heckscher. *Woodrow Wilson*. New York: Charles Scribner's Sons, 1991, 618, 619.

[35] FF to HG, October 4, 1919, Frankfurter Papers.

[36] RP to FF, April 28, 1919, Frankfurter Papers.

[37] RP to FF, May 17, 1919, Frankfurter Papers.

the urging of Louis Brandeis.[38] In September the Boston Police went out on strike and Massachusetts Governor Calvin Coolidge sent in the National Guard to police Boston. On September 14 Coolidge made the statement which was to catapult him to national prominence and ultimately the White House: "There is no right to strike against the public safety by anybody, anywhere, at any time."

Laski had spoken up for the striking policemen, only to be cruelly abused by the *Harvard Lampoon*. Referring to Laski as the "Great Indoor Agitator," the *Lampoon* observed that it "would be no mean blessing to have the next Soviet Ark that sailed transport this pseudo-instructor from the United States and from Cambridge."[39]

Despite the advice of Brandeis[40] to pay it no mind, the sensitive Socialist was deeply wounded, and the following spring he returned to the more congenial climes of the London School of Economics. Eventually Harold Laski became "the chief intellectual architect of the Labour Party" in Britain.[41] Before sailing with dignity on Cunard, Laski went to Washington to pay his respects to Mr. Justice Brandeis and apprise him of the faculty situation at Harvard Law School. "Harold thinks radicalism will not disturb Felix's position, that Pound & he will be firmly seated, but that the difficulty will come in getting others seated, that is new men," LDB reported to his wife.[42]

When the next term of the Supreme Court began in October of 1919, Solicitor General King moved "to advance this [Silverthorne] case for argument on an early day of the present term convenient to the Court."[43] Two weeks later Stephen T. Lockwood, the U.S. Attorney for the Western District of New York, received a wire informing him that John W. Ryan, a Buffalo lawyer in private

---

[38] LDB to Harold Joseph Laski, April 3, 1916, *Brandeis Letters*. "All of this increases my impatience to have you by Pound's and Felix's side for the upbuilding of the Law School and our law."

[30] *Harvard Lampoon*, January 16, 1920, 401.

[40] LDB to HJL, February 29, 1920, *Brandeis Letters*.

[41] See commentary following LDB to HL, April 3, 1916, *Brandeis Letters*.

[42] LDB to AGB, April 20, 1920, *Brandeis Letters*.

[43] "Motion by the United States to Advance" submitted October 13, 1919.

practice, had been appointed a Special Assistant to the Attorney General to take charge of the *Silverthorne* case. A lawyer for the Railroad Administration described this incident in a letter to his boss.

> On the afternoon of Monday [October 27th] U.S. Attorney Lockwood received a wire from the Attorney General advising him that John W. Ryan had been appointed Special Assistant to the Attorney General to take charge of and conduct all Silverthorne criminal prosecutions in all phases. The wire also directed the U.S. Attorney to render Mr. Ryan "every assistance within your power."[44]

Ryan was a friend and law school classmate of John Lord O'Brian. The obituary of Mr. Ryan in the *Buffalo Courier* of May 30, 1938, shows him to be a member of the Buffalo Law School Class of 1898, as was O'Brian. His obituary and the obituary of O'Brian in the *Buffalo Courier Express* of April 11, 1973, show that Ryan was a vestryman and O'Brian a trustee in the same church. Martindale-Hubbell Lawyers Directory for 1920 shows Ryan was in private practice in Buffalo at the time.

Henry W. Killeen, one of the lawyers for the Silverthornes, sent a telegram to the Attorney General alleging that Ryan had been appointed on O'Brian's recommendation. Killeen thought that the "prosecutions have been instigated and abetted by competitors of Silverthornes" and that O'Brian's interest in the matter was venal. "I understand that Ryan's appointment was made on recommendation of John Lord O'Brian and local railroad attorneys stop Did you know that O'Brian's law partner is interested in a lumber company which competes with Silverthorne for railroad business stop."[45] One can be sure that this protest never reached the eyes or ears of A. Mitchell Palmer.

---

[44] Dan B. Leonard to J.H. Howard, October 30, 1919, File 1627, Railroad Adm.

[45] Henry W. Killeen to A. Mitchell Palmer, February 2, 1920, File 1627, Railroad Adm.

What the *New York Times* had criticized as "the policy of tolerance that marked the attitude of the Department of Justice" towards the Bolshevik movement had come to an end that night of June 2, 1919, among the shards of glass at the home of a badly shaken Attorney General. Being the object of an attempted assassination has a wondrous way of concentrating the mind, and taking a larger view of things with respect to alien revolutionaries, Mitchell Palmer concentrated on rounding them up and shipping them out.

By the autumn of 1919 a large number were detained at Ellis Island in New York Harbor pending deportation. "By November [Roger] Baldwin was coordinating all of the legal efforts." His friend Harry Weinberger was kept so busy fending off deportations that "Judge Learned Hand began calling him 'Harry Habeas Corpus Weinberger.'"[46] In a letter written to his daughter, Justice Brandeis likened the Red Scare to the Spanish Inquisition.

> I have been daily renewing my apologies to Signor Torquemada for all the evil impressions I had harbored. He was doubtless a thorough patriot. The intensity of the frenzy is the most hopeful feature of this disgraceful exhibition;—of hysterical, unintelligent fear—which is quite foreign to the generous American nature."[47]

On November 10, 1919, the Court decided *Abrams v. United States*, 250 U.S. 616. *Abrams* was nothing more than a test of whether the same type of "speech" which "Congress had a right to prevent . . . so long as men fight" could still be prosecuted as a "clear and present danger" after the Armistice was signed and American soldiers fought only the Bolsheviks. A week after the *Abrams* decision, the Silverthornes' lawyers finished their brief. Both *Abrams* and *Silverthorne* arrived on writs of error, and between them they presented in two neat and discrete packages the precise issues the Justices had had before them in *Schenck*. An unfavorable

---

[46] Walker, 30.

[47] LDB to Susan Goldmark, December 7, 1919, *Brandeis Letters*.

decision in one could not prejudice a decision in the other. There was no search and seizure question in *Abrams*; it was a First Amendment case pure and simple.

Abrams was as weak a case of espionage as one could devise, and a gross miscarriage of justice as well. The defendants were given "sentences of twenty years" for the publication of what Mr. Justice Holmes aptly called a "silly leaflet." Nonetheless, the Court, with Holmes and Brandeis dissenting, upheld the convictions. "Mr. Assistant Attorney General [Robert P.] Stewart, with whom Mr. W[illiam] C. Herron was on the brief for the United States" in *Abrams* as soon they will be in *Silverthorne*. Roger Baldwin's ally, Harry Weinberger, briefed and argued the case for Abrams.

The *Abrams* decision evoked a storm of protest, and on the next day, the first anniversary of the Armistice, Red sympathizers held rallies throughout the country. The theme was "amnesty." *All* political prisoners must be released and *all* charges against radicals must be dropped. In Boston, at a rally held at Faneuil Hall, Felix Frankfurter made a speech condemning American intervention in the Russian Civil War and President Wilson's refusal to recognize the Bolshevik regime.[48] The front page of the *Boston Daily Globe* of November 12 gives an insight into what the first Armistice Day was like:

I.W.W. FIRE ON PARADE, 3 DEAD
Ex-Soldiers at Centralia Shot Down by Unseen Foe.

Centralia, Wash. November 11. Three ex-soldiers, members of the American Legion, were killed, two other service men were probably fatally wounded and several other soldiers were less seriously hurt, when persons said to be members of the Industrial Workers of the World fired an on Armistice Day parade today as it passed the I.W.W. hall.

---

[48] Michael E. Parrish. *Felix Frankfurter and His Times: The Reform Years.* New York: The Free Press, 1982, 121.

In Boston a guardsman performing police duty was shot dead. The National Guard was being phased out as new policemen were hired to replace those who had gone out on strike. "Ranks of New Police Force Nearly Full" is the subhead. An article titled "Says Intervention Began Red Terror" describes Frankfurter's speech to the faithful at Faneuil Hall. "On the Committee were John Graham Brooks . . . [and] Prof. Zecharia Chafee."

On November 22, 1919, the Silverthornes' attorneys filed a "Brief on Behalf of the Plaintiffs-in-Error," and on December 8 the Attorney General's Office filed a "Brief on Behalf of the United States." The latter demonstrates that the art of writing "tank briefs" had improved greatly since Winfred Denison took his penultimate dive in 1913.

> At the outset we desire to join counsel for plaintiffs in error in sincere and severe condemnation of the proceedings of the Federal officials in the execution of the first subpoenas. The Department of Justice never has approved of or condoned such lawless action, and it is to be hoped it never will. We can not, however, agree with counsel that such illegal action of subordinate public officials should forever prevent the United States from securing by legal process relevant testimony to a violation of its laws where no right under the fifth amendment can be successfully set up.[49]

The attorneys for the Silverthornes filed a "Reply Brief on Behalf of the Plaintiffs- in-Error" in which this "sincere and severe condemnation" is quoted *in toto* on pages 3 and 4. The "Brief on Behalf of the United States" was filed on December 8 and the "Reply Brief" which quoted from it was filed in printed form on December 10. The oral argument took place on December 12. Let those who complain of the law's delay take heed.

On December 21, 1919, the steamship *Buford* sailed from the Port of New York heavily laden with alien revolutionaries. Among

---

[49] Brief on Behalf of the United States, 47, 48.

their number was Emma Goldman, the "Red Queen of Anarchy," and her consort, Alexander Berkman, who had served 14 years in prison for the shooting of steelman Henry Clay Frick back in 1892. Their case had been argued unsuccessfully before the United States Supreme Court by Harry Weinberger. The *Buford* was expected to be the first "Red Ark" of many.

The decade which would become known as the "Roaring Twenties" began with a surprise on New Year's Day when Harvard, by a score of 7-6, beat Oregon in the Rose Bowl. The following day, January 2, 1920, Attorney General Alexander Mitchell Palmer gave the Reds a far bigger surprise. "Reds Raided In Scores Of Cities; 2,600 Arrests, 700 In New York; Deportation Hearings Begin Today" were the headlines atop the front page of the *New York Times* of January 3. From the tone of the article below, one would have to conclude that the *Times* was pleased that Palmer had finally given up playing "pussy-foot politics." An editorial appearing in the Sunday edition the following day under the headline "Reds By The Thousand" confirms that Mitchell Palmer had redeemed himself in the eyes of the *New York Times*.

> If some or any of us, impatient for the swift confusion of the Reds, have ever questioned the alacrity, resolute will, and fruitful, intelligent vigor of the Department of Justice in hunting down those enemies of the United States, the questioners and the doubters have now cause to approve and applaud. The agents of the department have planned with shrewdness and a large wisdom, and carried out with extraordinary success, the nabbing of nearly four thousand radicals, Communists and Communist Laborites, differentiated by name alone, all working for the destruction of the Government of the United States, and the establishing in its place of the Soviet State that has brought so much happiness and prosperity to Russia . . . The more of these dangerous anarchists are arrested, the more of them are sent back to Europe, the better for the United States. Let us hope that the Department of Labor will have no compassion for such of them as deserve deportation and are not, as most of them are not, American citizens.

Palmer's enforcement of the Deportation Act aroused a crescendo of protest among Progressives. On January 12, 1920, Francis Fisher Kane resigned as United States Attorney for the Eastern District of Pennsylvania, stating he was "entirely out of sympathy with the policy of the department." Kane's letter of resignation received wide publicity. This letter, as well as his picture, appeared in the *Survey* magazine of February 7, 1920, alongside that of John Lord O'Brian, who joined him in denouncing Palmer.

But this was distinctly a minority view. The *New York Times* was not alone in its sentiments as the newspapers of Sunday, January 4, 1920, attest. The lead editorial in the *Washington Post*—"The Red Assassins"—says there is no time to waste. The *Chicago Tribune* trumpeted "All Aboard For Next Soviet Ark." The *Boston Globe* announced with relish "Three Troopships To Carry Off Reds: More than 700 Rounded Up in Greater New York."

The crowning blow came on January 24, 1920, when in the case of an Austrian named Preis, Labor Secretary William Wilson found that the "Communist Party of America was such an organization as is described by the act of October 16, 1918, membership in which makes an alien liable for deportation." This is taken from the front page of the *New York Times* of January 25, 1920, under a column headlined "Finds Communist Membership Reason For Deportation: Decision by Secretary Wilson Affects More Than 3,000 Reds Now Under Arrest. More Arrests to Follow."

The deportation of Reds by the thousands now appeared imminent. But, as the saying goes, "it's always darkest before the dawn." At least that was the way Supreme Court Justice Louis Brandeis saw it from his vantage. On January 20 LDB assured his friend Learned Hand, the U.S. District Judge who had dubbed Roger Baldwin's friend "Harry Habeus Corpus Weinberger," that "we are over the worst of the reaction, or rather, we have a counter current moving."[50] This was to prove a most prescient observation.

---

[50] LDB to LH, January 20, 1920, *Brandeis Letters*.

Chapter X

THE COUNTER CURRENT

It was on Saturday, January 24, 1920, that Secretary of Labor Wilson announced his decision that membership in the Communist Party was grounds for deportation. On Monday, January 26, the Supreme Court handed down its decision in *Silverthorne v. United States*. In an opinion written by Justice Holmes the Court held that the evidence unconstitutionally seized from the corporate offices of the lumber company could not be used against Fred or Asa Silverthorne. In fact, it could not be used at all. The government had no right to avail itself of the knowledge it had obtained by virtue of the unconstitutional search and the examination of documents which it otherwise would not have had. Although few knew it at the time, the counter current Louis Brandeis had forecast had begun.

When Palmer's men pounced upon the Reds on January 2, 1920, they had in hand warrants which, from the newspaper accounts, met the specificity requirements of the Fourth Amendment. Apparently there was a policy of having one warrant for each prospective deportee based upon an affidavit which named that individual and the place where he was to be sought. According to the front page of the *New York Times* of January 7, 1920, "[I]t was announced that the raiding would continue until the last man [in the greater New York City area] named in the original 3,000 deportation warrants had been arrested"—"Novi Mir Raided."

The objection of the Reds to the Palmer raids was not that they were made without warrants or with warrants issued without probable cause. It was how the Justice Department obtained the probable cause originally which was called into question. "Industrial espionage" became a new term in our political lexicon.

> For months Department of Justice men, dropping all other work, had concentrated on the Reds. Agents quietly infiltrated into the radical ranks, slipped casually into centres of agitation, and went to work, sometimes as cooks in remote mining colonies, sometimes as miners, again as steel workers, and, where the opportunity presented itself, as "agitators" of the wildest type. *New York Times*, January 3, 1920, "Raids On 13 Centres Here."

The raids on the meeting places of the Reds were invariably preceded by intelligence work. Mitchell Palmer's men knew beforehand when and where meetings would be held, and who and what they were looking for, this information having been provided by undercover agents. "Undercover agent" is a more auspicious term than "spy," and "intelligence work" is another name for espionage. The Reds and their supporters, of course, denounced what they called industrial espionage as not only illegal but unconstitutional as well. Miraculously, however, they were spared the necessity of litigating this issue themselves by a case whose appearance could not have been more timely or fortuitous.

On February 10, 1920, approximately two weeks after the decision in *Silverthorne* and six weeks after the Palmer raids of January 2, the Second Circuit Court of Appeals determined *not* to decide the case of *Gouled v. United States*, which was then before them. *Gouled* presented a factual situation which was a perfect analogue to that of a Red facing deportation and raised questions of law which would appear to be identical.

Instead of deciding the case themselves, the Second Circuit, by stipulation of the parties, resorted to a rarely used procedure and certified to the Supreme Court the precise questions of law at issue. All the Supreme Court would have to do was to say yes or no. There were six questions, all of interest to a Red facing prosecution or deportation, the first two of which were the most significant.

Questions Certified.

First. Is the secret taking or abstraction without force by a representative of any branch or subdivision of the government of the United States of a paper writing, of evidential value only, belonging to one suspected of crime, and from the house or office of such person, a violation of the Fourth Amendment?

Second. Is the admission of such paper writing in evidence against the same person, when indicted for crime, a violation of the Fifth Amendment?[1]

The *modus operandi* of the Department of Justice was either to infiltrate one of their own into the ranks of a Communist organization or "turn" one of its members into an informer. The object was to secure evidence that groups such as the Union of Russian Workers were organizations in fact seeking to overthrow the government by force or violence and to identify their members. Under the cover of being a fellow Red, the agent would obtain access to documentary evidence and either filch it or abstract it in a handwritten summary. Memberships lists could be copied by hand.

These tactics raised questions of law of vital interest to a Red at bay during the Scare. The first question was whether the use of an agent in such a way constituted an unlawful search—one which might render the evidence inadmissible. Unlike the situation in *Silverthorne*, access to the premises and the papers was not gained by dint of legal authority. To the contrary, entry was obtained with the consent of the owner or occupant, albeit under the mistaken belief that the agent was a comrade.

If the government's agent is legally on the premises, does the covert taking of papers, of value only as evidence, violate the constitutional rights of the organization or its members? Does the surreptitious making of a handwritten synopsis of a document, or the copying of names from a list, constitute a "seizure" within the meaning of the Fourth Amendment? Does the use of such evidence

---

[1] *Gouled v. United States*, 264 F. 839, 841.

compel a person to be a witness against himself in violation of that provision of the Fifth Amendment? These were among the questions certified in *Gouled* on February 10, 1920. Two days later the precedent forged in *Silverthorne* made its debut.

On February 12, in a case arising out of the industrial warfare then raging in Butte, Montana, federal officers had raided the local IWW headquarters and the "adjacent living apartment" of John Jackson, an alien, who was "assistant secretary of the Butte union."[2] Documents were seized tending to show that Jackson was deportable under the Act of 1918, and he was arrested and held for deportation. Jackson sought habeas corpus alleging that the evidence against him in the deportation proceedings was unlawfully secured.

U.S. District Judge George M. Bourguin agreed. Citing "Silverthorne's case," Judge Bourquin held that "the deportation proceedings are unfair and invalid, in that they are based upon evidence and procedure that violate the search and seizure and due process clauses of the Constitution."[3] The order of deportation was set aside and Jackson freed.

Thomas Truss was an alien who had been a member of the IWW as well as the Communist Party and the Union of Russian Workers. On April 10, 1920, Louis F. Post, the Assistant Secretary of Labor, acting in the place of Labor Secretary William B. Wilson—who had taken sick leave—cancelled the deportation warrant against Truss. He then laid down the guidelines that would be followed in future cases. Henceforth evidence seized unlawfully "will be disregarded pursuant both to the principle and the precise decision in *In Re Jackson* and *Silverthorne v. U.S.*"

The following month, over the names of 12 lawyers, a newly formed organization called the National Popular Government League issued a *Report upon the Illegal Practices of the United States Department of Justice*, which condemned the Palmer raids and the persecution of foreign-born radicals. The "Decision of Louis F. Post, Assistant Secretary of Labor, *In Re* Thomas Truss, April 10, 1920" was attached as Exhibit 16. Six of the 12 signatories were

---

2 *Ex Parte Jackson*, 263 F. 110, 112 (1920).
3 Ibid., 112-113.

Felix Frankfurter, Zechariah Chafee, Roscoe Pound, Francis Fisher Kane, Swinburne Hale, and Jackson H. Ralston.

Swinburne Hale had represented the Communist Party in the proceedings which culminated in the finding of Secretary Wilson that the party was such an organization as is described by the Act of October 16, 1918, membership in which makes an alien liable for deportation. Jackson H. Ralston had been representing Louis Post before a committee of the House of Representatives where a move was afoot to impeach Mr. Post. No one, not even Mrs. Wilson, so it seems, was in command of the executive branch of government.

On June 1, 1920, Attorney General A. Mitchell Palmer appeared before the House Rules Committee to answer his critics, particularly Post, who by this time had cancelled thousands of deportation warrants for the reasons he stated in his decision in the case of Thomas Truss. According to the Attorney General, the Acting Secretary of Labor had "nullified" the will of Congress.

> It has become perfectly apparent that Mr. Post's course in all the deportation proceedings has been dictated by his own personal view that the deportation law is wrong, rather than by any desire or intention to carry out the law as enacted by the Congress. By his self-willed and autocratic substitution of his mistaken personal viewpoint for the obligation of public law; by his habitually tender solicitude for social revolutionists and perverted sympathy for the criminal anarchists of the country, he has consistently deprived the people of their day in court in the enforcement of a law of vital importance to their peace and safety. By his wholesale jail deliveries and his release of even self-confessed anarchists of the worst type he has utterly nullified the purpose of the Congress in passing the deportation statute and has set at large amongst the people the very public enemies whom it was the desire and intention of the Congress to be rid of.[4]

---

[4] "Attorney General A. Mitchell Palmer On Charges Made Against Department of Justice By Louis F. Post And Others. Hearings Before The Committee on Rules, House of Representatives, Sixty-Sixth Congress, Second Session, Part 1," 6.

The Attorney General pointed out to the committee that the precedent established in *Silverthorne*, quite wrongfully, was being used to accomplish this usurpation of power. *Silverthorne*, he said, was a criminal case which had no applicability in deportation cases.[5] But Palmer described the *Silverthorne* decision in language which makes one doubt that he ever read it. If indeed he did, Mitchell Palmer never made the "Buffalo connection."

> The Silverthorne case was a case arising in *New York City* and was appealed to the United States Supreme Court and involved the taking of certain papers belonging to the Silverthorne Lumber Co. *without warrant*, and the court held that papers so taken could not be used against an American citizen in a criminal charge.[6]

By June of 1920, thousands of Reds were being held close by ports of embarkation awaiting passage to the places whence they came. Some 700 of these aliens were in custody at Deer Island in Boston Harbor, where they had established "The Soviet Republic of Deer Island."[7] Writs of habeas corpus were obtained from the U.S. District Court in Boston requiring Henry J. Skeffington, that port's Commissioner of Immigration, to produce the deportees and to "show cause" why they were being held. This became the case of *Colyer v. Skeffington*, decided June 23, 1920, which the "dual biographer" of Brandeis and Frankfurter says straight out was a "setup."

> *Colyer v. Skeffington* was a setup. To head off a threatened deportation action before a judge friendly to the Palmer side, the anti-Palmer forces looked for a test case to produce a decision against Palmer. They wanted the right judge to hear the case, the appropriate lawyers to be involved, and evidence placed in the record to embarrass Palmer.[8]

---

[5] Ibid., 206.
[6] Ibid., 70 [emphasis added].
[7] *Colyer v. Skeffington*, 265 F. 17,45.
[8] Leonard Baker, 254.

The casting was flawless. The nominal plaintiffs were an English couple who were apparently the most presentable proletarians to be found in the new republic. They were "people of a high type, intelligent, [who] do not advocate violence." Nonetheless they qualified as "bona fide members of the Communist Party."[9] "The ACLU had played an important role in this case, providing associate counsel and arranging for news coverage."[10]

The Immigraton Commissioner, Henry J. Skeffington, was used to taking care of political chores for Louis Brandeis,[11] which may have had something to do with his appointment in 1913. "A Democratic labor man," Skeffington was a "good friend" of Justice Brandeis, as was the judge who was to try the case,[12] George Weston Anderson, the former Massachusetts Public Service Commissioner. You will recall it was he who cautioned Brandeis back in 1913 "that our activities, should be quiet—subterranean. Subterranean activities, you know, befit a Public Service Commissioner in Massachusetts." Apparently they befit federal judges as well.

Judge Anderson appointed Felix Frankfurter to serve as *amicus curiae* in the *Colyer* case and at Frankfurter's request named his colleague Zechariah Chafee as well. The two Harvard Law professors must have done a first-rate job because Anderson was unstinting in his praise and "appreciation of their unselfish and highly professional endeavors to assist in the proper determination"[13] of the case. Nothing less would suffice in a test case of this magnitude.

---

[9] Ibid.

[10] Donald Johnson. *The Challenge to American Freedoms: World War I and the Rise of the American Civil Liberties Union*. Lexington: University of Kentucky Press, 1963, 162, citing letters from Roger Baldwin to Anna L. Davis, March 29, 30, 1920 and Baldwin to Marian Sproule, April 2, 1920, ACLUP.

[11] LDB to Norman Hill White, May 29, 1909, *Brandeis Letters*: "My Dear Norman: *First:* I have just seen [Henry J.] Skeffington. He has arranged to spend the day Tuesday at the State House, and put himself under your instructions. He would like to have you then furnish him a list of the men whom you specifically wish him to see. He assumes that a large number of those on his old list have already been attended to by others" [brackets in original].

[12] LDB to Norman Hapgood, July 9, 1913, *Brandeis Letters*. "George W. Anderson . . . and Skeffington, a Democratic labor man,—both good friends of mine,—came to me separately yesterday to urge me . . . to run for the Massachusetts Attorney Generalship."

[13] *Colyer*, 22.

> At the opening of the trial the cases were said by counsel
> on both sides to be, in many important aspects, test cases
> of the legality of an undertaking of the government to
> deport several thousand aliens alleged to be proscribed
> by a portion of section 1 of the Act of October 16, 1918 .[14]

No one from the Attorney General's Office made an appearance. "No counsel from the departments in Washington has rendered the slightest assistance on the law or the facts," according to Judge Anderson. This does not mean, perish the thought, that the people of the United States went unrepresented.

> It should be added that, at the close of the hearing,
> Assistant United States Attorney Lewis Goldberg, who
> has presented the government's side of the cause with very
> great ability, urging every possible authority offering any
> support for the government's proceedings, expressed
> himself as fully content with the opportunity given the
> government to present all evidence and arguments which
> might sustain its view of the law and the facts.[15]

Now one would think counsel for the government, be that person from the Attorney General's Office in Washington or the U.S. Attorney's Office in Boston, would have asked Judge George W. Anderson to explain a public statement which, to say the very least, raised grave doubts about his ability to try the case of *Colyer v. Skeffington* fairly and objectively. Failing to receive a satisfactory explanation, an advocate for the United States, at all times keeping the Attorney General fully advised, would have asked Judge Anderson to recuse himself, and, if the Judge refused, would have pressed the matter before a higher tribunal. On January 12, 1920, as the Reds were being ferried to Deer Island, in an address to the Harvard Liberal Club, George Anderson had this to say of the "so-called 'Red menace.'"

> . . . It is a depressing,—almost appalling fact,—that, as

---

[14] *Colyer*, 21.
[15] *Colyer*, 22.

an aftermath of our "war to make the world safe for democracy," real democracy now seems unsafe in America. It is increasingly clear that America's loss of valuable lives and of money in this war was as nothing compared to her loss of moral, social, and political values.

. . . Many,—perhaps most,—of the agitators for the suppression of the so-called "Red menace," are, I observe, the same individuals, or class of forces, that in the years '17 and '18 were frightening the community to death about pro-German plots . . . .

There will be no sun-strokes in Massachusetts this month.

There will be no Red revolution this year . . . .

The heresy-hunter has throughout history been one of the meanest of men. It is time that we had freedom of speech for the just contempt that every wholesome-minded citizen has and should have for the pretentious, noisy, heresy-hunter of these hysterical times.[16]

But the advocate for the government was not in a very good position to challenge Judge Anderson's impartiality. Assistant United States Attorney Lewis Goldberg was a member of the Harvard College Class of 1911 and the Harvard Law School Class of 1913. It was United States Attorney for the District of Massachusetts George W. Anderson who had appointed Goldberg to his post in 1915. A naturalized citizen himself, the Lithuanian-born Goldberg must have felt a certain empathy with his adversaries and deserves full credit for his steadfastness in having "presented the government's side of the cause with very great ability."[17]

Right after the old English cases of *Wilkes v. Wood* and *Entinck v. Carrington* made a brief appearance on stage, Judge Anderson

---

[16] Dean Acheson. *Morning and Noon.* Boston: Houghton Mifflin Company, 1965, 116-117.

[17] The biographical material is taken from the obituaries of Judge Lewis Goldberg in the *New York Times* of April 14, 1974, and the *Boston Globe* of the same date.

cited, as "a careful review of the history of the spy system in industry and in dealing with political movements," *Labor's Challenge to the Social Order*, a monograph by his friend and fellow Cosmos Club member John Graham Brooks. The star performer had to wait in the wings until James Otis finished denouncing the writs of assistance.

Silverthorne brought down the house. Deciding every controverted question of fact in favor of the petitioners, Judge Anderson made its holding the cornerstone of his opinion. The precedent of *Silverthorne* fit *Colyer* like Cinderella's slipper.[18] These are the words of *Silverthorne* he quoted and held to be controlling.

> The proposition could not be presented more nakedly. It is that although of course its seizure was an outrage which the government now regrets, it may study the papers before it returns them, copy them, and then may use the knowledge that it has gained to call upon the owners in a more regular form to produce them; that the protection of the Constitution covers the physical possession but not any advantages that the government can gain over the object of its pursuit by doing the forbidden act . . .

> It reduces the Fourth Amendment to a form of words. 232 U.S. 393. The essence of a provision forbidding the acquisition of evidence in a certain way is that not merely evidence so acquired shall not be used before the court, but that it shall not be used at all.[19]

The government's case depended on proving that the Deer Island Soviet Republicans were members of the Communist Party and that the Communist Party was such an organization as is described in the Act of October 16, 1918. The evidence of the aims of the Communist Party, and of the deportees' membership in it, consisted for the most part of the manifestos and membership lists

---

[18] On pages 26 and 27 Judge Anderson quoted virtually the entire last half of the *Silverthorne* opinion.
[19] *Colyer*, 27, quoting *Silverthorne*.

found in searches of the party's headquarters and evidence later adduced therefrom.

This evidence, held Judge Anderson, had been seized in violation of the Fourth Amendment and, under the ruling of *Silverthorne,* could not be used "at all." It followed therefore that the government had not met its burden of proof by evidence which was constitutionally admissible. Contrary to the prior holding of Labor Secretary Wilson, Judge Anderson found that there was no evidence that the petitioners were members of the Communist Party or that the Communist Party was an organization advocating the overthrow of the government of the United States by force or violence. He ordered the petitioners discharged from the custody of the immigration authorities. *Colyer v. Skeffington* was the culmination of a six-month counter current that began with the *Silverthorne* decision on January 26, 1920.

Elizabeth Gurley Flynn was a friend of Roger Baldwin and a founding member of the American Civil Liberties Union.[20] In 1918, with funds secured by Baldwin, she founded the Workers Liberty Defense Union, dedicated to securing amnesty for all political prisoners. In her autobiography she relates how "the deportation delirium let loose by Palmer ran its course and was finally stopped by the pressure of public opinion."

> Louis F. Post, Assistant Secretary of the Department of Labor, cancelled 1,547 deportation warrants and made a principled stand against Palmer's lawlessness, when impeachment proceedings were lodged against him. Nothing came of the proceedings.
>
> There was tremendous protest against the Palmer raids. Francis Fisher Kane, U.S. Attorney of Philadelphia, resigned in protest. Federal Judge George W. Anderson spoke out strongly in Boston against the invasion of civil rights. A brochure entitled "Report on the Illegal Practices of the Department of Justice," signed by 12

---

[20] Annual Report No. 1, 1920-1921, shows Mrs. Flynn to be a national committeewoman of the ACLU, a post she held for many years.

eminent lawyers, was issued in May 1920. It was addressed "To the American People." Among those who signed were Professors Frankfurter, Pound, Freund and Chafee, Mr. Kane, Frank P. Walsh and Jackson H. Ralston, general counsel of the AFL. It was a scathing exposé of how these raids flouted the Constitution and all legal procedure.[21]

The week after Judge Anderson's decision in *Colyer v. Skeffington*, the 1920 Democratic National Convention opened in San Francisco. William Gibbs McAdoo and A. Mitchell Palmer were the leading contenders for the Presidential nomination. On the 38th ballot McAdoo had a delegate count of 405½, Palmer 383½, and Ohio Governor James M. Cox 211, with a two-thirds majority of the 1,000 delegates required for nomination.

Refusing to make a deal with McAdoo, Palmer threw his support to Cox, who was nominated on the 44th ballot. Cox then chose as his vice-presidential running mate Franklin Delano Roosevelt, the 38-year-old neighbor of the Palmers at whose home they had stayed the night they were bombed out by the Reds. While the ticket of Cox and Roosevelt will go down to defeat, it was this nomination which gave FDR the boost he needed to become governor of New York and ultimately President of the United States.

After the election Mr. Justice Brandeis began a behind-the-scenes public relations campaign against "espionage." On November 26, 1920, he wrote Frankfurter that he had told a journalist with *The New Republic* that "the N.R. ought to take up a continuous campaign against espionage . . . If [Editor Herbert] Croly takes up the fight for its eradication, the immorality, the ungentlemanliness, should be made the keynote, & not the industrial wrong or infringement of liberty as in the Red Campaign. *It is unAmerican. It is nasty. It is nauseating.*" In February and March of 1921, as a result of LBD's suggestion, the *New Republic* published a seven-part series entitled "The Labor Spy."[22]

---

[21] Elizabeth Gurley Flynn. *The Rebel Girl: An Autobiography.* New York: International Publishers, 1973, 257.
[22] See *Half Brother, Half Son*, No. 36 and commentary.

As Louis Brandeis penned these words, *Gouled,* the case which will resolve the constitutional implications of "industrial espionage," had taken its place on the Court's docket. He must have been aware of the case since the questions had been certified with great care and precision by the Court of Appeals of the Second Circuit over which Circuit Justice Brandeis presided. It became *Gouled v. United States,* Potter Stewart's next case on *The Road to Mapp v. Ohio and Beyond.*[23]

> [I]n January, 1918, it was suspected that the defendant, Gouled, and Vaughan were conspiring to defraud the Government through contracts with it for clothing and equipment; that one Cohen, a private in the Army, attached to the Intelligence Department, and a business acquaintance of defendant Gouled, under direction of his superior officers, pretending to make a friendly call upon the defendant, gained admission to his office and, in his absence, without warrant of any character, seized and carried away several documents . . . [24]

Gouled v. United States was argued January 4, 1921, and decided February 28, 1921, in the waning days of the Wilson administration. Before addressing the grave questions posed by the court below, the Supreme Court alluded to some of the darker pages of our Fourth and Fifth Amendment history. It was a stark reminder of the excesses of the past and evinced a firm resolve that such usurpations would be tolerated no longer.

> It would not be possible to add to the emphasis with which the framers of our Constitution and this court (in *Boyd v. United States,* 116 U.S. 616, in *Weeks v. United States* , 232 U.S. 383, and in *Silverthorne Lumber Co. v. United States,* 251 U.S. 385) have declared the importance to political liberty and to the welfare of our country of the due observance of the rights guaranteed under the Constitution by these two Amendments . . .

---

[23] P. Stewart, 1376.
[24] *Gouled v. United States,* 255 U.S. 298, 304 (1921).

> It has been repeatedly decided that these Amendments
> should receive a liberal construction, so as to prevent
> stealthy encroachment upon or "gradual depreciation"
> of the rights secured by them, by imperceptible practice
> of courts or by well-intentioned but mistakenly over-
> zealous executive officers.[25]

The Court then went on to answer all six questions in the affirmative. And so in February of 1921, rules were established which will be the salvation of the embattled Bolsheviks. As in *Silverthorne*, it came not in a case involving a Red, but in a case of another businessman trying to cheat the government.[26]

Silverthorne and *Gouled*—between them—made virtually every deportation a contestable proceeding. A warrant would be issued on probable cause, supported by an affidavit of an immigration officer, particularly describing a named individual as an alien deportable under the Act of October 16, 1918. The warrant would be served on that person and he would be arrested and held for deportation.

At this point the detainee would obtain a writ of habeas corpus on the ground that he was being held in violation of the Constitution. A hearing would be held to put the Immigration Department to their proof. Evidence would be introduced that the detainee—now called the relator—was a member of an organization advocating the overthrow of the government by force or violence. Necessarily this evidence would be in documentary form.

The relator would then object to its admission. Since the Communist Party had never released a list of its members, this evidence must have been obtained, so he alleges, in an unlawful search and accordingly must be excluded under the *Weeks* rule. The search to which he alludes does not pertain to his own arrest in which the requirements of the Fourth Amendment were scrupulously observed, but rather to an earlier search and seizure made at party headquarters, as to which, under the holding of

---

[25] Ibid., 303-304.

[26] For a small-time crook Felix Gouled certainly had eminent counsel. Former Associate Justice and future Chief Justice Charles Evans Hughes, the unsuccessful Republican candidate for President in 1916, argued the case on his behalf (255 U.S. 299).

Schenck v. United States, an individual Red had no standing to object. These two cases changed the rules of engagement so that with respect to Communist Party membership *Silverthorne* could be used to challenge evidence taken in searches made pursuant to a warrant and *Gouled* evidence obtained through the espionage Louis Brandeis so abhorred.

It was the colluded case of *Colyer v. Skeffington*, which rested on the colluded case of *Silverthorne v. United States*, which superseded the precedent established in *Schenck v. United States*, a fraud that failed, that gave the Reds the legal imprimatur they needed to turn the tables on the Attorney General. A court of law, so it would appear, after duly hearing all the evidence, had denounced the Red raids as unconstitutional. Thereafter, the raids rather than the Reds became the issue.

And so it was, during the so-called Red Scare, that the deportation of alien revolutionaries was thwarted by the manipulation and subversion of the rule of law. Legitimate inquiry into enforcement of the Deportation Act of 1918 thereafter would be shunted aside by the Reds and their "Parlor Pink" supporters and ridiculed as some sort of trauma—"delirium," "scare," "hysteria" or whatever—Americans suffered to their psyche in the aftermath of the World War.

Had Woodrow Wilson been in possession of his faculties, none of this would have come to pass. It is inconceivable that the President who had sent American troops to fight the Bolsheviks in Russia would have permitted an *Acting* Secretary of Labor to overrule his Attorney General and nullify the Deportation Act he had signed into law. But Mitchell Palmer on his own was not up to the occasion. Whatever his intellectual attainments, Palmer lacked the political acumen and the skills to fight back effectively.

Mitchell Palmer left office with the Wilson administration in 1921 and took up the private practice of law in Washington. While he never sought public office again, Palmer remained an influential figure in the Democratic Party. "He campaigned for John W. Davis in 1924 and for Al Smith in 1928. In 1932, as a delegate to the Chicago convention, he supported Franklin D. Roosevelt for the presidential nomination and is credited with writing most of the campaign platform."[27]

In January of 1922 *Colyer v. Skeffington* was reversed *in toto* by the First Circuit Court of Appeals in *Skeffington v. Katzeff*, as to each and every one of the petitioners. "The entry in each case must be: The decree of the District Court is reversed, the petition for writ of habeas corpus is denied, the writ is discharged, and the relators are remanded into the custody of the Commissioner of Immigration."[28] But few, if any, were ever deported. By then the Bolsheviks had turned Russia and the other countries they had seized into the Union of Soviet Socialist Republics, which this country did not recognize until 1933. International law made it impossible for the United States to deport an alien to a country with which it did not maintain diplomatic relations. LDB's counter current had bought the Reds the necessary time.

While the case of *United States v. Silverthorne Lumber Co. et al* had been wending its way through the legal process, other characters in this story had been having their own problems. In November of 1918 Roger Baldwin had been sentenced to prison for violating the Selective Service Act but "he emerged from prison on July 19, 1919, committed to the cause of radical though peaceful social change."[29] In August Baldwin married Madeline Doty and after a brief honeymoon left to work "as a wage-worker to study the psychology and conditions of labor at first-hand."[30] Roger Baldwin joined the IWW and sent Bill Haywood "the first dollar I ever earned at productive labor."[31] On July 28 Big Bill Haywood, like Frederick Silverthorne the month before, was released on bail pending his appeal. "For the next eighteen months he toured the country speaking on behalf of the IWW and those Wobblies still in jail."[32]

---

[27] *Dictionary of American Biography, supra.*

[28] *Skeffington v. Katzeff,* 277 F. 129, 133 (1922).

[29] Walker, 42.

[30] Letter RNB—"To my friends," July 31, 1919, Box 3, Roger Nash Baldwin Papers (cited hereafter as Baldwin Papers), Seeley G. Mudd Manuscript Library, Princeton University. Used by permission of the Princeton University Library.

[31] Walker, 46.

[32] Joseph R. Conlin. *Big Bill Haywood and the Radical Union Movement.* Syracuse: Syracuse University Press, 1969, 194.

On October 5, in the midst of the 1920 election campaign, the Seventh Circuit Court of Appeals decided the case of *Haywood v. United States*.[33] The defendants, said the Court, were correct in their contention that the search warrants issued by Judge Evans were deficient.

> The greater part [of the evidence] was taken in Chicago from the general headquarters in charge of Haywood. The affidavits, on which the search warrants issued, failed to describe the property to be taken except by reference to its general character, and failed to state any facts from which the magistrates could determine the existence of probable cause. If the proper parties had made prompt application, it may be assumed that they would have obtained orders quashing the writs and restoring the property.[34]

However "nothing of the sort occurred. Government attorneys, without objection or hindrance, used the property as evidence before the grand jury. Indictment was returned on September 28, 1917," and it was not until "February, 1918, [that the] defendants petitioned the court for an order to return the property." This was too late. Had Haywood et al. moved in a more timely manner, *Silverthorne* might have been their salvation.

> If, following restoration, Haywood and others were adjudged to be in contempt for refusing to obey subpoenas and orders of court to produce the files and documents before the grand jury, it may be assumed that such judgments would be reversed. *Silverthorne Lumber Company v. United States*, 251 U.S. 385 . . .[35]

On April 11, 1921, the Supreme Court of the United States denied certiorari in the case of *Haywood v. United States*.[36] The law

---

[33] 268 F. 795.
[34] Haywood, 801.
[35] Ibid.
[36] 256 U.S. 689.

had finally run its course for the Wobblies. But by this time Big Bill was in more congenial climes.

> Haywood dropped from sight in early March, 1921, shortly after speaking at the socialist Rand School and visiting old friends in New York. With the inevitable false passport, he boarded the *Oscar II*, Henry Ford's "peace ship" just a few years before. Hidden in the steerage until the ship cleared the piers, Haywood came up on deck as the *Oscar* passed the Statue of Liberty. "Saluting the old hag with her uplifted torch, I said: Good-by you've had your back turned on me too long. I am now going to the land of freedom."[37]

After receiving a hero's welcome, Big Bill Haywood lived out his life in the U.S.S.R. He died on May 17, 1928, and his funeral was a big event. "His body was taken in a red hearse to the front yard of the Club House of Political Prisoners, socially Moscow's *ne plus ultra*."[38] "Big Bill Haywood was cremated; half his ashes are buried in Chicago and half in Moscow."[39]

We cannot close until we put the Silverthornes to rest; the January 1920 decision of the Supreme Court did not end the case against them. The charge against the Silverthornes, you will recall, was that they had cheated the Lehigh Valley Railroad—and vicariously the U.S.A. since the railroads had been taken over by the federal government—by loading grain door boards on Lehigh Valley box cars in such a way that all of the boards were on the outside and the center was hollow. The box cars would appear fully loaded when they were not.

The Silverthornes' trial began in October of 1920. John W. Ryan, the Buffalo attorney in private practice who had been appointed a special federal attorney, prosecuted them with a tenacity unmatched in the history of the Western District of New York. "Silverthornes'

---

[37] Conlin, 197, 198.

[38] Conlin, 208.

[39] Bernard K. Johnpoll and Harvey Klehr. *Biographical Dictionary of the American Left.* Westport, Connecticut: Greenwood Press, 1986, 195.

case longest ever held in this District" was the title of an article in the *Buffalo Express* of November 12. On December 6 the *Buffalo Courier* carried a story—"That Silverthorne Trial . . . Today begins the ninth week of the trial, which has been one of the longest in this judicial district." But in the end the jury was unable to reach a verdict and a mistrial was declared. The *Buffalo Courier* of February 10, 1921, tells how it all ended:

> ASA SILVERTHORNE STRICKEN DEAD IN TONAWANDA OFFICE . . . Defendant in a Federal Suit . . . Mr. Silverthorne displayed a courage during this fight which was remarkable. He maintained an attitude that won him friends. At all times he protested his innocence of the charges against him. The case was noted for the number of motions and the various procedures taken before the case was brought to trial.

One of these "procedures" was the writ of error upon which the Supreme Court had ruled that the books and papers seized in the unlawful search of the offices of the Silverthorne Lumber Company, Inc., and evidence adduced therefrom, could not be used at all. Although it came too late to help Big Bill Haywood and the Wobblies, the ruling started the counter current which saved thousands of Reds from deportation and put an end to the Scare. Asa Silverthorne, like Mitchell Palmer, never knew what hit him.

Chapter XI

THE NOBLE EXPERIMENT

On January 16, 1919, the Eighteenth Amendment to the United States Constitution was ratified by the requisite number of states. It gave Americans one year to prepare for national Prohibition.

> 1. After one year from the ratification of this article, the manufacture, sale, or transportation of intoxicating liquors within, the importation thereof into, or the exportation thereof from the United States and all territory subject to the jurisdiction thereof for beverage purposes is hereby prohibited.
>
> 2. The Congress and the several States shall have concurrent power to enforce this article by appropriate legislation.

Prohibition was distinctly a creature of Protestant fundamentalism. "[R]ural, agricultural America with its large Protestant, native-born population thrust prohibition upon urban, industrial America, with its heterogeneity of races, religions and foreign backgrounds."[1] The "principal adherents" of the Anti-Saloon League, who spearheaded the temperance movement, "consisted of rural Methodists, followed, in order of importance, by Bible Belt

---

[1] John Kobler. *Ardent Spirits, The Rise and Fall of Prohibition*. New York: G.P. Putnam's Sons, 1973, 217.

Baptists, Presbyterians, Congregationalists and several smaller fundamentalists sects."[2] The League never deviated in its goal.

> Unlike those drys who . . . formed the independent Prohibition Party or unlike the WCTU, which divided and weakened itself bickering over moralistic issues, the Leaguers were prepared to strike a bargain with the devil if it advanced their grand design of drying up America . . . They hewed to the single purpose of making drinking a crime.[3]

The leader and general counsel for the Anti-Saloon League was an Ohio lawyer by the name of Wayne Wheeler. "Wheeler, more than any other man, was responsible for the strategy which inserted the liquor-banning Eighteenth Amendment into the U.S. Constitution."[4] His strategy was as simple as it was effective.

> Before an election the League would ask both Republican and Democratic candidates how they stood on temperance legislation. If both replied to its satisfaction, it would abstain from further interference in the race; if only one, it would back him; and if none, it would put forward an independent candidate of its own.[5]

The votes which led to the passage of Prohibition left no doubt of the political power of the Drys. The Eighteenth Amendment was adopted in the Senate by a vote of 65 to 20, and in the House of Representatives it passed by a majority of 282 to 128.[6] It ultimately was adopted by the legislatures of all states except Connecticut and Rhode Island.

The election of 1920 had given Wayne Wheeler an ally in the

[2] Kobler, 184.
[3] Kobler, 191.
[4] Thomas M. Coffey. *The Long Thirst—Prohibition in America: 1920-1933*. New York: W.W. Norton & Company, Inc., 1975, 8.
[5] Kobler, 195.
[6] Kobler, 211.

White House. "He was Sen. Warren G. Harding, another Ohioan, a proven friend of Wheeler's and of the prohibition cause. Harding, under Wheeler's guidance, had floor-managed the eighteenth Amendment ratification bill through the Senate in 1918."[7] The Anti-Saloon League backed the Republican ticket of Warren Harding and Calvin Coolidge over Democrats James M. Cox and Franklin D. Roosevelt. Cox, the incumbent governor of Ohio, was, in Wheeler's opinion, "more wet than dry."[8]

> When Harding went to the White House, Wheeler's influence in national affairs already great, doubled overnight. He installed one of his protégés, Roy Asa Haynes, as Federal Prohibition Commissioner. The Prohibition Bureau was forced on the Treasury Department, which did not want it, instead of the Justice Department, which specialized in law enforcement. Wheeler appears to have feared that the Justice Department would have tried to run the Prohibition Bureau, instead of letting him do it by remote control.[9]

Prohibition had but a limited impact on the drinking habits of those on high. Wheeler tried to get the President to take the pledge without success. Harding explained that he drank for medicinal purposes only. "His drinking had been a lifelong habit, he pleaded, and therefore it might be harmful to his health if he were suddenly to stop it."[10] Congressional drinking was a bipartisan policy.

> Under the Capitol dome itself, a few steps from the chamber where Congress passed the Volstead Act, there nestled a small, inconspicuous room . . . It was designated "the Board of Education" room, but initiates knew it better as "the Library." What took place there bore scant relation to either education or literature. Set up jointly by Congressmen Nicholas Longworth,

---

[7] Coffey, 37.
[8] Coffey, 36.
[9] Geoffrey Perrett. *America in the Twenties - A History*. New York: Simon and Schuster 1982, 170.
[10] Coffey, 117.

Republican of Ohio, and John Nance Garner, Democrat of Texas, whose common fondness for whiskey enabled them to surmount their political antagonism, it provided a snug retreat . . . The books concealed an abundance of liquor.[11]

The Eighteenth Amendment gave "Congress and the several states . . . concurrent power to enforce this article by appropriate legislation." The Volstead Act, passed by Congress in 1919, created a federal agency—the Prohibition Bureau—with the power and the duty of enforcing Prohibition throughout the United States. But it was never contemplated that the task of keeping America dry would be the responsibility of the federal government alone. The individual states were expected to do their share.

Most states in fact did pass enforcement legislation. In 1921, for example, New York passed a replication of the Volstead Act called the Mullan-Gage Law. During the first three years of its existence 6,904 Prohibition cases were presented to grand juries, of which only 20 resulted in a conviction.[12] The dearth of convictions was not because New Yorkers suddenly had become abstemious.

The clandestine drinking establishments which proliferated during Prohibition were called "speakeasies." In 1922 New York City Police Commissioner Grover Whalen estimated that there were 32,000 in that city alone. "'All you need is two bottles and a room and you have a speakeasy,' he observed."[13] It did not take long for New Yorkers to catch on.

> In certain New York social circles the line between hospitality and profit grew thin. The *New York Times* of June 6, 1922, reported:
>
> Many individuals, some prominent socially, have fitted up regular bars in their living apartments and have engaged drink mixers. The patronage is restricted to the

---

[11] Kobler, 242.

[12] Kobler, 236.

[13] Kobler, 224.

set in which the owner of the place moves. Several persons have greatly added to their finances through the operation of the apartment bar. At some places drinks of the best grade are sold for 40 to 50 cents.[14]

Speakeasies ranged from "blind pigs" to full-fledged nightclubs that catered to well-heeled revelers out for a night on the town. But for every nightclub like Sherman Billingsley's Stork Club or El Fey where Mary Louise "Texas" Guinan hailed guests with her trademark greeting— "hello, suckers"—there were probably a thousand speakeasies which could be characterized as a "mom and pop" operation.

Few people had automobiles in the 1920s. The shopping center was a thing of the future. In the big cities all but a few relied on public transportation. Housewives shopped on foot and, since there were no refrigerators, did so on a daily basis. They bought meat from the butcher, seafood from the fishmonger, and groceries from the grocer. Most of these stores fronted on the street and were usually located on the ground floor of a walk-up apartment building. They were owned and operated by independent tradesmen, and, as often as not, the living quarters of the proprietor and his wife—"mom and pop"—were appurtenant to their place of business. The same was true of the neighborhood speakeasy.

Illicitly manufactured whiskey was called "moonshine" and most was made in the home. All one had to do was to set up a still in the kitchen or basement and let fermentation take care of the rest. What was not used for home consumption might be sold to the local speakeasy. The home brewing of beer could be a family enterprise. "Mother's in the kitchen, washing out the jugs; Sister's in the pantry, bottling the suds; Father's in the cellar, mixing up the hops; Johnny's on the porch, watching for the cops," went a 1920s ditty. But according to Commissioner Roy Asa Haynes, Prohibition was a conspicuous success.

As Wheeler's puppet Prohibition Commissioner, a position he filled for six years, Haynes consistently

---

[14] Kobler, 235, 236.

issued glowing progress reports. "The Amendment is
being enforced to an even greater extent than many of its
devoted friends anticipated [January, 1922] . . . . [The]
home brew fad is taking its last gasp [December, 1922]
. . . . Bootleg patronage has fallen off fifty per cent [April,
1923] . . . . There is little open and above-board drinking
anywhere [December, 1923] . . . . " Scandal, meanwhile,
continued to erupt at every level of Haynes' command.[15]

The Volstead Act had "exempted prohibition agents from the
civil service rules, leaving it to the party in power to dispense
appointments as spoils . . . patronage loaded the personnel rolls of
the Prohibition Bureau with illiterates, incompetents, misfits and
criminals."[16] "Few instruments of law enforcement ever aroused
greater contempt and loathing than the prohibition agents."
"Swinish"—so one newspaperman characterized them.[17]

Chester Mills, the Prohibition administrator of greater New
York City, "found himself saddled with a staff of 228 Republican
spoilsmen and only 12 Democrats, many of them corrupt, stupid or
both. He protested . . . to a national committeeman of the
Republican Party, who bluntly informed him that the patronage
system existed everywhere, and that the Second District would be
no exception."[18] Mills was forced to reinstate four agents he had just
fired for corruption. Bribery and extortion were the rule rather than
the exception.

> However meager the salary, many an agent found
> compensation in the opportunities for graft. During a
> dispute with Agent Levy's political sponsor Major Mills
> asked somewhat ingenuously how anybody as valuable
> as the sponsor claimed Levy to be could content himself
> with such paltry [$1,200-$2,800 per annum] pay.
> "We're all over twenty-one," Mills was told. "He wants
> the job to get his the same as the rest of them in this

---

[15] Kobler, 274.
[16] Kobler, 275.
[17] Kobler, 272.
[18] Kobler, 276.

prohibition racket." Agent Kerrigan once had the temerity to estimate publicly that a dry agent's job was worth $40,000 to $50,000 a year.[19]

Smuggling was rife. The Great Lakes and the St. Lawrence River teemed with small, swift craft plying their way from newly built Canadian warehouses to the thousands of small coves and inlets that dot the coast from Maine to Minnesota. Smugglers were active on the high seas as well. Foreign ships lay off the coast to wholesale whiskey to "rumrunners" in speed boats. The three-mile limit became known as "Rum Row." A boat builder named William McCoy achieved fame and fortune smuggling in genuine Scotch whiskey from the British West Indies. Whiskey bearing the label of traditional foreign distillers became known as "the real McCoy."

But "the real McCoy" was expensive and most imbibers had to rely on home-fermented spirits. Homeowners became vintners as well. At the grocery store one could buy bricks of grape concentrate with instructions of what not to do lest you violate the law and cause them to ferment. Caution!—Do not add water and leave in jar or these grapes will turn into a delicious Burgundy wine, the possession of which is forbidden by the Volstead Act. "From 1925 to 1929 Americans drank more than . . . three times as much as all of the domestic and imported wine they drank during the five years before prohibition."[20] But moonshine was by far the biggest cottage industry.

> Far simpler than brewing beer or fermenting wine at home was distilling alcohol . . . Steam cookers, coffee percolators and wash boilers were also commonly used as receptacles for mash. But at a cost of only $5 or $6 the home distiller could buy the more sophisticated portable one-gallon copper still . . . By 1921 the one-gallon still had become a commonplace domestic utensil, and over some sections of the big cities the reek of sour mash hung like a miasma.[21]

---

[19] Kobler, 277.

[20] Kobler, 240.

[21] Kobler, 240, 241.

The operations of those who made a business of violating the Prohibition laws, and the location of their establishments, were well known to local law enforcement authorities. City policemen, however, did not consider the enforcement of the Volstead Act to be one of their obligations. To the contrary, they did everything they could to thwart it. Of course, these immunities did not come without a fee. Syndicates of hoodlums backed by politicians carved out territories in all of the major cities of the United States. Their sovereignty was enforced by the bomb and the Thompson submachine gun. So long as they killed only each other, no one really cared. The police and the politicians were paid to look the other way. Prohibition corrupted law enforcement nationwide and at every level.

While the minions of the Prohibition Bureau were lining their pockets, an upheaval was taking place at the very top of the administration whose campaign slogan was "A Return to Normalcy." Charles A. Forbes, a friend of President Harding, had been appointed to head the Veterans' Bureau. "Charlie" was a regular at the biweekly poker sessions held at the White House and thus a member of what the President called his "poker cabinet." In early 1923 rumors surfaced that Forbes had been taking bribes; he thereupon resigned and was later convicted of fraud and sent to prison. His resignation was not preceded by the customary exchange of letters.

> [A] visitor to the White House with an appointment to see the President was directed by mistake to the second floor. As he approached the Red Room he heard a voice hoarse with anger and on entering saw Harding throttling a man [Colonel Forbes of the Veterans Bureau] against the wall as he shouted: "You yellow rat! You double-crossing bastard! If you ever . . . " Whirling about at the visitor's approach, Harding loosed his grip and the released man staggered away, his face blotched and distorted. "I am sorry," Harding said curtly to his visitor. "You have an appointment. Come into the next room."[22]

---

[22] Francis Russell. *The Shadow of Blooming Grove: Warren G. Harding in His Times*. New York: McGraw Hill, 1968, 558.

The following month, soon after the Senate began an investigation into the Veterans' Bureau, Charles F. Cramer, Forbes' chief assistant, committed suicide in his home in Washington. The fact that this house had formerly been the residence of Senator Warren Harding, and that Cramer had purchased it from Harding, fueled speculation that the President was somehow involved.[23] In June a worried President, wanting desperately to get away from Washington, left on a transcontinental trip to Alaska. It was to be his last journey.

On the night of August 2, 1923, Warren Gamaliel Harding, the 29th President of the United States, died suddenly at the Palace Hotel in San Francisco, shortly after returning from Alaska. He had become ill aboard ship after eating a dinner of crab, and the cause of death was said to be food poisoning. The torch was passed early the next morning in a Vermont farmhouse when Vice-President Calvin Coolidge took the oath of office by candlelight. In his first press release, in an effort to reassure the American people of the continuity of their government, the new President reported that he had asked Harding's appointees to remain in office. Coolidge had no idea of what lay ahead.

The previous year Secretary of the Interior Albert B. Fall had entered into oil and gas leases with companies controlled by Harry Sinclair and Edward L. Doheny. The leases covered U.S. lands within the known geologic structures of the Teapot Dome Oil Field in Wyoming and the prolific Elk Hills Field in California, petroleum reserves set aside for the use of the Navy. Contrary to the Mineral Leasing Act of 1920, Fall did not call for public bids, but instead negotiated the terms of the leases in private meetings. Sinclair got Teapot Dome and Doheny Elk Hills.

A Senate committee chaired by Democrat Thomas J. Walsh undertook an investigation into these transactions and 18 months later, in October of 1923, called the first public hearing. It quickly transpired that Doheny and Sinclair had "lent" the Secretary of the Interior some $400,000 while the "negotiations" were in progress.

---

[23] Mark Sullivan. *Our Times: The Twenties*. New York: Charles Scribner's Sons, 1935, 363.

The timing of these "loans" was quite propitious for the recipient, who was on the verge of losing his New Mexico ranch. Doheny and Fall were old friends, Doheny testified, and he simply wanted to help him out. He was a rich man, and to him the money was a mere bagatelle. The first installment was $100,000 in cash placed in a black bag and delivered by Doheny's son.

Albert Fall was convicted of taking a bribe and sent to prison. The oil leases were cancelled and Sinclair, but not Doheny, went to jail. Doheny was represented by an array of lawyers including William Gibbs McAdoo. This was to prove fatal to McAdoo's chances for the Democratic Presidential nomination in 1924.

Another Cabinet member asked to hold over by an unsuspecting Coolidge was Attorney General Harry M. Daugherty, the man most responsible for Warren Harding's becoming President of the United States. Daugherty, a lawyer and politician from the town of Washington Court House, Ohio, had prevailed on Harding to forgo an easy reelection to the Senate in order to run for President in 1920.[24]

Harry Daugherty maintained a house at 1509 H Street, halfway between the White House and the Department of Justice, where he lived with his friend and factotum, Jess Smith. Prohibition stopped at its portals. Nothing but the best of spirits was served, and departing guests were usually favored with a bottle or two of the "real McCoy" confiscated from those who dared flout the law of the land. The "Little House on H Street, became a social as well as a patronage center," where favors were dispensed and all sorts of deals made.[25]

A frequent visitor to the house on H Street was Thomas W. Miller, the Alien Property Custodian, who had charge of the property seized from enemy aliens during the war. One such property was the American Metal Company, which was said to have been German owned. The assets of the company had been seized and sold, and the proceeds impounded. In 1921 a petition for

---

[24] Russell, 334.
[25] Russell, 449, 450.

restitution was made by individuals claiming to be the true owners of the American Metal Company on the ground that they were Swiss rather than German nationals. Their contention was upheld by Alien Property Custodian Miller and the release of some $6,500,000 authorized by Attorney General Daugherty. A handsome fee was paid to John King, a prominent New York Republican, for handling this transaction, of which $50,000 found its way into the pockets of Thomas W. Miller. King died shortly thereafter; Miller was tried, convicted, and sent to prison. But that was not the end of it.

In early 1924, concurrently with the Teapot Dome investigation, Senate investigators discovered that another $50,000 of the American Metal Company honorarium had gone to a bank in Washington Court House, Ohio, run by the Attorney General's brother. It came to rest in an account entitled "Jess Smith No. 3" to which Harry Daugherty was a signatory. By this time Smith had taken his life at the house on H Street by shooting himself through the head. He was found with a revolver in one hand and his head in a metal wastepaper basket which contained the ashes of some freshly burned papers.

The Attorney General refused to appear before the Senate Committees investigating corruption or to permit them to examine Justice Department files. Daugherty offered no explanation for the "Jess Smith No. 3" account. On March 28 "Coolidge sent him a blunt note requesting his immediate resignation." Daugherty complied. Bitterly he blamed his troubles on the Reds and their sympathizers.

> As he walked down the steps of the Justice Department for the last time, tough and truculent, he again saw the red hand of Moscow in his difficulties. [Certain Senators] were, he explained in his apologia, communists at heart, "received in the inner Soviet circles as comrades," and he had withheld his files from them in the interest of national security.[26]

---

[26] Russell, 620.

Daugherty's disgrace came as a windfall to the American Civil Liberties Union. A raid on a Communist Party Convention at Bridgman, Michigan, had brought about full-scale hostilities between the ACLU and what it labeled the "Nation-wide Spy System Centering in the Department of Justice." Daugherty and his chief of investigation, William J. Burns—the detective who had broken the McNamara case—were under constant attack. But the new President, five months in office, had already taken steps to ameliorate the situation.

> Though President Harding had not seen fit to oppose the American Legion and reactionary officials (especially the Attorney-General) by releasing the political prisoners, President Coolidge at once showed a different attitude, and set about finding a method of releasing the prisoners which would *have the least possible political come-back*.[27]

The President took advantage of this opportunity to make peace with the ACLU. "On April 2, 1924, President Coolidge nominated Harlan F. Stone of New York, as Attorney General, to succeed Mr. Daugherty, resigned. The nomination was confirmed by the Senate on April 7, 1924, and Mr. Stone took the oath of office on April 9, 1924."[28] The President and his new Attorney General were fellow New Englanders who had known each other from college days. Stone graduated from Amherst College in 1894 and Coolidge a year later.

Harry Daugherty's legacy was a scandal-racked Department of Justice in great disarray. Harlan Fiske Stone took it over, swept it out with a big broom, and in less than a year transformed it into a respected and effective force. His most notable achievement was the replacement of a patronage-laden Bureau of Investigation headed by William J. Burns with a professionally staffed organization with John Edgar Hoover at the helm. The ACLU noted these changes with much satisfaction.

---

[27] ACLU Annual Report No. 3, 5 [emphasis added].
[28] 264 U.S., III.

> [T]he activities of the Bureau were radically changed
> after the resignations of Attorney-General Daugherty
> and William J. Burns. Their policies were reversed by
> Attorney-General Stone. The Bureau was put in its
> proper place as a legal investigating agency . . .
>
> The complete transformation of the Bureau of
> Investigation under Attorney-General Stone was
> indicated in his announcement soon after taking public
> office, and in the resignation of William J. Burns shortly
> thereafter. It was understood that Mr. Stone totally
> disapproved of Mr. Burns' attitude and methods.[29]

The complete transformation of the Bureau of Investigation
(later the FBI) was preceded by some strenuous lobbying by Roger
Baldwin during the summer of 1924. On Monday, August 4,
Baldwin met with Stone and Hoover and came away satisfied that
they had instituted the necessary reforms. What had been
accomplished, he wrote the Attorney General, "meets every
suggestion which any of us could possibly make." Baldwin was
particularly impressed with the young Acting Director of the FBI.
Of J. Edgar Hoover he wrote to Stone, "I think I owe it to him and
to you to say that I think we were wrong in our estimate of his
attitude."[30] In a memorandum to the Attorney General, Hoover
reported that Baldwin "seemed to be fully satisfied . . . and I believe
that the Bureau of Investigation will no longer be the subject of
attack by either himself or his organization."[31]

Hoover had read the situation correctly. The following January,
after the transformation was complete, the Executive Committee of
the ACLU met in New York City. In response to a letter from the
Attorney General the committee agreed to comply with his
suggestion that the "radical and labor papers should be correctly
advised of the facts regarding the Bureau under Mr. Hoover's and

---

[29] ACLU Annual Report No. 4, 9.
[30] RNB to Harlan F. Stone, August 6, 1924, Reel 38, Vol. 271, ACLUP.
[31] "Hoover—Memorandum for the Attorney General," August 5, 1924. "FBI Documents About
ACLU—Vol. 3." ACLU Archives, 132 West 43rd Street, New York, New York (cited by
Walker at 66).

Attorney General Stone's direction."[32] Two days later Roger Baldwin advised Hoover, by now the Director of the FBI, that the ACLU had issued several press releases "commending the present administration of the Bureau" and that any time Hoover saw publications which were "at variance with the facts," he should call them to the ACLU's attention, "so that we may correct them."[33]

On August 14, 1924, 10 days after he met with Baldwin, Attorney General Stone selected William J. Donovan, the United States Attorney for the Western District of New York, to be his special assistant.[34] The arrival of Donovan and his wife, Ruth, caused quite a splash in Washington society. "In all, the Donovans were invited to social events at the White House or aboard the [Presidential] yacht no fewer than six times in their first month in the capital."[35] But this is not all that surprising since the new Assistant Attorney General was a celebrity in his own right.

William J. "Wild Bill" Donovan had commanded New York's "Fighting 69th" Regiment of World War I fame. Upon his return to Buffalo, the 36-year-old colonel resumed the practice of law with the firm of O'Brian, Hamlin, Donovan and Goodyear. A protege of John Lord O'Brian,[36] Wild Bill had been the unsuccessful Republican candidate for lieutenant governor of New York in an election marred by a most unseemly controversy.

In October of 1918, while commanding his regiment in the Argonne Forest, Colonel Donovan had been wounded in action and as a result of this engagement had been recommended for the Congressional Medal of Honor. In the fall of 1922 the War Department belatedly decided to award him the medal. While not officially announced until after the election, the decision was leaked while the campaign was in progress. The medal—whether or not its

---

[32] Executive Committee Minutes, January 19, 1925, Reel 40, Vol. 281, E-10, ACLUP.

[33] RNB to JEH, January 21, 1925, Reel 38, Vol. 271, ACLUP.

[34] The William J. Donovan Papers, U.S. Army Military History Institute, Carlisle Barracks, Pennsylvania, hereinafter Donovan Papers, Diary.

[35] Anthony Cave-Brown. *The Last Hero: Wild Bill Donovan.* New York: Times Books/Random House, 1982, 91.

[36] Cave-Brown, 28.

award was politically motivated—became a campaign issue.[37]

A fine speaker as well as a war hero, Wild Bill Donovan was a man with great political potential, particularly during Prohibition. An Irish Catholic Republican from upstate New York as well as a lifelong abstainer from alcohol, William Joseph Donovan was a ticket balancer's dream. Like most Republican politicians, Colonel Donovan straddled the issue of Prohibition. "His heart is wet, his head is moist and on his feet he has the galoshes of the Anti-saloon League,"[38] complained one of his opponents.

It was a widely held suspicion among working men that Prohibition was a plot to keep them sober and industrious, and that while they were being deprived of having a legitimate drink in the neighborhood bar, businessmen were sipping whiskey and wine at their private clubs while discussing new ways to exploit them. Wild Bill had won their grudging respect by his even-handed enforcement of the Volstead Act. Of working class origins himself, Donovan had been introduced into Buffalo society by John Lord O'Brian[39] and had married a girl from a wealthy and socially prominent family.

One of the most exclusive clubs in Buffalo was the Saturn Club. On the night of August 23, 1923, some 30 federal agents, acting on U.S. Attorney Donovan's orders, raided the club, arrested the bartender, broke open the private lockers of some 118 members with sledgehammers, and seized a large quantity of intoxicating liquors. The next day the members of Donovan's law firm held an acrimonious meeting after which one of them withdrew from the firm. Donovan, himself a member of the Saturn Club, was ostracized.[40]

Calvin Coolidge managed to keep from being personally involved with Prohibition problems. "Silent Cal," as he became called, "referred inquiries to either the Secretary of the Treasury or the Attorney General, who were respectively in charge of prohibition enforcement and prosecution. Letters that could not be

---

[37] Cave-Brown, 82. The medal was presented on January 18, 1923.
[38] "Lehman Says Donovan Vague on Prohibition," *Buffalo Courier Express*, October 20, 1932. "Scrapbook," Donovan Papers.
[39] Cave-Brown, 28.
[40] Cave-Brown, 84-87.

referred elsewhere, Coolidge had one of his secretaries answer." The President was well aware of the corrosive effect of Prohibition in general, and he thought that "any law which inspires disrespect for the other laws—the good laws—is a bad law."[41]

Prohibition had an impact on the political parties which on the national level worked much to the disadvantage of the Democrats. The core constituencies of the Democratic coalition were the states of the old Confederacy—the "Solid South"—and the party apparatus— "machines" as they were called—in the large cities of the North. Prohibition rent this coalition asunder. Southern Democrats were overwhelmingly Protestant and Dry while big city Democrats outside the South were predominantly Catholic and Wet.

In 1924 the leading contender for the Democratic nomination once again was William Gibbs McAdoo. "McAdoo would go into the convention with firm pledges from about one-half of the delegates"[42] with a two-thirds majority required for the nomination. With the notable exception of Alabama, McAdoo was the choice of the South. His chief rival and *bete noir* was New York Governor Alfred E. Smith.

Al Smith was, as the saying went, "as wet as the Atlantic Ocean" and made no bones about it. "The Happy Warrior" was his sobriquet and 'The Sidewalks of New York' his theme song. He wore a derby, smoked cigars, and spoke with a rasping lower East Side accent. An Irish Catholic and a product of Tammany Hall, Smith was emblematic of all that Drys opposed. Nor did he try to build bridges.

In 1923 the New York state legislature passed a bill repealing the Mullan-Gage Law—that state's counterpart of the Volstead Act— and sent it to Governor Smith for his signature. After hearing the views of all concerned—Wayne Wheeler spoke for the Drys— Smith signed the repeal into law.[43] Henceforward, the enforcement of Prohibition in the Empire State will be the job of the federal government alone. If Al Smith had gotten the Democratic

---

[41] Donald R. McCoy. *Calvin Coolidge: The Quiet President.* New York: Macmillan, 1967, 303.

[42] William H. Harbaugh. *Lawyer's Lawyer: The Life of John W. Davis.* New York: Oxford University Press, 1973, 204.

[43] Coffey, 112, 113.

nomination in 1924, as he will in 1928, there was no doubt but that the South and Dry Democrats in every region would have bolted the party. They were mortally offended.

> Wayne Wheeler . . . issued a statement which virtually declared war against New York's governor. "The action of Governor Smith will stir the nation as did the shot on Fort Sumpter," Wheeler declared. "Tammany dictated the signature along with the liquor interests. But the governor's action will array the country and enforcement will become stronger than ever. New York will stay in the union in spite of Governor Smith."[44]

In June of 1924, at the Democratic National Convention held in New York City, Smith and McAdoo fought each other to a stalemate. After a record 103 roll call votes the delegates settled on John W. Davis as a compromise candidate. The courtly Mr. Davis, formerly ambassador to the Court of St. James, was a Wall Street lawyer whose clientele included J.P. Morgan, a fact which was much used against him. Davis never had a chance. "Fighting Bob" LaFollette ran as a third party candidate and garnered one-sixth of the total vote, helping to bring about the "Coolidge Landslide" in November.

In the 1924 elections the American people opted to "Keep Cool with Coolidge." They did not hold Calvin Coolidge responsible for the gang of thieves Warren Harding had appointed, and the President was better able to position himself on the Prohibition issue than was his opponent. "By luck and by design the President slipped neatly between the wets and the drys . . . The drys did not have the courage to attack Coolidge for fear that he would do less than he was doing and the wets largely left him alone for fear he might just get his back up and try to do more."[45]

The repeal of the Eighteenth Amendment at this time was politically impossible. It will take the Great Depression and the election of Franklin Roosevelt to bring about repeal. The issue in 1924 was "enforcement." Republican candidates for Congress had

---

[44] Coffey, 114, 115.
[45] McCoy, 303.

been as Wet or Dry as their political exigencies required. Where taking a definitive stand was politically unwise they hedged. "I'm not for Prohibition, but so long as it is the law, it must be enforced," was the thrust. Said properly, it was calculated to mollify Drys while Wets would vote secure in the knowledge that liquor would continue to flow.

The *Weeks* rule requires a judge in a federal criminal trial, upon application by the defendant, to exclude evidence taken in an unreasonable search. The question during Prohibition was not *whether* a judge must pass on the reasonableness of a search, but *when*. Was it sufficient that searches and seizures be subjected to judicial scrutiny after they have taken place and that the fruits be admitted or excluded accordingly? Or must this adjudication be done beforehand? In 1924 this was not an arcane question of interest only to an esoteric few; it was of vital importance to Prohibition's enforcers and violators alike.

In *Amos v. United States*, decided in 1921, Treasury agents, acting without a warrant, arrived at the defendant's house and told his wife, Amos not being at home, that they had "come to search the premises 'for violations of the revenue law.'"[46] What reasons they had for making this search, and whether it amounted to probable cause, is not stated in the Court's opinion. Gaining admittance, the agents made a search and seized two bottles of illegally distilled whiskey found under a quilt on a bed. Before his trial began, Amos moved to exclude the bottles, and any testimony as to their being found, from being used as evidence against him. The motion was denied and the defendant tried and convicted. Amos sought review by the Supreme Court on a writ of error.

The conviction was reversed. The evidence had been taken in an unreasonable search made in violation of the Fourth Amendment, held the Court, and therefore should have been excluded under the *Weeks* rule. The result might have been different had there been probable cause to believe illegal whisky was on the premises. In *McBride v. United States* [47] federal agents smelled the distinct odor

---

[46] 255 U.S. 313, 315.
[47] 284 F. 416 (1922).

of fermenting whiskey wafting from a stable where they found and seized a still. The Fifth Circuit Court of Appeals held the warrantless search to be valid. It is a common law rule, predating the Constitution, that an officer may arrest, without a warrant, a person who commits a crime in his presence. And when an officer is apprised by his senses that a crime—in this case the illicit manufacture of whiskey—is being committed, that crime will be deemed to have been committed in his presence.

But what if the aroma was coming from a still in McBride's home instead of an outbuilding? The home, after all, is the very citadel of privacy and deserves special protection. Certainly Congress thought so when in 1921 they amended the Volstead Act. Section 6 of the Act Supplemental to the National Prohibition Act, approved November 23, 1921, generally known as the Willis-Campbell Act (Comp. St. Ann. Supp. 1923, § 10184a) provided

> that any officer, agent, or employee of the United States, engaged in the enforcement of this act or the National Prohibition Act, or any other law of the United States, who shall search any private dwelling as designated in the National Prohibition Act, and occupied as such dwelling without a warrant directing such search . . . shall be guilty of a misdemeanor, and upon conviction thereof shall be fined . . .

If the Willis-Campbell Act deterred Prohibition agents from making warrantless searches of homes, that fact seems to have eluded the commentators of that era. For one thing, the words *private dwelling . . . occupied as such* raise questions which make difficult the successful prosecution of an officer in the situation where some rooms in the home are used as a speakeasy or to distill whiskey while the rest is used as living quarters. A trial would degenerate into a farce. A tort action for trespass is impractical for the same reason.

> When it is said that a home may never be searched without a warrant . . . the problem is only half solved. What is a home? . . . It is obvious that some line must be drawn; its precise location is not so obvious. "Home" for

this purpose does not necessarily include the entire domestic establishment, the common law messuage, because the same interest in privacy does not prevail throughout.[48]

In cities like New York or Chicago, where ethnic enclaves were the rule rather than the exception, the typical neighborhood speakeasy was a family operation. "Mom and Pop" were usually related to many of their customers and had a common bond with others that went back to the old country. This took on added significance during Prohibition for it was of critical importance when buying whiskey, by the drink or by the bottle, to buy it from a supplier who cared about his customers' well-being.

The Volstead Act permitted the manufacture of ethyl alcohol for industrial purposes because the economy could not function without it. To prevent its being used as a beverage, the Treasury Department required that it be denatured by the addition of wood alcohol and other poisonous substances. Much bootleg whiskey produced during the 1920s was made from industrial alcohol from which the denaturants had been distilled out, or so one hoped.

It was best not to deal with strangers. "But many bootleggers, untroubled by the danger to the consumer, were satisfied to market an alcohol that didn't smell or taste too dreadful, however deleterious the denaturants, after coloring and flavoring it to simulate whiskey or gin." In 1923 the Surgeon General "reviewed the analyses made by government chemists of samples collected from confiscated bootleg liquor. Most of it showed traces of one or more poisons, including wood alcohol." In one year alone almost 12,000 people died of drinking denatured alcohol.[49]

Not all Americans thought this a tragedy. " But the fatalities drew no sign of regret from Wayne Wheeler. 'The government is under no obligation to furnish people with alcohol that is drinkable when the Constitution prohibits it,' he argued, adding, 'the person

---

[48] Wood. *The Scope of the Constitutional Immunity Against Searches and Seizures*, 34 West Virginia Law Quarterly 137, 138 (1928).
[49] Kobler, 308, 309.

who drinks this industrial alcohol is a deliberate suicide.'"[50] Nor was the label of a prestigious foreign distiller on a bottle a guarantee that its contents were genuine. Bottles could be refilled, and the counterfeiting of seals and tax stamps had risen to an art. The best assurance that you would not be poisoned was to deal with someone you knew, who would vouch for the provenance of his merchandise.

It was in the family home that the vast majority of Prohibition violations were taking place. Most speakeasies and stills were "mom and pop" operations. It was a simple matter for a team of agents to locate and stake them out. Observation and their senses would tell them when the time was ripe for a raid. A leader with badge in sight, another with a crowbar, and a third with his hand resting on a holstered pistol would be a sufficient show of force.

One readily can empathize with "Pop" when confronted by such a trio. He knows that if he does nothing he will be ruined. They will break every bottle in sight save one, and trash the place looking for more. When they leave, it will be with him under arrest and behind will be a freshly padlocked door with a seal warning of the dire consequences of removing it. It would not take long for "Pop" to ask the question that the raid was meant to elicit. "Can't we work something out?" There would be no need for a repeat performance. The operation would be permitted to continue in return for a periodic "license fee." The amount will be within reason; after all, there is no point in putting "Mom and Pop" out of business.

The biggest obstacle to an enlightened policy was the Prohibition Bureau of the Treasury Department run by Commissioner Roy Asa Haynes. Any instruction to ease up on enforcement would be reported by him to his patron, Wayne Wheeler. Were Haynes to be dismissed—and the corruption in the Bureau was certainly grounds for his dismissal—the wrath of Wheeler and the Drys would fall upon the Coolidge administration. But if one thinks about it, and you can be sure they thought about it long and hard, there was a way to undercut Haynes and the Bureau, a way *which would have the least possible political comeback.*

---

[50] Kobler, 310.

Chapter XII

AGNELLO v. UNITED STATES

The Fourth Amendment does not require that a search or seizure be made pursuant to a warrant; it requires only that it not be *unreasonable*. All that is said with respect to warrants is by way of limitation on their issuance. But in the 1920s, the text of the Fourth Amendment notwithstanding, there were good and sufficient reasons of public policy why a warrant should be required to search a dwelling place.

The problem was that Prohibition searches were such pushovers. If the reasonableness of a search was to be judged by probable cause, all would have passed muster. A still emitted an unmistakable odor, and no one could observe the comings and goings from a speakeasy without knowing for an absolute certainty that a violation of the Volstead Act was in progress. If searches could be made without warrants, and Prohibition agents didn't take bribes, the "Noble Experiment" might have succeeded, for a while at least.

Raids on those Prohibition offenders we have called "Mom and Pop" were the most numerous and the most egregious. They were the most divisive as well. To city dwellers, a raid on a neighborhood still or speakeasy, invariably appurtenant to the proprietor's living quarters, was an attack on one's family and friends. In political terms, seen through the ethnic eyes of the Irish, Italians, Jews, or Poles of Boston, Chicago, or New York City, honest hard-working Democrats were being victimized by a swinish constabulary of shakedown artists recruited from the ranks of the Republican organization. The resentment ran deep.

Any law which would inhibit raids by Prohibition agents on speakeasies or stills located in buildings used in part as living quarters would have been a good thing. A decision of the Supreme Court holding that a search of a dwelling of any sort is *unreasonable* unless made pursuant to a judicially issued warrant, if not textually sound, was most definitely in the public interest.

These raids were almost invariably warrantless. Probable cause, however, was there in abundance. In each case a Prohibition agent truthfully could say that his senses told him that a violation of the Volstead Act was going on. Since this constituted a crime committed in his presence, no warrant was thought to be required. A warrant requirement would bring such raids to a halt. They would be pointless since the fruits of such a search would be excluded under the *Weeks* rule. It would never even come to that; the Assistant U.S. Attorney assigned to the case would simply refuse to prosecute. He, after all, is not going to waste his time and the court's time trying a case he cannot win.

A warrant requirement would require a Prohibition agent, who had probable cause to believe that a violation was taking place, to set forth the relevant facts in an affidavit and take it to a judge. The judge, finding probable cause, would then issue a warrant to search the premises described in the affidavit, seize any intoxicating liquor and arrest anyone found violating the Volstead Act. Warrant in hand, the agent would return to the place in which the still or speakeasy was located, gain entry, arrest the culprits, and seize any alcoholic beverages. Thereupon the agent would be obliged to *return* the warrant to the judge who issued it along with his *indorsement*.

> *Return.* The act of a sheriff, constable, marshal, or other
> ministerial officer, in delivering back to the court a writ,
> notice, process or other paper, which he was required to
> serve or execute, with a brief account of his doings under
> the mandate, the time and mode of service or execution,
> or his failure to accomplish it, as the case may be. Also
> the indorsement made by the officer upon the writ or
> other paper, stating what he has done under it, the time

and mode of service, etc.[1]

A warrant requirement, in the nature of things, would impede Prohibition searches by making them more difficult. But to whatever degree it would hinder Prohibition agents in the performance of their duties, it would be a far greater hindrance to their extortions. And for every warrantless search that led to the courtroom, there were probably a hundred that led to a bribe. Once the parties had "worked something out," of course, there was nothing to show that a raid had ever taken place. Warrants, on the other hand, leave a paper trail.

There will always be some searches that will be fruitless. And a factual situation which gave rise to probable cause sometimes will change so that a search is no longer necessary or advisable. A judge who upon the application of a law enforcement officer issues a search warrant understands these facts of life and will accept that officer's returning a warrant unexecuted or with an indorsement stating that the search proved to be unsuccessful. He would accept it once or twice, at any rate.

But an officer—in this case an agent of the Prohibition Bureau—who made a practice of returning warrants empty-handed is another matter. A judge soon would realize that he and the judicial process were being used as instruments of extortion. It would only be a matter of time before a judge would refer the matter to the United States Attorney and ask that he investigate. Bear in mind that federal judges and U.S. Attorneys didn't like Prohibition agents any more than did ordinary Americans, the kind who serve on juries. Nor would the victims be hard to find. They would be the persons whose names and addresses were on the unexecuted warrants and in the affidavits that led to their issuance.

The enforcement of Prohibition was the joint responsibility of the Treasury and Justice Departments. Those who made the raids and arrests were usually Treasury agents. It was the United States Attorneys of the Justice Department whose task it was to prosecute

---

[1] *Black's Law Dictionary.*

violators. A warrant requirement would give Justice the upper hand. Inevitably, U.S. Attorneys would have to pass on the sufficiency of affidavits of probable cause and see that any warrants that issued complied with the requirements of the Fourth Amendment. Warrants also must be executed promptly. A "stale" warrant is no warrant at all. And with this oversight it would be a lot more difficult for Wayne Wheeler to enforce Prohibition by remote control through his puppet, Roy Asa Haynes.

A warrant requirement would severely limit a Prohibition agent's ability to raid a "Mom and Pop" operation. Heretofore, an agent, having learned through his senses that the Volstead Act was being violated, could use force to gain entry. He had nothing to fear by way of a tort suit since a crime had been committed in his presence. Now his badge would no longer get him past the door. He would not dare to make a forcible entry because a warrantless search of premises in part used as a dwelling house would now be unreasonable and therefore unconstitutional notwithstanding the probable cause his eyes, ears, and nose were transmitting to his brain.

Were such a warrant requirement to be "read in" to the Fourth Amendment by the Supreme Court, a Prohibition agent who wished to raid a speakeasy or still located in a building used in part as living quarters would first have to obtain a search warrant; once he obtained a search warrant he would have to execute it, and once he executed the warrant he would have no choice but to arrest "Mom and Pop" and close down their operation. And this, of course, would not make anybody any money.

However, there still would be opportunities for graft. Like the Willis-Campbell Act, the warrant requirement would apply only to a home. Warrantless searches, as before, if based on probable cause, would not be unreasonable if made of a person, car, truck, or boat. It would make sense, therefore, for the avaricious legions of Commissioner Roy Asa Haynes to turn their attentions to those who imported and transported whiskey in bulk. And this would be a lot less controversial.

No one cared about the rumrunners who matched speed and wits with the federal authorities on the Great Lakes or high seas nor the toughs who by night trucked their cargo to the cities. They made their money and they took their chances. The highjackings and the nightly shootouts they had with rival gangs and the law made good cocktail conversation. And most would shrug their shoulders if some Prohibition agents bit the dust. More than likely, the customers of a speakeasy would expect the house to buy a round to toast the latest to join the ranks of what Commissioner Haynes had called "our little band of martyrs."[2]

Calvin Coolidge was a contemplative man who put great value on tranquillity. He slept "up to ten and eleven hours a day." Of "Silent Cal" H. L. Mencken wrote that "his ideal day is one on which nothing whatever happens." The President avoided stress wherever he could and saw to it that everything was "under control—his control."[3] Thanksgiving Day of 1924 fell on November 27. It would have been a good time for the President to take stock of his accomplishments and chart his course. Now would be a good time for us to do it for him.

Coolidge had restored the people's confidence in their government and in return they had given the President his own mandate. What had been most in his favor was the economy. "The business of America is business," went a Coolidge aphorism, and business was booming. Wage earners were producing and consuming goods and services as never before. It was the golden age of sports and working men were a lot more interested in the exploits of Babe Ruth and Jack Dempsey than in the ideology of Marx and Lenin.

The Red Star was on the wane. The Bolsheviks who in 1919 were a clear and present danger to public safety were now a ragtag band of soapbox orators searching desperately for an audience. Ignoring them was the best policy. The one big problem was Prohibition and the hypocrisy and corruption it had wrought. And in that area, in the minds of many, it was not Calvin Coolidge who was really in charge. In a biography entitled *Wayne Wheeler Dry Boss*, T. Justin Steuart wrote:

[Wheeler] controlled six Congresses, dictated to two

---

2 Kobler, 291.
3 McCoy, 290, 291.

Presidents of the United States, directed legislation for the most important elective state and federal offices, held the balance of power in both Republican and Democratic parties, distributed more patronage than any dozen other men, supervised a federal bureau from the outside without official authority, and was recognized by friend and foe alike as the most masterful and powerful single individual in the United States.[4]

A decision by the Supreme Court, at this moment in American history, that the Fourth Amendment required a search, if made of a *private dwelling . . . occupied as such*, be made pursuant to a warrant, would have been very much in the public interest. Moreover, its effects would be mostly invisible. Commissioner Roy Asa Haynes could continue to issue his glowing reports on how truly effective enforcement has become, noting that arrests for home-distilling have fallen precipitously. In pulpits throughout the land Dry leaders could righteously point with pride in having reduced the flow of "demon rum" to a trickle. Who is to tell them different? Certainly not the ethnics in the big cities. In the long run they will have to wait for the country to come to its senses, but, in the meanwhile, they can muddle through with moonshine.

Calvin Coolidge started off the new year by filling a seat on the Supreme Court. "On January 5, 1925, President Coolidge nominated Harlan Fiske Stone of New York"[5] to the Supreme Court. The office of Attorney General was vacant from January 12, the day Justice Stone took his seat on the Court, to March 17 when Calvin Coolidge appointed his friend and fellow Vermonter, John Garibaldi Sargent.[6] For the next four years Sargent served as Attorney General and Wild Bill Donovan his chief assistant. But behind the scenes "Garibaldi," as the press liked to call Sargent, was a figurehead and Donovan the de facto Attorney General. Sargent, "who in size, dress, and bearing reminded one of a St. Bernard dog

---

[4] Cited by Kobler at 182.
[5] 267 U.S., III.
[6] 267 U.S., III.

just back from a romp in the Alps,"[7] was about as communicative with newspapermen as was the President.

> Often he varied his customary simple answers of "I don't know" and "I can't discuss that" by saying "Colonel Donovan has charge of that," but he wouldn't let Donovan, who was regarded as the real attorney general, open his mouth. And thus the Justice Department worked in nearly absolute secrecy; it seemed as if Sargent regarded correspondents as more dangerous than the nation's criminals.[8]

Almost every case in which the exclusionary rule is invoked today involves a search which, if judged by the circumstances which attend it, would satisfy the Fourth Amendment's standard of reasonableness. When a search is held to be unlawful, it is almost invariably held to be unlawful, not because "probable cause" was lacking, but because the search was not made pursuant to a warrant. The Court has declared its "preference" that reasonableness be determined before the fact by a judge and that, with certain exceptions, a search and seizure made without a judicially issued warrant is invalid no matter how probable the cause which prompted it. This so-called "judicial preference for a warrant" was originally established in the 1925 case of *Agnello v. United States*. As Potter Stewart noted along *The Road to Mapp v. Ohio and Beyond*, it was *Agnello* which gave us "a full-blown rule of exclusion at federal trials."

> The *Silverthorne* and *Gouled* opinions went far towards converting the limited rules of the *Boyd* and *Weeks* cases into a full-blown rule of exclusion at federal trials. But the conversion was not yet complete. Four years after the *Gouled* decision, in *Agnello* v. *United States,* the Court was presented with an opportunity to re-evaluate each of the remaining limitations on the exclusionary rule imposed in the *Boyd* and *Weeks* opinions.[9]

---

[7] McCoy, 280.

[8] *Little Falls N.Y. Times*, February 2, 1929, Scrapbook, Donovan Papers.

[9] Stewart, 1376, citing *Agnello v. United States*, 269 U.S. 20 (1925).

Frank Agnello and his brother, Thomas, had been convicted of conspiring to sell cocaine in violation of the Harrison Act of 1914. In January of 1922 "Pasquale Napolitano and Nunzio Dispenza, employed by government revenue agents for that purpose," had set up a "buy" at the home of Alba, a codefendant of the Agnellos. "Six revenue agents and a city policeman followed them and remained on watch outside." From their vantage point they were able to see the defendants Alba, Centerino, Pace, and the two Agnellos sitting at a table with Napolitano, who had been provided with marked money to pay for the narcotics.

> Looking through the windows, those on watch saw Frank Agnello produce a number of small packages for delivery to Napolitano and saw the latter hand over money to Alba. Upon the apparent consummation of the sale, the agents rushed in and arrested all the defendants. They found some of the packages on the table where the transaction took place and found others in the pockets of Frank Agnello. All contained cocaine. On searching Alba, they found the money given him by Napolitano.[10]

Frank Agnello had come to Alba's directly from his own home and, after arresting him, "several of the agents went to No. 167 Columbia street, Brooklyn, which was occupied as a grocery store and also as a residence by the Agnellos . . . [I]n the room occupied by Frank Agnello there was found a can containing cocaine."[11] Frank Agnello had a defense separate and apart from those of his co-defendants. At the trial he testified that he did not know the packages contained narcotics and would not have carried them if he did. On cross-examination he was confronted with the cocaine found in his bedroom. It was admitted into evidence for the purpose of impeaching his credibility and he was convicted along with the rest. All of the defendants appealed their conviction.

"The question thus raised," said the Second Circuit Court of Appeals, "is one of great importance. May an agent of the

---

[10] 269 U.S. 28, 29.

[11] *Agnello v. United States*, 290 F. 671, 673 (1923).

government, in a case where he can arrest without a warrant and search the person without a warrant, search also without a warrant the home of the person so arrested"?[12] That court decided the question in favor of the government, and the defendants sought review by the Supreme Court. "The United States deeming the question of search and seizure decided below to be one of general public importance," joined "with petitioners in requesting that the writ of certiorari issue as prayed for."[13] On April 30, 1923, the Supreme Court of the United States granted a writ of certiorari in the case of *Agnello v. United States.*[14]

At their trial in March of 1922, Frank and Thomas Agnello had been represented by two Brooklyn lawyers named Wackerman and Kesselman. Each defendant was found guilty and sentenced to two years in prison and a $5,000 fine. Shortly thereafter, on behalf of all of the defendants, Kesselman sought review from the Second Circuit Court of Appeals and at the same time obtained a 90-day stay of execution. On June 5, 1922, the firm of O'Gorman, Battle, Vandiver & Levy took over the defense and were able to get another stay. Successive stays of execution will enable the Agnellos to remain free on bond throughout the pendency of the appeal.

George Gordon Battle was a prominent New York City lawyer and it is he who will argue the case of *Agnello v. United States* on behalf of the defendants.[15] A "familiar figure in New York's public and social life for more than thirty-five years," Battle, a Democrat, was a man of considerable political influence in New York politics and a friend and supporter of Al Smith. He was, when he died, the chairman of the Law Committee and Grand Sachem of Tammany Hall.[16] His adversary will be William J. "Wild Bill" Donovan, the

---

[12] 290 F. 673, 674.

[13] "Concurrence By United States in Issuance of Writ" filed April 16, 1923.

[14] 262 U.S. 738.

[15] "Mr. George Gordon Battle with whom Mr. Isaac H. Levy, was on the briefs for petitioners . . . " *Agnello v. United States*, 269 U.S. 21.

[16] "George G. Battle, Lawyer, 80, Dead, Senior Partner of Noted Firm Here was Tammany Leader—Known as 'Mr. Chairman,'" *New York Times*, April 30, 1949. The quotations and the information in this paragraph are from this source as well as *George Gordon Battle*, a memorial by Ludlow S. Fowler and Morris E. Lasker, Association of the Bar of the City of New York, Vol. 102, 9-15.

scourge of Buffalo's Saturn Club.[17]

Agnello v. United States was argued before the Supreme Court on April 23, 1925. The argument—the "plain meaning" argument—that should have been made on behalf of the United States was as simple as it was unanswerable: The Fourth Amendment does not require that searches be made pursuant to a warrant; it requires only that they not be *unreasonable.* The test in each case, therefore, is whether or not, under the totality of the circumstances, the search met the Fourth Amendment's standard of reasonableness. The opinion in the court below laid out what should have been the government's argument before the Supreme Court.

> Whether a search or seizure in a criminal case is or is not unreasonable must necessarily be determined according to the facts and circumstances of the particular case. In the instant case we think that what the defendants did in the presence of the agents of the government was sufficient to justify not only the arrest and search of their persons and that it also constituted such probable cause as justified the search of the home of one of them under the circumstances disclosed.[18]

No one could doubt that the search of Alba's house at 138 Union Street was valid. It was there that the officers witnessed the exchange of the marked money and the narcotics, a crime committed in their presence. The seizure of both fell within the common law maxim that a police officer, contemporaneously with a valid arrest, may search the persons arrested and the area around them for weapons or contraband. That he needs no warrant to do so is an accepted rule of

---

[17] The name of Solicitor General James M. Beck also appears on the brief. But Beck had resigned effective April 1, 1925, three weeks before the case was argued. According to 269 U.S. 20, 23, *Agnello* was argued by "Assistant to the Attorney General Donovan, with whom Solicitor General Mitchell was on the brief for the United States." But William D. Mitchell, Beck's successor, according to 268 U.S. III, did not take office until June 8, a month and a half after Angello was argued. Given the flux in the Solicitor General's Office, it is highly unlikely that either Beck or Mitchell had anything to do with the case and that the appearance of their names was strictly *pro forma.*

[18] *Agnello v. United States*, 290 F. 671, 682-683.

law. It is also, one might add, one that sanctions searches and seizures wherein reasonableness is self-evident.

It was only the search of Frank Agnello's home at 167 Columbia Street, several blocks from Alba's, which was at issue. The search for and the seizure of the can of cocaine used to discredit his testimony was made subsequent to and at a distance from the scene of the arrest. "The one important question involved is as to the admission in evidence of a can of cocaine hydrochloride found by government agents, immediately after the arrest of the defendants, in the bedroom of the defendant Frank Agnello."[19] Essentially what the "Brief on Behalf of the United States" attempted to do was to bring the search of Frank Agnello's home within the common law maxim—an impossible task. The court declined to make the stretch.

> The legality of the arrests or of the searches and seizures made at the home of Alba is not questioned. Such searches and seizures naturally and usually appertain to and attend such arrests. But the right does not extend to other places. Frank Agnello's house was several blocks distant from Alba's house, where the arrest was made. When it was entered and searched, the conspiracy was ended and the defendants were under arrest and in custody elsewhere. That search cannot be sustained as an incident of the arrests. See *Silverthorne Lumber Co. v. United States*, 251 U.S. 385, 391 . . . [20]

"The search of Frank Agnello's house and seizure of the can of cocaine violated the Fourth Amendment," held the Court, and the evidence should have been excluded. They then grafted unto the *Weeks* rule a warrant requirement not to be found in the text of the Fourth Amendment. "Belief, however well founded, that an article sought is concealed in a dwelling house furnishes no justification for a search of that place without a warrant. And such searches are held unlawful notwithstanding facts unquestionably showing probable cause."[21]

---

[19] "Brief on Behalf of the United States," 14.
[20] 269 U.S. 30, 31.
[21] 269 U.S. 33.

What is most significant about Donovan's brief is the argument it did *not* make. The common law maxim that a search without a warrant is lawful when made by an officer contemporaneously with and at the scene of a valid arrest was not a rule of constitutional dimension. And in any event it does *not* mean that searches made otherwise are unlawful. The maxim is but another way of saying that searches made under these circumstances are *ipso facto* reasonable.

It does not automatically brand as unlawful searches made some time after, or at a distance from, the scene of the arrest. Each such search must be judged on its own merits. The officers had every reason to believe a search of Frank Agnello's residence would turn up a cache of cocaine, and every reason to believe it would disappear if they did not act immediately. The search of 167 Columbia Street, at a distance from the scene of the arrest, was not unreasonable and therefore it was not unconstitutional. In the context of the Fourth Amendment these two words are interchangeable.

There is nothing novel about this argument; it cried out to be made. That it did not occur to the man who briefed and argued the case on behalf of the United States is astounding. And so a warrant requirement became part of our Fourth Amendment jurisprudence without the most cogent argument against it ever being advanced. *Agnello v. United States* introduced to our law of search and seizure a false standard which has plagued it ever since.

Prima facie, like any other decision of the nation's highest court, *Agnello v. United States* must be presumed to be a genuine "case" or "controversy." And a postmortem critique, which calls into question the sufficiency of the legal argument made on behalf of the United States, standing alone, is not enough to rebut this presumption. But before we leave the case which established the warrant requirement, let us lay out the facts and let the reader be the judge.

As strange as it may seem today, drugs were not considered a problem in the 1920s. By popular belief, addiction was confined to "drug fiends" who pursued a bohemian style of life and Chinese who smoked opium in "dens." It was not a matter which concerned ordinary people. There was no mass movement or crusade to prohibit people from using drugs if that was their will. The consumption of intoxicating liquors was an emotionally and politically charged issue while the use of narcotics was not. If the idea was to obtain a precedent establishing a warrant requirement, a drug scenario was far less controversial than one involving alcohol.

The appearance of George Gordon Battle is in itself noteworthy. While Battle spent the first 14 years of his career in the practice of criminal law, he and "then United States Senator James A. O'Gorman" formed in 1912 the firm that became O'Gorman, Battle, Vandiver and Levy. "By far the largest part of his professional career [thereafter] was devoted to civil matters."[22] Battle's office address at all times relevant to this discussion was 37 Wall Street. It is highly unusual to find a Wall Street lawyer like George Gordon Battle representing two Brooklyn drug merchants like Frank and Thomas Agnello.

There had to be an ulterior motive. George Gordon Battle did not get involved to earn a fee. What he saw in *Agnello* was the opportunity to gain a precedent which would ameliorate the excesses of Prohibition, a worthy objective if ever there was one. If raids on family-run stills and speakeasies could be curbed, Prohibition would take on a more human face. What the Coolidge administration got was a plausible explanation for their inability to keep America Dry.

Inquiries by Dry leaders to the President would be referred to "Garibaldi," who in turn would refer them to Colonel Donovan. The answer would come back that the Supreme Court had spoken. The enforcement of Prohibition, like the enforcement of other laws, is subject to constitutional limitations, and if some moonshiners and bootleggers go free as a result, that is the price we pay to protect the privacy of the home.

What Calvin Coolidge got out of it was tranquility. The detenté Harlan Stone had forged with the ACLU would stand Coolidge in good stead in the event of trouble from the left. Prohibition and its enforcement remained as the chief source of aggravation. An order to Commissioner Roy Asa Haynes to lay off of "Mom and Pop" stills and speakeasies would have brought down the wrath of the

---

[22] Fowler and Lasker, 12, 13.

Drys on his head. The Court's holding in *Agnello v. United States* gave him a way of accomplishing the same thing *which would have the least possible political comeback.*

If Wheeler thought anything was amiss, he never let on. In an article in the *New York Times* on October 13, 1925, the day after *Agnello* was decided—"High Court Defines House Search Right"—there is a subtitle, "Wheeler Comments." "Commenting on the Supreme Court decision, Wayne B. Wheeler, general counsel of the Anti-Saloon League, said it was correct, and added that his organization looked with disfavor on Government agents who would violate the law." Wheeler, however, was a dying man.

> What the public didn't realize was that Wheeler was now a diminishing man. His extraordinary power in national politics, which had seemed to reach its zenith with the dry Republican sweep in the 1924 elections, had been gradually fading since then, and Wheeler's health was fading with it. Always slender, he was now so bony and wrinkled that he looked ten or fifteen years older than his age, which was fifty-seven. His face was gaunt and his eyes were tired. His clothing hung loose on him.[23]

The President took charge. "Coolidge, occupying the White House no longer as Harding's inheritor but with his own mandate, began proving himself as stubborn as he was silent." He revamped the entire system of Prohibition enforcement and appointed General Lincoln Andrews as Prohibition "czar" with powers superseding those of the Prohibition Commissioner.[24] Wheeler, who was fading fast, was in no condition to object. He died the following year.

It is the behavior of the representatives of the United States which militates most against the authenticity of *Agnello*. With regard to Frank Agnello, it was only the can of cocaine found in his room which was in controversy. The testimony of the officers who witnessed the exchange of the money and the narcotics, and the

---

[23] Coffey, 185.
[24] Coffey, 185.

packages of cocaine "found in the pockets of Frank Agnello" at Alba's—the same evidence used to convict his four co-defendants—would have been admissible in a second trial. Frank Agnello is reminiscent of "King of Policy" Albert Adams. All he stood to gain from a successful appeal to the Supreme Court of the United States was a new trial in which he was sure to be convicted.

There was no legitimate reason to permit Frank Agnello's co-defendants to remain at large during the appeal and beyond. Dilatory tactics come naturally to convicted felons, and the appellate process offers a means of deferring the dreaded day the prison gate slams behind them. There is a countervailing duty on the part of the prosecution to see that they do not get away with it. The only search and seizure at issue, states Donovan's brief, "tended to prejudice only one of the defendants—namely, Frank Agnello—in whose room the search was made . . . Even if it could be conceded that its admission was error as to him, the other defendants are not entitled to object."[25] Why was this simple point not made back in 1922 when they applied to be released on bail?

The decision of the Second Circuit Court of Appeals in March of 1923 removed the last trace of a doubt, if ever there was one before, that the convictions of Thomas Agnello *et al* must stand. Any further appeals on their behalf had to be considered dilatory, yet on April 16 when George Gordon Battle filed a petition to have the Supreme Court review the convictions of all five defendants, the United States joined him "in requesting that the writ of certiorari issue as prayed for." Why did they not try to have the case of Frank Agnello severed?

It hardly needs to be stressed that convicted felons enlarged on bail must pursue their appeal diligently or be incarcerated as long as it is pending. Were this not generally so, the appellate courts would be awash with protracted appeals along with, one would suspect, a concomitant reduction in the nation's prison population. Through successive stays, all granted with the concurrence of the U.S. Attorney, Thomas Agnello and the others remained at large for

---

[25] Brief on Behalf of the United States, 18, 19.

12-1676.

DEPARTMENT OF JUSTICE

UNITED STATES ATTORNEY
EASTERN DISTRICT OF NEW YORK
ROOM 211 FEDERAL G
BROOKLYN,

WAD/FLK

Mr. Ramsey

M. ___

April 21, 1926.

The Attorney General,
Washington, D. C.

RECORDED

12-1676-26

APR 22 ___ A.

LUHRING-RAMSEY

S i r : -

The matter of Thomas and Frank Agnello, et al., a

narcotic case in which the defendants were convicted over

four years ago, went through an appeal to the Circuit Court

of Appeals and a certiorari to the Supreme Court, the judg-

ment being affirmed throughout as to all except one defendant,

Frank Agnello. The order on the mandate was duly entered and

the defendants were booked to commence their respective terms

several months ago. On the request of representatives of Mr.

Nutt, Chief of the Narcotic Division, we have deferred the

apprehension and imprisonment of the defendants who are at

large on heavy bail. This request for delay has been confirmed

by telephone and I asked today that it be confirmed in writing by

the Chief of the Narcotic Division.

In the meantime, Thomas Agnello who has grown rich in

this business, is living in ostensible luxury and we have reason

to believe has been doing business in the same line, but has

been too cunning to be arrested on a new charge. How much harm

he has done will never be known. If he professes reform and de-

sires to help the Government, he has had over four years to show

it. If he continues at large and still plies his nefarious craft

-3-

who can say that it may be for no better purpose than to seek revenge, eliminate his competitors or graft on others in his line? One might assume that true penitence and a disposition to help the Government to stamp out this damnable trade would be better proven in Atlanta than in parading in fine livery about the country as an object of envy while we may justly be held in contempt of the people whom we serve for allowing him to remain at large in the full enjoyment of his ill gotten gain.

Generally speaking, I have no objection to follow any reasonable suggestion of responsible officials which may be helpful to them in the performance of their duties, but in this instance I do not feel justified in assuming any responsibility for further delay in this matter without express authority from the Department of Justice. A very few lines from you will be appreciated and of course is all that will be required to settle my mind as to the course of duty which confronts me.

Respectfully,

WILLIAM A. DeGROOT,
U. S. Attorney.

more than four years. The writ of certiorari enabling the Supreme Court to review the lower court's findings was issued April 30, 1923, but George Gordon Battle did not file his brief until December 3, 1924. During this time the United States made no attempt to have the writ dismissed for lack of diligence.

The Court's decision on October 12, 1925, reversed the conviction of Frank Agnello alone. The convictions of the other defendants were upheld and there was no valid reason why they should not have been immediately remanded. Nevertheless, at the request of the Attorney General's Office, their commitment was further deferred. In April of 1926 William DeGroot, the U.S. Attorney for the Eastern District of New York, asked the Attorney General how long this intolerable situation would have to be endured.

> In the meantime, Thomas Agnello who has grown rich in this business, is living in ostensible luxury and we have reason to believe has been doing business in the same line, but has been too cunning to be arrested on a new charge. How much harm he has done will never be known. If he professes reform and desires to help the Government, he has had over four years to show it. If he continues at large and still plies his nefarious craft who can say that it may be for no better purpose than to seek revenge, eliminate his competitors or graft on others in his line? One might assume that true penitence and a disposition to help the Government to stamp out this damnable trade would be better proven in Atlanta than in parading in fine livery about the country as an object of envy while we may justly be held in contempt of the people whom we serve for allowing him to remain at large in the full enjoyment of his ill gotten gain.[26]

DeGroot asked that any further instructions to defer the execution of the sentence be given in writing. This letter had the intended effect. Two weeks later the case file for *Agnello v. United*

---

[26] William. A. DeGroot to Attorney General, April 21, 1926. Justice Department correspondence regarding *Agnello v. United States* bears the prefix 12-1676 followed by a distinguishing number. This letter is No. 12-1676-26, R.G. 60, DJA, #112, Straight Numerical Files, 1904-37.

States notes: "Deft. Thomas Agnello present and remanded to custody of Marshal for Execution of sentence from May 4, 1926."[27]

But the U.S. Penitentiary Inmates Systems Management, 601 McDonough Blvd., Atlanta, Georgia 30315, in response to the author's inquiry as to Thomas Agnello, stated that they "have no information concerning this individual." In any event, Agnello did not have to serve out his time; he had friends in high places.

June 3, 1927

In re
Thomas Agnello.

———

Honorable William J. Donovan,
    Assistant to the Attorney General,
      Washington, D.C.

My dear Colonel Donovan:-

Please accept my hearty thanks for your courteous telegram reading as follows:

"Case went to President today with recommendation that sentence be commuted to expire at once on condition that fine be paid."

I greatly appreciate your prompt attention to this matter.

With warm personal regards, I am

Faithfully yours,

George Gordon Battle[28]

One would assume such a recomendation would be made in

———

27 Criminal Docket No. 8188, U.S. District Court, EDNY, Federal Record Center, Bayonne, New Jersey.
28 George G. Battle to William J. Donovan, June 3, 1927, No. 12-1676-32, DJA.

writing by either Donovan or Attorney General Sargent. Certainly it would have given the President the reasons why Agnello's sentence should be commuted. If Calvin Coolidge had followed the example of Woodrow Wilson, the original letter of recomendation would be among his papers together with a copy of his response. Neither can be found in the Calvin Coolidge Papers in the Library of Congress.

One would expect to find in the Department of Justice case file for *Agnello v. United States*, along with Battle's letter of June 3, a copy of the "courteous telegram" for which he thanked Donovan, as well as a copy of the letter to the President recommending the commutation of Thomas Agnello's sentence and the President's reply. They are neither there nor anywhere else. All correspondence now extant between Coolidge on one hand and Donovan and Sargent on the other has been catalogued alphabetically and indexed chronologically in the Calvin Coolidge Papers. No such letter or reply is there to be found. But for a faceless clerk who filed Battle's note no one would ever know that the sentence of Thomas Agnello was commuted by the President.

What the Agnellos got out of the deal was leniency. Thomas Agnello was to remain at large until after the election of 1928 when something might be done for him. Then an exasperated U.S. Attorney put Donovan on the spot by writing a caustic letter demanding that his instructions to defer the commitment of Thomas Agnello be confirmed in writing. And so Thomas Agnello had to take a fall until the heat was off and Battle could spring him, but his brother Frank went unscathed. The file for *Agnello v. United States* tells us what became of the case against the drug dealer whose conviction the Justice Department deemed of sufficient importance to see its appeal through the Supreme Court of the United States. On December 5, 1928, as time was running out on the Coolidge administration, the case against Frank Agnello was dismissed. "Case called as to Frank Agnello and dismissed as to him on motion Asst. U.S. Atty."[29]

---

[29] Criminal Docket No. 8188, U.S. District Court, EDNY, Federal Records Center, Bayonne, New Jersey.

It is not to be supposed that the Justices of the Supreme Court were taken in by all of this. They knew that whatever they decided in *Agnello* with respect to federal drug agents would apply to federal Prohibition agents with equal force. But we must bear in mind that these men could see the world only in the context of their times. To them it was a trade-off. While to subvert the judicial process was not a good thing, it was a lesser evil than the corruption Prohibition engendered.

Whatever they did, they did with the understanding that the false standard they forged could be applied only to the federal government. If, as a result, an occasional bootlegger, smuggler, tax evader, and the like went unwhipped of justice, that was a tolerable price to pay. They could not have imagined that it would be applied to the individual states and that its chief beneficiaries would be the robbers, rapists, and murderers who roam our streets today. When the Eighteenth Amendment was repealed in 1933, the precedents it spawned should have been repealed along with it.

Chapter XIII

THE WARRANT REQUIREMENT

The warrant requirement established in *Agnello v. United States* in 1925 lasted some 22 years. During that time, as we shall see, the application of the *Weeks* rule, of which it had become a part, was almost exclusively the concern of those engaged in violating or enforcing Prohibition. Then in 1947 the plain meaning of the text of the Fourth Amendment—the simple and unanswerable truth not advanced in *Agnello*—prevailed in *Harris v. United States*.

George Harris had been arrested at his home by agents of the FBI on a charge that he had caused a forged check to be transported in interstate commerce. The FBI held a valid warrant to arrest him but no warrant to search his home. After arresting Harris, the agents proceeded to search his apartment for stolen checks they had probable cause to believe were there, and, in the process, found a considerable number of Selective Service "draft cards." Draft cards were the universal form of identification men carried at that time and would be of use to a professional check forger and passer. There were no such things as credit cards.

Indicted for the illegal possession of draft cards, under federal law a felony, Harris moved to suppress the evidence. The motion was denied and Harris tried and convicted. He then appealed on the grounds that the admission into evidence of the draft cards violated his rights under the Fourth Amendment. By a vote of five to four, the Supreme Court upheld his conviction in a statement of the law we must not forget.

> This Court has also pointed out that it is only unreasonable searches and seizures which come within the constitutional interdict. The test of reasonableness cannot be stated in rigid and absolute terms. "Each case is to be decided on its own facts and circumstances." *Go-Bart Importing Company v. United States*, 282 U.S. 344, 357 (1931).

> The Fourth Amendment has never been held to require that every valid search and seizure be effected under the authority of a search warrant.[1]

If the "reasonableness" of a search or seizure in *each case is to be decided on its own facts and circumstances*, "reasonableness" always would be a question of fact rather than a question of law. The circumstances of each case are unique; those in the case at bar will always differ from those in any other. A judge would *never* be bound by the doctrine of *stare decisis* to say that a murderer like Edward Coolidge *must* go free because of a decision in a prior case said to be "the law."

If the "reasonableness" of a search or seizure in *each case is to be decided on its own facts and circumstances,* the nature and scope of the intrusion on one hand would be weighed against the exigencies of law enforcement on the other. In *Coolidge v. New Hampshire* the police had the most probable of cause to believe that the suspect's 1951 Pontiac automobile was the scene of the murder of Pamela Mason. Under the facts and circumstances that then prevailed, how could anyone say that the vacuuming of that automobile and the seizure of the dust it accumulated was such an intrusion into the privacy of Edward Coolidge as to constitute an unreasonable search and seizure forbidden by the Fourth Amendment?

If the "reasonableness" of a search or seizure in *each case is to be*

---

[1] *Harris v. United States*, 331 U.S. 145, 150 (1947).

decided on its own facts and circumstances, a judge must necessarily decide what is reasonable and what is not by empathy. What kind of treatment would he have expected were he in the suspect's shoes? Faced with the scenario of the search in question, what would he have done were he the policeman?

If the "reasonableness" of a search or seizure in *each case is to be decided on its own facts and circumstances*, a judge must in each case necessarily pit his assessment of the facts and circumstances against that made by the police. The police made their call as to reasonableness when they went ahead with the search or seizure. The judge must now decide *post facto* whether or not they acted unreasonably.

In this regard a judge would be accountable, in the bar of public opinion, at least, for the consequences of his decision. Should a miscarriage of justice be the result—as in *Coolidge v. New Hampshire*—he could not shield himself from criticism by laying it at the feet of the Framers. The onus would be upon him—that judge—to explain why he thought that under the facts and circumstances of that case the murder conviction of Edward Coolidge should be reversed. And who in the opinion of most Americans are better finders of fact in such situations: a judge or the detectives who have been working on the case?

Finally, if the "reasonableness" of a search or seizure in *each case is to be decided on its own facts and circumstances*, a judge who wished to exclude evidence would be in a most uncomfortable position. More often than not, the evidence which the defense is seeking to suppress, when taken together with the probable cause which led the police to believe it would be found, is the very evidence which proves beyond a reasonable doubt that the defendant is guilty of the crime of which he is charged. The guilt of the defendant and the reasonableness of the search are usually mutually supportive.

It is no accident that the scenarios in *Weeks* and the other cases which went into the formation of the exclusionary rule were faked. Truly unreasonable searches invariably come up empty-handed so that there is no evidence to exclude. If the reasonableness of a search or seizure in *each case is to be decided on its own facts and circumstances*—the holding in *Harris*—the impact of the exclusionary rule on criminal justice would be so minimal as to make a study of it a waste of time.

Weeks and *Harris* could not coexist; one or the other had to go. A year later *Harris* died under mysterious circumstances in *Johnson v. United States.*[2] *Johnson*, along with *Weeks*, are the two pillars of the exclusionary rule *Mapp v. Ohio* will apply to the states. Unlike *Harris*, whose precedent lasted but a year, the precedent of *Johnson* has been long-lived and, after the passage of half a century, binds us today. Its importance cannot be overstated.

The case began in a corridor of the Europe Hotel in Seattle, Washington, where five men with educated noses were sniffing around. One was a city detective and the other four were federal narcotics agents. "All were experienced in narcotic work and recognized at once a strong odor of burning opium which to them was distinctive and unmistakable. The odor led to Room 1." They knocked on the door, identified themselves, and after a slight delay and some rustling or shuffling around, were admitted. They searched the room and found "incriminating opium and smoking apparatus, the latter being warm, apparently from recent use."

Anne Johnson was indicted, tried, and convicted of possession of narcotics, a felony, and sentenced to 18 months in prison and a fine of $250. She sought review by the Supreme Court on the grounds that the evidence against her had been unlawfully seized and should have been suppressed under the *Weeks* rule. The search of her room, she claimed, had been made in violation of the Fourth Amendment. The Court agreed.

Johnson v. United States held that probable cause must be determined not by the police, but by a magistrate before the search is conducted. This decision has been used time and time again to justify the release of defendants all men acknowledge are guilty of the most heinous of crimes. *Coolidge v. New Hampshire*, the case with which we began, is one example. In memorial to the murdered Pamela Mason and the countless victims of vicious crimes whose perpetrators will escape justice after the exclusionary rule and its

---

[2] *Johnson v. United States*, 333 U.S. 10, 12 (1948).

warrant corollary are applied to the states in 1961, we will reargue *Johnson v. United States*. Let us review the facts before we plan our strategy.

The question before the Court is this: Is a search and seizure made by a federal officer upon "probable cause"—cause probable enough to convince any magistrate to issue a search warrant—an unreasonable search and seizure forbidden by the Fourth Amendment simply because that officer did not obtain a warrant beforehand? One year before in *Harris v. United States* (1947), by a vote of five-to-four, the Supreme Court answered this question in the negative overruling by implication *Agnello v. United States* (1925).

Mr. Justice Frankfurter had dissented in *Harris*. Felix Frankfurter had taken his seat on the Supreme Court in 1939 after stormy confirmation hearings which focused on his activities on behalf of those his critics saw as subversives. Felix Frankfurter was for the exclusionary rule so long as it was applied only to the federal government, and, it is appropriate to note, both *Harris* and *Johnson* were decided at a time when revelations about Communist infiltration into the federal government were the issue of the day. Inveighing in his dissent against fear and repression, FF recalled the excesses of the Red Scare.

> The dangers are not fanciful. We too readily forget them. Recollection may be refreshed as to the happenings after the first World War by the "Report upon the Illegal Practices of the United States Department of Justice," which aroused the public concern of Chief Justice Hughes (FN8) (then at the bar), and by the little book entitled "The Deportations Delirium of Nineteen-Twenty" by Louis F. Post, who spoke with the authoritative knowledge of an Assistant Secretary of Labor.[3]

ACLU Annual Report No. 3, on page 25, states that "the union made possible the publication . . . of Deportations Delirium of 1920, by Louis F. Post, published by Charles H. Kerr and

---

[3] *Harris*, 173-174.

Company," the "little book" to which Justice Frankfurter refers. The annual report lists, as did the previous two, Felix Frankfurter as a national committeeman. He was also, as you will recall, one of the authors of "Report upon the Illegal Practices of the United States Department of Justice," the other work he cites to refresh our recollection of the Red Scare.

In footnote 8 above, after citing a 1920 address by former Supreme Court Justice Charles Evans Hughes before the Harvard Law School Association, Mr. Justice Frankfurter recalled *Colyer v. Skeffington*, a case in which Professor Frankfurter had played a role. He neglected, however, to mention his part in it or that Judge George W. Anderson's decision was subsequently reversed on appeal in the 1922 case of *Skeffington v. Katzeff*, a fact of which Frankfurter had to be aware.

> FN 8. For a contemporaneous judicial account of searches and seizures in violation of the Fourth Amendment in connection with the Communist raids of January 2, 1920, see Judge George W. Anderson's opinion in *Colyer v. Skeffington*, 265 F. 17.

Frankfurter was joined in his dissent by Frank Murphy and Wiley Rutledge. Justice Murphy wrote a separate dissenting opinion, with which Rutledge and Frankfurter concurred, that also raised the specter of Mitchell Palmer.

> The principle established by the Court today can be used as easily by some future government determined to suppress political opposition under the guise of sedition as it can be used by a government determined to undo forgers and defrauders. See *United States v. Kirschenblatt*, 16 F.2d 202, 203. History is not without examples of the outlawry of certain political, religious and economic beliefs and the relentless prosecution of those who dare to entertain such beliefs. And history has a way of repeating itself.[4]

---

[4] *Harris*, 194.

When a law admits of more than one interpretation, it is useful to look at the history which brought it about to see what it was that its enactors sought to accomplish. This is especially true in the case of a constitutional amendment.

> The safe way is to read its language in connection with the known condition of affairs out of which the occasion for its adoption may have arisen, and then to construe it, if there be therein any doubtful expressions, in a way so far as is reasonably possible, to forward the known purpose or object for which the amendment was adopted. *Maxwell v. Dow*, 176 U.S. 581, 602 (1900),

And this was what Felix Frankfurter, in his dissent in *Harris*, purported to do. "Thus, one's views" regarding the warrant issue, wrote FF, "ultimately depend upon one's understanding of the history and the function of the Fourth Amendment . . . The provenance of the Fourth Amendment bears on its scope. It will be recalled that James Otis made his epochal argument against general warrants in 1761. Otis' defense of privacy was enshrined in the Massachusetts Constitution of 1780 in the following terms":

> XIV. Every subject has a right to be secure from all unreasonable searches, and seizures of his person, his houses, his papers, and all his possessions. All warrants, therefore, are contrary to this right, if the cause or foundation of them be not previously supported by oath or affirmation; and if the order in the warrant to a civil officer, to make search in suspected places, or to arrest one or more suspected persons, or to seize their property, be not accompanied with a special designation of the persons or objects of search, arrest, or seizure: and no warrant ought to be issued but in cases, and with the formalities, prescribed by the laws.[5]

It was the Massachusetts form, according to Frankfurter, upon

---

[5] *Harris*, 158.

which James Madison drew when he came to deal with safeguards against searches and seizures in the United States Constitution.[6] We shall see directly what Madison thought on this subject, but in the meanwhile it is sufficient to say that nothing in Justice Frankfurter's understanding of the "history and the function of the Fourth Amendment," including the "Massachusetts Form" above, remotely justified his conclusion that:

> The plain import of this is that searches are "unreasonable" unless authorized by a warrant, and a warrant hedged about by adequate safeguards. "Unreasonable" is not to be determined with reference to a particular search and seizure considered in isolation. The "reason" by which search and seizure is to be tested is the "reason" that was written out of historic experience into the Fourth Amendment. This means that, with minor and severely confined exceptions, inferentially a part of the Amendment, every search and seizure is unreasonable when made without a magistrate's authority expressed through a validly issued warrant.[7]

The Solicitor General is the officer whose task it is to represent the Executive Branch of the United States in the Supreme Court. He "is the only governmental official specifically charged by statute with being 'learned in the law.'"[8] It is December of 1947 and the case on the docket is *Johnson v. United States*. We shall put ourselves in the place of Solicitor General Philip B. Perlman and his fellow advocates and see how well law-abiding Americans were served by their counsel.[9]

Let us begin by noting that we will be arguing the same issue before a Court composed of the same nine Justices who decided *Harris* seven months before. In *Harris*, the majority—Chief Justice

---

[6] *Harris*, 158.
[7] Ibid., 161, 162.
[8] Edward Lazarus. *Closed Chambers*. New York: Times Book/Random House, 1998, 230.
[9] "*Robert S. Erdahl* argued the cause for the United States. With him on the brief were *Solicitor General Perlman, Assistant Attorney General Quinn* and *Irving S. Shapiro*." *Johnson v. United States*, 11.

Vinson and Associates Black, Reed, Burton, and Douglas—simply stated the obvious fact that the Fourth Amendment does not say that searches and seizures must be made under the authority of a warrant. There is no sense in belaboring that point, a recitation of the holding in *Harris* will be sufficient. If the unadorned text of the Fourth Amendment is to prevail, so also will we. That there was probable cause to believe that Anne Johnson was in possession of narcotics need not be overstressed either; a simple statement of the facts and circumstances makes the case against her. What we must concern ourselves with is *history*.

The dissenters in *Harris* were Felix Frankfurter, Frank Murphy, Wiley Rutledge, and Robert Jackson. Their dissents were grounded, in one way or another, in the history and events which led to the passage of the Fourth Amendment. It was Frankfurter's contention that when interpreted in the context of that "historic experience," a warrant requirement should be implied. "[E]very search and seizure is unreasonable when made without a magistrate's authority expressed through a validly issued warrant," constitutional historian Frankfurter wrote authoritatively.

But his argument seems lacking in substance. For one thing, *Wilkes v. Wood*, the English case Frankfurter emphasized, involved a search and seizure which *was* made pursuant to a warrant. At issue was whether this search warrant—broad and open-ended—could be used as a shield to protect the defendant officials against liability in a suit by those they had wronged. And if there was anything specific to show that the Founding Fathers had an abiding concern as to warrantless searches, Frankfurter did not come up with it. Undoubtedly the Court's decision in *Johnson v. United States* will, as FF put it in *Harris*, "ultimately depend upon one's understanding of the history and the function of the Fourth Amendment." So we had better make our own excursion into colonial history and challenge his synthesis with one of our own.

The logical place to start is with the accession to the throne of George III in October of 1760, the first in the series of events which led to the Revolutionary War. No account is complete, and none ever made, without recalling James Otis. But Otis said nothing of warrantless searches; what he addressed was the evil of the "writ of assistance," the name given a form of general warrant issued to customs officers, and the power and immunity it conferred upon its bearer. A man possessing such a writ, said Otis, "is accountable to no person for his doings."

> It is a power, that places the liberty of every man in the hands of every petty officer . . . Every one with this writ may be a tyrant in a legal manner . . . a person with this writ, in the day time, may enter all houses, shops, etc. at will, and command all to assist him. Fourthly, by this writ, not only deputies, etc. but even their menial servants, are allowed to lord it over us.[10]

Warrants were issued in the name of the king and when George II died in 1760, by law all warrants in the British Empire then extant terminated six months thereafter.[11] For the legal system to operate new ones were required in the name of the new king. Those issued by George III were anything but limited and specific, and their legality was challenged on both sides of the Atlantic. In America the case was argued in February of 1761 before the colonial judges in the Old Town House in Boston. "May it please your honours," Otis began:

> I was desired by one of the Court to look into the books, and consider the question now before them concerning Writs of Assistance . . .

> I will to my dying day oppose with all the powers and faculties God has given me, all such instruments of slavery on the one hand, and villainy on the other, as this writ of assistance is. It appears to me the worst instrument of arbitrary power, the most destructive of English liberty and the fundamental principles of law, that ever was found in an English law book.[12]

---

[10] William Tudor. *The Life of James Otis of Massachusetts*. Originally published in 1823, this book was reprinted in 1970 by Da Capo Press of New York City. Quotes are at page 66.

[11] "But these writs continued in force only until the demise [of George II on October 25, 1760] and for six months afterward." American Law Review, Vol. 3, *James Otis*, 641, 649 (1868).

[12] Tudor, 63.

> Now one of the most essential branches of English liberty is the freedom of one's house. A man's house is his castle; and whilst he is quiet, he is as well guarded as a prince in his castle. This writ, if it should be declared legal, would totally annihilate this privilege.[13]

A warrant, in this context, is a writ directing or authorizing an officer of the law to make a search or seizure. An officer may make a search and seizure without a warrant, but if he does so, he does so at his peril. An officer making a warrantless search without probable cause has committed a trespass. If the seizure is of a person—an arrest—it is an assault. Such an officer is personally liable for these torts in a civil action for damages brought against him by an aggrieved party. This is not true of a search or seizure made pursuant to a warrant. An officer executing a warrant acts under a cloak of immunity. In the event the facts thought to constitute probable cause turn out to be false, he is not liable for the indignities the victim may have suffered.

This is why it is imperative that warrants be narrowly drawn and supported by affidavit. If a warrant does not specify who or what is sought and no one vouches for the probable cause which prompts the search, there is no accountability. What the British had done was to issue, on the basis of facts unsworn, if stated at all, warrants so broad and sweeping as to give its agents authority to search at will without having to worry about personal liability. A victim of even a malicious search or seizure had no recourse.

Otis gave the court an example. A customs officer named Ware held a writ of assistance to search for uncustomed goods. Ware was arrested "by a constable, to answer for a breach of the sabbath-day acts, or that of profane swearing" and brought before a judge.

> As soon as [the judge] had finished, Mr. Ware asked him if he had done. He replied, Yes. Well then, said Mr. Ware, I will shew you a little of my power. I command

---

[13] Ibid., 66, 67.

you to permit me to search your house for uncustomed
goods; and went on to search the house from the garret
to the cellar; and then served the constable in the same
manner![14]

It was the writ of assistance—a general warrant—which gave
Ware the power he showed the judge and the constable. He would
not have dared to make the search without it. For had he done so,
Ware would have been sued straight away, and, given his outrageous
behavior, a jury most likely would have awarded the plaintiffs
exemplary damages. An officer making a search or seizure without
benefit of a warrant was then, as he is now, liable for the
consequences of his actions. It was the warrant that placed the
liberty of every man in the hands of a petty officer like Ware and
permitted him to be a tyrant in a legal manner.

The story then moves across the Atlantic to Manchester,
England, and the 1763 case of *Wilkes v. Wood*,[15] cited by
Frankfurter in support of his case. John Wilkes, a noted wit and
member of Parliament, was suspected of being the author of a
pamphlet deemed libelous of George III.

A warrant was issued by Lord Halifax, the secretary of
state, to four messengers, ordering them "to make strict
and diligent search for the authors, printers, and
publishers of a seditious and treasonable paper, entitled,
The North Briton No. 45, . . . and them, or any of them,
having found, to apprehend and seize, together with
their papers."[16]

Armed with "this 'roving commission,' they proceeded to arrest
upon suspicion no less than forty-nine persons in three days, even
taking some of them from their beds in the middle of the night"[17]

---

[14] Tudor, 67.

[15] *Wilkes v. Wood*, 3 Geo. 3, 98 Eng. Rep. 489 (1763).

[16] Nelson B. Lasson. *The History and Development of the Fourth Amendment to the United States Constitution*. Baltimore: John Hopkins Press, 1937, 43.

[17] Ibid., 43,44.

before arresting John Wilkes and seizing his papers. Wilkes brought suit against Robert Wood, who had led the expedition into his privacy, as well as Lord Halifax, who had issued the warrant.

Wilkes v. Wood was tried before Chief Justice Charles Pratt.[18] The defendants pleaded the general warrant in their defense, but the warrant was held to be illegal.

> [The Chief Justice] then went upon the warrant, which he declared was a point of the greatest consequence he had ever met with in his whole practice. The defendants claimed a right, under precedents, to force persons houses, break open escritoires, seize their papers, etc. upon a general warrant, where no inventory is made of the things thus taken away, and where no offenders names are specified in the warrant, and therefore a discretionary power given to messengers to search wherever their suspicions may chance to fall. If such a power is truly invested in a Secretary of State, and he can delegate this power, it certainly may affect the person and property of every man in this kingdom, and is totally subversive of the liberty of the subject.[19]

Pratt quashed the warrant and the defendants, thus stripped of their immunity, were held liable for trespass and false imprisonment. Wilkes was awarded a judgment for 1,000 pounds against Wood and 4,000 against Lord Halifax, enormous sums at the time. "These decisions were greeted with the wildest acclaim all over England. 'Wilkes and Liberty' became the byword of the times, even in far-away America."[20] Chief Justice Pratt left no doubt that he considered the tort remedy the proper deterrent.

> [A] jury have it in their power to give damages for more than the injury received. Damages are designed not only

---

[18] "Pratt, Charles, 1st Earl Camden, 1714-94, English jurist, Lord chancellor (1766-70). Declared the prosecution of John Wilkes illegal. Denounced British policy toward American colonists." *The Columbia Viking Desk Encyclopedia*, New York: Viking Press, 1968.

[19] *Wilkes*, 498.

[20] Lasson, 45, 46.

as a satisfaction to the injured person, but likewise as a
punishment to the guilty, to deter from any such
proceeding for the future, and as a proof of the
detestation of the jury to the action itself.[21]

The exclusion of evidence was never considered. At the time his
case was decided, Wilkes had a charge of criminal libel pending
against him. As to any evidence seized by the trespassers, Pratt
"[o]bserved, that if the jury found Mr. Wilkes the author or
publisher of No. 45 [the offending pamphlet], it will be filed, and
stand upon record in the Court of Common Pleas, and of course be
produced as proof, upon the criminal cause . . ."[22]

There is yet another argument we must meet. While grounded
in colonial history, it arises nevertheless from the text of the Fourth
Amendment. To Justice Robert H. Jackson, the problem with the
Fourth Amendment was its syntax. He wrote a dissenting opinion
in *Harris* which pointed out the curious fact that while the Fourth
Amendment imposes specific limitations on searches and seizures
made pursuant to a warrant, it requires no such limitations of those
made without a warrant.

As to warrantless searches and seizures, the Fourth Amendment
requires only that they not be "unreasonable," which Jackson found
anomalous.

> The Fourth Amendment first declares in bold broad terms:
> "The right of the people to be secure in their persons,
> houses, papers, and effects, against unreasonable searches
> and seizures, shall not be violated . . . ." Our trouble arises
> because this sentence leaves debatable what particular
> searches are unreasonable ones. Those who think it their
> duty to make searches seldom agree on this point with those
> who find it in their interest to frustrate searches.

The Amendment, having thus roughly indicated the

---

[21] *Wilkes,* 498, 499.
[22] *Wilkes,* 499.

immunity of the citizen which must not be violated, goes on to recite how officers may be authorized, consistently with the right so declared, to make searches: " . . . and no Warrants shall issue, but upon probable cause, supported by Oath or affirmation, and particularly describing the place to be searched, and the persons or things to be seized."

Here endeth the command of the forefathers, apparently because they believed that by thus controlling search warrants they had controlled searches.[23]

Jackson did not think the Framers "intended to leave open an easy way to circumvent" the more specific requirements of the Fourth Amendment and proposed to remedy this textual deficiency by declaring warrantless searches inherently unreasonable. "The fair implication . . . is that no search of premises, as such, is reasonable except the cause for it be approved and the limits of it fixed and the scope of it particularly defined by a disinterested magistrate."

Of course, this, like each of our constitutional guarantees, often may afford a shelter for criminals. But the forefathers thought this was not too great a price to pay for that decent privacy of home, papers and effects which is indispensable to individual dignity and self-respect. They may have overvalued privacy, but I am not disposed to set their command at naught.[24]

Nothing is more insightful into the mind of the Framers than the prior drafts of the Fourth Amendment and the changes which brought about the final product passed in the First Session of the First Congress. James Madison wrote the first draft of what became the Bill of Rights, and in June of 1789 his proposals were submitted to the House of Representatives. The first version of what became the Fourth Amendment—drafted by the "Father of the Constitution"—was this:

---

[23] *Harris*, 195, 196.
[24] *Harris*, 198.

> The rights of the people to be secured in their persons; their houses, their papers, and their other property, from all unreasonable searches and seizures, shall not be violated by warrants issued without probable cause, supported by oath or affirmation, or not particularly describing the places to be searched, or the persons or things to be seized.[25]

On July 21[26] the House referred the proposed amendments to a "Committee of Eleven" it had formed which consisted of one member from each state.[27] "On August 13 the House resolved itself into a Committee of the Whole to consider the report and the debate upon the proposed amendments, each being considered separately, lasted ten days."[28] On August 17, 1789, the Committee of Eleven reported Madison's proposals to the Committee of the Whole with the search and seizure provision now reading as follows:

> The right of the people to be secured in their persons, houses, papers, and effects, shall not be violated by warrants issuing without probable cause, supported by oath or affirmation, and not particularly describing the place to be searched, and the persons or things to be seized.[29]

It was then proposed by Congressman Elbridge Gerry that the word "secured" be changed to "secure" and the phrase "unreasonable searches and seizures" be reinserted. These proposals were adopted.[30] Congressman Benson of New York then moved the following amendment:

> Mr. Benson objected to the words "by warrants issuing." This declaratory provision was good as far as it went, but

---

[25] *The Debates and Proceedings in the Congress of the United States,* Vol. 1. Washington D.C.: Gales and Seaton (1834), hereinafter *Annals of Congress* or *Annals,* 252.

[26] *Annals,* 690.

[27] Two of the original 13 colonies—Rhode Island and North Carolina—had not yet ratified the Constitution.

[28] Lasson, 100.

[29] *Annals,* 783.

[30] *Annals.*

he thought it was not sufficient; he therefore proposed to alter it so as to read "and no warrant shall issue."

The question was put on this motion, and lost by a considerable majority.[31]

The Fourth Amendment, of course, had to be passed by the Senate as well. This the Senate did, without amendment. What debate there was we will never know. "Little information concerning the deliberations of the Senate is available, due to the fact that until 1794 the Senate sat behind closed doors and that there are consequently no reports of its debates."[32] The amendment will be ratified by state legislatures or conventions. But it was, after all, submitted to them—necessarily so—on a "take it or leave it" basis. So whatever opinion or reservation state legislators or delegates might have expressed, if any there were, are not really important.

The Committee of the Whole, on the other hand, was composed of the entire House, men who for the most part had endured the Revolutionary War and the troubles which preceded it. When they spoke, they expressed the collective will of the House of Representatives and their understanding of the colonial experience with respect to search and seizure. We will never find a better or more pure distillation of what was the intent of the Framers of the Fourth Amendment than by tracing its progress through the House of Representatives.

This then was the text of the proposed Fourth Amendment approved by the Committee of the Whole after the acceptance of the Gerry proposal and the rejection of the Benson amendment on August 17, 1789:

> The right of the people to be secure in their persons, houses, papers, and effects, against unreasonable searches and seizures, shall not be violated by warrants issuing without probable cause, supported by oath or

---

[31] *Annals.*

[32] Lasson, 102, footnote 86.

affirmation, and not particularly describing the place to be searched, and the persons or things to be seized.

In 1937 Dr. Nelson B. Lasson published *The History and Development of the Fourth Amendment to the United States Constitution.* It was his research that uncovered what amounts to the "hijacking" of the Fourth Amendment for, you see, it is the Benson version—which lost by a considerable majority—which is today the Fourth Amendment to the Constitution of the United States.

> The right of the people to be secure in their persons, houses, papers, and effects, against unreasonable searches and seizures, shall not be violated [by warrants issuing without], *and no warrants shall issue, but upon* probable cause, supported by oath or affirmation, and not particularly describing the place to be searched, and the persons or things to be seized. [Emphasis added]

Egbert Benson (1746-1833) served in the House of Representatives from 1789 to 1793.[33] A New Yorker, he was chairman of the Committee of Three. Lasson tells the story.

> However, on August 24, when Benson as chairman of a Committee of Three, which had been appointed to arrange the amendments, reported an arrangement of the [first ten] amendments as they were supposed to have been agreed upon by the House, the *clause appeared as he had proposed it and as the House had rejected it.*

> And so it stands today. The records do not show that the alteration was ever noticed or assented to as such by the House. In this form it was received and agreed to by the Senate. And the only remaining discussion by the House and Senate concerned those [other] amendments upon which the two houses were not in accord.[34]

With respect to warrantless searches, two ironic truths emerge from

---

[33] *Congressional Quarterly's Guide to Congress,* 4th Ed.
[34] Lasson, 101, 102 [footnotes omitted].

the *Annals* of the First Congress. The first one is that the Fourth Amendment which is the law today does not represent the intent of the Framers. The second is that the August 17, 1789, draft it supplanted, which did—"by a considerable majority"—represent the intent of the Framers, is not part of the Constitution we have sworn to uphold. This does not mean, however, that it is without significance.

While the prior drafts are not "the law," they are a source—indeed the best source—from which to resolve ambiguity into what did become the Fourth Amendment when ambiguity in its text arises. They are most certainly an important part of the history the proponents of the warrant requirement invoke to "find" in the Fourth Amendment a requirement which cannot be discerned from its tenor. Let us look once again at the three drafts of the Fourth Amendment which preceded the Benson coup:

MADISON'S DRAFT
July, 1789

The rights of the people to be secured in their persons; their houses, their papers, and their other property, from all unreasonable searches and seizures, shall not be violated by warrants issued without probable cause, supported by oath or affirmation, or not particularly describing the places to be searched, or the persons or things to be seized.

COMMITTEE OF ELEVEN

The right of the people to be secured in their persons, houses, papers, and effects, shall not be violated by warrants issuing without probable cause, supported by oath or affirmation, and not particularly describing the place to be searched, and the persons or things to be seized.

FINAL DRAFT
COMMITTEE OF THE WHOLE
August 17, 1789

The right of the people to be secure in their persons, houses, papers, and effects, against unreasonable searches and seizures, shall not be violated by warrants issuing without probable cause, supported by oath or affirmation, and not particularly describing the place to be searched, and the persons or things to be seized.

Two salient facts fairly leap out of the text of these drafts. In all three, the *right of privacy*—that is "the right of the people to be secure in their persons, houses, papers, and effects"—is protected only as against searches and seizures made pursuant to what the Framers knew as "general warrants"—that is "warrants issuing without probable cause, supported by oath or affirmation, and not particularly describing the place to be searched, and the persons or things to be seized." In none of the drafts is the *right of privacy* protected as against searches and seizures made without warrants. Officers acting without warrants were always amenable to civil suit, and one can only conclude that the Framers were quite content to rely on the law of torts to deter them from acting arbitrarily. And this is in perfect consonance with the colonial experience.

Our forefathers were not as fortunate as John Wilkes. The ringing words of James Otis, while they may have kindled a revolution, did not sway the colonial judges. By upholding the writs of assistance, they left Americans subject to invasions of privacy by British officials thereby rendered impervious to any tort remedy. And it was this which was in the minds of the First Congress when they met in spring of 1789.

To deter the agents of the newly formed federal government from visiting on posterity the same usurpations the British had inflicted on them, the Framers sought to enshrine in the Constitution the rule of law established in *Wilkes v. Wood*. Henceforward, any warrant not meeting the specifications of the Fourth Amendment would be quashed as unconstitutional and void. Should the victim of an arbitrary search or seizure bring an action for trespass, or, if the seizure was of his person, for assault or false imprisonment, such a warrant would provide no immunity for the American counterparts of Robert Wood and Lord Halifax.

So not only does history not support the view that the Framers "preferred" that a search and seizure be made pursuant to a warrant, it clearly shows that it was quite the other way around. Under the

Fourth Amendment originally intended by the Framers, a search or seizure made without a warrant—no matter what the circumstances—would not be unconstitutional. Benson's surreptitious substitution of, *and no warrants shall issue, but upon* in place of *by warrants issuing* changed things, but only to this extent. Whereas before a warrantless search made without probable cause was simply a tort, it now was a constitutional violation as well. But a warrantless search based upon probable cause remained constitutional and, if fruitful, a commendable example of police work.

This little known episode in American constitutional history would have answered all of Justice Jackson's questions including the one he asked rhetorically. "Here endeth the command of the forefathers, apparently because they believed that by thus controlling search warrants they had controlled searches" ironically was absolutely true. Benson's coup had disjointed the text of the Fourth Amendment right along the line of cleavage Jackson found puzzling.

Jackson, had he known the provenance of the enigma he was parsing, never would have imputed to the Framers an intention that warrantless searches were inherently unreasonable. A logical man and an objective one as well, Justice Robert H. Jackson would have recognized that such a conclusion was untenable. For once one knows that the Framers did not intend to interdict warrantless searches at all, all theories for a warrant requirement evaporate.

In *Johnson v. United States* Justice William O. Douglas switched sides to give Frankfurter, Murphy, Rutledge, and Jackson a majority of five. It was Jackson who wrote the Court's opinion, essentially a restatement of the thesis he had expounded in his *Harris* dissent. "At the time entry was demanded the officers were possessed of evidence which a magistrate might have found to be probable cause for issuing a search warrant."

> The point of the Fourth Amendment, which often is not grasped by zealous officers, is not that it denies law enforcement the support of the usual inferences which reasonable men draw from evidence. Its protection consists in requiring that those inferences be drawn by a

neutral and detached magistrate instead of being judged by the officer engaged in the often competitive enterprise of ferreting out crime. Any assumption that evidence sufficient to support a magistrate's disinterested determination to issue a search warrant will justify the officers in making a search without a warrant would reduce the Amendment to a nullity and leave the people's homes secure only in the discretion of police officers.[35]

"There are exceptional circumstances in which . . . a magistrate's warrant for search may be dispensed with. But this is not such a case . . . If the officers in this case were excused from the constitutional duty of presenting their evidence to a magistrate, it is difficult to think of a case in which it should be required."[36] By a vote of five to four, the decision in *Johnson v. United States* resurrected the warrant requirement created by *Agnello* which *Harris* had vitiated.

The mystery is how Felix Frankfurter's exegesis into colonial history—pure buncombe—passed unchallenged. FF came up with absolutely nothing that suggested an intent on the part of the Framers that searches be deemed the more reasonable if made pursuant to a warrant or that warrantless searches were inherently unreasonable. All he did was recall incidents and cases which condemned overly broad and unattested warrants while saying nothing whatever about warrantless searches.

In *Harris*, the text of the Fourth Amendment—that it makes no warrant requirement—was held to be controlling, and the majority simply ignored the historical expositions made in the dissents. In *Johnson*, reduced to a minority by the defection of Douglas, the same four Justices dissented without opinion. This is all the more curious since their number included Justice Black, an adversary of both Frankfurter and Jackson[37] and, as we shall see, a lifelong critic of the warrant requirement. One can only conclude that Hugo Black

---

[35] *Johnson*, 13-14, citing *Agnello v. United States.*
[36] Johnson, 14,15.
[37] See H. N. Hirsch, *The Enigma of Felix Frankfurter*, New York: Basic Books, 1981, 185, 186, for an account of the personal animosity between Black and Jackson. With respect to Black and Frankfurter, see James F. Simon, *The Antagonists*. New York: Simon and Schuster, 1989.

never heard of Egbert Benson.

Of course Felix Frankfurter knew more about colonial history than what he wrote, and he was far too intelligent not to realize that what he did write did not support his conclusion. And that conclusion had nothing to do with James Otis or John Wilkes; they were just window dressing. Frankfurter's allusions to the Red Scare and *Colyer v. Skeffington* betray his true motive. His votes in *Harris* and *Johnson* were simply a continuation of his lifelong proclivity to subvert the law to protect subversives. And Frankfurter made clear that Harris and his ilk would be but the incidental, undeserving beneficiaries of the warrant requirement.

> If only the fate of the Davises and the Harrises were involved, one might be brutally indifferent to the ways by which they get their deserts ... The implications of such encroachment, however, reach far beyond the thief or the black-marketeer. I cannot give legal sanction to what was done in this case without accepting the implications of such a decision for the future ... [38]

Harris and *Johnson* were decided in a political arena in which charges and countercharges of "Communist subversion" and "witch hunts" were daily fare. Felix Frankfurter was quite supportive of those accused of Communist connections, two of his proteges—Lee Pressman[39] and Alger Hiss[40]—among them. And Frank Murphy and Wiley Rutledge left little doubt of where their sympathies lay with respect to "the outlawry of certain political, religious and economic beliefs [read Marxism] and the relentless prosecution [read Red Scare] of those who dare to

---

[38] *Harris*, 156.

[39] "Pressman, Lee (1906-1969). Lee Pressman was a member of the Communist Party in 1934 and 1935 ... He graduated from Harvard Law School in 1929, a protege of Felix Frankfurter." Johnpoll and Klehr.

[40] In 1949, in the first trial of Alger Hiss on a charge of perjury, Justice Frankfurter testified as a character witness to the "integrity, loyalty and veracity" of the defendant. Allen Weinstein, *Perjury—The Hiss-Chambers Case.* New York: Alfred A. Knopf, 1978, 447.

entertain such beliefs."[41]

> It therefore takes no stretch of the imagination to picture law enforcement officers arresting those accused of believing, writing or speaking that which is proscribed, accompanied by a thorough ransacking of their homes as an "incident" to the arrest in an effort to uncover "anything" of a seditious nature. Under the Court's decision, the Fourth Amendment no longer stands as a bar to such tyranny and oppression.[42]

The Solicitor General filed a 40-page brief in the *Johnson* case which argued in detail how the facts and circumstances that led to the search of Anne Johnson's hotel room gave the investigating officers probable cause to believe that someone was smoking opium in Room 1. It made no attempt to rebut Frankfurter's argument that "an understanding of the history and function of the Fourth Amendment" compels the conclusion that "every search or seizure is unreasonable when made without a magistrate's authority expressed through a validly issued warrant." The brief contributed absolutely nothing to our knowledge of constitutional history.

So it came to pass that *Harris v. United States*, a precedent not only true to the text of the Fourth Amendment but faithful to the intent of the Framers as well, was "superseded" by *Johnson v. United States*, a decision false to both. "Superseded" is a word more apt than "overruled," for not only was *Harris* not expressly overruled in *Johnson*; *Harris* was never so much as mentioned. There is more to be said, but it is better said amid the miscarriages of justice *Johnson* will leave strewn along our judicial highway. Now we must get back on the road to *Mapp v. Ohio*.

---

[41] *Harris*, 194.
[42] Ibid.

Chapter XIV

OUR FOURTH BRANCH OF GOVERNMENT

On January 19, 1920, one week before the case of *Silverthorne Lumber Co. v. United States* was decided, the American Civil Liberties Union was born. Its founding father was Roger Baldwin, who went on to serve as its executive director for the next 30 years. After his retirement in 1950, Baldwin remained on the board of directors for more than 30 years and was the guiding spirit of the union until his death in 1981.

In his obituary[1] the *New York Times* eulogized this "amiable Boston aristocrat [who] for decades . . . battled ceaselessly for the concept that the guarantees of the Constitution and the Bill of Rights apply equally to all." From the tenor of the article the reader is left with the distinct impression that the American counterpart to Voltaire has just passed away. Nothing could be further from the truth.

The ACLU has gone to great lengths to foster the image that they are guardians of the rights of everyone and not just those on the left, as their critics claim. They maintain that it is their willingness to stand up for the rights of all, including radicals, that has led to false charges that the organization is pro-Communist. Nor are such accusations anything new.

> The American Civil Liberties Union, in the last analysis, is a supporter of all subversive movements; its

---

[1] "Roger Baldwin, 97, Is Dead: Crusader for Civil Rights Founded the A.C.L.U.," *New York Times*, August 27, 1981.

propaganda is detrimental to the interests of the State. It attempts not only to protect crime, but to encourage attacks upon our institutions in every form . . . [Its] main work is to uphold the communists in spreading revolutionary propaganda and inciting revolutionary activities to undermine our American institutions and overthrow our Federal Government.[2]

The ACLU's first Annual Report (1920-21) is entitled the "Fight for Free Speech." It points out that the ACLU "makes no distinction as to whose liberties it defends; it puts no limit on the principle of free speech."[3] This is certainly a reaffirmation of Voltaire's aphorism: "I may disapprove of what you say, but will defend to the death your right to say it." How then could fair-minded people accuse the ACLU of supporting the Communists in their "revolutionary activities to undermine our American institutions"?

In 1934 "Roger N. Baldwin, Director, American Civil Liberties Union," published an article in a magazine sponsored by the Soviet government comparing freedom in our country with freedom in the U.S.S.R. If the opening statement—"we will, on occasion, even defend the rights of reactionaries to free speech and unhindered assemblage"—does not sound very Voltairesque, the rest of this screed leaves no doubt that the touchstone of the ACLU was Marx, not Voltaire, and their concern for civil liberties a facade.

> I, too, take a class position. It is anti-capitalist and pro-revolutionary. I believe in non-violent methods of struggle as most effective in the long run for building up successful working class power. Where they cannot be followed or where they are not even permitted by the ruling class, obviously only violent tactics remain. I champion civil liberty as the best of the non-violent means of building the power on which workers' rule must be based. If I aid the reactionaries to get free speech now and then, if I go outside the class struggle to fight against censorship, it is only because those liberties help

---

[2] "American Civil Liberties Union and Communist Activity," *Law and Labor*, February 1931, 23, 24, citing a committee of the New York State Legislature.

[3] ACLU Annual Report No. 1, 7, 8.

to create a more hospitable atmosphere for working class liberties. *The class struggle is the central conflict of the world; all others are incidental.*

Proletarian Liberty in Practice

When that power of the working class is once achieved, as it has been only in the Soviet Union, I am for maintaining it by any means whatever. Dictatorship is the obvious means in a world of enemies, at home and abroad. I dislike it in principle as dangerous to its own objects. *But the Soviet Union has already created liberties far greater than exist elsewhere in the world.*[4]

In its 1981 obituary of Roger Baldwin, the *New York Times* quoted the encomiums of Ira Glasser, the ACLU's director, and Norman Dorsen, its President, to the departed. Baldwin was "one of the titans of American history [and] in a way one of our country's founding fathers—they wrote the Constitution, and he invented a way to enforce it." This is a curious statement; what could they mean?

The *Report of Activities* of the American Civil Liberties Union for 1986-87 offers a more definitive restatement of the Baldwin approach to constitutional law: "It is the job of the courts to enforce the Bill of Rights, but they cannot act on their own initiative. While Congress and the president can initiate action, the courts are powerless to fulfill their function unless an aggrieved person complains by filing a lawsuit." The report hastens to tell us who stepped into the constitutional void so thoughtlessly left by our Founding Fathers:

The ACLU was the missing ingredient that made our

---

[4] "Freedom in the U.S.A. and the U.S.S.R.," *Soviet Russia Today*, September 1934, 11. This article is hard to come by. It is missing from the microfilmed copy of the 1934 issue of *Soviet Russia Today* at the New York Public Library, and for some reason the Library of Congress had given it an erroneous call number, an error which happily has been corrected. For the record, a copy of the article appears opposite. You will note that Baldwin is joined in his opinion of the "workers' democracy" by a former instructor from Harvard, the lampooned Laski. "Harold Laski, British socialist, has just written from the Soviet Union his opinion that *liberty of the individual to develop his powers to the full—the test of any social system—is greater there than in any county in the world.*"

constitutional system finally work. Most of what we today recognize as constitutional rights were established within the past 35 years—barely more than the last 15 percent of the bicentennial period. In a very real sense, the ACLU and other organizations outside the government function, in effect, as a fourth and truly independent branch, part of the system that checks abuses of power. *We are the ignition for the constitutional engine*, the key that makes it run.

The "key" which is inserted in the "constitutional engine" is what the ACLU itself openly calls a "manipulated test case."[5] As an example Roger Baldwin told his biographer, Peggy Lamson, how they set up what became the famous "Scopes Monkey Trial."

In 1925 Tennessee passed a law prohibiting the teaching of the theory of evolution. This came to the notice of an ACLU functionary whose job it was to comb the newspapers for litigation opportunities. She passed it on to Baldwin, who "saw its import in a flash." The ACLU board met and voted a "special fund" to finance a test case to defend "free speech" and issued a press release stating they considered it "important enough to be carried to the Supreme Court of the United States." "A few days later came a telegram from the town of Dayton, Tennessee, announcing, 'J.T. Scopes, teacher of science, Rhea Central High School, Dayton, will be arrested, charged with teaching evolution . . . for test case to be defended by you.'"[6]

What followed was no more a trial of a "case" or "controversy" than the moving picture *Inherit the Wind* was an accurate portrayal of what really went on. Clarence Darrow and William Jennings Bryan were no more adversaries than were Spencer Tracy and Frederic March; they were just actors. "The ACLU had rented and furnished an unoccupied house—known locally as The Mansion— to accommodate their legal staff and the numerous eminent scientists they had brought to Tennessee as expert witnesses on the

---

[5] Peggy Lamson. *Roger Baldwin—Founder of the American Civil Liberties Union.* Boston: Houghton Mifflin Company, 1976. "In many instances the ACLU acted to achieve what they referred to as a 'manipulated test case,'" 157.

[6] Lamson, 164.

FREEDOM

in the U.S.A. and the U.S.S.R.

By ROGER N. BALDWIN

Director, American Civil Liberties Union.

THOSE of us who champion civil liberties in the United States and who at the same time support the proletarian dictatorship of the Soviet Union are charged with inconsistency and insincerity. "How can you consistently support the right of free agitation in capitalist countries when you defend a dictatorship that tolerates no agitation against its rule?" we are asked.

On the face of the argument, our critics have a case. If we were Communists, they say, our position would be defensible. But we champion civil liberties for all without taking a class position, without confining them, as do the Communists, to the working class. We will, on occasion, even defend the rights of reactionaries to free speech and unhindered assemblage. We go outside the class struggle to oppose all forms of censorship over radio, books, movies and the theatre.

But our critics are in error in denying to us a class position. Everybody takes a class position, consciously or unconsciously. Even our critics do. They are advocates of those liberties which are freely exercised *only* in a capitalist society *when the system is safe.* And by insisting on them in any and all circumstances they become in effect the upholders of the system of political democracy which is in practice only a mask for capitalist dictatorship.

All my associates in the struggle for civil liberties take a class position, though many don't know it. There are the conservatives who figure that the interests of property are better maintained in the long run by letting the opposition blow off steam. There are the liberals who believe that capitalism can be modified, its abuses checked, and a transition effected to some vague "new social order" through peaceful agitation. There are pacifists so wedded to methods of non-violence that *they would rather tolerate the colossal violence of the existing system than upset it by overt violence by the working class.* All of them are in effect pro-capitalist for they have no program directed toward abolishing capitalism.

I, too, take a class position. It is anti-capitalist and pro-revolutionary. I believe in non-violent methods of struggle as most effective in the long run for building up successful working class power. Where they cannot be followed or where they are not even permitted by the ruling class, obviously only violent tactics remain. I champion civil liberty as the best of the non-violent means of building the power on which workers' rule must be based. If I aid the reactionaries to get free speech now and then, if I go outside the class struggle to fight against censorship, it is only because those liberties help to create a more hospitable atmosphere for working class liberties. *The class struggle is the central conflict of the world; all others are incidental.*

Proletarian Liberty in Practice

When that power of the working class is once achieved, as it has been only in the Soviet Union, I am for maintaining it by any means whatever. Dictatorship is the obvious means in a world of enemies, at home and abroad. I dislike it in principle as dangerous to its own objects. *But the Soviet Union has already created liberties far greater than exist elsewhere in the world.* They are liberties that most closely affect the lives of the people—power in the trade unions, in peasant organizations, in the cultural life of nationalities, freedom of women in public and private life, and a tremendous development of education for adults and children. I saw these liberties in practice. I have followed carefully their aspects since I was in the Soviet Union. While I have some reservations about party policy in relation to internal democracy, and some criticisms of the unnecessary persecution of political opponents, the fundamentals of liberty are firmly fixed in the USSR. And they are fixed on the only ground on which liberty really matters—economic. No class to exploit the workers and peasants; wide sharing of control in the economic organizations; and the wealth produced is common property.

The rigid suppression of any opposition to the program of socialism is a measure of the difficulties and in part of the sense of insecurity in a world of enemies. But so unbiased a student of the Soviet Union as Dr. Harry Ward, reported a marked let-up in the pressures from on top and a considerable extension of the "area of consent" between his two stays of almost a year each in 1924 and 1931. Harold Laski, British socialist, has just written

from the Soviet Union his opinion that *liberty of the individual to develop his powers to the full—the test of any social system—is greater there than in any country in the world.*

I saw in the Soviet Union many opponents of the regime. I visited a dozen prisons—the political sections among them. I saw considerable of the work of the OGPU. I heard a good many stories of severity, even of brutality, and many of them from the victims. While I sympathized with personal distress I just could not bring myself to get excited over the suppression of opposition when I stacked it up against what I saw of fresh, vigorous expressions of free living by workers and peasants all over the land. And further, no champion of a socialist society could fail to see that some suppression was necessary to achieve it. It could not all be done by persuasion. Doubtless there has been at times far more coercion than was necessary. The Party has itself repeatedly said so. But "workers' democracy" in action is no product of coercion. *It is genuine, and it is the nearest approach to freedom that the workers have ever achieved.*

How long the proletarian dictatorship will last, only world conditions and internal success in building socialism can determine. Highly centralized authority will give way. The State and police power will eventually disappear. Civil liberties will exist again, within the confines of a socialist society; but not to oppose it, for who will want to? The extension of education, the bringing up of a generation to take active responsibility all over the Soviet Union will lessen power at the center and from on top.

If American workers, with no real liberties save to change masters or, rarely, to escape from the working class, could understand their class interests, Soviet "workers' democracy" would be their goal. And if American champions of civil liberty could all think in terms of economic freedom as the goal of their labors, they too would accept "workers' democracy" as *far superior to what the capitalist world offers to any but a small minority. Yes, and they would accept—regretfully, of course—the necessity of dictatorship while the job of reorganizing society on a socialist basis is being done.*

Roger Baldwin describes himself:

I have continued directing the unpopular fight for the rights of agitation, as director of the American Civil Liberties Union, on the side engaging in many efforts to aid working-class causes. I have been to Europe several times, mostly in connection with international radical activities, chiefly against war, fascism, and imperialism; and have traveled constantly in the United States to areas of conflict over workers' rights to strike and organize . . . . I have been active in the fight for the conservation of birds and animals and forests. My chief aversion is the system of greed, private profits, privilege, and violence which makes up the control of the world today, and which has brought it to the tragic crisis of unprecedented hunger and unemployment. I am opposed to the New Deal because it strives to strengthen and prolong production for private profit. At bottom, I am for conserving the full powers of every person on earth by expanding them to their individual limits. Therefore I am for socialism, disarmament, and ultimately for abolishing the state itself as an instrument of violence and compulsion. I seek social ownership of property, the abolition of the propertied class, and sole control by those who produce wealth. Communism is the goal. It all sums up into one single purpose—the abolition of the system of dog-eat-dog under which we live, and the substitution by the most effective nonviolence possible of a system of cooperative ownership and use of all wealth.
—30th Anniversary Yearbook
Harvard College Class of 1905 (1935)

The above quotation appears on page 27 of Volume 2 of *Recollections of a Life in Civil Liberties,* Robert Nash Baldwin, 1972, Columbia University Oral History Department.

facts of evolution."[7] The carnival had come to Dayton.

In the meanwhile "the money poured in" and the ACLU got a lot of good publicity. The Monkey Trial was not really about Scopes and the theories of Charles Darwin; they were just props. It was a great public relations success, lending substance to the ACLU's claim that they were indeed the protector of the civil liberties of all people and not, as their enemies claimed, just those who were then known generically as Reds.

To the ACLU at this time the greatest threat to "free speech" was the enforcement of criminal syndicalist laws by state governments. On the basis of evidence unearthed in a 1922 raid on a Communist Party convention at Bridgman, Michigan, Charles Ruthenberg, the executive secretary of the Communist Party USA, had been convicted by the state of Michigan of such an offense, and his was the test case,[8] so it seemed, which would determine whether the Communist Party would suffer the same fate as the IWW. While the Monkey Trial was taking place in Tennessee in July of 1925, Ruthenberg's appeal was pending before the Supreme Court in Washington.

Scopes v. Tennessee, had the ACLU prevailed, would have been the perfect stalking horse for *Ruthenberg v. Michigan.* For if the teaching and advocacy of the doctrines of Charles Darwin are "free speech," vouchsafed as against the states by the Fourteenth Amendment, they would have been able to argue, why then is not the teaching or advocacy of the doctrines of Karl Marx equally protected? The ACLU might have obtained in a case involving evolution a precedent which could have been used in a case involving revolution—the class struggle which to Roger Baldwin was the central conflict of the world. The plan was foiled by the Tennessee Supreme Court.[9] A half century later Roger Baldwin was still bitter.

> But then, deliberately, they *reversed* the conviction of Scopes on a blatantly specious detail. The fine on

---

[7] Lamson, 168.

[8] *People v. Ruthenberg,* 229 Mich. 315, 201 N.W. 358 (1924). The case was "Disposed of Without Consideration by the Court" after Ruthenberg's death in 1927. 273 U.S. 782.

[9] See *Scopes v. State,* 154 Tenn. 105, 121, 289 S.W. 363, 367 (1927).

Scopes, they said, had been imposed by the presiding judge instead of, as the law of the state provided (inexplicably), by the jury. The strategy was obvious; Scopes's conviction was thus overturned. There was no possible justification for him to take his case up through the federal courts on appeal.[10]

The ACLU's metaphor of the constitutional engine can be carried further. In urban areas throughout the country wholesalers supply automobile parts to garages where people's cars are fixed. Some wholesalers buy straight from the factory. Factory prices are listed in catalogues and are not usually discounted. While these wholesalers keep on hand a certain amount of inventory, they are frequently out of stock, and the garages and their customers often suffer inconvenient delays as a result.

Other wholesalers specialize in supplying used or hardly used automobile parts. Although they keep little or no inventory on hand, they will guarantee one-day service. They are never out of stock, and never will be, so long as people park their cars on the city streets. In most places such an operation is known as a "chop-shop."

The highly motivated and skilled operatives of those wholesalers, once given an order, will comb the streets and locate and strip a vehicle in a hour. Before the parking meter runs out of time it is just another abandoned derelict. The ACLU, the "fourth and truly independent branch" of our federal government, has been running a nationwide constitutional chop-shop since it opened its doors in 1920. This is as illegal as it is unethical.

About 150 years ago two characters named Lord and Veazie tried to pull a fast one on the City Bank of Boston. What they did was to set up a case between themselves in the federal court in Maine for the purpose of settling legal questions upon which they and the bank had a large amount of property depending. Veazie being the designated winner in the lower court, Lord had it brought up, by writ of error, for review by the Supreme Court of the United States.

The idea was to obtain an opinion of the Court in a test case

---

[10] Lamson, 167.

manipulated by the two spurious litigants which later could be used as a precedent to control the outcome when they came to grips with their real adversary, the City Bank of Boston. "The existence of this suit was kept from the knowledge of the parties really interested," for a while at any rate. But when the writ of error was entered in the Supreme Court, the bank got wind of it and exposed the fraud for what it was.

> The court is satisfied . . . that there is no real dispute between the plaintiff and defendant. On the contrary, it is evident that their interest in the question brought here for decision is one and the same, and not adverse; and that in these proceedings the plaintiff and defendant are attempting to procure the opinion of this court upon a question of law, in the decision of which they have a common interest opposed to that of other persons, who are not parties to this suit, who had no knowledge of it while it was pending in the Circuit Court, and no opportunity of being heard there in defence of their rights. [11]

"The objection in the case before us is," continued the Court, "that there is no real conflict of interest" between the parties, "that the plaintiff and defendant have the same interest, and that interest adverse and in conflict with the interest of third persons, whose rights would be seriously affected if the question of law was decided in the manner that both of the parties to this suit desire it to be." The Court set aside the judgment as a fraud and dismissed the writ of error. "A judgment in form, thus procured, in the eye of the law is no judgment of the court. It is a nullity . . ."

> It is the office of courts of justice to decide the rights of persons and of property, when the persons interested cannot adjust them by agreement between themselves,— and to do this upon the full hearing of both parties. And any attempt, by a mere colorable dispute, to obtain the opinion of the court upon a question of law which a party desires to know for his own interest or his own purposes, when there is no real and substantial controversy between

---

[11] *Lord v. Veazie,* 49 U.S. (8 How.) 251, 254 (1850).

those who appear as adverse parties to the suit, is an abuse
which courts of justice have always reprehended, and
treated as a punishable contempt of court.[12]

Similarly in 1889 Michigan passed an act regulating the rates a
railroad could charge for passenger traffic. "On the very day on which
the law took effect, to wit, October 2, 1889, the defendant in error,
plaintiff below, went to the defendant's office in Port Huron, and
tendered $3.20 for a ticket from that place to Battle Creek, which was
refused. Thereupon he brought this action in damages, to which the
railroad company promptly answered."[13]

The Supreme Court of Michigan had "felt constrained to make
[the] observation" that the evidence suggested "that this was a
friendly suit between the plaintiff and the defendant to test the
constitutionality of this legislation." The counsel for the railroad
did not deny this, but stated: "This may be conceded; but what of
it? There is no ground for the claim that any fraud or trickery has
been practised in presenting the testimony."[14]

The Court refused to rule on the constitutional question. Only
when "the court must, in the exercise of its solemn duties, determine
whether the act be constitutional or not" would it exercise that
"ultimate and supreme" power, and then only in a case when after
"an honest and actual antagonistic assertion of rights by one
individual against another, there is presented a [constitutional]
question . . ."[15] Beware of friendly lawsuits, a unanimous Court
cautioned its posterity.

> We do not mean to insinuate aught against the actual
> management of the affairs of this company. The silence
> of the record gives us no information, and we have no
> knowledge outside thereof, and no suspicion of wrong.
> Our suggestion is only to indicate how easily courts may
> be misled into doing grievous wrong to the public, and
> how careful they should be to not declare legislative acts

---

[12] Ibid., 255.

[13] *Chicago & Grand Trunk Railway Company v. Wellman*, 143 U.S. 339, 340 (1892).

[14] Ibid., 344.

[15] Ibid., 345.

unconstitutional upon agreed and general statements, and without the fullest disclosure of all material facts. Judgment affirmed.[16]

Half a century later, during World War II, much the same caper was tried. In 1942 Congress had passed the War Emergency Price Control Act which regulated among other things the rents a landlord could charge for residential properties in certain areas. Johnson, a landlord, contrived to have Roach, one of his tenants, institute a friendly suit for damages in the U.S. district court.[17]

In his answer Johnson challenged the constitutionality of the law and was successful in obtaining an order from the district court dismissing the tenant's complaint on the ground that the rent control law was unconstitutional. At this point the United States intervened and moved that the case be dismissed on the grounds that it was collusive. When the district court denied this motion, the government appealed to the Supreme Court. It did not contend that "any false or fictitious state of facts was submitted to the court," only that "one of the parties has dominated the conduct of the suit" by controlling the attorneys on each side.

> Here an important public interest is at stake—the validity of an Act of Congress having far-reaching effects on the public welfare in one of the most critical periods in the history of the country. That interest has been adjudicated in a proceeding in which the plaintiff has had no active participation, over which he has exercised no control, and the expense of which he has not borne. He has been only nominally represented by counsel who was selected by appellee's counsel and whom he has never seen. Such a suit is collusive because it is not in any real sense adversary. It does not assume the "honest and actual antagonistic assertion of rights" to be adjudicated—a safeguard essential to the integrity of the judicial process, and one which we have held to be indispensable to adjudication of

---

[16] Ibid., 346.

[17] *Roach v. Johnson*, 48 F. Supp. 833 (1943).

constitutional questions by this Court.[18]

The Supreme Court dismissed the suit as collusive. "It is the court's duty to do so where, as here, the public interest has been placed at hazard by the amenities of parties to a suit conducted under the domination of only one of them."[19] With these cases in mind we will take another stroll down *The Road to Mapp v. Ohio and Beyond* and see how they apply.

Enough has been said of the whited sepulchre that is *Weeks*, and the dead men's bones it conceals.[20] But while they lie a'moldering in their graves, their rule goes marching on, insulating the guilty from conviction so they can prey upon the law abiding. Cases connived to thwart the prosecution of Dynamiters, the deportation of Bolsheviks, and the enforcement of Prohibition will come to be used to free the robbers, rapists and murderers who are the plague of our cities.

We shall see some funny cases make their way to the Supreme Court. Seeing a case all the way up the ladder of the law costs a lot of money—more than most defendants normally would be willing to spend. While prosecutors and attorneys general don't, of course, spend their own money, budget constraints and limited manpower impose the same discipline on them. The volume of crime compels them to compromise cases they would prefer to prosecute to the limit of the law. Of necessity they must cull the venial from the grievous and those cases where circumstances make conviction doubtful from those where it is sure. The same applies to appeals. Prosecuting attorneys always know that when they elect to pursue any one case on the trial or appellate level, they are letting another go by the boards.

The natural consequence of these limitations of time and money is that criminal cases normally reach the appellate level only when the stakes are high. That capital cases come to be heard by the court of last resort is not surprising. To see cases of lesser turpitude,

---

[18] *United States v. Johnson*, 319 U.S. 302, 305 (1943).

[19] Ibid.

[20] "Whited sepulchres, which indeed appear beautiful outward, but are within full of dead men's bones" (Matthew 23:27).

such as nonviolent felonies, make their appearance ought to raise an eyebrow or two. But when cases of misdemeanor, or infractions punishable by a small fine, present themselves before the Court and receive plenary consideration, something very strange is going on. Such a scenario immediately suggests collusion.

In 1917 Roger Baldwin gave a comrade some advice on how they could fool most of the people some of the time and some of the people most of the time. Essentially it was to wrap themselves in the flag and the Constitution and to get others to front for them. The ACLU has practiced what he preached from its inception.

> 1st. Do steer away from making it look like a Socialist enterprise. Too many people have already gotten the idea that it is nine-tenths a Socialist movement. You can of course avoid this by bringing to the front people like Senator Works, Miss Addams and others who are known as substantial Democrats . . .
>
> 4th. We want to also look like patriots in everything we do. We want to get a lot of good flags, talk a good deal about the constitution, and what our forefathers wanted to make of this country, and to show that we are the folks that really stand for the spirit of our institutions.[21]

In law, as in politics, appearances are important, and the ACLU realized long ago they could not afford to argue criminal cases on their merits. Whenever the discussion turns to guilt or innocence, they don the mantle of the Founding Fathers, take the constitutional high ground and hold it against the Philistines who would betray our most hallowed institutions for the trifle of justice in the case at hand. They portray themselves as the defenders of the Bill of Rights, making the tough decisions in the hard cases, and their adversaries as the misguided, who would sacrifice our most cherished institutions on the altar of expediency.

---

[21] Letter from Roger Baldwin to Louis Lochner, August 21, 1917, *Lusk Report*, Vol. I, exhibit following page 1120.

Johnson v. United States, the case which resurrected the warrant requirement, was decided February 2, 1948. The highest priority of the ACLU thereafter was to apply the *Weeks* rule, along with its *Johnson* corollary, to the states. The obstacle they had to overcome is that the exclusionary rule rests on the Fourth Amendment, and that the Fourth Amendment, like the rest of the Bill of Rights, does not apply to the states. An attempt to rewrite history failed on the last day of the 1948/49 term in *Wolf v. Colorado*.

Julius Wolf was convicted of abortion, a felony under Colorado law. The police knew for a certainty that an abortion had taken place and had the most probable of cause to believe that Wolf, a Denver doctor, had committed it. Without further ado, they went to his office and placed him under arrest. In the process they seized his appointment book, which was used at the trial to connect him with a woman on whom an abortion had been committed.

State authorities had always proceeded on the assumption that the Fourth Amendment, the *Weeks* rule, and the warrant requirement applied only to the federal government and that they had only to satisfy the Fourteenth Amendment's guarantee of due process. So that if a felony in fact had been committed and state officers, without using excessive force, made a search and seizure based on probable cause, they had not deprived any person of his liberty or property without due process of law simply because they had not gotten a warrant beforehand.

To apply the *Weeks* rule, with its *Johnson* proviso, to state criminal prosecutions would be nothing short of revolutionary. The first attempt to do so was in *Wolf*, even though that search had taken place prior to the *Johnson* decision. The difficulty of posing the question to be decided is evidenced by the length of the first sentence of the opinion.

Mr. Justice Frankfurter delivered the opinion of the Court.

> The precise question for consideration is this: Does a conviction by a State court for a State offense deny the "due process of law" required by the Fourteenth Amendment, solely because evidence that was admitted at the trial was obtained under circumstances which would have rendered

it inadmissible in a prosecution for violation of a federal law in a court of the United States because there deemed to be an infraction of the Fourth Amendment as applied in *Weeks v. United States,* 232 U.S. 383? . . .

Unlike the specific requirements and restrictions placed by the Bill of Rights (Amendments I to VIII) upon the administration of criminal justice by federal authority, the Fourteenth Amendment did not subject criminal justice in the States to specific limitations. The notion that the "due process of law" guaranteed by the Fourteenth Amendment is shorthand for the first eight amendments of the Constitution and thereby incorporates them has been rejected by this Court again and again, after impressive consideration. See, e.g., *Hurtado v. California,* 110 U.S. 516; *Twining v. New Jersey,* 211 U.S. 78; *Brown v. Mississippi,* 297 U.S. 278; *Palko v. Connecticut,* 302 U.S. 319. Only the other day the Court reaffirmed this rejection after thorough reexamination of the scope and function of the Due Process Clause of the Fourteenth Amendment. *Adamson v. California,* 332 U.S. 46. The issue is closed.[22]

To say that the Fourth Amendment does not apply to the states through the Fourteenth is not to say that the states are free to do all that which the Fourth Amendment forbids. What it does mean is that whatever can be comprehended within the ambit of the Fourth Amendment—so swollen by the exclusionary rule and its rigid warrant corollary—is not to be the determinant of what due process of law requires of the states in the area of search and seizure. The measure of due process is more fluid.

For purposes of ascertaining the restrictions which the Due Process Clause imposed upon the States in the enforcement of their criminal law, we adhere to the views expressed in *Palko v. Connecticut, supra,* 302 U.S. 319. That decision speaks to us with the great weight of the authority, particularly in matters of civil liberty, of a

---

[22] *Wolf v. Colorado,* 338 U.S. 25, 26 (1949).

court that included Mr. Chief Justice Hughes, Mr. Justice Brandeis, Mr. Justice Stone and Mr. Justice Cardozo, to name only the dead. In rejecting the suggestion that the Due Process Clause incorporated the original Bill of Rights, Mr. Justice Cardozo reaffirmed on behalf of that Court a different but deeper and more pervasive conception of the Due Process Clause. This Clause exacts from the States for the lowliest and the most outcast all that is "implicit in the concept of ordered liberty." 302 U.S. at 325.

Due process of law thus conveys neither formal nor fixed nor narrow requirements. It is the compendious expression for all those rights which the courts must enforce because they are basic to our free society.[23]

While the Fourteenth Amendment did not make the Fourth applicable to the states, both amendments—for different constitutional reasons—share some common ground. An unnecessarily intrusive search made by federal agents without probable cause would be a classic example of an unreasonable search proscribed by the Fourth Amendment. Were a state affirmatively to sanction intrusive searches made without probable cause, such a search by a state officer would be the *deprivation* of a *liberty* guaranteed by the Fourteenth Amendment without *due process of law*.

The security of one's privacy against arbitrary intrusion by the police—which is at the core of the Fourth Amendment—is basic to a free society. It is therefore implicit in "the concept of ordered liberty" and as such enforceable against the States through the Due Process Clause . . . Accordingly, we have no hesitation in saying that were a State affirmatively to sanction such police incursion into privacy it would run counter to the guaranty of the Fourteenth Amendment.[24]

---

[23] *Wolf,* 26, 27.
[24] *Wolf,* 27, 28.

But the search of Wolf's office was by no means arbitrary. It was made on the best of probable cause and was no more intrusive than it had to be. Does such a search *deprive* a *person* of a *liberty* "basic to a free society" simply because a warrant was not obtained beforehand? How was Wolf prejudiced? Let us restate Mr. Justice Frankfurter's opening sentence in *Wolf*:

> The precise question for consideration is this: Does a conviction by a State court for a State offense deny the "due process of law" required by the Fourteenth Amendment, solely because evidence that was admitted at the trial was obtained under circumstances which would have rendered it inadmissible in a prosecution for violation of a federal law in a court of the United States because there deemed to be an infraction of the Fourth Amendment as applied in *Weeks v. United States,* 232 U.S. 383?

The Court held that the search of Wolf's office was not, under the facts and circumstances of that case, an *arbitrary* intrusion by the police. By no means is the right to have evidence of one's guilt excluded at one's trial a right "implicit in the concept of ordered liberty" or "basic to a free society." Frankfurter compiled an appendix which demonstrated that the *Weeks* rule was an aberration that the rest of the English-speaking world rejected.

> The jurisdictions which have rejected the *Weeks* doctrine have not left the right to privacy without other means of protection [citations omitted.] Indeed, the exclusion of evidence is a remedy which directly serves only to protect those upon whose person or premises something incriminating has been found. We cannot, therefore, regard it as a departure from basic standards to remand such persons, together with those who emerge scatheless from a search, to the remedies of private action and such protection as the internal discipline of the police, under the eyes of an alert public opinion, may afford.[25]

---

[25] *Wolf,* 30, 31.

> We hold, therefore, that in a prosecution in a State court
> for a State crime the Fourteenth Amendment does not
> forbid the admission of evidence obtained by an
> unreasonable search and seizure.[26]

The notion that the Fourteenth Amendment made applicable to the states the first eight amendments, or any of their provisions, is called "incorporation." As Justice Frankfurter stated in *Wolf,* the incorporation doctrine had been rejected by the Court "again, and again after impressive consideration." Undaunted, the ACLU saw the problem in its proper perspective. Incorporation was a strategic imperative which must be taken by whatever means necessary.

But *Wolf v. Colorado* appeared to be their high-water mark. In *Wolf* they mustered three votes to apply the *Weeks* rule to the states and four for incorporation, the idiosyncratic Justice Black having voted for the latter, but not the former. After that everything went wrong. Frank Murphy and Wiley Rutledge, two of the ACLU's most stalwart Justices, died during the 1949 summer recess. And December saw the publication of two law review articles which laid waste to the incorporation theory.[27]

What "due process of law" did require of the states in the administration of criminal justice was known in shorthand as "fundamental fairness." Anything done in a state court which might have convicted an innocent man was viewed under fundamental fairness with the gravest suspicion and the defendant given the benefit of every doubt. Where, however, his guilt was clearly established, he was not permitted to escape his just deserts. Fundamental fairness had as its underlying purpose the protection of the innocent from wrongful conviction.

On one side in this contest are those who believe the purpose of a criminal trial is to determine the truth of the accusation against the defendant. The innocent must be exonerated and the guilty convicted and punished. These people believe not only that

---

[26] *Wolf,* 33.

[27] *"Does the Fourteenth Amendment Incorporate the Bill of Rights?"* 2 Stanford Law Review. (1949), 5. *The Original Understanding,* by Charles Fairman, 5-139. *The Judicial Interpretation,* by Stanley Morrison, 140-173.

punishment deters crime, but also that society should exact from the criminal a penalty for the harm he has done. Poorly organized and ineptly led, they constitute the vast majority of the American people—the silent and impotent majority.

On the other side are the ACLU and their allies—a cohesive and highly motivated minority skilled in masking their true intentions. They care not whether incorporation is a historical truth or a valid interpretation of the Fourteenth Amendment. They see it as a means—the only means—to their ends. Well-placed and unscrupulous, their tentacles reach into the inner sanctum of the law. They want the exclusionary rule applied to the states, and to this end will do whatever they must.

Over the next 12 years a continuous constitutional struggle will take place between fundamental fairness and a swindle which will come to be known as "selective incorporation." Cases will be duly briefed and gravely argued before the bar of the Supreme Court. The Justices will then deliberate and in due course announce their decision. There will always be a dissenting opinion. The opinions on both sides will be dissected by certified constitutional gurus who will tell us what they really mean. Each case will become another milestone in our Fourth Amendment jurisprudence.

Unbeknownst to all but a few, a very different game was being played *sub rosa*. None of the milestones was a genuine case or controversy; they were shams setup to subvert fundamental fairness. The "adversaries," to paraphrase Shakespeare,[28] who appear to "strive so mightily" against each other are in reality on the same side, working to the same end. When they meet later to "eat and drink as friends," they can have a good laugh at the gullibility of the American people in general and of certain members of the Court in particular.

Pulling the puppet strings in these "Punch and Judy" shows will be the American Civil Liberties Union. Their only real adversary, behind the scenes, will be an aging constitutional smithy who does not want it on his conscience that the precedents he helped forge to

---

[28]   The Taming of the Shrew.

protect anarchists and Communists will come to be used to free robbers and murderers. It is the supreme irony of his life that Felix Frankfurter, who knew what was going on and dared not speak, will lead the battle against incorporation and the ACLU he served so well and so long.[29]

What the ACLU did was to follow in the footsteps of Winfred Denison and Leslie Lyons. Their strategy was to get the precedent in a case in which the law would be perceived as a bully and a persecutor, one in which no one would be offended that the defendant got off. What the ACLU needed was a post-*Wolf* manipulated test case in which, like *Weeks,* there was no victim. The defendant broke a law, but nobody got hurt, except perhaps the defendant himself.

Southern California seems to be a breeding ground for suborned cases. Coincidentally it is the habitat of a particularly virulent chapter of the ACLU. As the implications of *Wolf* were being pondered, a case was being connived in Los Angeles destined to go into the books as *Rochin v. California.*[30] It seems that "three deputy sheriffs entered defendant's bedroom after having forced the bedroom door open. They were not authorized by search warrant or at all to enter the room."[31] After Rochin swallowed two capsules, the deputies took him to a hospital and had his stomach pumped out. Rochin was charged with possession of a small amount of morphine, a misdemeanor.

No one can accuse the prosecution of playing hardball. They stipulated with the defense that "if he [the defendant] were a witness he would testify that the two capsules were taken from him by use of a stomach pump and without his consent and against his will."[32] One has to wonder whether a prosecutor who will stipulate what a

---

[29] "Felix Frankfurter," to quote Roger Baldwin, "was one of our staunchest founding members. He had been on the War Labor Board, and he had labor connections too. He stuck with us until he went on the Supreme Court. Then my differences with some of his decisions alienated us until his retirement, when we resumed relations again." Lamson, 130.

[30] *Rochin v. California,* 342 U.S. 165 (1952).

[31] *People v. Rochin,* 101 Cal. 2d 140, 225 P. 2d (1951).

[32] 225 P. 2d 2.

defendant's testimony would be if he testified, in a case in which he does *not* testify, will strive all that mightily against his adversary when the chips are down before the Supreme Court. Most prosecutors like to cross-examine defendants who decide to take the witness stand.

If Rochin had testified, he would have been convicted of possession of morphine by his own voluntary testimony. Without his testimony, the case for an unreasonable search and seizure could not have been made. In either instance there would be no constitutional issue to appeal. This concordat did not just come about by itself; you can imagine the hard bargaining and arm's length negotiations which preceded it.

One would think that the first thing a lawyer representing Rochin would do would be to bring a civil suit for damages against the deputies, the County of Los Angeles, and the doctor who pumped out Rochin's stomach. Between such parties defendant there are pockets deep enough to pay substantial damages and there seems to be no question of liability.

> Under the record here, deputy Jack Jones and the alleged doctor of medicine, Mier, were guilty of unlawfully assaulting, battering, torturing and falsely imprisoning the defendant at the alleged hospital. A remedy of defendant for such highhanded and reprehensible conduct is an action for damages.[33]

Damages, of course, would deter such aggression and certainly the money would help a person like Rochin. On the other hand, this would be inconsistent with the position that only the *Weeks* rule can save us from rampaging deputy sheriffs. Furthermore, a suit for damages might spoil an otherwise perfect adversarial relationship with the prosecutor. Suppose he simply dropped the charges against Rochin? After all, the prosecutor doesn't need a precedent; he already has *Wolf v. Colorado.*

Following a discussion—first on and then off the record—as to whether a probated sentence might cause appellate problems, the

---

[33] 225 P. 2d 3.

defendant withdrew his application for probation. Immediately thereafter, Judge W. Turney Fox sentenced him to 60 days.[34] Antonio Richard Rochin was a most unusual man; a defendant who prefers jail to being free on probation is a rarity.

On appeal to the Supreme Court of the United States, California was represented by Attorney General Edmund G. "Pat" Brown and his deputies. The ACLU appeared *amicus curiae* through eight lawyers, including A.L. Wiren.[35] Wiren also represented Rochin. Rochin prevailed, but one doubts his legal staff was pleased. What the ACLU wanted was a decision that the morphine pills were inadmissible, not because the use of them was unfair under the circumstances of Rochin's case but because the Fourth and Fifth Amendments require the exclusion of such evidence in all cases.

They were foiled by the wily Justice Frankfurter. It was on grounds of "equity"[36] that the defendant's conviction was set aside. The conviction was obtained by "conduct that shocks the conscience" and methods which "offend a sense of justice." Neither the Fourth nor the Fifth Amendment was brought to bear. The use of the disgorged pills was analogized to the use of a coerced confession: "[I]n order to convict a man the police cannot extract by force what is in his mind [nor can they] extract what is in his stomach."[37]

Nevertheless, *Rochin* was a perfect scenario. Had Justices Black and Douglas been able to gain three adherents, a precedent for incorporation would have been set in a case where fundamental fairness required the same result. It was just a question of votes. President Eisenhower's appointment of Earl Warren as Chief Justice in 1953 and his election eve appointment of William J. Brennan Jr. in 1956 will bring the number of incorporationists back up to four.

---

[34] See Transcript of Record, 176-179.

[35] "Al Wiren, First Full-Time ACLU Lawyer, Dies at 77," *Los Angeles Times*, February 5, 1978. The article states that Abraham Lincoln (Al) Wiren had served as legal director of the local ACLU from 1941 to 1972.

[36] **Equity.** Justice administered according to fairness . . . It is . . . based on what was fair in a particular situation. *Black's Law Dictionary.*

[37] *Rochin*, 342 U.S. 172-173.

Meanwhile, led by saber-toothed Attorney General Brown, California entered into an era in which the suppression of horse-race bookmaking became the Golden State's highest legal priority. *Irvine v. California* was a case in which Los Angeles police officers had, without a warrant, broken into the defendant's house to plant a microphone. Irvine was convicted of bookmaking, a misdemeanor, after a trial in which the officers testified to conversations in Irvine's bedroom that they had overheard. Deploring their conduct, the Supreme Court nevertheless upheld Irvine's conviction, having this to say of the exclusionary rule:

> There is no reliable evidence known to us that inhabitants of those states which exclude the evidence suffer less from lawless searches and seizures than those of states that admit it. Even this Court has not seen fit to exclude illegally seized evidence in federal cases unless a federal officer perpetrated the wrong. Private detectives may use methods to obtain evidence not open to officers of the law . . .

> That the rule of exclusion and reversal results in the escape of guilty persons is more capable of demonstration than that it deters invasions of right by the police. The case is made, so far as the police are concerned, when they announce that they have arrested their man. Rejection of the evidence does nothing to punish the wrong-doing official, while it may, and likely will, release the wrong-doing defendant. It deprives society of its remedy against one lawbreaker because he has been pursued by another. It protects one against whom incriminating evidence is discovered, but does nothing to protect innocent persons who are the victims of illegal but fruitless searches. The disciplinary or educational effect of the court's releasing the defendant for police misbehavior is so indirect as to be no more than a mild deterrent at best. Some discretion is still left to the states in criminal cases, for which they are largely responsible, and we think it is for them to determine which rule best serves them.[38]

---

[38] *Irvine v. California*, 347 U.S. 128, 136-137 (1954).

People v. Cahan[39] was a California case with a factual situation suspiciously similar to *Irvine*. Aside from the names of the eavesdropping policemen and the horse-race bookmaker, the only discernible difference is that the bedroom conversations were picked up by a microphone planted under a chest of drawers instead of in the bedroom closet. Cahan was convicted after a trial in which officers testified to these conversations. By a vote of four to three the California Supreme Court overruled all prior California precedent. Henceforward, California would use the exclusionary rule.

It was in *Irvine* that Justice Tom C. Clark began to waver. "In light of the 'incredible' activity of the police here, it is with great reluctance that I follow *Wolf*." He opined that the "extinction" of *Wolf* might come about "when five Justices are sufficiently revolted by local police action." His decision to switch sides in 1961 will be greatly influenced by *Cahan*. The ACLU got a lot of action out of what appears to be a single investigation of horse-race bookmaking in Los Angeles; six will get you five it was the same microphone.

In *Rochin, Irvine,* and *Cahan* California was represented by Attorney General Brown and his assistant, Clarence A. Lynn. Assistant Attorney General Elizabeth Miller appeared in both *Irvine* and *Cahan*. Morris Lavine represented Irvine and together with A.L. Wiren appeared *amicus curiae* in *Cahan*. Wiren represented Rochin and also appeared *amicus curiae* for the ACLU in that case. It is fair to say of the three cases that they had interlocking lawyers.

At this point in our constitutional history, the focus of the Fourth Amendment moved from bookmaking to housing inspections. In 1958 Aaron David Frank was fined $20 by the city of Baltimore for a violation of that city's health code. A section of the code required a homeowner to allow, during the daytime, an inspection by a health inspector who had reason to believe a health violation existed. In Frank's case the request was made in the middle of the afternoon and for ample reason. The house was "in an

---

[39] 44 Cal. 2d 434; 282 P. 2d 905 (1955).

extreme state of decay," and large deposits of "rodent feces" were found nearby, giving the inspector probable cause to believe rats were in residence.

Mr. Justice Frankfurter delivered the opinion of the Court.

> Acting on a complaint from a resident of the 4300 block of Reisterstown Road, Baltimore, Maryland, that there were rats in her basement, Gentry, an inspector of the Baltimore City Health Department, began an inspection of the houses in the vicinity looking for the source of the rats. In the middle of the afternoon of February 27, 1958, Gentry knocked on the door of appellant's detached frame home at 4335 Reisterstown Road. After receiving no response he proceeded to inspect the area outside the house. This inspection revealed that the house was in an "extreme state of decay," and that in the rear of the house there was a pile later identified as "rodent feces mixed with straw and trash and debris to approximately half a ton." During this inspection appellant came around the side of the house and asked Gentry to explain his presence. Gentry responded that he had evidence of rodent infestation and asked appellant for permission to inspect the basement area. Appellant refused.[40]

That "a man's house is his castle" is one of this country's most cherished beliefs. We do not, however, live in this world by ourselves, and along with this right of privacy go certain obligations. To say one man has certain obligations is but another way of saying he must respect the rights of others. The Right Not To Have Your Children Bitten by Rats Breeding in Your Neighbor's Basement, while not specifically enumerated in the Constitution, should be a right of which due process takes cognizance—*a fortiori*, when your neighbor's castle and yours are connected to a common sewer system.

The Court's majority applied due process of law. When these rights clash, as they did here, one right cannot at all times prevail at the expense of the other. They must be accommodated, and Baltimore's

---

[40] *Frank v. Maryland*, 359 U.S. 360, 361 (1959).

attempt to do this was not unreasonable. The four dissenters—
Warren, Black, Douglas, and Brennan—took quite a different view.

> The decision today greatly dilutes the right of privacy
> which every homeowner had the right to believe was part
> of our American heritage. We witness indeed an inquest
> over a substantial part of the Fourth Amendment.

> The question in this case is whether a search warrant is
> needed to enter a citizen's home to investigate sanitary
> conditions.[41]

Nowhere does it appear that any entry was ever made into
Frank's house, with or without a warrant. The sole issue was
whether Baltimore could fine Frank $20 for unreasonably denying
its health inspector permission to inspect his basement for rat
infestation. The Court held that it could. To make sure tyranny did
not pass unnoted, the dissent reminded us of the bitter lessons of
history starting, of course, with the Star Chamber. No. 45 of the
North Briton and its putative author, John Wilkes, made their
obligatory appearance. The elder Pitt is quoted: "The poorest man
may in his cottage, bid defiance to all the force of the Crown. It may
be frail" etc. We hear James Otis denouncing the writs of assistance
at the old Town House. No histrionic base was left untouched.

Ohio ex rel Eaton v. Price was a case pending on the Court's
docket that bore an uncanny resemblance to *Frank v. Maryland.* It
seems that a housing inspector in Dayton, Ohio, also had been
refused entry by a homeowner. As in *Frank,* and as required by the
law, the request was made at a reasonable hour in the daytime and
there was no hint or suggestion of harassment.

The *Frank* case had been decided May 4, 1959. Two weeks later
four of *Frank's* five-man majority found the Ohio case controlled by
that decision. They therefore voted to dismiss the appeal of the
homeowner. The fifth member of the *Frank* majority, Potter
Stewart, recused himself because his father had been a member of

---

[41] *Frank,* 359 U.S. 374.

OUR FOURTH BRANCH OF GOVERNMENT

the Ohio Supreme Court from which the appeal was taken. Chief Justice Warren and the other three *Frank* dissenters voted to hear the Ohio case, which would now have to be argued before an eight-man Court deadlocked at four-four. This aroused the ire of the other Justices, who found this behavior unseemly.

> Mr. Justice Frankfurter, Mr. Justice Clark, Mr. Justice Harlan and Mr. Justice Whittaker are of the view that this case is controlled by, and should be affirmed on the authority of, *Frank v. Maryland*, 359 U.S. 360.

> The *Frank* case was decided on May 4. Application to review this case came before us within two weeks of the *Frank* decision. Since we deem the decision in the Maryland case to be completely controlling upon the Ohio decision, we are of the opinion that it would manifest disrespect by the Court for its own process to indicate its willingness to create an opportunity to overrule a case decided only a fortnight ago after thorough discussion at the bar and in the briefs and after the weightiest deliberation within the Court.[42]

This case brought to the forefront the power struggle going on behind the scenes. On the surface the issue appears to be whether the Fourteenth Amendment forbids a state to fine a homeowner for unreasonably denying entry to a health inspector. At bottom it is a search for a precedent to overrule *Wolf v. Colorado* and to apply the Fourth Amendment—and in due course the *Weeks* exclusionary rule—to the states. *Frank v. Maryland* could have accomplished this but failed by one vote.

It is at least remarkable that *Frank* came to be argued before the nation's highest tribunal. Frank appears to be eccentric, but not so much so that he would spend his life savings to defend a principle of some sort. High-minded he is not. Baltimore, on the other hand, could simply let the case go. If this retreat from civic virtue leads to a spate of

---

[42] *Ohio ex rel Eaton v. Price* 360 U.S. 246, 248-249, (1959).

health inspection refusals, Baltimore can deal with that problem when it comes.

With respect to Frank, health officials can do what he says they must: scoop up a sufficient amount of "probable cause" and present it, with supporting affidavits, to a local magistrate. A search warrant will issue forthwith and they can then search and seize, or search and destroy as the facts indicate. When all is said and done, this is a $20 case. That's what it is worth to Maryland and that's what it is worth to Frank. Yet as far as the record is concerned, Frank took on Maryland by himself.

The same is true of the Ohio case which was, as Justice Clark put it, "on all fours" with *Frank v. Maryland*. This is quite curious. All of a sudden appear two litigious-minded homeowners, of apparently limited financial circumstances, who appear determined to resist at all costs, including attorney's fees, what to the ordinary eye appear to be well-founded and reasonable searches by health inspectors.

Had either homeowner, the one in Ohio or the one in Maryland, sought legal advice, he would have been told to let the inspector in and stop acting like a jackass. A lawyer who had that client's interest at heart, and no ulterior motive, could not in good conscience advise him to go to court and charge him for his time.

As for the taxpayers of Baltimore and Dayton, did they pick up a tab entitled "Legal services rendered—Appeal to state and U.S. Supreme Courts"? If they did, they had a right to complain. Instead of running up a monstrous bill, the city attorney simply could have gotten a warrant before inspecting the house. Never mind that he is not constitutionally required to do so; the circumstances of the case do not merit litigating the matter. It is simply not worth it to the client municipality. No one, including city attorneys, is required to do battle with every crank who comes along.

A suspicious person searching for an explanation would see the hidden hand of the ACLU at work behind the scenes, even though its name does not appear of record in either case. That person's suspicions would be confirmed if he looked at the ACLU Annual Report for 1959 under the category "Illegal Searches and Seizures," where we find the following discussion.

> The dissenting view [in the Maryland case] feared the
> decision would open the door to Fourth Amendment
> violations. Standing alone, said the minority, the ruling
> "greatly dilutes the right of privacy which every homeowner
> had the right to believe was part of our American heritage."
> *An Ohio case before the court, supported by the ACLU, raised*
> *the same constitutional issue.*[43]

What does "supported by the ACLU" comprehend in financial terms? Does it mean they paid attorney's fees? If so, how much and to whom? More to the point, did they pay attorneys on both sides in the case? And why did not the ACLU sail under its own colors? The record in the Ohio case makes no mention of the ACLU. Anyone reading the case would think that the homeowner was acting independently. Of course, the Annual Report doesn't admit "support" in the Maryland case. Here we must rely, like the inspector at Frank's door, on evidence aliunde.

On June 27, 1960, more than a year after the decision to hear the Ohio case, the Maryland case notwithstanding, the Court deadlocked four-four.[44] On the same day, in *Elkins v. United States*, they abolished the so-called "silver platter" rule established in *Weeks*. Henceforth evidence unlawfully seized by state authorities will be inadmissible in a federal criminal trial. The decision, however, did not reach the constitutional threshold.

> What is here invoked is the Court's supervisory power
> over the administration of criminal justice in the federal
> courts, under which the Court has "from the very
> beginning of its history, formulated rules of evidence to
> be applied in federal criminal prosecutions." *McNabb v.*
> *United States*, 318 U.S. 332, 341. In devising such
> evidentiary rules, we are to be governed by "principles of
> the common law as they may be interpreted . . . in the
> light of reason and experience."[45]

---

[43] American Civil Liberties Union, Annual Report No. 39, 91. [emphasis added.] The quote within the quote is taken from Justice Douglas's dissent in *Frank v. Maryland*.

[44] *Ohio ex rel Eaton v. Price*, 364 U.S. 263.

[45] *Elkins v. United States*, 364 U.S. 206, 216.

So ended the 1959-1960 term of the Supreme Court of the United States. The ACLU's "constitutional engine" was fired up and ready to roll. All that was needed was the right vehicle and that would turn up in the next term, fittingly enough, in the debris of another bomb blast.

Chapter XV

MAPP v. OHIO

The official version of *Mapp v. Ohio*, the one accepted by the Supreme Court of the United States, was this put forth by A.L. Kearns and Walter L. Greene in the jurisdictional statement these two attorneys filed on behalf of Dollree Mapp on July 14, 1960:

Statement Of The Case

On the 23rd day of May, 1957, police officers, without the benefit of a search warrant, ostensibly looking for an individual who was wanted in connection with an extortion bombing, forced their way into defendant's private residence, which was the upper portion of a two-family house. Twelve (12) police officers had surrounded the private residence of the defendant where she lived with her 13-year old daughter and forced their way into it. Upon demand of a search warrant, a piece of paper was held before the defendant without giving her an opportunity to view or read same. She was then handcuffed to the banister of the stairway while the search of her private residence was made. This alleged search warrant was never proved or even tendered in the trial court upon request of the defendant. Nor was there any evidence introduced that any search warrant was ever issued.

Thereafter, the police officers, frustrated in their attempt to find any individual involved in an extortion bombing, illegally and in violation of defendant's constitutional rights, searched her private dwelling, and found lewd and lascivious documents belonging to a former roomer. The evidence showed that these documents were found by the defendant while she was cleaning a room which had been vacated by the former roomer. She stored these documents until such a time as the roomer would have returned to claim his property. It was for possession of the *roomer's* documents that the defendant was convicted of violation of Section 2905.34 Ohio Revised Code, and sentenced to from one (1) to seven (7) years in the Ohio State Women's Reformatory.

Mr. Justice Clark had stated in *Irvine* that had "I been here in 1949 when *Wolf* was decided, I would have applied the doctrine of *Weeks v. United States*, 232 U.S. 383 (1914), to the states." He predicted this would come about in some case "when five Justices are sufficiently revolted by local police action." In *Mapp* he accepted the official version and was himself "sufficiently revolted" to become one of the needed converts for *Wolf's* extinction. Enough is enough, he cried, throwing up his hands in disgust. Americans have a constitutional "right to be secure against rude invasions of privacy by state officers," and "we can no longer permit that right to remain an empty promise."[1] What he regurgitated was *Mapp v. Ohio*.

This story of the indignities suffered by Miss Mapp would turn the strongest of judicial stomachs. If this is what state policemen do to someone like Dollree Mapp, heaven knows what they would do when they're on the trail of a real desperado. So it is important to know what actually happened in Cleveland, Ohio, on that afternoon of May 23, 1957. Let's see how the official version stacks up against the newspaper accounts of the time.

The real case of *Mapp v. Ohio* began with a bang at 3:45 on the morning of Monday, May 20, 1957. In fact it was a very big bang caused by a bomb planted under the residence of one of Cleveland's leading policy bankers, Donald "The Kid" King, now the world's most successful boxing promoter. The headlines of that day's

---

[1] *Mapp v. Ohio*, 367 U.S. 643, 660 (1961).

Cleveland Press, in large block letters, running from one side of the front page to the other, read: "Birns is Jailed in Bombing; Charge $1000-a-Week Plot." Underneath is a picture of "Donald King's home at 3713 E. 151st St." looking considerably the worse for wear.

Also on the front page are side-by-side photos of a youthful and short-haired Don King and one Shondor Birns. The bomb blast "opened what police believed is a new offensive by Shondor Birns to control Cleveland's numbers racket . . . 'Shondor was one of the five pistols who bombed me,' King told reporters." The bomb didn't kill Mr. King, but it did give him quite a fright. Instead of tending to the matter himself, in the tradition of the numbers racket,[2] he did what a good citizen should—he went to the police.

The *Plain Dealer* reported the next day that "King made history yesterday when he openly turned to police with information he said would help send someone to jail . . . King also linked the death of Tommy Boyce last month to the numbers racket." Boyce "was shot to death in his home on April 12." King seemed to think this chap Birns was involved. "The cast of characters in the bombing plot investigation . . . includes five clearinghouse operators,[3] two musclemen and Birns. All have police records."[4]

One of these characters was Virgil Ogletree, a clearinghouse operator. Not in residence at his usual haunts, he was thought to be doing his clearing in the house of one Dollree Mapp. It was Ogletree for whom a special investigation unit led by Sgt. Carl Delau were looking when they arrived at 14705 Milverton Avenue S.E. that Thursday afternoon. Carl Delau was the policeman Don King called to report the bombing. "At 3:40 a.m. King called Sgt. Delau at home and refused to talk with anyone but him."[5] Perhaps Delau had been

---

[2] "Shondor Birns Is Bomb Victim," *Plain Dealer*, March 30, 1975, and "Quiz 3 In Birns Slaying," the following day.

[3] In "policy," "runners" make their daily rounds in allotted areas collecting bets. The bettor picks a number from 1 to 999. The number and the amount of the wager are recorded on a policy slip with a carbon counterpart. The bettor gets the copy and the runner keeps the original. Every day by a certain hour, and after deducting a commission, the runners turn in their bets and slips to a clearinghouse. Later in the day, when "the number" has been "picked," people at the clearinghouse sort through the slips looking for "hitters."

[4] "5 Now Held in Bombing of King's Home," *Plain Dealer*, May 21, 1957.

[5] Ibid.

told by a visibly shaken but otherwise reliable informant that where Ogletree was, so also would be a large amount of policy paraphernalia.

It seems reasonable to assume Mr. Justice Tom Clark—who wrote the Court's opinion—was not aware that policy paraphernalia was ever a consideration. He gives the impression that but for the obscene material the police came up empty-handed. The appellants' "Statement of the Case" tells us only that the police were "ostensibly looking for an individual who was wanted in connection with an extortion bombing." No mention is made of policy paraphernalia whatever, much less any finding of it.

The only statement in point is found in Ohio's brief on page 5. "A trunk of policy paraphernalia was found in the basement by Patrolman Dever." But this is equivocal because the same brief on page 3 says of "the home of the Appellant" that it "is a two-family brick dwelling and the Appellant lived on the second floor." The Cleveland *Plain Dealer* of May 24, 1957, is somewhat more explicit. On page 11 is a picture of a policeman in plain clothes with a handful of slips of paper. He is peering into a large trunk containing a lot more of the same. Underneath is the caption "'California Gold' Strike":

> Sgt. Carl J. Delau examines a trunkful of policy slips found in the home of Miss Dollree Mapp, ex-wife of boxer Jimmy Bivens and former girl friend of Archie Moore, light heavyweight champion of the world.

This is a continuation of a story on page one—"Policy House Closed After 3-Hour Siege"—which opens: "The 'California Gold' policy house abruptly went out of business yesterday after a three-hour police siege of the house of Miss Dollree Mapp." It states the raid was made on the basis of a tip that one of the persons involved in the King bombing was hiding out at the house:

> The informant also [said] that Miss Mapp's home was being used as a policy house.

> This, it turned out, was the "California Gold" policy house. The officers seized a large trunk full of slips and records and other policy paraphernalia. They also

discovered a quantity of books, pamphlets and photographs they described as "obscene."

The appellant's "Statement of the Case" avers that "the police officers [were] frustrated in their attempt to find any individual involved in an extortion bombing." This does not jibe with the *Plain Dealer's* report that "Ogletree, who had sneaked down the back stairs, was found in the downstairs home. A woman who lived there said he had threatened her. Miss Mapp gave her home address as the one on Lee Road."

Now one of Miss Mapp's lawyers was a witness to this incident. According to the *Plain Dealer*, "Her lawyer, Walter L. Greene, was on hand at the final stages of the siege. She [Miss Mapp] had phoned him. He followed the police entourage downtown." Greene testified for the defense at the trial. The preliminary questions on direct examination established that Walter L. Greene was an attorney associated in the practice of law with his father and with A.L. Kearns, the other lawyer who is representing Miss Mapp. On cross-examination the following exchange took place:

> Q. While you were out there, Mr. Green [*sic*], did you observe somebody being taken away from there?
> A. Yes.
> Q. Do you know who it was?
> A. There were two people.
> Q. Do you know who they were?
> A. I know, of course, Mrs. Mapp, and I later learned the other was Virgil Ogletree. I saw him the first time in the downstairs suite.
> Q. On the first floor suite?
> A. Yes, ma'am.
> Q. And he was taken away in a patrol wagon?
> A. That would be my best recollection.[6]

---

[6] Transcript of Record—Supreme Court of the United States, *Mapp v. Ohio*, Docket No. 236, filed July 14, 1960. The transcript has an index which makes citation by page number unnecessary.

How then could Kearns and Greene, when they came to write their "Statement of the Case," say "the police officers [were] frustrated in their attempt to find any individual involved in an extortion bombing"? Let us be charitable and say they have an odd way of expressing themselves, a way which might be confusing to people like Potter Stewart, for example.

> Let us pick up the threads of our story at the home of Dollree Mapp, in Cleveland, Ohio, on May 27 [*sic*], 1957. Mapp lived on the second floor of a two-family brick house and rented out rooms to boarders. In mid-May, three police officers appeared at her home and demanded entrance, explaining that they were searching for a man in connection with a recent bombing. After consulting by telephone with her attorney, Mapp refused to admit them without a search warrant. The officers returned later, with others, and forced their way in. After Mapp asked to see the officers' search warrant, the officers produced a piece of paper, which Mapp grabbed and placed down the front of her blouse. A fracas ensued when one of the officers tried to retrieve the piece of paper. After handcuffing Mapp, the officers searched the house. No bombing suspect was ever found and no search warrant was ever produced. The officers did, however, find four books—*Affairs of a Troubadour, Little Darlings, London Stage Affairs*, and *Memories of a Hotel Man*—as well as a hand-drawn picture described in the state's brief as being "of a very obscene nature."[7]

All cases given plenary review are discussed by the full Court in private conference. Justice Stewart's understanding of the facts, the only one speaking to the point, must be taken as that of the whole Court. Indeed, this is the almost universal impression of the case. Wisconsin Judge Ralph Adam Fine, for example, wrote an excellent book in which he tells of the iniquities brought about by the application of the exclusionary rule to the states.

In discussing the *Mapp* decision he had this to say of the goings-on at Milverton Avenue that afternoon. "Although the man for

---

[7] *The Road to Mapp v. Ohio and Beyond*, 1366-1367.

The Cleveland Press

The Newspaper That Serves Its Readers

NO. 26980

CLEVELAND, MONDAY, MAY 20, 1957

Phone CHerry 1-1111

Home

★★★★★★

52 Pages — 7 Cents

Birns Is Jailed in Bombing; Charge $1000-a-Week Plot

A bomb blast at 3:45 a. m. today on the front porch of a numbers gambling figure opened what police believe is new offensive by Shondor Birns to control Cleveland's numbers racket.

Birns was linked to the bombing by Donald King, 25, of N.E. 131st St., whose front door was ripped open by dynamite.

"Shondor was one of the five pistols who bombed me," King told reporters.

The numbers operator, freed only 5 months ago from federal prison, was jailed after King charged him with collecting $1000 a week from a numbers racket ring.

King, a numbers operator who says he retired a few weeks ago, told police that his business partner bombed because he stopped paying Birns his $200-a-week share of the money.

He said that he and two other policy operators agreed last October to pay Birns to keep the numbers business flowing smoothly.

Birns denied the charge.

"I don't know these guys and I don't want to know them," he said.

"They tell the police anything, the police believe them. I've got a job and a family."

The job, he said, is with Union Towel & Supply Co. There was a lot of flammable fluids in Birns' home, Lieut. Martin Cooney, said Birns said for $200 a week from each of us he would see that the odds stayed the same, around four per cent.

He explained that by controlling the odds, the operators could gradually reduce the size of the payoffs and Birns would make the most money.

He said he paid Birns this weekly bill January when he cut it to $100. He said the payments were made

to Birns' "representative." A few weeks ago he stopped paying altogether.

The other "pistols who bombed me," he said, were Edward Keeling, 31, of 3193 E. 134 St., Dan Boone, 1613 E. 115th St., Buckeye Jackson, 1497 E. 100th St., and Truman Turk, 1507 E. 100th St.

King said he called up Jackson and Boone after the bombing. "I know you did it and I'll see to it that you go to the penitentiary," police quoted him as saying to Jackson and Boone.

Police could not find Jackson and Boone. Turk was found at home, sick in bed. He is to be questioned later.

Birns was arrested less than three hours after the bombing in his home, 16913 Judson Dr. He appeared jovial and confident when he was booked. Also locked up were Keeling and Samson Powell, 36, of 2329 E. 97th St., a "musicleman."

King said the final break with the ring came when the others decided to change the number system used to pay off. The number, he said, was taken from stock.

Turn to Page 9, Column 1

SHONDOR BIRNS is linked to bombing of policy figure's home.

BOMBED because he quit the racket, he says, was Donald King, 25.

Beck Is Ousted as Veep of AFL-CIO at Union Trial

Teamster President Charged With "Gross Misuse" of Funds

WASHINGTON —(UP)— Teamster President Dave Beck was ousted as an AFL-CIO vice president today by the AFL-CIO high command on grounds of "gross misuse" of union funds.

The action came shortly after Beck refused at an unprecedented closed-door AFL-CIO trial to answer charges that he had brought the labor movement into "disrepute."

AFL-CIO President George Meany announced that the 35 members of the AFL-CIO Executive Council who were present today had unanimously voted Beck's ouster with unprecedented action.

"There is not the faintest ... could be arranged on the Am...

Atlantic Winds Delay New Gripsholm Liner

...(UP)— the heavy ...but the Gripsholm today ...ocean voyage across the Atlantic.

...of Sweden's ...to reach here, ...will discharge 115 ...The original Gripsholm had ...as a repatriation ship. It ...postwar ...

Save 4 Trapped in Car by [Fire]

...four persons, including two children, were attended ...for an hour today in an automobile on Dexter Avers. ...trapped while several teachers, William Dobbs, ...Dewaty Smith, 5635 Rob-mond Rd., Solon...

...and inadequate ... camed County of Solon Road. ...With them were Jimmy ... half feet of water in the bac...

Pictures on Page 27

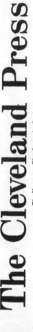

DYNAMITE BLAST ripped open the front porch on ...floors (bearing) of Donald King's home at 3713 E. 131st St.

Bureau of Special Investigation

DIST: 2981

May 23, 19 57

EXAMINED BY _____ RANK **Lieut.**   May 24, 19 57

FROM **Carl I. Delau, Sgt.**   TO   **Martin P. Cooney, lieut.**

SUBJECT Daily duty report for Thursday, May 23, 1957.

COPIES TO

Sir:

Reported for duty at 8:30 A.M. this date in company with Ptls. Dover #990 and Haney #258, read reports, complaints and performed the following assignments.

At this office requestioned Elijah Abercrombie, 773 E. 93 St. relative to the malicious destruction of property of Donald King, 3713 E. 151 St. Subject against denied thathe had ever received money from King and had seen him only abour six times in his life. Subject was then booked at the Detective Bureau on the warrant that was issued, this was for violation of R.C. 2901.38, (blackmail-felony). Subject was taken to the statement room but he refused to make a statement.

Made reports which are connected with the investigation of Donald King and the bombing of his home. Report made on the questioning of Sampson Powell, known muscle man and suspected of working for Alex Birns. Report made on the telephone numbers which were confiscated from Elijah Abercrombie.

Went to the residence of Sam Elmore, 3189 E. 132 St., reported clearing house figure who had been given a beating by muscle men of Alex Birn This subject wanted for questioning and possible statement, failed to find this person at home, word was left with his wife for Sam Elmore to come to this office.

On information received from a confidential source, went to 147 05 Milverton Ave., the residence of Dollree Mapp who is known to this office and has previous arrest for clearing house violations. Information had been obtained that a person was hiding out at this address who was wanted in connection with the bombing of Donald King and that certain evidence was conveye to this address. Dollree Mapp resides on the second floor, subject was at home but refused to let us into her home. After considerable delay a search warrant was obtained and entrance gained. Arrested Dollree Mapp and a Vergil Ogletree for investigation, they were conveyed to the Detective Bureau where they were booked. Ogletree is known to be connected with a clearing house operation and also the California Gold policy house. In the basement we found a foot locker which contained a large amount of policy paraphernalia in the form of balls and business from the California Gold and Interstate policy houses. In the second floor residence of Dollree Mapp we found a number of books of a pornographic nature. Special report to be made of this and the prosecutor to be consulted.

Reported off duty at 8:00 P.M.

Respectfully:

Sgt.

POLICE DEPARTMENT
CLEVELAND, OHIO

Bureau of Special
Investigation

DEPARTMENTAL INFORMATION

May 23, , 57

EXAMINED BY_____ RANK **Lieut.**

May , 57

FROM **Carl I. Delau, Sgt.**   TO **Martin P. Cooney, Lieut.**

SUBJECT **Arrest of DOLLREE MAPP, 14705 Milverton Ave., investigation in connec-**
COPIES TO **Files, Detective Bur.**   **tion with the malicious destruction of property**
of Donald King, 3713 E. 151 St.

Sir:

In company with Patls. Devor #890 and Haney #258, at approximately 4:45 P.M. this date, arrested DOLLREE MAPP, also known as DOLLREE DIVENS, DOLLREE MOORE, 14705 Milverton Ave., F, C, age 29 and VIRGIL OGLETREE, 1355 E.115 St. for investigation. Subject were conveyed to Central Station and booked at the Detective Bureau, to be photoed and printed.

Information was obtained from a confidential source which stated that a person wanted in connection with the bombing of Donald Kings home at 37-13 E. 151 St. was confining himself to this address and that there also was a lot of clearing house evidence at this location. This address of 14705 Milverton Ave. is a two family brick home which has been known to be the property of the above Dollree Mapp with the subject residing on the second floor. Dollree Mapp had previous arrest for possession of clearinghouse slips M.C. 13.1318.

Checked 14705 Milverton Ave. at about 1:00 P.M. this date at which time we observed her auto parked in the garage. In the drive of this address we noticed an auto which is the property of Vergil Ogletree, MA-981, this person known to be a clearing house operator and had been connected with the operation of the California Gold policy when it was in operation. Detailed on this address until approximately 1:45 P.M. during which time neither Mapp or Ogletree left the premises. At this time we then made an effort to gain entrance to the residence of Mapp, on ringing the doorbell this subject would not come to the door but spoke to us through the second floor window. Mapp stated that she would not let us in unless we had a search warrant and said that she was the only person at home and that the woman who resides on the first floor was away for the day.

Remained in the vicinity of this home until a search warrant was obtained by Lieut. Thomas White who then came to this address. With the warrant in our possession we then gained entrance via the side door and found the above Dollree Mapp on the stairway between the first and second floor. Subject was placed under arrest and a search was made of the premises. In the basement we found a large foot locker which contained considerable policy paraphernalia, later examination showed that it contained the following, 5 sets of policy ball 1 marked chart sheet, a bag of box car seals, one counter, 14 bundles of California Gold day policy drawings, 14 bundles of Interstate day policy drawings, the California Gold drawings were of class 2247 thru 2260, the Interstate drawings were of class 2147 thru 2160. There were 7 bundles of California Gold night drawings, class 1124 to 1129, policy books, rubber bands and other equipment. This evidence was confiscated, tagged and turned in to the property room.

Made search of the second floor in company with Dollree Mapp and found the following which was confiscated and taken to Central Station. In one bedroom we found four books of a pornographic nature and several pictures, the books are titled as follows: London Stage Affairs, Affairs of a Troubadour, Memories of a Hotel Man, Little Darlings. This evidence was found in a suitcase which is Dollree Mapps and contained evidence with her name on it.

DIST. ZONE   _____ 19 ____

EXAMINED BY _____ RANK _____   _____ 19 ____

FROM   TO

SUBJECT   Arrest of DOLLREE MAPP, 14705 Milverton Ave.

COPIES TO   (continued)

In this same bedroom in a dresser drawer we found a weapon, a Colt make "Bronco" automatic, 7.65 MM, serial number 10410. This gun contained a magazine and no cartridges. Special report made on this gun and the weapon to be checked out by the Bureau of Scientific Identification.

In this same bedroom, various other photographs and material were confiscated including tapes for a tape recording machine. These will be played to determine if they contain anything of interest to this department.

From the kitchen of the second floor we confiscated policy books and pads and from a desk we confiscated three address books. Questioned Dollree Mapp while on the premises who stated that she resides on the second floor with her daughter Barbara Mapp, age 13 and Maurice Jones, age 26 and Margarette Cortos, age 22. These persons were not on the premises and there was no clothing to indicate that they live at this address.

Made search of the first floor and in the kitchen we arrested Vergil Ogletree, this subject was searched but we failed to find any clearing house or policy evidence. This subject was seated in the kitchen with Flavera Fitzpatrick Lockheart, age 32. This person stated that she had lived at this address for 10 months and pays her rent to Dollree Mapp. Subject also stated that she was told by Mapp not to open the door for the police and for her to let Ogletree stay in her quarters.

At Central Station we requestioned Dollree Mapp, subject has no CPD photo number at present time. Subject stated that she has owned this home at 14705 Milverton for a year and nine months and had moved back to this address in Nov., 1956. She added that she collected rent of $100 per month from the woman on the first floor. Dollree Mapp has phone 98-2-3833 on the second floor listed to Deloreo Moore, subject no longer resides at this address. Mapp denies that the obscene literature or policy evidence are hers. She stated that the Maurice Jones who moved away from her home five weeks ago had brought the foot locker to her home and that he also had left the obscene books behind when he left. Subject admits to be the girl friend of Edward Keeling who is a known clearing house figure. Mapp admitted to knowing Donald King and other clearing house figures but could give no help relative to the bombing of King's home. Subject is very evasive in her answers and was not making an effort to be helpful to the police.

Vergil Ogletree, our CPD #80236 was questioned at our office. This person admits to one arrest for clearing house violations but states that he has no connection with any clearing house or policy operations. He told us that he was at 14705 Milverton Ave. as he was picking up some cleaning and came to this address several minutes before the police. He denied that he had any connection with the clearing house business which was found in the basement. This subject stated that he had no information on the bombing and was home at the time.

Prosecutor to be consulted on the arrest of these two subjects.

Respectfully,

whom they were looking was not found, they did come across some booklets, pictures, and a drawing, all of which the officers thought were obscene."[8] More recently, in a book with a similar thesis— *Guilty: The Collapse of Criminal Justice*—New York criminal court Judge Harold J. Rothwax expressed the same understanding. "The bombing suspect was not found, and the piece of paper turned out not to be a search warrant."[9]

This is not meant by way of criticism of either judge. To the author's knowledge, the only account that Ogletree was found— apart from the contemporaneous newspaper reports and the transcript of the trial—is a book by Fred W. Friendly and Martha J.H. Elliott.[10] The authors, who interviewed Miss Mapp, state:

> Meanwhile, the bombing suspect, Virgil Ogletree, was finally found in the first-floor apartment.*
>
> _____
>
> *Miss Mapp told the authors she knew Ogletree was downstairs. [footnote in original]

If the "Statement of the Case" by Kearns and Greene misled the Supreme Court as to the existence of Virgil Ogletree, did it also mislead the Court into believing the police did not have a warrant to search for Ogletree or for policy paraphernalia? Take, for example, their statement: "Upon demand of a search warrant, a piece of paper was held before the defendant without giving her an opportunity to view or read same." Let us examine this a bit more closely.

If you are confronted by a police officer in plain clothes and you question his identity, he will hold his credentials up in front of your eyes. He will not hand them to you nor permit you to take them from him. This is standard police procedure. Before the advent of the Xerox process, the same practice was followed with respect to warrants. With this in mind, read the *Plain Dealer's* description of the "fracas":

> Reinforcements arrived from the Fourth District. The

_____

[8]   Ralph Adam Fine. *Escape of the Guilty*. New York: Dodd, Mead & Company, 1986, 152.
[9]   Harold J. Rothwax. *Guilty: The Collapse of Criminal Justice*. New York: Random House, 1996, 43.
[10] *The Constitution: That Delicate Balance*. New York: Random House, 1984, 132.

warrant arrived from Central Police Station. Again Delau demanded that Miss Mapp let them in. Again Miss Mapp refused.

This time, armed with the warrant plus some brawn, the officers pried open a screen door, broke the glass on an inner door and entered Miss Mapp's home. They found the trunk, opened it, saw what was inside.

But not without one desperate last-ditch act of defiance from Miss Mapp. She met the policemen on the stairs. She grabbed the warrant from the hand of one of them. Then she stuffed it down the front of her dress. The raiders were startled, to say the least. But one of them rolled up a sleeve and said to her "If you don't get it for us, I will." She returned the warrant.[11]

Police reports made contemporaneously with the arrests confirm the existence of a search warrant. A report dated May 23, 1957, by "Carl I. Delau, Sgt. to Martin P. Cooney, Lieut." concerning the "Arrest of Dollree Mapp, 14705 Milverton Ave., investigation in connection with the malicious destruction of property of Donald King, 3713 E. 151 St." states that Delau, Dever and Haney:

Checked 14705 Milverton Ave. at about 1:00 P.M. this date at which time we observed her auto parked in the garage. In the drive of this address we noticed an auto which is the property of Virgil Ogletree, MA-981, this person known to be a clearing house operator . . .

At "approximately 1:45 p.m." they rang the doorbell. The "subject would not come to the door but spoke to us through the second floor window. Mapp stated that she would not let us in unless we had a search warrant." The report continued:

Remained in the vicinity of this home until a search warrant was obtained by Lieut. Thomas White who then came to this address. With the warrant in our possession

---

[11] *Plain Dealer*, May 24, 1957, 11.

we gained entrance via the side door and found the above Dollree Mapp on the stairway between the first and second floor. Subject was placed under arrest and a search was made of the premises.

Dollree Mapp and Virgil Ogletree were arrested at approximately 4:45 p.m. In the basement the police found and seized "a large foot locker which contained considerable policy paraphernalia." On the second floor they found "four books of a pornographic nature" and a "Colt make 'Bronco' automatic, 7.65[?], serial number 10410." Ogletree was found and arrested in the first floor apartment. The tenant "stated that she was told by Mapp not to open the door for the police and for her to let Ogletree stay in her quarters." Delau's "Daily duty report for Thursday, May 23, 1957" says much the same thing:

> Information had been obtained that a person was hiding out at this address who was wanted in connection with the bombing of Donald King and that certain evidence was conveyed to this address. Dollree Mapp resides on the second floor, subject was at home but refused to let us into her home. After considerable delay a search warrant was obtained and entrance gained.

A search warrant is not simply a piece of paper to be discarded when it has served its purpose. A police officer who obtains a warrant must return it within a given time to the judicial authority who issued it. The warrant must be "endorsed" by the officer upon its "return." He must write on the warrant itself the time and place of its execution or that he failed to execute it, as the case may be. In the event a search warrant is executed, the return must be accompanied by an inventory of what was seized.

Judges keep a record of the warrants they issue, for a period of time at least, so that should a warrant be lost, there is still an official record of its existence. If there is no such record, the presumption would be there that was no such warrant. Ohio law was clear on the consequences of warrantless searches. "Therefore, a law officer who proceeds to make a search and seizure without a warrant, or under a defective warrant, is a trespasser, amenable to civil and perhaps criminal action."[12]

Let us say you are a lieutenant in the Cleveland Police Department. A woman of known litigious disposition[13] has told the police in no uncertain terms that they are not getting into her house without a warrant. In the person of Don King you have a affiant ready, willing, and able to sign the supporting affidavit needed to obtain a warrant. A call over the police radio will fetch him.[14] It is early Thursday afternoon, and in the Cuyahoga County Courthouse in downtown Cleveland, judges and magistrates are to be found in abundance.

It is your job to get a search warrant and go out to Milverton Avenue and execute it. In the meanwhile, the three policemen awaiting the warrant are keeping both Miss Mapp's house and Ogletree's car, which is parked in her driveway, under observation. If you were a police lieutenant, would you get the warrant? Or would you go out there with a meaningless piece of paper, wave it under her nose, and bluff it out?

According to the "Statement of the Case," this "alleged search warrant was never proved or even tendered in the trial court upon request of the defendant." On oral argument Kearns told the Supreme Court of the United States; "We asked during the trial of the case that the search warrant be produced and it was not." "But the prosecutor promised—and we have the prosecutor here—that the search warrant would be produced and it never was."[15]

---

[12] *State v. Lindway*, 131 Ohio State 166, 2 N.E. 2d 490, 493 (1936).

[13] It was widely known in Cleveland that Dollree Mapp was suing light heavyweight champion Archie Moore for breach of contract. Kearns and Greene were her attorneys in this action.

[14] "Police Chief Frank W. Story refused King permission to carry a gun but took steps to provide him around-the-clock protection," "5 Now Held in Bombing of King's Home," *Plain Dealer*, May 21, 1957.

[15] The official transcript of the oral argument in *Mapp v. Ohio* may be found in *Landmark Briefs and Arguments of the Supreme Court of the United States: Constitutional Law* —University Publishing of America, Bethesda, Maryland. A.L. Kearns, on behalf of Dollree Mapp, was the first lawyer to address the Court and his argument and exchanges take up the first 12 pages. He gave the rest of his alloted time to Bernard A. Berkman, speaking for the ACLU, who finished up on page 19. The rest of the oral argument in this transcript of 43 pages was made by Gertrude Bauer Mahon, who represented Ohio. The two sentences cited above may be found respectively on pages 2 and 3 of the transcript. The remaining excerpts quoted herein can easily be found and for that reason are not identified by page numbers.

If that is so, further discussion is pointless. Any police lieutenant who really did have a search warrant would have produced it when it counted—at the trial. The matter would have been settled then and there, once and for all. But in the real case of *State v. Mapp*, the real lieutenant, Thomas White, from whose hand Dollree Mapp snatched that "piece of paper," was never asked anything by anybody.

In fact the existence of a warrant to search the Mapp house for policy paraphernalia and for Ogletree was never once challenged. The defense *never* "asked during the trial of the case that the search warrant be produced"—then, or any other time either. The statements Kearns made to the Supreme Court of the United States were not just misleading they were out-and-out lies.

Suppose they were? This case was decided almost 40 years ago; whether or not Lt. White actually had a warrant is moot. *Mapp v. Ohio* is *res judicata*: the case is closed. True, but there is another *Mapp v. Ohio* that lives on under the doctrine of *stare decisis*. It keeps applying that earlier fraud, the *Weeks* rule, to confer immunity upon murderers and armed robbers. *That* case of *Mapp v. Ohio* is very much alive; we live with it every day.

The validity of *stare decisis* depends on both sides of a legal argument being fairly and adequately represented by counsel. The question pressed here is whether the *Mapp v. Ohio* that affects our daily lives was a genuine "case" or "controversy" meeting this standard *or* whether in truth it was a fraud in which the prosecution acted in concert with the defense to mislead the Supreme Court of the United States by presenting a false state of facts.

If you want to believe *Mapp v. Ohio* was not a setup, you have to make a lot of assumptions which, especially when taken together, are contrary to human experience. First of all, you have to envision a prosecutor who really wants to put someone like Dollree Mapp in prison for one to seven years, when accommodations are short and there are so many more deserving tenants out and about. Why a district attorney would prosecute a private possessor of "dirty booklets"—a bailee at that—on a felony statute which, however its text may be read literally, is aimed at those who traffic in pornography is beyond understanding.

Miss Mapp was arrested on May 23, 1957. Not until September

19 was she indicted for "possession obscene[?]." The following day she pleaded "not guilty" and posted a bail bond in the amount of $2,500. On the 8th of July, 1958, she retracted her plea of "not guilty" and entered a plea of "guilty." She remained free on bond, and her case was "referred to Probation Dept. for report." This suggests a disposition in her case had been reached. Something changed her mind. On August 1 the Court gave her leave to withdraw the plea of "guilty" and plead "not guilty" once again.[16]

More than 15 months after the episode at her house, Dollree Mapp was put on trial in the Cuyahoga County Court of Common Pleas for the "possession of obscene material." She will be represented at all times by A.L. Kearns and Walter L. Greene. The state of Ohio will be represented by Assistant Prosecutor Gertrude Bauer Mahon.[17] Like Kearns and Greene, she will not only try the case but argue it on all levels of appeal. Mrs. Mahon's husband, Court of Common Pleas Judge John J. Mahon,[18] was a colleague of Donald F. Lybarger, the judge who will preside over the trial of Dollree Mapp.

The prosecution is not required as part of its *prima facie* case to prove the evidence it uses was *not* unconstitutionally obtained. The defense must first raise that issue. If the defendant makes no objection, it is presumed he has none, and the trial proceeds accordingly. A defendant who wishes to claim evidence was taken from him in an illegal search and seizure must do so seasonably. He may not let it pass at the trial and later assert the claim on appeal after the trial court and the prosecution have relied upon his silence.

On September 3, 1958, before the trial began, attorney A.L. Kearns filed this motion on behalf of the defendant:

[16] All information in this paragraph is taken from Court of Common Pleas, Criminal Docket 137 (1957).

[17] The name of John T. Corrigan, the Cuyahoga County Prosecutor, appears on the brief along with that of Mrs. Mahon. There is no reason to think, however, that this was anything else but *pro forma*.

[18] See obituary of Gertrude Mahon, *Cleveland Press*, September 27, 1979, B-6.

STATE OF OHIO	)	IN THE COURT
		OF COMMON
		PLEAS
	)	CASE NO. 68326
COUNTY OF CUYAHOGA)		SS.

STATE OF OHIO	)	
	)	
Plaintiff)		
	)	
vs.	)	MOTION TO
		SUPPRESS
	)	
DOLLY MAPP	)	<u>EVIDENCE</u>
	)	
Defendant	)	

Now comes the defendant by her attorney, A.L. Kearns and moves this honorable court for an order suppressing the evidence procured by the police officers, to wit:

Certain claimed lewd and lascivious Books, Pictures and Photographs and intended to be used in evidence in the trial of the aforesaid cause.

For the reason that the aforesaid evidence was not procured by a proper search warrant as submitted [*sic*] by Section 2905.35 of the Ohio Revised Code.

<u>/s/ A.L. Kearns</u>
Attorney for Defendant

This motion to suppress may be found in the case file for *Ohio v. Mapp*—Docket No. 68326—in the Court of Common Pleas for Cuyahoga County. The prosecution filed no papers in opposition. Nor did the prosecution offer oral argument. According to the transcript it was only Kearns who argued the motion, and this is the way he explained it to the trial court:

Now we say that the State of Ohio did not have a search warrant *setting forth the items that are mentioned in this indictment*, and which the State of Ohio intends to use in

329

this cause against this defendant, and for that reason we
are asking that particular evidence be suppressed.[19]

Note that this does not allege that the state of Ohio did not have
a search warrant to search for persons or for things other than
obscene materials. The defense did not request the prosecution to
produce any warrant it did have, so that it might be examined. They
raised no question of "probable cause." There was no allegation that
an unreasonable search or seizure had ever taken place. All Kearns
said was that there was no warrant which specified "lewd and
lascivious books, pictures and photographs." That being the case
Memories of a Hotel Man and the rest of the anthology, according to
Kearns, could not be used in evidence against the defendant. Judge
Lybarger overruled the motion and the trial began.

The prosecutor called only two witnesses, Patrolman Michael
Haney and Sgt. Carl Delau. They both testified to the finding of the
lascivious material. With respect to the warrant Haney testified that
a "search warrant was brought out after an hour and a half or two
hour delay, brought to the premises, and the officers admitted by
Miss Mapp from the sidewalk." During Haney's cross-examination
by Kearns, the following exchange occurred:

By Mr. Kearns:
Q. Where is that search warrant?
A. I don't know.
Q. Do you have it here?
A. I don't have it.
Q. Would you tell the jury who has it?
A. I can't tell the jury who has it; no, sir.
Q. And you were one of the investigating officers in the
   investigation by the police department?
A. Yes.
Q. But you can't tell us where the search warrant is?
A. No, I cannot.
Q. Or what it recites?
A. No.

---

[19] Transcript of Record, 2, 3 [emphasis added].

Q. You yourself did not obtain the search warrant, did
you, officer?
A. No, I did not.
Q. Do you know who did?
A. I was told Lieutenant White obtained it.

Sgt. Carl Delau on direct examination testified:

A. (continuing) Close to four p.m. that afternoon
Lieutenant White arrived on the scene with a search
warrant. When we told her we had a search warrant she
opened the door. Before that she said she wouldn't; at
that time we did pry the screen door to gain entrance to
the building itself. We went upstairs, myself and
Lieutenant White; Inspector Barrett had arrived on the
scene. She demanded to see the warrant; that is when
she grabbed it out of his hand and concealed it on her
person. We recovered the warrant, and she was quite
belligerent at that particular time.

The only questions the defense asked Sgt. Delau about the warrant
on cross-examination were these:

Q. Well, as a matter of fact she told you then that she
had talked to her lawyer, and asked you if you had a
search warrant?
A. Yes, she did.
Q. And you said no, but we can get one?
A. That is correct.
Q. And then she told you that you better get a search
warrant, then you could go into her house?
A. Correct.
Q. And it was then that you called Lieutenant White
and told him you were having trouble getting in,
and she insists on a search warrant?
A. I didn't call White; I called Lieutenant Cooney, my
boss.
Q. Then sometime later when you and the other two
police officers were on the scene, someone came out
with a search warrant, didn't they?
A. That is correct.
Q. And who was it?

A. That was Lieutenant White.
Q. Lieutenant White came with a search warrant?
A. Yes.

Miss Mapp testified on her own behalf. This is what she said happened:

A. When they came in I said, "Inspector, I want to see the search warrant." And I was standing on the top landing of the stairs, and I didn't know who the inspector was when he was in plain clothes. He said, "Here is the search warrant." He held it back from me, and I remember Mr. Green told me I should see it and read it, and I told him I wanted to see it. He said, "You can't see it." At that I reached over, took the search warrant from his hand and put it down in my bosom.

There is nothing suspicious about Haney's testimony. He was a patrolman under the command of Sgt. Delau. When Lt. White appeared with the warrant, there was no reason for him to show it to a junior officer or for Haney to ask his superior officer to see it. To do so would have been quite out of line. Haney never read or had possession of the warrant, and there was no reason he should know where it was at the trial, as defense counsel no doubt knew. Nor is there anything unusual about Miss Mapp's account. Lt. White held the search warrant up in front of her eyes close enough for her to be able to snatch it from him. If what Lt. White said to Miss Mapp was, "You can't *see* it," he no doubt meant, "You can't *have* it." Defense counsel probably knew this also.

Lt. White was not a witness to the search of Miss Mapp's room nor to the discovery and seizure there of the lewd literature. He could contribute nothing to the prosecution's *prima facie* case. The defense did not contend at the trial that the piece of paper Miss Mapp snatched from his hand was anything other than a search warrant. Under these circumstances there was absolutely no reason for the prosecution to call Lt. White.

If the police had a warrant, and under the circumstances we are entitled to presume that they did, they acted entirely within the law. They were empowered to execute the warrant by entering the house, by force if necessary, and to overcome Miss Mapp's resistance by handcuffing and arresting her. Evidence encountered in the search for Ogletree or for policy paraphernalia—the lewd booklets and a "25 caliber Colt automatic gun"—could lawfully be seized and used as evidence.

The case would be a virtual replication of *Adams v. New York* in 1904. Albert J. Adams, as you will recall, was convicted of the knowing possession of 3,500 policy slips which had been seized by the police in searching his office under a search warrant for "gambling paraphernalia." In doing so they came across a letter, unrelated to gambling, which was later used as a specimen of Adams' handwriting at the trial. Adams was convicted and appealed to the Supreme Court. The only question presented, said the Court, was whether the letter found in the execution of the search warrant, which had a legal purpose in the attempt to find gambling paraphernalia, was competent against the accused. The Court found that it was and upheld the defendant's conviction.

If Kearns had asked the prosecution to produce the warrant, all presumptions would run in favor of Dollree Mapp. If the state of Ohio didn't come up with a search warrant, or explain its absence, we would have to presume there was no warrant *at all*. It would be as simple as that. But at no time did the defense contend at the trial, as they later will on appeal, that the piece of paper held up by Lt. White was anything else but a warrant to search for "persons" or "things" other than "lewd and lascivious books, pictures, and photographs." The existence of a warrant to search for Ogletree and policy paraphernalia was never challenged.

In the Office of the Clerk of the Court of Common Pleas, Cuyahoga County, Ohio, in the file entitled *State v. Mapp*, Docket No. 68326, there is no search warrant to be found. But this is not surprising. The warrant was issued—according to the police reports and the testimony—by an unnamed judge or magistrate on May 23, 1957, three months before Mapp's indictment on September 19. From the very beginning the warrant was a document extrinsic to that case.

It is the indictment which marks the commencement of a felony case. The Clerk of the Court, upon receiving an indictment, sets up a file in which it and all subsequent papers pertaining to that case will be kept. Each file has a tab bearing the name of the defendant and the number his case has been assigned on the court's docket. Thereafter, any document filed in the clerk's office by either side— Kearns's motion to suppress evidence is an example—must be captioned with the title of the case and the docket number. The staff of the clerk's office then will see to it that these papers are placed in the proper file. While under no obligation to do so, the prosecutor could have filed the warrant with the clerk's office. All Mrs. Mahon had to do was to caption it—*State v. Mapp*, No. 68326—and pass it over the counter at the clerk's office. But the warrant would never have made its way into the case file without that affirmative act.

For that matter, the lewd and lascivious books, pictures and photographs of which Dollree Mapp was convicted of possessing are not to be found in the case file either, yet they were included in the inventory. According to the testimony of Patrolman Michael Haney, all of the "books and pictures, and so forth" seized at the home of Mrs. Mapp "were marked for identification and turned over to the property room at Central Police Station." At the trial *The Affairs of a Troubadour, Little Darlings, London Stage Affairs,* and *Memories of a Hotel Man* became States Exhibits 1, 2, 3, 4 respectively and other miscellanea became Exhibits 5-13.[20]

The Cuyahoga County Prosecutor's Office, one notes, maintains its own case files keyed by name and docket number to the files of the Court of Common Pleas. The natural repository, therefore, for both the evidence and the warrant under which it was seized is the file belonging to the County Prosecutor's Office. Unfortunately, according to incumbent [1998] Cuyahoga County Prosecutor [now Congresswoman] Stephanie Tubbs Jones, no file designated *State v. Mapp*, No. 68326 is to be found. Also missing, she added, was the prosecutor's file for Mrs. Mahon's other famous case—the trial of Dr. Sam Shepard for the murder of his wife.

We have distinguished searches and seizures made without "probable cause" from those held unconstitutional simply because

---

[20] Transcript, 7-9.

they were made without a warrant. We need not concern ourselves with that issue here. For at no time at any stage in the development of the law of search and seizure in the English-speaking world has it ever been held in any forum that there is anything unconstitutional, illegal, or wrong about a search made by a policeman upon "probable cause" pursuant to a warrant issued by a magistrate. And such a case, we are entitled to presume, was *Mapp v. Ohio.*

Chapter XVI

SILVER BLAZE

ilver Blaze is a story by Sir Arthur Conan Doyle in which Sherlock Holmes solved the mystery of a missing racehorse who was the favorite in the coming race for the Wessex Cup. The horse, named Silver Blaze for his white forehead, had been kidnapped in the middle of the night and the stableboy on guard found in a drugged sleep. His supper of curried mutton had been laced with powdered opium. In the stable that night there was also a dog, a dog that did not bark. Holmes had this familiar colloquy with the owner of the missing horse:

> "Is there any point to which you would wish to draw my attention?" [asked the owner]
>
> "To the curious incident of the dog in the night time."
>
> "The dog did nothing in the night time."
>
> "That was the curious incident," remarked Sherlock Holmes.

The search warrant and the probable cause which prompted the search of Miss Mapp's house are the metaphorical equivalent of the white forehead of the horse; the hearts and minds of the Supreme Court are the Wessex Cup. But paint over the blaze, as did Holmes's antagonists, and you have a horse of a different color. As she left the trial court, *State v. Mapp* was a horse all would perceive to be Silver

Blaze: a reasonable search made on probable cause pursuant to a warrant.

It was a horse of a different color that emerged from the paddock on the banks of the Scioto River a year and a half later. The silver blaze had been painted over. It was a nag that was paraded before the Ohio Supreme Court in Columbus, and they were snookered into believing that the search was not only unreasonable and warrantless but, except for the lascivious material, fruitless as well. Cuyahoga County Prosecutor Gertrude Bauer Mahon was the dog that did not bark.

There is nothing in that court's opinion to indicate that the judges were cognizant of the fact that a bombing, a felony, had occurred or that the search of Miss Mapp's house was for a suspect. Quite the contrary, it is clear they knew nothing of this. They did not know of the existence of Ogletree, much less his apprehension by the police. A judge of the Ohio Supreme Court could only conclude, from the record before him, that the police had made, by means of a forced entry, an unwarranted search of Miss Mapp's home for policy slips, the possession of which is a misdemeanor, and found instead "lewd and lascivious" books, the possession of which is, under the Ohio statute, a felony.

> There is, in the record, considerable doubt as to whether there ever was any warrant for the search of defendant's home. No warrant was offered in evidence, there was no testimony as to who issued any warrant or as to what any warrant contained, and the absence from evidence of any such warrant is not explained or otherwise accounted for in the record. There is nothing in the record tending to prove or from which an inference may be drawn, and no one has even suggested that any warrant that we may assume that there may have been described anything other than policy paraphernalia as things to be searched for . . . Admittedly therefore there was no warrant authorizing a search of defendant's home for any "lewd, or lascivious book . . . print, [or] picture."[1]

---

[1] *State v. Mapp*, 170 Ohio St. 427, 166 N.E. 2d 387, 389 (1960).

What had happened in the meanwhile was that Kearns and Greene—Miss Mapp's lawyers—had been permitted to go far beyond the scope of the objection they had made in their motion to suppress evidence and been allowed to take free swipes at the Cleveland police. They had told the Ohio Eighth District Court of Appeals that there "were from 7 to 12 police officers involved, they came according to Patrolman Haney to find some man for questioning as to a bombing, which some unknown said might be at the address. No such man ever was there."[2]

They painted the same picture to the Supreme Court of Ohio. Since "the alleged 'warrant' was never presented in evidence or shown to exist," said Kearns and Greene, "the conclusion is that the paper was a ruse."

> There was no proof of any "person hiding out in her home who was wanted for questioning in connection with a . . . bombing"—that was a sham proposed to justify the inexcusable conduct of the officers in handcuffing her and going through the home of this mother and her young daughter . . .[3]

Mrs. Mahon never brought to the attention of either of the Ohio appellate courts the fact that the constitutional question framed at the trial by the defendant's motion to suppress evidence did not reach beyond that settled in *Adams v. New York*. The *Adams* case was never cited. The misrepresentations of facts were left unrefuted. All that Mrs. Mahon said is that however beastly the actions of the Cleveland police may have been, the items seized must be admitted as evidence because Ohio does not have the exclusionary rule.

As it turned out, *State v. Mapp* was not decided on the search and seizure issue. The Ohio Supreme Court, by a vote of four to three, found that the statute under which Miss Mapp had been convicted was constitutionally invalid because it placed an

---

[2] Transcript of Record, 72.

[3] In the Supreme Court of Ohio, *State v. Mapp*, No. 36,091. Brief of Defendant—Appellant in Reply and Opposing Motion to Dismiss, 2.

intolerable burden on the rights of free speech, press, and the dissemination of ideas protected as against the states by the Fourteenth Amendment. This is a view, one would certainly think, that would be endorsed by the highest appellate tribunals in the rest of the United States. It is hard to imagine a state supreme court which would uphold the constitutional validity of such a law.

Ohio, however, had a unique provision in its own constitution which said that "[n]o law shall be held unconstitutional and void by the supreme court without the concurrence of at least all but one of the judges . . . Since more than one of the judges of this court are of the opinion that no portion of the statute upon which defendant's conviction was based is unconstitutional and void," said the Ohio Supreme Court, "the judgment of the Court of Appeals must be affirmed."[4] This meant that despite the majority's opinion to the contrary, the defendant's conviction was upheld. Miss Mapp, therefore, because the state court upheld a state statute against a claim that it violated the United States Constitution, was enabled to appeal to the Supreme Court of the United States as a matter of right. Such a scenario could have happened only in Ohio.

On July 14, 1960, Kearns and Greene filed their jurisdictional statement in the United States Supreme Court. It was this that contained the official version of the "facts" recited at the beginning of the previous chapter. Here, as a general proposition, the appellant is required to show that the constitutional question he is now asking the Court to review was raised below in the trial court. This is the way Kearns and Greene fudged it: "The matter of the conduct of the police in procuring the evidence was first raised in the trial court in a 'Motion to Suppress' filed September 3, 1958."

Of course, the motion to suppress said nothing of the sort. The constitutional question Kearns and Greene had posed to the trial court was an *Adams* horse with a silver blaze. The constitutional question they are now asking the Supreme Court to review is a horse of a different color. Mrs. Mahon let it pass unchallenged, and then became stern.

---

[4] *State v. Mapp*, 391.

Several statements are made in the Jurisdictional
Statement of the Appellant that are not supported by the
record. There was no evidence that twelve police officers
surrounded and forced their way into the residence of
the Appellant. The testimony established that seven
police officers arrived on the scene, but other than the
Sergeant who testified at the trial, and his two men, the
other officers did not play any part in the search of the
Appellant's premises . . .

Nor was there any evidence that the Appellant was
handcuffed to the banister of the stairway while a search
of her private residence was made.

Who cares whether the number of police officers who
surrounded and forced their way into the residence of the appellant
was 12, 7, or 3? One would be too many. What difference does it
make whether Miss Mapp was handcuffed to the banister of the
stairway or to one of the officers, as she had already testified?

On October 24, 1960, the Supreme Court decided to hear the
case of *State v. Mapp* by noting "probable jurisdiction."[5] Kearns and
Greene filed their brief, essentially a rehash of the jurisdictional
statement, on February 1, 1961. While the brief posed a search and
seizure question, it was argued most perfunctorily. You cannot tell
whether their position is that there was no warrant at all or that the
search was made pursuant to a warrant in which "obscene materials"
were not specified. It is deliberately vague.

Mrs. Mahon responded with a growl. Her brief disputed anew
the assertion "that twelve police officers had surrounded the private
residence of the defendant, and forced their way into it. This is
predicated upon the unsupported testimony of one of the attorneys
for the defendant, Walter L. Greene, who 'estimated' that there
were that number."[6] Then she said what she should have said in her
response to the jurisdictional statement. That she did so at this point
must be regarded as a protective measure well known to all

---

[5]   364 U.S. 868.
[6]   "Supplemental Brief of Appellee on the Merits," 4.

bureaucrats by the acronym C.Y.A.

> There was no request by the defense during the trial for the production of the search warrant or that it be tendered, and their statement to that effect at page 5 of their brief on the merits is unsupported by the record. The police officers who made the search and who were the witnesses in this case, testified that they did not obtain the search warrant. Their testimony shows that they awaited the arrival of Lt. White with a search warrant and upon his arrival, the appellant resisted execution of the warrant (R. 16, 18). No question was raised on the trial that no search warrant had been obtained and Lt. White was as available to the defense on subpoena as to the State. It was not incumbent upon the State to offer a search warrant into the evidence as an element of the offense to be proven on this trial. The only issue raised on the motion to suppress the evidence was that a proper search warrant was not secured setting forth the confiscated evidence on which the appellant was charged by indictment (R. 2). And it is admitted that such a search warrant was not secured.[7]

There was a third brief filed in *Mapp v. Ohio*:

> This brief is submitted on the merits of the Appeal. Both Appellant and Appellee have consented to the filing of this brief *amici curiae* by the American Civil Liberties Union and the Ohio Civil Liberties Union.[8]

Nothing in this brief is in any way relevant to the law of search and seizure or the exclusionary rule, except this single paragraph:[9]

> D. USE OF EVIDENCE OBTAINED IN AN IL-
> LEGAL SEARCH AND SEIZURE VIOLATES THE
> DUE PROCESS CLAUSE OF THE FOURTEENTH
> AMENDMENT.

---

[7] Ibid., 3.
[8] "Brief Amici Curiae on Behalf of American Civil Liberties Union and Ohio Civil Liberties Union."
[9] Ibid., 20.

> This case presents the issue of whether evidence obtained in an illegal search and seizure can constitutionally be used in a State criminal proceeding. We are aware of the view that this Court has taken on this issue in *Wolf v. Colorado*, 338 U.S. 25. It is our purpose by this paragraph to respectfully request that this Court re-examine this issue and conclude that the ordered liberty concept guaranteed to persons by the due process clause of the Fourteenth Amendment necessarily requires that evidence illegally obtained in violation thereof, not be admissible in state criminal proceedings.

This paragraph is worth reading twice. Note how artfully it is crafted. The ACLU and the Ohio CLU did not elaborate on what "view" it was that the Court had taken "on this issue in *Wolf v. Colorado*"; they say only that they are "aware" of it. It does not say *why* the Court should "conclude that the ordered liberty concept guaranteed to persons by the due process clause of the Fourteenth Amendment *necessarily requires* that evidence illegally obtained in violation thereof, not be admissible in state criminal proceedings." Most importantly it does not even assert, much less advocate, that the Fourth Amendment applies to the states through the Fourteenth. Nothing in the brief would give one an inkling that the case had any bearing on the incorporation issue.

You must keep in mind that all of this is taking place in a sea of ink about obscenity. "The substantial federal question that prompted the Supreme Court to hear the appeal was whether the Ohio statute was vague and overbroad in violation of the first and fourteenth amendment's free press guarantee; the overwhelming portion of the briefs and virtually all of the oral argument were devoted to this issue," recalled Potter Stewart.[10]

To the outside world, *Mapp v. Ohio* appeared to be a case involving the constitutionality of the Ohio statute,[11] a question which hardly

---

[10] *Road to Mapp v. Ohio and Beyond*, 1367.

[11] The *Cleveland Press* on March 24, 1960, the day after the Ohio Supreme Court decided *State v. Mapp*, had a short article on page 59 entitled "Court Upholds Woman's Guilt in Smut Case." Nothing was found in the *Plain Dealer*.

could be called a legal toughie. You would find few judges or other people who would disagree with the proposition that the "mere private possession of such literature by an adult should [not] constitute a crime. The right of the individual to read, to believe or disbelieve, and to think without governmental supervision is one of our basic liberties."[12] A judge would not have to ponder many an ancient volume of forgotten lore to weigh the equities here and make his call. There are no rights of others to weigh in the balance. Nor would he have to look back to Magna Carta for the answer. *Smith v. California*, 361 U.S. 147, decided unanimously by the Supreme Court of the United States just 16 months before, is dispositive of the question.

Mapp v. Ohio was but a deception wrapped inside a deception; one ringer inside of a larger ringer, so to speak. The scam would not work unless insulated from intruders. To pull it off certain precautionary measures had to be taken. The most likely whistle blowers were those Cleveland police officers who had personal knowledge of the events of May 23, 1957. It would not do for them to learn Silver Blaze had been abducted, so they were served a curried *Adams* scenario to throw them off the scent.

In a nine-paragraph article, which, as we will see, was manipulated by the Ohio Civil Liberties Union, it is stated no less than three times that the search of Mrs. Mapp's house *was* made pursuant to a warrant—a warrant that did not specify obscene materials—as opposed to a search made with no warrant at all.

**Extract from *Cleveland Press News*, March 27, 1961
"Obscenity Conviction Goes to Highest Court"**

Bernard Berkman, chairman of the legal committee of the Civil Liberties Union here, said he will argue before the high court *that the search warrant did not include obscene materials* . . .

In their search for a suspect, police went to Dollree Mapp's home. Refused entry, *they obtained a search*

---

[12] This quotation is from Judge Herbert's opinion in *State v. Mapp*, 393.

warrant for gambling gear.

In the basement detectives found a trunk full of policy slips and other betting materials. In Dollree's room they found four lewd books and obscene pictures.

Berkman said that the basis for his charges of violating the constitution is that the search warrant did not mention obscene material.[13]

Now did this story just happen, or did it just happen to be planted? The answer to this horticultural question is to be found in Princeton, New Jersey. There, in the Seeley G. Mudd Manuscript Library, are kept the archives of the ACLU and its affiliates. In a file entitled "Ohio—1961" appears correspondence between Mrs. Vivian Donaldson, the executive secretary of the Ohio CLU in Cleveland, and Leanne Golden of the ACLU's New York City office.

One item consists of a copy of the foregoing article with a note typed underneath in which "Vivian" tells "Leanne" that the "story was released to the Cleveland-Press News for today (3/27/61)." It also says: "The above story is not quite correct in parts." Underneath is a handwritten note: "P.S. Our man at the Press did not make up a release in written form."

On March 29 Vivian again writes Leanne, who she assumes by now has gotten the *Press* story. She tells her that there was "no official written release. Hence no copies available. We have a man at the press who took the facts and wrote the story without much ado." When *Mapp v. Ohio* was argued two days later, it was an entirely different story, with much ado about the apparent lack of a warrant. We have already seen Kearns's statements that:

"We asked during the trial of the case that the search warrant be produced and it was not."

"But the prosecutor promised—and we have the prosecutor here—that the search warrant would be produced, and it never was."

---

[13] ACLUP, "Ohio—1961" [emphasis added].

Moving along we see:

> THE COURT: Did you raise the question of no search warrant in the trial court?

> MR. KEARNS: I did. I even filed a motion to suppress the evidence in the trial court, which motion was overruled.

Bernard Berkman of the ACLU opened by saying that he was "asking this Court to reconsider *Wolf* versus *Colorado* and to find that evidence which is unlawfully and illegally obtained should not be permitted into a state proceeding." As in the brief, this came in the form of a request rather than by way of argument. The *amicus curiae* advanced no reasons why this should be so nor did he say how he arrived at the conclusion that any evidence against Dollree Mapp was "unlawfully" or "illegally" obtained. Aside from these opening remarks, his argument was directed toward the obvious unconstitutionality of the Ohio obscenity law.

Mrs. Mahon took much the same course. There was a lively discussion about whether college librarians or "the head of a university" might fall under the proscription of the Ohio obscenity statute. One Justice observed that he had a rare book:

> THE COURT: ... And any book on his shelves, on my shelves, which I know to be obscene in content, but a matter of great indifference to me because I'm interested in the fact that it was published in 1527—that makes me a violator of this statute? Is that correct?

> MRS. MAHON: I would say so, Your Honor; any collector of obscenity would be—

> [General laughter]

> THE COURT: Does the question of purpose—

> MRS. MAHON: —would be violating this statute.

> THE COURT: Well, Uncle Sam has one of the biggest collections, and I can tell you now where it is, but it's

345

outside of your jurisdiction.

[General laughter]

Perhaps this delightful banter distracted Mrs. Mahon. With respect to the search and seizure question her duty was clear. She was under an obligation to make absolutely certain the Court understood that:

a) A bombing suspect and a trunk full of policy slips were found in Miss Mapp's house.

b) The statements of the defense attorneys in this regard were false and misleading.

c) The motion to suppress evidence made in the trial court did not place at issue the question of whether or not there existed a lawful warrant to search for Virgil Ogletree or policy paraphernalia.

d) Opposing counsel is therefore limited to arguing the question of whether or not evidence incidentally found during an otherwise lawful search for someone or something else may be seized and used in evidence, and that *Adams v. New York* is authority that it may.

Mrs. Mahon had to have realized that it would not suffice to say that the alleged misconduct of the police does not matter because Ohio does not use the exclusionary rule; the very point the ACLU was trying to make was that the exclusionary rule must be applied to the states to deter just such police misconduct. She should have affirmatively stated that evidence incidentally found during an otherwise warranted and lawful search is admissible everywhere, including those jurisdictions which do employ the rule.

Mrs. Mahon did none of these things. Instead she further beclouded the issue by drawing no distinction whatever between

346

Silver Blaze and the horse of a different color. To her undiscerning eyes, both were equally unlawful and equally irrelevant.

> The record doesn't show, and we have admitted, and as the supreme court held, this was an unlawful search insofar as this particular evidence was concerned, at least. There was no search warrant to cover it . . .

> And so, in the Ohio Constitution and under the Ohio laws, the fact that there was a search warrant would not make the evidence any the more competent or the fact that there was no search warrant would not make it any the less competent . . .

> And we respectfully submit that there has been no violation of any constitutional right of the defendant in this case on the trial, by reason of there having been no proper search warrant.

Near the end of her allotted time she was asked a direct question:

> **THE COURT:** Is the search warrant in existence?

> **MRS. MAHON:** Insofar as the record is concerned, it doesn't show any.

The "record" she is referring to is the "record on appeal." But each member of the Court has a copy of that record before him, and already knows without having to ask Mrs. Mahon that "it doesn't show any" warrant. This led to a follow-up question which the lady cut off in midsentence with a rambling, obfuscating answer:

> **THE COURT:** Is there any record of it in the records as to whether—

> **MRS. MAHON:** There's no record that there was a search warrant. The two officers who testified, who were the only ones, Mr. Chief Justice, you find in the record who made this particular search and found this evidence—they talk about twelve police officers being there and surrounding the place and making the search.

But the only officers who turned up with this evidence were Sergeant Delau and the patrolman who testified in this case. They had nothing to do with obtaining a search warrant. When the defendant requested, told them to get one, the officers said they waited and that Lieutenant White came out there. They thought he had a search warrant. Now, that's what the record shows.

MR. CHIEF JUSTICE WARREN: All right, thank you.

So ended the oral "argument" on behalf of Ohio. It was obvious that this line of questioning inevitably would have led to Mrs. Mahon being faced with a direct question as to whether or not there was *any* record at *any* place of *any* warrant being issued by *any* judicial authority to search the premises on Milverton Avenue for *anyone* or *anything*. Mrs. Mahon did not want to be confronted with that question. When she was saved by the bell she had at least 41 seconds of her allotted time remaining[14] in which to tell the Court whether or not there was a warrant to search Miss Mapp's house for a suspected bomber or policy paraphernalia and that, contrary to the statements of opposing counsel, both had been found at 14705 Milverton Avenue on the afternoon of Thursday, May 23, 1957.

Mrs. Mahon had to tread a fine line. If it came to light that there was a warrant to search for Ogletree or policy paraphernalia, some well-laid plans would have gone awry. Justice Clark, for example, proceeded on the assumption that there was no warrant *at all* or he would not have written "the officers, having secured their own entry, and continuing in their defiance of the law."[15]

It was within the bounds of plausible denial to let pass the misrepresentations of her adversaries. If called to account, Mrs. Mahon could always dismiss them as irrelevant. The evidence was admissible, warrant or no, she would have explained, because the exclusionary rule did not apply to the states. Such a posture also created the proper illusion. The natural inference one would draw

---

[14] The Supreme Court Archives have audio tapes of the oral argument for those who wish to time it.
[15] *Mapp*, 644.

from such evasiveness is that there was no warrant *at all* and that Mrs. Mahon was covering it up.

But if she was brought to bay on whether there was *any* warrant to search for *anyone* or *anything*, Mrs. Mahon would have had to admit of its existence. After all, she would not have been the only one to know about it. The police officer who obtained the warrant as well as the magistrate who issued it would have known of its existence for a certainty. Those in Cleveland and environs, therefore, were led to believe that there was a warrant—one that did not specify "obscene materials"—while the rest of the country was led to believe that *Mapp v. Ohio* was a case about freedom of speech.

Mapp v. Ohio was argued on Wednesday, March 29, 1961. The following Monday, April 3, Alan Reitman, an associate director of the ACLU in New York, wrote the Ohio CLU about the difficulties encountered in their joint press release. One suspects he is miffed over the fact the Cleveland article alluded to a search and seizure issue at all. "I think I have a good idea of the problems you face," says Reitman to Mrs. Donaldson,[16] "but I would like to suggest the following publicity procedure on joint briefs in the future." To show how the job should have been done, he enclosed an article clipped from the *New York Times* of the day before:

HIGH COURT HEARS OBSCENITY CASE
Weighs Validity of Ohio Law Making It a Crime to Own Salacious Literature

By ANTHONY LEWIS

Special to *The New York Times*

WASHINGTON, April 1—May a state make it a crime for a citizen to have obscene literature in his own home, with no intention of selling or showing it to anyone?

---

[16] He also said, "I gather that you are getting some help from a reporter on the Cleveland *Press-News* in the preparation of news releases."

Anthony Lewis is still that newspaper's in-house legal expert known for his penetrating analysis and his ability to see things in a certain way. He has never been known to be out of step with the ACLU. Nothing in this article of 23 paragraphs would give the reader the slightest hint that *Mapp v. Ohio* involved a search and seizure question.

To those interested in constitutional cases bearing on law enforcement—to an organization like the National District Attorneys' Association, for example—*Mapp v. Ohio* looked like a real yawner. They would have no reason to suspect that a case involving the prosecution of a citizen for having obscene literature in her own home, with no intention of selling it or showing it to anyone, would become, along with *Weeks v. United States*, one of the two most important cases in our Fourth Amendment jurisprudence. Twenty-two years later Potter Stewart still didn't have an inkling of what really happened.

> In fact, until the circulation of the first draft of the majority opinion, the issue that the Court ultimately was to decide had been mentioned only by an amicus curiae, the ACLU. Its twenty-page brief included only a three-sentence paragraph at the very end asking the Court to overrule its 1949 decision in *Wolf v. Colorado*, which had held that the state courts were not required to exclude evidence seized in violation of the fourth and fourteenth amendments. That the ACLU's argument was not regarded by the parties as even a remotely important issue in the case was made clear at the oral argument. The appellant's lawyer was asked whether he was requesting the Court to overrule the *Wolf* case and, thus, to exclude the fruits of an illegal search at a state trial. He answered, quite candidly, that he had never heard of the *Wolf* case.[17]

On June 19, 1961, the Court handed down its decision. The constitutionality of the obscenity statute, the basis on which the case was briefed and argued, was airily dismissed in a footnote.

---

[17] *The Road to Mapp v. Ohio*, 1367.

Other issues have been raised on this appeal but, in the view we have taken of the case, they need not be decided. Although appellant chose to urge what may have appeared to be the surer ground for favorable disposition and did not insist that *Wolf* be overruled, the *amicus curiae*, who was also permitted to participate in the oral argument, did urge the Court to overrule *Wolf*.[18]

In a rhetorical *tour de force*, a plurality of four members of the Supreme Court of the United States—Clark, Warren, Douglas, and Brennan—abrogated an elementary tenet of constitutional law going back to the earliest days of the Republic that the first eight amendments to the Constitution apply only to the federal government and are not limitations on the powers of the several states. This fundamental question was never addressed—even peripherally—in the briefs or in oral argument.

Wolf explicitly held that the "notion that the 'due process of law' guaranteed by the Fourteenth Amendment is shorthand for the first eight amendments of the Constitution and thereby incorporates them has been rejected by this Court again and again, after impressive consideration . . . The issue is closed."[19] In the face of this holding, the *Mapp* plurality reached the astonishing conclusion "that the Court held in *Wolf* that the [Fourth] Amendment was applicable to the States through the Due Process Clause."[20] That being the case:

> Since the Fourth Amendment's right of privacy has been declared enforceable against the States through the Due Process Clause of the Fourteenth, it is enforceable against them by the same sanction of exclusion as is used against the Federal Government. Were it otherwise, then just as without the *Weeks* rule the assurance against unreasonable federal searches and seizures would be "a form of words," valueless and undeserving of mention . . . so too, without that rule the freedom from state in-

---

[18] *Mapp*, 646.

[19] *Wolf v. Colorado*, 26.

[20] *Mapp*, 655.

vasions of privacy would be so ephemeral . . . [21]

While the decision did not get the headlines accorded the bomb blast which began this chain of events, *Mapp v. Ohio* nevertheless got good coverage in the Cleveland newspapers. An editorial in the *Cleveland Press* of June 21, 1961, saw it for exactly what it was: "A Landmark Decision." "No one would have dreamed it, but a filthy book and picture case originating in Cleveland in 1957 has just resulted in a decision by the U.S. Supreme Court that will influence law enforcement all over the country." An article the previous day had elicited the fact that a certain sergeant in the vice squad had no idea that he and the Cleveland P.D. had been taken in a shell game. "The man who arrested Miss Mapp in 1957, Sgt. Carl Delau, said the decision was devastating."

> "If we have a search warrant for clearing-house material and find a counterfeiting operation, are we to disregard it?"

> Delau had a search warrant for clearing-house material when he raided Miss Mapp's home, 14705 Milverton Rd. In addition to evidence of policy operations, he found obscene pictures and printed material that Miss Mapp said she was merely holding for a roomer.[22]

Others saw it differently. "Bernard A. Berkman, who represented the American and Ohio Civil Liberties Unions in arguments before the Supreme Court," told the same reporter that "it appears to be a historical landmark of tremendous importance to the entire nation. The decision in the Mapp case now prevents evidence obtained by official lawlessness from being used in a state court and we hope this ruling will deter official efforts in the future from obtaining evidence by unconstitutional methods."

The National District Attorneys' Association filed a petition for a rehearing. It was denied October 9, 1961 (368 U.S. 871). Too

---

[21] *Mapp*, 655.

[22] "Hail Search Decision As Blow For Liberty," *Cleveland Press*, June 20, 1961.

late, one would guess. If they had wanted to appear *amicus curiae* they should have come forward earlier. But then maybe they thought it was a case involving free thought and free expression. Come to think of it, everyone else did too, except, of course, the people who set up *Mapp v. Ohio* in the first place.

It is in retrospect that one can see most clearly the planning that went into this coup. It began in 1949 when the Court handed down its decision in *Wolf v. Colorado* over dissenting opinions which had a critical bearing on how we got to *Mapp and Beyond*. Three Justices—Douglas, Murphy, and Rutledge—thought that evidence used at Wolf's trial was unlawfully seized and should have been excluded. When the Court met again in October, Frank Murphy and Wiley Rutledge were dead, and, so it seemed, was the campaign to apply the exclusionary rule to the states.

By 1959, thanks to the appointments made by President Eisenhower, the Court was divided along the same lines with the same numbers as it had been 10 years earlier. Chief Justice Earl Warren and Associate Justices William O. Douglas and William J. Brennan Jr. were a cabal of three bent upon applying the Fourth Amendment and the *Weeks* rule to the states, the former being the *sine qua non* of the latter. Wavering in the wings was Justice Tom Clark, who had stated in *Irvine* that "had I been here in 1949 when *Wolf* was decided, I would have applied the doctrine of *Weeks v. United States*, 232 U.S. 383 (1914), to the states." Clark predicted that the "extinction" of *Wolf* might come about "when five Justices are sufficiently revolted by local police action."[23]

Justice Hugo Black was *sui generis*. Against all evidence, he maintained as a historical fact that the Framers of the Fourteenth Amendment intended it to incorporate the first eight amendments and to thereby make them applicable to the states. But he saw in the Fourth Amendment no exclusionary rule. "[T]he federal exclusionary rule is not a command of the Fourth Amendment but is a judicially created rule of evidence which Congress might negate," he wrote in *Wolf*. And so Hugo Black voted to uphold the conviction of Dr.

---

[23] *Irvine*, 138.

Wolf. Any "manipulated test case" had to take into account Justice Black's singular views.

Frank v. Maryland was a Fourth Amendment case in which no search or seizure ever took place. That way the exclusionary rule never came into play. In *Frank* there was a health inspector who had probable cause to search a house for rat infestation. In the middle of the day he knocked on the door asking to inspect the premises. Permission was refused. The owner was then cited, tried, and fined $20 under a municipal ordinance for unreasonably refusing admittance to a health inspector.

This enabled Frank to appeal on the grounds that the ordinance was unconstitutional. His argument would be that the Fourth Amendment applies to the states and that it obliges a state, if it wishes to enter a house over the owner's objection, to obtain a warrant beforehand. The ordinance is unconstitutional, it can be argued, because it imposes a penalty for exercising a constitutional right. *Frank v. Maryland* was a scenario set up to compensate for Hugo Black's myopia by presenting only the incorporation issue. To that extent, it succeeded. The problem with *Frank* was that it didn't "revolt" Tom Clark so that the cabal came up one vote short.

Ohio ex. rel. Eaton v. Price was a back-up health-inspection case, especially crafted to deal with a certain contingency. "Brother Stewart, who was with the majority in *Frank* recused himself because the case came from Ohio's Supreme Court, where his father then served." This statement was made June 8, 1959, but the case was not decided until more than a year later. With Potter Stewart sitting on the sidelines, the Court split four-four.[24] Had the fading Felix Frankfurter died in the year that intervened or become incapacitated as he will in 1962, the cabal would have gotten the precedent they so coveted by a vote of four to three.

Frank v. Maryland and *Ohio ex rel Eaton v. Price* were not genuine "cases" or "controversies," but mere vehicles used to transport a specific issue to the Supreme Court. Neither the Maryland nor the

---

[24] *Ohio ex rel Eaton. v. Price*, 364 U.S. 263 (1960)

Ohio case could have been set up without the ACLU's co-optation of the local authorities. The sole purpose of these two shams was to obtain surreptitiously, in a petty case, a precedent which later could be used in cases involving serious crime.

While Justice Black had not deviated from the opinion he expressed in *Wolf* that "the federal exclusionary rule is not a command of the Fourth Amendment," he had modified his position in a way that would prove significant. In *Rochin* in 1954 and again in *Irvine* in 1956, he filed separate opinions which indicated he felt that the use of evidence taken in a search or seizure forbidden by the Fourth Amendment violated the Fifth Amendment's commandment that "no person . . . shall be compelled in any criminal case to be a witness against himself."

But this raised yet another obstacle. Not only could Hugo Lafayette Black not find the exclusionary rule in the Fourth Amendment; he couldn't find the warrant requirement either. In 1947, in *Harris v. United States*, a case with which we are familiar, he had joined in the majority's opinion that:

> This Court has also pointed out that it is only unreasonable searches and seizures which come within the constitutional interdict. The test of reasonableness cannot be stated in rigid and absolute terms. "Each case is to be decided on its own facts and circumstances."
>
> The Fourth Amendment has never been held to require that every valid search and seizure be effected under the authority of a search warrant.[25]

A year later Black dissented in *Johnson v. United States*, the case which resurrected the warrant requirement created by *Agnello* which *Harris* had vitiated. Justice Black read the Fourth Amendment to interdict only *unreasonable* searches and seizures. And in the mind of Hugo Black, a search or seizure, otherwise reasonable, was not unconstitutional simply because a warrant was not obtained beforehand.

---

[25] *Harris*, 150 [citation omitted].

To succeed, therefore, a scenario had to present a search and seizure—a *fruitful* search and seizure—unreasonable enough under the totality of the circumstances so that Hugo Black would deem it unconstitutional and egregious enough to touch just the right spot in the viscera of Tom Clark. It was the same problem faced by those who gave us the exclusionary rule in the first place and it was solved the same way.

In *Weeks v. United States* Leslie Lyons and Winfred Denison saw to it that the probable cause which prompted the search never came to light. From the record before it the Court could only conclude that the Kansas City police just showed up at 1834 Penn Street one day looking for lottery tickets. The Justices had no idea of the arrest of Olla Weeks for shoplifting or the seizure of the women's apparel including twelve pairs of silk hose in her chiffonier. Shorn of probable cause, the actions of the police officers appear to be not only unreasonable but an outrageous violation of home and person.

In *Mapp v. Ohio* Gertrude Bauer Mahon saw to it that the probable cause which prompted the search never came to light. From the record before it the Court could only conclude that the Cleveland police just showed up at 14705 Milverton Avenue one day ostensibly looking for a supposed bomber. The Justices had no idea of the policy-related bombing of Don King's house or that it was a suspected bomber who was found in the first floor apartment along with a trunk full of policy paraphernalia. Shorn of probable cause, the actions of the police officers appear to be not only unreasonable but an outrageous violation of home and person. It worked perfectly.

The previous June, in *Elkins v. United States*, decided less than one year before, Justice Clark had joined in Frankfurter's opinion that *Wolf v. Colorado* did *not* make the Fourth Amendment applicable to the states. In *Mapp v. Ohio,* Tom Campbell Clark, made an abrupt 180-degree turn and "found" that it did after all. It was not Frankfurter's words in *Wolf v. Colorado* that had changed, but Clark's appreciation of them. Hugo Black helped him with this problem of semantics.

Only four days before the *Mapp* decision came down,

Black wrote to Clark saying, "I am disturbed by the sentence . . . in your opinion that 'Since the Fourth Amendment's *right of privacy* has been declared enforceable against the States through the Due Process Clause of the Fourteenth, it is enforceable against them by the same sanction of exclusion as is used against the Federal Government.' [Emphasis supplied] [*sic*]. This, I think, makes it necessary for me to say that my agreement to your opinion depends upon my understanding that you read *Wolf* as having held, and that we are holding here, that the Fourth Amendment *as a whole* is applicable to the States and not some imaginary and unknown fragment designated as the 'right of privacy.'"

Black said that his concurrence in Clark's opinion was based upon this understanding. "If I am wrong in this and your opinion means that the Fourth Amendment does not apply to the States *as a whole*, I am unwilling to agree to decide this crucial question in this case . . . In other words, I am agreeing to decide this question in this case and agreeing to yours as the opinion for the Court on the basis of my understanding that the holding and opinion mean that hereafter the Fourth Amendment, when applied either to the state or federal governments, is to be given equal scope and coverage in both instances. If this is not correct, I think the case should be set down for reargument as the dissenters suggest."[26]

Reargument, as it turned out, was unnecessary. Mr. Justice Clark was revolted sufficiently to write an opinion which, after excoriating the actions of the Cleveland police, applied the *Weeks* rule to the states. "We hold that all evidence obtained by searches and seizures in violation of the Constitution is, by that same authority, inadmissible in a state court."[27]

Having once recognized [in *Wolf v. Colorado*] that the

---

[26] Bernard Schwartz. *Super Chief, Earl Warren and His Supreme Court—A Judicial Biography.* New York: New York University Press, 1983, 397-398, citing Tom C. Clark Papers, Tarlton Law Library, University of Texas, Austin, Texas.

[27] *Mapp*, 655.

right to privacy embodied in the Fourth Amendment is enforceable against the States, and that the right to be secure against rude invasions of privacy by state officers is, therefore, constitutional in origin, we can no longer permit that right to remain an empty promise. Because it is enforceable in the same manner and to like effect as other basic rights secured by the Due Process Clause, we can no longer permit it to be revocable at the whim of any police officer who, in the name of law enforcement itself, chooses to suspend its enjoyment.[28]

In *Mapp v. Ohio*, Warren, Douglas and Brennan concurred in Clark's opinion. Black responded as predicted to supply the swing vote. The "Fourth Amendment, standing alone," he said, is not "enough to bar the introduction into evidence against an accused of papers and effects seized from him in violation of its commands." The "Fourth Amendment does not itself contain any provision expressly precluding the use of such evidence," and Justice Black did not see how any such rule "could properly be inferred."[29]

Reflection on the problem, however, in the light of cases coming before the Court since *Wolf*, has led me to conclude that when the Fourth Amendment's ban against unreasonable searches and seizures is considered together with the Fifth Amendment's ban against compelled self-incrimination, a constitutional basis emerges which not only justifies but actually requires the exclusionary rule.[30]

And so emerged a majority to apply the Fourth Amendment and the *Weeks* rule to the states. The remaining four Justices— Harlan, Frankfurter, Whittaker, and Stewart—voted to reverse Miss Mapp's conviction on the grounds that a statute "making criminal the *mere* knowing possession or control of obscene material . . . is [not] consistent with the rights of free thought and ex-

---

[28] *Mapp*, 660.
[29] *Mapp*, 661, 662.
[30] *Mapp*, 662.

pression assured against state action by the Fourteenth Amendment. That was the principal issue . . . which was briefed and argued in this Court."[31] Instead, "five members of this Court have simply 'reached out' to overrule *Wolf*,"[32] wrote Justice Harlan, "in the context of a case where the question was briefed not at all and argued only extremely tangentially."[33] "In any event, at the very least, the present case should have been set down for reargument, in view of the inadequate briefing and argument we have received on the *Wolf* point. To all intents and purposes the Court's present action amounts to a summary reversal of *Wolf*, without argument."[34]

The majority, according to Harlan, misapprehended the role of the Supreme Court in reviewing criminal convictions obtained in state courts. "Here we review state procedures whose measure is to be taken not against the specific substantive commands of the Fourth Amendment but under the flexible contours of the Due Process Clause." The fundamental fairness of the trial is the only question to be considered.

> [O]ur task, far from being one of over-all supervision, is, speaking generally, restricted to a determination of whether the prosecution was Constitutionally fair. The specifics of trial procedure, which in every mature legal system will vary greatly in detail, are within the sole competence of the States. I do not see how it can be said that a trial becomes unfair simply because a State determines that evidence may be considered by the trier of fact, regardless of how it was obtained, if it is relevant to the one issue with which the trial is concerned, the guilt or innocence of the accused.[35]

The framers of *Mapp* saw to it that the facade they presented to the Court would not be penetrated by any probing adversary. The entry of an opposing *amicus curiae*—like the National District

---

[31] *Mapp*, 673.
[32] *Mapp*, 674.
[33] *Mapp*, 676.
[34] *Mapp*, 677.
[35] *Mapp*, 682, 683.

Attorneys' Association—would have blown their cover. The ACLU finessed this problem by making it look like a case involving freedom of speech and expression. Trying Miss Mapp on a statute that was patently unconstitutional also insured that the Justices who opposed the application of the *Weeks* rule to the states would vote to reverse her conviction as well.

Naturally the Fourth Amendment had to make an appearance. The most important search and seizure decision in our history could not very well be justified if the issue was never mentioned. And so it was, but just barely. One paragraph in the ACLU brief and two in its oral argument, both couched in precatory terms, were just right: enough so that no one could say the issue was never raised but not enough to alert the opposition. They never could have permitted the search and seizure question to be briefed or argued any more than "extremely tangentially."

For had the true facts emerged, Hugo Black surely would have found the search and seizure was not *unreasonable* and voted as he had before and would do again. Shortly before his retirement and death in 1971 he wrote:

> The majority rejects the test of reasonableness provided in the Fourth Amendment and substitutes a *per se* rule— if the police could have obtained a warrant and did not, the seizure, no matter how reasonable, is void. But the Fourth Amendment does not require that every search be made pursuant to a warrant. It prohibits only "unreasonable searches and seizures." The relevant test is not the reasonableness of the opportunity to procure a warrant, but the reasonableness of the seizure under all the circumstances. The test of reasonableness cannot be fixed by *per se* rules; each case must be decided on its own facts.

> For all the reasons stated above, I believe the seizure and search of petitioner's car was reasonable and, therefore, authorized by the Fourth Amendment. The evidence so obtained violated neither the Fifth Amendment which does contain an exclusionary rule, nor the Fourth Amendment which does not. The jury of petitioner's peers, as conscious as we of the awesome gravity of their decision, heard that evidence and found the petitioner

guilty of murder. I cannot in good conscience upset that verdict. *Coolidge v. New Hampshire*, 403 U.S. 443, 509-10.

The vehicle called *Mapp* came with an additional option—it was a "convertible." Had the attempt to cozen Tom Clark and Hugo Black failed, it would have turned into a case involving freedom of expression. The cabal simply would have ignored the search and seizure issue and voted along with the rest of the Justices to sustain the Ohio Supreme Court's opinion that the "right of the individual to read, to believe or disbelieve and to think without government supervision is one of our basic liberties." *Mapp v. Ohio*, to the extent it would be remembered at all, would be remembered as a case which "clarified" *Smith v. California*. It was a no-lose situation.

There was one Justice sitting on the bench that day who was uncharacteristically silent. Certainly the occasion must have evoked a flood of memories. The previous October had marked the 50th anniversary of the dynamiting of the *Los Angeles Times*. And now the chain of causality that began with that awful event had come full circle. The chief beneficiary of a case tailored by blithe young progressive spirits for political radicals of a bygone era henceforth will be the common criminal. Rules fashioned in the cases of lottery ticket sellers, grain door board grifters, and bootleggers now will be used to loose robbers, rapists, and murderers to prey upon an unsuspecting society. Mr. Justice Frankfurter must have snorted over Tom Clark's restatement of the history of the exclusionary rule:

> Thus, in the year 1914, in the *Weeks* case, this Court "for the first time" held that "in a federal prosecution the Fourth Amendment barred the use of evidence secured through an illegal search and seizure." *Wolf v. Colorado, supra,* at 28. This Court has ever since required of federal law officers a strict adherence to that command which this Court has held to be a clear, specific, and constitutionally required—even if judicially implied— deterrent safeguard without insistence upon which the Fourth Amendment would have been reduced to "a form of words." Holmes, J., *Silverthorne Lumber Co. v. United States*, 251 U.S. 385, 392 (1920). It meant, quite

simply, that "conviction by means of unlawful seizures . . . should find no sanction in the judgments of the courts . . .," *Weeks v. United States, supra,* at 392, and that such evidence "shall not be used at all." *Silverthorne Lumber Co. v. United States, supra,* at 392.[36]

If they wanted to talk about *Weeks* and *Silverthorne,* Felix Frankfurter could have given his brethren a lecture that would have made their hair stand on end. The House of Truth, so near and yet so far, surely was etched in his memory. They were all gone now— Valentine, Denison, Christie and Percy—he was the only one left and he would not be left for long. FF would have remembered the hot summer of 1913 when he and Denison were so happy and the Thanksgiving Win departed for the Philippines in high spirits, leaving *Weeks v. United States* waiting at the altar of the Supreme Court. What had they wrought?

---

[36] *Mapp,* 648.

Chapter XVII

THE ROAD BEYOND *MAPP v. OHIO*

M*app v. Ohio* held that evidence taken in an unreasonable search and seizure is inadmissible in a state criminal trial. Actually it did a lot more than that. Under the doctrine established in the 1948 case of *Johnson v. United States*, it was not sufficient that a search or seizure simply be reasonable under the facts and circumstances of the case. Federal agents, absent exceptional circumstances, had to present their evidence to a magistrate beforehand and obtain a warrant. If they did not, no matter how minimal the intrusion, or probable the cause, any evidence thereby secured would be inadmissible in a federal criminal trial.

Johnson v. United States created a false standard. The Fourth Amendment does not require that searches or seizures be made pursuant to a warrant; it requires only that they not be *unreasonable*. And what is reasonable and what is not, in law as in life, can be judged only by the totality of the facts and circumstances with which one is confronted. *Harris v. United States*, decided the year before *Johnson*, made this clear.

> This Court has also pointed out that it is only unreasonable searches and seizures which come within the constitutional interdict. The test of reasonableness cannot be stated in rigid and absolute terms. "Each case is to be decided on its own facts and circumstances."
>
> The Fourth Amendment has never been held to require

that every valid search and seizure be effected under the
authority of a search warrant.[1]

Then, as now, all states had laws identical or similar to the
Fourth Amendment.[2] In all jurisdictions an unreasonable search
was tortious and the offending officer liable in a civil suit against
him by the aggrieved party. Under certain circumstances it could be
a violation of the criminal law as well. Under state law, therefore,
searches and seizures unreasonable in the true sense of that word
were deterred by the same sanctions used by the law to deter any
other type of tortious or criminal behavior. The perpetrators were
subject to civil liability and criminal punishment.

Where the facts giving rise to probable cause were within his
knowledge, a state police officer generally acted on his own. It was
where he had to rely on information provided by others that he
obtained a warrant. In such cases he marshalled his evidence and took
affidavits from witnesses, most particularly a complainant, and
presented them to a magistrate. If the magistrate saw "probable cause,"
he issued a warrant to search or arrest and the police executed it.

In the event the complaint and affidavits turned out to be
malicious falsehoods, and the accused person innocent of any
wrongdoing, the policeman executing the warrant, if he acted in
good faith and without unnecessary force, was exonerated from any
liability, civil or penal. The aggrieved had to look to his accuser for
recompense. Making a false affidavit is also a crime and the accuser
then might well become the accused on a charge of perjury.

So that before 1961, a state police officer, more often than not,
obtained a warrant not because he needed the wisdom or objectivity
of a magistrate in drawing the proper inferences from the evidence,
but for two entirely different reasons. One was to put the witnesses
to a test. If, after being told of the consequences of perjury, an
accuser was unwilling to swear out a warrant against the accused, the
police probably would proceed no further. The word of any witness
who would not sign an affidavit was suspect.

---

[1] *Harris,* 150, *supra* [citation omitted].

[2] Fraenkel. *Concerning Searches and Seizures,* 34 Harvard Law Review 361 (1920). See footnotes 1, 2.

The other reason was to protect himself from liability or prosecution should his "facts" prove false. He knew that if he acted without a warrant, he did so at his peril. If he searched and found the loot there would, as a practical matter, be no comebacks. But if he came up empty-handed or arrested an innocent man, he had better be able to show he had probable cause to do so. This is somewhat hard to do *post facto*. Success has many fathers, but failure is an orphan—as the saying goes.

Then in 1963, two years after *Mapp*, a case was decided which made the finality of all criminal convictions open to question. In *Fay v. Noia*, 372 U.S. 391, a petitioner convicted of murder, who had acquiesced in his conviction by failing to appeal it, challenged it collaterally in a federal habeas corpus proceeding. Twenty-one years after his conviction had become final under state law, Frank Noia successfully relitigated and reargued the validity of his confession in a federal forum on the same facts and points of law decided against him by a trial court and jury.

"If I had the wings of an angel, over these prison walls would I fly," were the words to a prisoner's lament. To many a felon doing his time in a state penitentiary in 1965, *Mapp* and *Noia* appeared to be the two wings of that angel. Countless thousands of them had been convicted after trials in which physical evidence, such as a weapon or the fruits of the crime, had been used to prove their guilt. While almost invariably this evidence was obtained as a result of a search which to the ordinary eye would appear reasonable, few were made pursuant to a warrant. Under the warrant requirement most such searches therefore would be invalid.

The question opened by *Noia* was whether the *Weeks* rule and its *Johnson* corollary would be applied retrospectively to state cases in which the search and seizure was made before the *Mapp* decision. A burglar named Linkletter was the first to test it. "This case presents the question of whether this requirement [the exclusionary rule] operates retrospectively upon cases finally decided in the period prior to *Mapp*."[3]

---

[3] *Linkletter v. Walker*, 381 U.S. 618, 619-620 (1965).

The petitioner was convicted in a Louisiana District Court on May 28, 1959, of "simple burglary." At the time of his arrest he had been under surveillance for two days as a suspect in connection with another burglary. He was taken to the police station, searched, and keys were taken from his person. After he was booked and placed in jail, other officers took his keys, entered and searched his home, and seized certain property and papers. Later his place of business was entered and searched and seizures were effected. These intrusions were made without a warrant. The State District Court held that the arresting officers had reasonable cause for the arrest under Louisiana law and finding probable cause to search as an incident to arrest it held the seizures valid. The Supreme Court of Louisiana affirmed in February 1960.[4]

The Court traced the history of the exclusionary rule, focusing on some of its milestone cases.

The Court [in *Wolf*] went on to say that the federal exclusionary rule was not "derived from the explicit requirements of the Fourth Amendment . . . . The decision was a matter of judicial implication." At 28. Since "we find that in fact most of the English-speaking world does not regard as vital to such protection the exclusion of evidence thus obtained, we must hesitate to treat this remedy as an essential ingredient of the right."[5]

[Later] the Court emphasized that the exclusionary rule was "calculated to prevent, not to repair. Its purpose is to deter—to compel respect for the constitutional guaranty in the only effectively available way—by removing the incentive to disregard it."[6]

The Court in *Linkletter* agreed with the *Wolf* Court that the exclusionary rule was not a constitutional right included within the command of the Fourth Amendment, but rather a deterrent, the

[4] Ibid., 621.
[5] Ibid., 630.
[6] Ibid., 633.

only effective deterrent to lawless police action. The purpose of *Mapp*, they pointed out, "was to deter the lawless action of the police and to effectively enforce the Fourth Amendment. That purpose will not at this late date be served by the wholesale release of the guilty victims."[7]

By a vote of seven to two Linkletter's petition was denied. Neither he nor thousands of other state convicts will fly the coop on the wings of *Mapp* and *Noia*. Unlike *Noia* and other confession cases, "there is no likelihood of unreliability or coercion present in a search-and-seizure case." Nothing in such a case is relevant to

> the fairness of the trial—the very integrity of the fact-finding process. Here, as we have pointed out, the fairness of the trial is not under attack. All that petitioner attacks is the admissibility of evidence, the reliability and relevancy of which is not questioned, and which may well have had no effect on the outcome.[8]

The avowed purpose of the *Weeks* rule is the protection of the security of our home and person. It is to deter police officers from unlawful entry and arbitrary arrest. There is no evidence more probative than certain physical evidence found in the possession of the accused. If such evidence cannot be used, it is argued, the police will refrain from such unconstitutional conduct.

The *Weeks* rule does not, however, vest the defendant personally with a constitutional right to have such evidence excluded. Its *raison d'etre* is the protection of the right of privacy of us all. This being the case, the defendant's guilt is quite irrelevant. It is the belief of its proponents that the *Weeks* rule deters most effectively when evidence is excluded which *does* incriminate the defendant. The rule accepts as the price of liberty, as the Court did in the case of *Weeks*, that guilty men as a result will go free. But how much deterrence do we need? What price are we willing to pay?

Suppose a defendant asserts his claim for exclusion in the trial

---

[7] Ibid., 637.
[8] Ibid., 638-639.

court and it is found wanting. The search and seizure in question occurred after *Mapp*. The trial court finds the evidence was legally seized and admits it. The defendant is convicted and does not exercise his right to appeal. The sun has set on his day in court.

Should he later, perhaps years later, be permitted to reargue his case in a habeas corpus proceeding in federal court? Can he properly say that he is being held in custody in violation of the Constitution? No constitutional right of *his* has been violated. To protect the right of privacy of the public, is it necessary to permit a collateral attack after final conviction by a convict whose guilt is beyond question? Must we allow him to litigate anew the facts decided against him? In 1968 Justice Brennan, speaking for a majority of five, answered both these questions affirmatively.[9] But first we will listen to Justice Black state the facts in his dissent:

> Petitioner Kaufman was convicted of robbing a federally insured savings and loan association while armed with a pistol. Part of the evidence used against him was a revolver, some of the stolen traveler's checks, a money-order receipt, a traffic summons, and gasoline receipts. During the trial petitioner's counsel conceded that petitioner had committed the robbery but contended he was not responsible for the crime because he was mentally ill at the time.[10]

> Of course one important factor that would relate to whether the conviction should be vulnerable to collateral attack is the possibility of the applicant's innocence. For illustration, few would think that justice requires release of a person whose allegations clearly show that he was guilty of the crime of which he had been convicted.[11]

> It is seemingly becoming more and more difficult to gain acceptance for the proposition that punishment of the guilty is desirable, other things being equal.[12]

[9] *Kaufman v. United States*, 394 U.S. 217 (1969).
[10] Ibid., 231.
[11] Ibid., 232-233.
[12] Ibid., 240-241.

I would always require that the convicted defendant raise the kind of constitutional claim that casts some shadow of a doubt on his guilt. This defendant is permitted to attack his conviction collaterally although he conceded at the trial and does not now deny that he had robbed the savings and loan association and although the evidence makes absolutely clear that he knew what he was doing. Thus, his guilt being certain, surely he does not have a constitutional right to get a new trial. I cannot possibly agree with the Court.[13]

The proponents of the exclusionary rule, when addressing the general public, tend to insinuate that its purpose is somehow to protect the innocent against wrongful conviction. Of course, that is untrue. There is but one purpose of the rule, and Justice Brennan, taking issue with the dissent of Justice Black, tells us what it is. Mark his words.

> More fundamentally, the logic of his [Black's] dissent cannot be limited to the availability of post-conviction relief. It brings into question the propriety of the exclusionary rule itself. The application of that rule is not made to turn on the existence of a possibility of innocence; rather, exclusion of illegally obtained evidence is deemed necessary to protect the right of all citizens, not merely the citizen on trial, to be secure against unreasonable searches and seizures.[14]

Being a judicially created remedy rather than a personal constitutional right, the measure of the *Weeks* rule is utilitarian. Is it cost effective? Are the incremental deterrent effects of its application in habeas corpus proceedings worth the cost to society of setting obviously guilty criminals free to ply their trade? *Kaufman* was just a wild turn in the exclusionary rule roller-coaster track, and in 1976 it was overruled.

Respondent Lloyd Powell was convicted of murder in June 1968 after trial in a California state court. At about

---

[13] Ibid., 242.
[14] Ibid., 229.

midnight on February 17, 1968, he and three companions entered the Bonanza Liquor Store in San Bernardino, Cal., where Powell became involved in an altercation with Gerald Parsons, the store manager, over the theft of a bottle of wine. In the scuffling that followed Powell shot and killed Parsons' wife. Ten hours later an officer of the Henderson, Nev., Police Department arrested Powell for violation of the Henderson vagrancy ordinance, and in the search incident to the arrest discovered a .38-caliber revolver with six expended cartridges in the cylinder.

Powell was extradited to California and convicted of second-degree murder in the Superior Court of San Bernardino County. Parsons and Powell's accomplices at the liquor store testified against him. A criminologist testified that the revolver found on Powell was the gun that killed Parsons' wife. The trial court rejected Powell's contention that testimony by the Henderson police officer as to the search and the discovery of the revolver should have been excluded because the vagrancy ordinance was unconstitutional.[15]

In an opinion written by Justice Lewis Powell the Court decided "that where the State has provided an opportunity for full and fair litigation of a Fourth Amendment claim, a state prisoner may not be granted federal habeas corpus relief on the ground that evidence obtained in an unconstitutional search or seizure was introduced at his trial. In this context the contribution of the exclusionary rule, if any, to the effectuation of the Fourth Amendment is minimal and the substantial societal costs of application of the rule persists with special force."[16] Justices Brennan and Marshall, on the other hand, felt that the cost cannot be a consideration when it comes into conflict with the original intent of the Framers of the Constitution. They were appalled by this decision

that habeas relief for non-"guilt-related" constitutional

---

[15] *Stone v. Powell*, 428 U.S. 465, 469-470 (1976) [footnotes omitted].
[16] Ibid., 494-495 [footnotes omitted].

claims is not mandated because such claims do not affect the "basic justice" of a defendant's detention, this is presumably because the "ultimate goal" of the criminal justice system is "truth and justice ..." This denigration of constitutional guarantees and *constitutionally mandated procedures*, relegated by the Court to the status of mere utilitarian tools, must appall citizens taught to expect judicial respect and support for their constitutional rights. Even if punishment of the "guilty" were society's highest value—and procedural safeguards denigrated to this end—in a constitution that a majority of the Members of this Court would prefer, that is not the ordering of priorities under the Constitution forged by the Framers, and this Court's sworn duty is to uphold that Constitution and not to frame its own.[17]

Chief Justice Warren Burger wrote a separate opinion concurring with the majority in which he pointed out how the *Weeks* rule differs from rules of evidence whose purpose is to screen out unreliable evidence. "In evaluating the exclusionary rule," wrote the Chief Justice, "it is important to bear in mind exactly what the rule accomplishes. Its function is simple—the exclusion of truth from the fact-finding process."[18]

> The operation of the rule is therefore unlike that of the Fifth Amendment's protection against compelled self-incrimination. A confession produced after intimidating or coercive interrogation is inherently dubious ... This is not the case as to *reliable* evidence—a pistol, a packet of heroin, counterfeit money, or the body of a murder victim—which may be judicially declared to be the result of an "unreasonable" search. The reliability of such evidence is beyond question; its probative value is certain.[19]

Prior to the *Mapp* decision in *Walder v. United States,* the Court

---

[17] Ibid., 523-524 [footnote omitted].
[18] Ibid., 496.
[19] Ibid., 496-497.

had created an exception to the federal exclusionary rule. If at his trial the defendant lied on direct examination, the prosecutor would be permitted, under the *Walder* exception, to impeach his testimony by introducing evidence unlawfully obtained. He did not have a constitutional "shield against contradiction of his untruths. Such an extension of the *Weeks* doctrine would be a perversion of the Fourth Amendment."[20]

In 1974 another exception to the exclusionary rule was created. After an extensive investigation of suspected illegal gambling operations, FBI agents obtained a warrant authorizing a search of respondent John Calandra's place of business in Cleveland, Ohio, for wagering paraphernalia. In executing the warrant they found no gambling paraphernalia but did find evidence of extortionate credit transactions, commonly called loansharking, which related to another ongoing investigation.

Calandra was subpoenaed by a federal grand jury investigating loansharking. He appeared but refused to testify even after being offered immunity. The district court found that the search warrant had been issued without probable cause and that the search had exceeded the scope of the warrant. The court held that Calandra need not answer the grand jury's questions, a decision which the government appealed. In another opinion by Justice Lewis Powell, the Supreme Court reversed.

> The duty to testify [before a grand jury] has long been recognized as a basic obligation that every citizen owes his Government . . . It may on occasion be burdensome and even embarrassing. It may cause injury to a witness' social and economic status. Yet the duty to testify has been regarded as "so necessary to the administration of justice" that the witness' personal interest in privacy must yield to the public's overriding interest in full disclosure.[21]

The *Weeks* rule is no more than "a judicially created remedy designed to safeguard Fourth Amendment rights generally through

---

[20] *Walder v. United States*, 347 U.S. 62, 65 (1954).
[21] *United States v. Calandra*, 414 U.S. 338, 345 (1974).

its deterrent effect, rather than a personal constitutional right of the party aggrieved."[22] Therefore, reasoned Justice Powell, in "deciding whether to extend the exclusionary rule to grand jury proceedings, we must weigh the potential injury to the historic role and functions of the grand jury against the potential benefits of the rule as applied in this context."[23] "In the context of a grand jury proceeding," Powell concluded, "we believe that the damage to that institution from the unprecedented extension of the exclusionary rule urged by respondent outweighs the benefit of any possible incremental deterrent effect."[24]

Justice Brennan, joined by Douglas and Marshall, dissented. It was not the deterrent effect of the *Weeks* rule which was uppermost in the minds of the framers of that rule, but rather the "imperative of judicial integrity." "When judges appear to become 'accomplices in the willful disobedience of a Constitution they are sworn to uphold,'" wrote Brennan, "we imperil the very foundation of our peoples' trust in their Government on which our democracy rests."[25] He rested his case on that paradigm of judicial integrity— *Silverthorne v. United States:*

> *Silverthorne* plainly controls this case. Respondent, like plaintiffs in error in *Silverthorne*, seeks to avoid furnishing the grand jury with evidence that he would not have been called upon to supply but for the unlawful search and seizure . . . Only if *Silverthorne* is overruled can its precedential force to compel affirmance here be denied.[26]

Sadly Justice Brennan observed that "official lawlessness has not abated" and he was "left with the uneasy feeling that today's decision may signal that a majority of my colleagues have positioned themselves to reopen the door still further and abandon altogether the exclusionary rule in search-and-seizure cases . . ."[27]

---

[22] Ibid., 348.
[23] Ibid., 349.
[24] Ibid., 354.
[25] Ibid., 360.
[26] Ibid., 362-363 [footnote omitted].
[27] Ibid., 365.

Justice Brennan must have been reassured four years later when the Court had before it another case of what he likes to call "official lawlessness." In *Mincey v. Arizona*, Mincey, a drug dealer, shot and killed an Arizona narcotics officer. Responding to a radio call, homicide detectives arrived at Mincey's apartment, the scene of the murder, and took charge of the investigation.

> They supervised the removal of Officer Headricks and the suspects, trying to make sure that the scene was disturbed as little as possible, and then proceeded to gather evidence . . . In short, Mincey's apartment was subjected to an exhaustive and intrusive search. No warrant was ever obtained.[28]

The Arizona Supreme Court had held that "a reasonable, warrantless search of the scene of a homicide—or of a serious personal injury with likelihood of death where there is reason to suspect foul play—does not violate the Fourth Amendment to the United States Constitution where the law enforcement officers were legally on the premises in the first instance."[29] The Supreme Court of the United States thought otherwise and, speaking through Justice Potter Stewart, reversed Mincey's conviction for murder.

The "warrantless search of Mincey's apartment was not constitutionally permissible simply because a homicide had recently occurred there,"[30] wrote Stewart. "If the warrantless search of a homicide scene is reasonable, why not the warrantless search of the scene of a rape, a robbery, or a burglary?"[31] What protection would this "afford a person in whose home a homicide or assault occurs?"[32]

Bear in mind that the official lawlessness in this case did not consist of the entry of the homicide detectives. That they were legally and constitutionally on the premises all agree. It is the search that followed which violated Mincey's Fourth Amendment rights.

---

[28] *Mincey v. Arizona*, 437 U.S. 385, 389 (1978).
[29] Ibid., 389-390.
[30] Ibid., 395.
[31] Ibid., 393.
[32] Ibid., 394.

This familiar passage from *Johnson v. United States* was held to control:

> "The point of the Fourth Amendment, which often is not grasped by zealous officers, is not that it denies law enforcement the support of the usual inferences which reasonable men draw from evidence. Its protection consists in requiring that those inferences be drawn by a neutral and detached magistrate instead of being judged by the officer engaged in the often competitive enterprise of ferreting out crime." *Johnson v. United States, supra,* at 13-14.[33]

As the law developed, a criminal prosecution became as much a contest as to whether evidence should be excluded as to whether the defendant had committed the crime with which he was charged. Trial courts were obliged to hold pretrial hearings to determine whether evidence should be suppressed because of an alleged violation of the exclusionary rule. The trial of three bank robbers— Simmons, Andrews, and Garrett—is an example.

> At about 5:15 p.m. the same day, two FBI agents came to the house of Mrs. Mahon, Andrews' mother, about half a block from the place where the car was then parked. The agents had no warrant, and at trial it was disputed whether Mrs. Mahon gave them permission to search the house. They did search, and in the basement they found two suitcases, of which Mrs. Mahon disclaimed any knowledge. One suitcase contained, among other items, a gun holster, a sack similar to the one used in the robbery, and several coin cards and bill wrappers from the bank which had been robbed.[34]

Before trial, Garrett moved to suppress the suitcase full of evidence. To establish his standing to do so, he testified at a hearing that he was the owner of the suitcase. The district court denied the motion to suppress. Garrett was thereafter convicted in a trial in

---

[33] Ibid., 395.

[34] *Simmons v. United States,* 390 U.S. 377, 380 (1968) [footnote omitted].

which not only the suitcase and its contents were in evidence, but his pretrial testimony as well.

The Supreme Court, in an opinion written by Justice Harlan, reversed Garrett's conviction. To do otherwise, wrote Harlan, would put him in the intolerable position of having to surrender one constitutional right in order to assert another. "Garrett was obliged either to give up what he believed, with advice of counsel, to be a valid Fourth Amendment claim or, in legal effect, to waive his Fifth Amendment privilege against self-incrimination."[35] Justice Black, joined by Justice White, dissented.

> The Court makes new law in reversing Garrett's conviction on the ground that it was error to allow the Government to use against him testimony he had given upon his unsuccessful motion to suppress evidence allegedly seized in violation of the Fourth Amendment. The testimony used was Garrett's statement in the suppression hearing that he was the owner of a suitcase which contained money wrappers taken from the bank that was robbed. The Court is certainly guilty of no overstatement in saying that this "was undoubtedly a strong piece of evidence against [Garrett]." *Ante*, at 391. In fact, one might go further and say that this testimony, along with the statements of the eye-witnesses against him, showed beyond all question that Garrett was one of the bank robbers. The question then is whether the Government is barred from offering a truthful statement made by a defendant at a suppression hearing in order to prevent the defendant from winning an acquittal on the false premise that he is not the owner of the property he has already sworn that he owns. My answer to this question is "No."[36]

There are limited exceptions to the warrant requirement. Under exigent circumstances, a policeman may arrest without a warrant someone he has probable cause to believe has committed a felony and search that person and the immediate area around him for

---

[35] Ibid., 394.
[36] Ibid., 396.

evidence in plain view. But whenever an arrest or search is made without a warrant, the defense will argue that the circumstances were not all that exigent and that the policeman could have obtained a warrant beforehand if he had tried a little harder. This, as we have seen in the case of *Mincey*, is quite a different proposition from asserting that an arrest or search was made on less than probable cause and therefore was unreasonable.

Where there is a warrant, the defense will attack it on the grounds that the affidavits supporting it did not show probable cause. In all the factual situations we will see in subsequent search and seizure cases, it would appear to a reasonable person—if the author is one, at any rate—that there was probable cause for the officer to act as he did. In each case the cops caught the guy with the goods, and everyone knows he is guilty, but the only thing that matters is what was written into the affidavits before the warrant was issued.

The same process of reasoning used to determine what is probable or reasonable is used to determine guilt or innocence. Whether or not the defendant is guilty beyond a reasonable doubt is in itself nothing more than a judgment of what is both probable and reasonable in a given case. Such a judgment must *always* depend on the circumstances of the case at hand and can *never* be done by rule. Indeed, this truth would seem too self-evident to require restatement. This, however, is not the case.

Instead of judging probable cause by the facts and circumstances of the case at bar, the Court attempted to do it by formula. Not only was this contrary to right reason, it was the substitution of rigid, artificial, judicially crafted standards in place of the fluid test of human experience ordained in the Fourth Amendment—"a substitution of technicality for practicality."[37] This resulted in rules, exceptions, prongs and jargon incomprehensible to the general public. Take for example Justice Brennan's explanation in the 1983 case of *Illinois v. Gates* of the *Aguilar-Spinelli* two-pronged test for

---

[37] "But in Fourth Amendment cases findings of reasonableness or of probable cause necessarily rest on the facts and circumstances of each particular case." Clark, J., dissenting in *Aguilar v. Texas*, 378 U.S. 108, 118 (1964). The "Court has substituted a rigid, academic formula for the unrigid standards of reasonableness and 'probable cause' laid down by the Fourth Amendment itself — a substitution of technicality for practicality . . . " Id., 122.

determining probable cause:

> Properly understood, therefore, *Spinelli* stands for the proposition that corroboration of certain details in a tip may be sufficient to satisfy the veracity, but not the basis of knowledge, prong of *Aguilar*. As noted, *Spinelli* also suggests that in some limited circumstances considerable detail in an informant's tip may be adequate to satisfy the basis of knowledge prong of *Aguilar*.[38]

By a vote of six to three the "two-pronged test" was overruled in *Illinois v. Gates* in an opinion written by Justice Rehnquist. "For all these reasons, we conclude that it is wiser to abandon the 'two-pronged test' established by our decisions in *Aguilar* and *Spinelli*. In its place we reaffirm the totality-of-the-circumstances analysis that traditionally has informed probable-cause determinations . . . The task of the issuing magistrate is simply to make a practical, common-sense decision."[39]

Justice Brennan saw in this the seeds of totalitarianism. Quoting from our old friend *Johnson v. United States,* he warned that "today's decision threatens to 'obliterate one of the most fundamental distinctions between our form of government, where officers are under the law, and the police-state where they are the law.'"[40]

It is the warrant requirement of *Johnson* which stigmatizes eminently reasonable searches made as a result of practical, common-sense decisions. In 1975, for example, California highway patrolmen stopped the defendant's station wagon "because he had been driving erratically . . . When the petitioner opened the car door to get out the registration, the officers smelled marihuana smoke." They made what was concededly a valid search of the vehicle and found "a totebag and two packages wrapped in green opaque plastic. The police unwrapped the packages; each one contained 15 pounds of marihuana."[41]

Having concluded that automobiles have "inherent mobility,"

---

[38] *Illinois v. Gates*, 462 U.S. 213, 282 (1983), Brennan J., dissenting.
[39] Ibid., 238 [footnote omitted].
[40] Ibid., 291.
[41] *Robbins v. California*, 453 U.S. 420, 422 (1981) [footnote omitted].

the Court had created an exception to the warrant requirement especially for cars. But it had also held in previous cases that this exception did not allow the warrantless search of everything found in an automobile during a lawful warrantless search of the vehicle itself. There is, after all, "no reason to believe that the privacy expectation in a closed piece of luggage taken from a car is necessarily less than the privacy expectation in closed pieces of luggage found elsewhere."[42]

Plastic bags are hardly luggage, contended California; they are different—at least in a marijuana case. Wrong, said the Court. While the contents of some containers, like a gun case, can be inferred from their outward appearance, this is not true of opaque green plastic bags. "What one person may put into a suitcase, another may put into a paper bag." "Once placed within such a container, a diary and a dishpan are equally protected by the Fourth Amendment."[43]

In 1971 Justice Harlan had stated that until the Court overrules *Mapp v. Ohio,* "no solid progress in setting things straight in search and seizure law will . . . occur." In *Robbins* Justice Rehnquist put himself squarely in that corner.

> The 10 years which have intervened since Justice Harlan made this statement have only tended to confirm its correctness.
>
> The harm caused by the exclusionary rule is compounded by the judicially created preference for a warrant as indicating satisfaction of the reasonableness requirement of the Fourth Amendment. It is often forgotten that nothing in the Fourth Amendment itself requires that searches be conducted pursuant to warrants. The terms of the Amendment simply mandate that the people be secure from unreasonable searches and seizures, and that any warrants which *may* issue shall only issue upon probable cause . . .[44]

[42] Ibid., 425.
[43] Ibid., 426.
[44] Ibid., 437, 438.

In 1978 a visibly nervous young man was observed in Miami
Airport by two plainclothes detectives. "Royer's appearance, man-
nerisms, luggage, and actions fit the so-called 'drug courier profile.'"
He had purchased a one-way ticket to New York City, paying cash,
and checked two large suitcases with a name identification of "Holt."
The two detectives approached, identified themselves, "and asked if
Royer had a 'moment' to speak with them; Royer said 'Yes.'" "Upon
request, but without oral consent, Royer produced for the detectives
his airline ticket and his driver's license."

When asked about the discrepancy between the two names,
"Royer explained that a friend had made the reservation in the name
of 'Holt.' Royer became noticeably more nervous during this
conversation . . ." One detective asked Royer to accompany him to
a small room off the concourse while the other retrieved the
suitcases from the airline. They told him "they had reason to suspect
him of transporting narcotics."

> Royer was asked if he would consent to a search of the
> suitcases. Without orally responding to this request,
> Royer produced a key and unlocked one of the suitcases,
> which one detective then opened without seeking further
> assent from Royer. Marihuana was found in that suitcase.[45]

By a vote of five to four the Court held that Royer was the victim
of an illegal search and seizure because the detectives lacked
probable cause to arrest him. "We cannot agree," wrote Justice
White for the majority, "that every nervous young man paying cash
for a ticket to New York City under an assumed name and carrying
two heavy American Tourister bags may be arrested and held to
answer for a serious felony charge."[46]

Justice Rehnquist again dissented. "The question we must
decide is what was *unreasonable* about the steps which *these officers*
took with respect to *this* suspect in the Miami Airport on this
particular day."[47]

---

[45] *Florida v. Royer*, 460 U.S. 491, 494 (1983).
[46] Ibid., 507.
[47] Ibid., 528-529.

The opinion nonetheless, in my view, betrays a mind-set more useful to those who officiate at shuffleboard games, primarily concerned with which particular square the disc has landed on, than to those who are seeking to administer a system of justice whose twin purposes are the conviction of the guilty and the vindication of the innocent. The plurality loses sight of the very language of the Amendment which it purports to interpret:

"The right of the people to be secure in their persons, houses, papers, and effects, against *unreasonable* searches and seizures, shall not be violated . . ." (Emphasis added).

Analyzed simply in terms of its "reasonableness" as that term is used in the Fourth Amendment, the conduct of the investigating officers toward Royer would pass muster with virtually all thoughtful, civilized persons not overly steeped in the mysteries of this Court's Fourth Amendment jurisprudence. Analyzed even in terms of the most meticulous regard for our often conflicting cases, it seems to me to pass muster equally well.[48]

While cases involving searches and seizures often resemble one another, they always vary in circumstance. What is reasonable or probable in a given case can only be determined by a synthesis of its facts and circumstances. It can never be done by using previous cases as axioms from which what is probable or reasonable may be deduced. The futility of trying to do so is illustrated by *Arizona v. Hicks*. Justice Antonin Scalia delivered the opinion of the Court.

On April 18, 1984, a bullet was fired through the floor of respondent's apartment, striking and injuring a man in the apartment below. Police officers arrived and entered respondent's apartment to search for the shooter, for other victims, and for weapons. They found and seized three weapons, including a sawed-off rifle, and in the course of their search also discovered a stocking-cap mask.

---

[48] Ibid., 520.

One of the policemen, Officer Nelson, noticed two sets of expensive stereo components, which seemed out of place in the squalid and otherwise ill-appointed four-room apartment. Suspecting that they were stolen, he read and recorded their serial numbers—moving some of the components, including a Bang and Olufsen turntable, in order to do so—which he then reported by phone to his headquarters. On being advised that the turntable had been taken in an armed robbery, he seized it immediately. It was later determined that some of the other serial numbers matched those on other stereo equipment taken in the same armed robbery, and a warrant was obtained and executed to seize that equipment as well. Respondent was subsequently indicted for the robbery . . . It was conceded that the initial entry and search, although warrantless, were justified by the exigent circumstance of the shooting.[49]

In *Mincey* the Court had held that while the police may seize evidence that is in "plain view" during the course of their legitimate emergency activities, a "warrantless search must be 'strictly circumscribed by the exigencies which justify its initiation.'" Here, Officer Nelson's moving of some of the stereo components constituted "a 'search' separate and apart from the search for the shooter, victims, and weapons that was the lawful objective of his entry into the apartment."[50] Moreover, the "plain view" exception does not apply because while the turntable itself was in plain view, the serial numbers were not.

> But taking action, unrelated to the objectives of the authorized intrusion, which exposed to view concealed portions of the apartment or its contents, did produce a new invasion of respondent's privacy unjustified by the exigent circumstance that validated the entry. This is why, contrary to Justice Powell's suggestion . . . the "distinction between 'looking' at a suspicious object in plain view and 'moving' it even a few inches" is much more than trivial for purposes of the Fourth Amendment. It matters not that the search uncovered

---

[49] *Arizona v. Hicks*, 480 U.S. 321, 323-324 (1987).
[50] Ibid., 324-325.

nothing of any great personal value to respondent—
serial numbers rather than (what might conceivably have
been hidden behind or under the equipment) letters or
photographs. A search is a search, even if it happens to
disclose nothing but the bottom of a turntable.[51]

It is true that suppression of this evidence may make it
impossible to prosecute Hicks. "But there is nothing new in the
realization that the Constitution sometimes insulates the
criminality of a few in order to protect the privacy of us all."[52] This
is indeed reassuring to those of us who keep our *billets doux* under
the stereo turntable. For the record, Justices O'Connor, Rehnquist,
and Powell dissented.

If it is the purpose of the exclusionary rule to deter unlawful
police conduct, it is manifestly ineffectual to apply it to cases where
the police, in perfectly good faith, and for very good reason, believe
they are acting within the law. To do so simply results in the freeing
of a criminal with no corresponding benefit on the Fourth
Amendment side of the ledger. This is particularly true when the
police are acting under the aegis of a superior legal authority upon
which perforce they must rely.

United States v. Leon, 468 U.S. 897 (1984) and *Massachusetts v.
Sheppard,* 468 U.S. 981 (1984) were companion cases argued and
decided on the same days. Each involves much the same principle of
law and *Sheppard* follows *Leon* on consecutive pages of Volume 468
of the *U.S. Reports*. Justice Brennan's dissenting opinion in *Leon,*
pages 928-960, in which Justice Marshall joined, is expressly made
applicable by him to *Sheppard* as well. *Leon* involved a search and
seizure in a drug case after extensive surveillance of the defendants.
The search warrants were issued on the basis of affidavits showing
"probable cause" which had been examined by several deputy
district attorneys and a superior court judge and found by them to
be legally sufficient. The facts and circumstances of *Leon* are too
complicated to admit of concise discussion. Suffice it to say that in

---

[51] Ibid., 325.
[52] Ibid., 329.

Leon the officers acted in good faith on legal advice upon which they should be entitled to rely.

Massachusetts v. Sheppard was a murder case. Justice White, who delivered the opinion of the Court, gives us the facts. "The badly burned body of Sandra Boulware was discovered in a vacant lot in the Roxbury section of Boston at approximately 5 a.m., Saturday, May 5, 1979. An autopsy revealed that Boulware had died of multiple compound skull fractures caused by blows to the head. After a brief investigation, the police decided to question one of the victim's boyfriends, Osborne Sheppard."[53] Sheppard had an alibi. He had been at a card game from 9:00 p.m. Friday to 5:00 a.m. Saturday. There were several people, he told police, who would substantiate this.

> By interviewing the people Sheppard had said were at the gaming house on Friday night, the police learned that although Sheppard was at the gaming house that night, he had borrowed an automobile at about 3 o'clock Saturday morning in order to give two men a ride home. Even though the trip normally took only 15 minutes, Sheppard did not return with the car until nearly 5 a.m.

> On Sunday morning, police officers visited the owner of the car Sheppard had borrowed. He consented to an inspection of the vehicle. Bloodstains and pieces of hair were found on the rear bumper and within the trunk compartment. In addition, the officers noticed strands of wire in the trunk similar to wire strands found on and near the body of the victim. The owner of the car told the officers that when he last used the car on Friday night, shortly before Sheppard borrowed it, he had placed articles in the trunk and had not noticed any stains on the bumper or in the trunk.

> On the basis of the evidence gathered thus far in the investigation, Detective Peter O'Malley drafted an affidavit designed to support an application for an arrest

---

[53] *Sheppard*, 984.

warrant and a search warrant authorizing a search of Sheppard's residence.[54]

"Detective O'Malley showed the affidavit to the District Attorney, the District Attorney's first assistant, and a sergeant, who all concluded that it set forth probable cause for the search and the arrest." But because "it was Sunday, the local court was closed, and the police had a difficult time finding a warrant application form. Detective O'Malley finally found a warrant form . . . entitled 'Search Warrant—Controlled Substance.'"[55]

> Realizing that some changes had to be made before the form could be used to authorize the search requested in the affidavit, Detective O'Malley deleted the subtitle "controlled substance" with a typewriter . . . However, the reference to "controlled substance" was not deleted in the portion of the form that constituted the warrant application and that, when signed, would constitute the warrant itself.[56]

O'Malley then took the affidavit and the warrant form to the residence of a judge who "examined the affidavit and stated that he would authorize the search as requested." The detective pointed out to the judge that the form dealt with controlled substances.

> After unsuccessfully searching for a more suitable form, the judge informed O'Malley that he would make the necessary changes so as to provide a proper search warrant. The judge then took the form, made some changes on it, and dated and signed the warrant. However, he did not change the substantive portion of the warrant, which continued to authorize a search for controlled substances; nor did he alter the form so as to incorporate the affidavit. The judge returned the affidavit and the warrant to O'Malley, informing him that the warrant was sufficient authority in form and

---

[54] Ibid.
[55] Ibid., 985.
[56] Ibid.

content to carry out the search as requested. O'Malley
took the two documents and, accompanied by other
officers, proceeded to Sheppard's residence. The scope
of the ensuing search was limited to the items listed in
the affidavit, and several incriminating pieces of
evidence were discovered.[57]

To say that several incriminating pieces of evidence were
discovered was certainly no overstatement. To be more precise, in
the basement of Sheppard's house "[t]he police found a pair of
bloodstained boots, bloodstains on the concrete floor, a woman's
earring with bloodstains on it, a bloodstained envelope, a pair of
men's jockey shorts and women's leotards with blood on them,
three types of wire, and a woman's hairpiece, subsequently
identified as the victim's."[58] Sheppard was tried and convicted of
murder in the first degree. He appealed to the Supreme Court on
the grounds that the use of this evidence violated his rights under
the Fourth Amendment.

Sheppard's argument was that the search warrant was
constitutionally infirm in that while the affidavit upon which the
warrant was based described the persons or things to be seized, the
warrant itself did not. In oral argument the defense had conceded
"that if the judge had crossed out the reference to controlled
substances, written 'see attached affidavit' on the form, and attached
the affidavit to the warrant, the warrant would have been valid."[59] It
would have incorporated by reference the items listed in the
affidavit for which the search warrant was sought.

The case was decided on the basis of good faith. "If an officer is
required to accept at face value the judge's conclusion that a warrant
form is invalid, there is little reason why he should be expected to
disregard assurances that everything is all right, especially when he
has alerted the judge to the potential problems." Suppressing the
evidence in such a situation "will not serve the deterrent function

---

[57] Ibid., 986-987 [footnotes omitted].
[58] Ibid., 987 [footnote 4].
[59] Ibid., 990 [footnote 7].

that the exclusionary rule was designed to achieve."[60] By a vote of seven to two the Court upheld the conviction of Osborne Sheppard.

This prompted a lengthy and vigorous dissent by Justice Brennan in which Mr. Justice Marshall joined. As in *Stone v. Powell* Brennan invoked the original intention of the Framers.

> The majority ignores the fundamental constitutional importance of what is at stake here. While the machinery of law enforcement and indeed the nature of crime itself have changed dramatically since the Fourth Amendment became part of the Nation's fundamental law in 1791, what the Framers understood then remains true today— that the task of combating crime and convicting the guilty will in every era seem of such critical and pressing concern that we may be lured by the temptations of expediency into forsaking our commitment to protecting individual liberty and privacy. It was for that very reason that the Framers of the Bill of Rights insisted that law enforcement efforts be permanently and unambiguously restricted in order to preserve personal freedoms. In the constitutional scheme they ordained, the sometimes unpopular task of ensuring that the government's enforcement efforts remain within the strict boundaries fixed by the Fourth Amendment was entrusted to the courts. As James Madison predicted in his address to the First Congress on June 8, 1789:
>
> "If [these rights] are incorporated into the Constitution, independent tribunals of justice will consider themselves in a peculiar manner the guardians of those rights; they will be an impenetrable bulwark against every assumption of power in the Legislative or Executive; they will be naturally led to resist every encroachment upon rights expressly stipulated for in the Constitution by the declaration of rights." 1 Annals of Cong. 439.[61]

If James Madison ever said anything to import the existence of an exclusionary rule or a warrant requirement into the Fourth

---

[60] Ibid., 990-991.
[61] 468 U.S. 929, 930.

Amendment, it most surely was not in the passage just quoted from the Annals of the First Congress. But if Justice Brennan wished to acquaint himself with Madison's thinking in this regard, he had only to read another 13 pages of the Annals. There, on page 452, in the same speech from which Justice Brennan has just quoted— Madison's "address to the First Congress on June 8, 1789"—the Father of the Constitution read to that assembly the Bill of Rights he had drafted for their consideration. With respect to what became the Fourth Amendment that draft read:

> The rights of the people to be secured in their persons; their houses, their papers, and their other property, from all unreasonable searches and seizures, shall not be violated by warrants issued without probable cause, supported by oath or affirmation, or not particularly describing the places to be searched, or the persons or things to be seized.[62]

The obvious conclusion was that Madison was predicting that independent tribunals of justice would follow the example of Chief Justice Charles Pratt and quash general warrants, thus exposing those issuing and executing the warrants to tort liability. The intruders then could be sued—as Wilkes sued Wood—and the victims awarded exemplary damages—as was Wilkes—in an amount sufficient to deter future transgressors.

Nevertheless, Mr. Justice Brennan, "compelled by the language of the Fourth Amendment and the history that led to its adoption," was able to discern the original intent of the Framers and to follow that intention in resolving the case of Osborne Sheppard. He and Mr. Justice Marshall would have reversed the conviction and required the commonwealth, should they elect to try Sheppard again, to do so in a trial uncontaminated by the grisly evidence found in his subterranean abattoir. That this was the Framers' idea, and not his own, Justice Brennan was emphatic.

What the Framers of the Bill of Rights sought to

---

[62] 1 Annals of Congress, 452.

accomplish through the express requirements of the Fourth Amendment was to define precisely the conditions under which government agents could search private property so that citizens would not have to depend solely upon the discretion and restraint of those agents for the protection of their privacy. Although the self-restraint and care exhibited by the officers in this case is commendable, that alone can never be a sufficient protection for constitutional liberties . . .

These convictions spring not from my own view of sound criminal law enforcement policy, but are instead compelled by the language of the Fourth Amendment and the history that led to its adoption.[63]

Brennan's opinion is as lengthy as it is apocolyptic. It begins on page 928, where, after referring to his dissent in *Calandra* in 1974, he states: "I have witnessed the Court's gradual but determined strangulation of the [*Weeks*] rule."

It now appears that the Court's victory over the Fourth Amendment is complete. That today's decisions represent the *pièce de résistance* of the Court's past efforts cannot be doubted, for today the Court sanctions the use in the prosecution's case in chief of illegally obtained evidence against the individual whose rights have been violated—a result that had previously been thought to be foreclosed.[64]

The opinion ends with a valediction bearing a remarkable similarity to the end of Cooper's novel, *The Last of the Mohicans*— the closing scene in which Hawkeye and his friend, Sagamore, weep over the open grave of the warrior Uncas. That scene, as well as the book, closes with this lament: "My day has been too long. In the morning I saw the sons of Unamis happy and strong; and yet, before the night has come, have I lived to see the last warrior of the wise race of the Mohicans."

---

[63] 468 U.S. 948.
[64] 468 U.S. 929.

In the case of Osborne Sheppard, *Weeks* lies in the place of the fallen Uncas. It takes Justices Brennan and Marshall a lot longer—almost 42 pages—to bear witness to the burial of The Last of the Fourth Amendment. But this should not be surprising because both Justices were noted for their prolixity while frontier scouts and Indian sachems tended to be men of few words. Unlike the poor Mohicans, however, the Fourth Amendment still has a chance. It may rise again in the misty dawn of a day the bereaved may never see.

> Once lost, such rights are difficult to recover. There is hope, however, that in time this or some later Court will restore these precious freedoms to their rightful place as a primary protection for our citizens against overreaching officialdom.

> I dissent.[65]

---

[65] 468 U.S. 960.

Chapter XVIII

POISONED PRECEDENTS

Justices Brennan and Marshall were joined in their lugubrious lament over the case of Osborne Sheppard by a host of constitutional scholars. A spate of law review articles made their appearance with such titles as:

> *Massachusetts v. Sheppard: When the keeper leads the flock astray—a case of good faith or harmless error.*
> 59 Notre Dame L. Rev. 665-84 (1984)

> *I came not to praise the exclusionary rule but to bury it—United States v. Leon; Massachusetts v. Sheppard.* 18 Creighton L. Rev. 819-75 (1984-85)

Then in 1990 the Court decided *James v. Illinois* and the tenor of legal writing became decidedly more sanguine:

> *An unexpected departure from the steady erosion of the Fourth Amendment exclusionary rule. James v. Illinois.* 22 Univ. of Toledo L. Rev. 839-869 (1991).

> *Whither the exclusionary rule? Not quite yet. James v. Illinois.* 24 John Marshall L. Rev. 493-507 (1991).

James v. Illinois limited the exception to the exclusionary rule created in 1954 case of *Walder v. United States, supra,* which permits the prosecution to introduce evidence which would be inadmissible in their case-in-chief to contradict perjured testimony given by the defendant.[1] *James* held that this exception did not extend to testimony given by defense witnesses other than the defendant— perjury by proxy—to use the words of the Illinois Supreme Court. Mr. Justice Brennan delivered the Court's opinion:

> On the night of August 30, 1982, eight young boys returning home from a party were confronted by a trio of other boys who demanded money. When the eight boys refused to comply, one member of the trio produced a gun and fired into the larger group, killing one boy and seriously injuring another.[2]

Witnesses had described the shooter as having reddish, shoulder-length hair in a slicked back "butter" style. Five members of the group of boys who were fired upon recalled having seen the defendant some weeks before "at which time James had the aforementioned hair color and style. At trial, however, his hair was black and worn in a 'natural' style."[3]

> The next evening, [after the murder] two detectives of the Chicago Police Department took 15-year-old Darryl James into custody as a suspect in the shooting. James was found at his mother's beauty parlor sitting under a hair dryer; when he emerged, his hair was black and curly. After placing James in their car, the detectives questioned him about his prior hair color. He responded that the previous day his hair had been reddish brown, long, and combed straight back. The detectives questioned James again later at the police station, and he further stated that he had gone to the beauty parlor in order to have his hair "dyed black and curled in order to change his appearance." App. 11.

> The State subsequently indicted James for murder and attempted murder. Prior to trial, James moved to suppress the statements regarding his hair, contending

---

[1] See *Walder v. United States,* 347 U.S. 62 (1954), *supra.*

[2] *James v. Illinois,* 493 U.S. 307, 309 (1990).

[3] Ibid., 310.

that they were the fruit of a Fourth Amendment violation because the detectives lacked probable cause for his warrantless arrest. After an evidentiary hearing, the trial court sustained this motion and ruled that the statements would be inadmissible at trial.[4]

"James did not testify in his own defense. He called as a witness Jewel Henderson, a friend of his family. Henderson testified that on the day of the shooting she had taken James to register for high school and that, at that time, his hair was black."[5] The state sought to impeach this testimony by introducing James's statements about changing his appearance—statements the trial court had excluded from the prosecution's case-in-chief. The statements were admitted for this limited purpose and James was convicted of murder. The Supreme Court of the United States—by a vote of five to four—reversed the conviction.

> Expanding the class of impeachable witnesses from the defendant alone to all defense witnesses would create different incentives affecting the behavior of both defendants and law enforcement officers . . . [T]hreat of a subsequent criminal prosecution for perjury is far more likely to deter a witness from intentionally lying on a defendant's behalf than to deter a defendant, already facing conviction for the underlying offense, from lying on his own behalf . . . [E]xpanding the impeachment exception to encompass the testimony of all defense witnesses likely would chill some defendants from presenting their best defense . . . Whenever police obtained evidence illegally, defendants would have to assess prior to trial the likelihood that the evidence would be admitted to impeach the otherwise favorable testimony of any witness they call.[6]

"There is no gainsaying that arriving at the truth is a fundamental goal of our legal system," Justice Brennan reminded

---

[4] Ibid., 309-310.
[5] Ibid., 310.
[6] Ibid., 313-315.

us. "But various constitutional rules limit the means by which government may conduct this search for truth in order to promote other values embraced by the Framers and cherished throughout our Nation's history."[7] Let us examine this statement.

There is no gainsaying that arriving at the truth should be a fundamental goal of our legal system. But what "values embraced by the Framers" limit this search? Certainly none that the Framers chose to express in the Fourth Amendment. There is nothing in those 54 words which requires that evidence be excluded or that searches be made pursuant to a warrant. The plain fact is that neither an exclusionary rule nor a warrant requirement can be found in the text of the Fourth Amendment. And that cannot be gainsaid.

To circumvent this manifest truth, the proponents of the exclusionary rule and the warrant requirement invoke phony history. In *Massachusetts v. Sheppard*, for example, Justice Brennan would have reversed the conviction of Osborne Sheppard and precluded Massachusetts, should the commonwealth elect to try him again, from using the grisly evidence found in Sheppard's basement, the scene of the murder. The most likely result of such a decision—had it commanded a majority—would have been that the torturer and murderer of Sandra Boulware would have gotten off scot-free. To Mr. Justice Brennan, this is the price the Framers were willing to pay to keep our homes and persons secure against what he likes to call "official lawlessness." In 1976 he took the same position in *Stone v. Powell* when he voted to set aside the conviction of Lloyd Powell, the man who murdered Mrs. Gerald Parsons during the robbery of her liquor store in San Bernadino, California.

> Even if punishment of the "guilty" were society's highest value—and procedural safeguards denigrated to this end—in a constitution that a majority of the Members of this Court would prefer, that is not the ordering of priorities under the Constitution forged by the Framers, and this Court's sworn duty is to uphold that Constitution and not to frame its own.[8]

---

[7] Ibid., 311 [citation omited].

[8] *Stone v. Powell, supra* 523-524.

Should an Osborne Sheppard or a Lloyd Powell go free and murder once again, who would be accountable? Certainly not William J. Brennan Jr. He made clear that his decision in *Sheppard* was not based upon his "own view of sound criminal law enforcement policy," presumably made of sterner stuff than that of the Framers, but was "instead compelled by the language of the Fourth Amendment and the history that led to its adoption."[9] Mr. Justice Brennan was but doing his sworn duty to uphold the Constitution forged by the Framers.

Now murderer Darryl James goes unscathed—or at least the Court accepts that possibility—to promote other values embraced by the Framers and cherished throughout our nation's history. But never has Brennan, or any other proponent of the exclusionary rule, produced a scrap of evidence that lends support to the notion that the Framers ever even thought of enforcing the Fourth Amendment by letting the guilty go free. History to people like Justice William J. Brennan Jr. is never a search for the truth. It is an exercise in dissimulation the purpose of which is to coat their opinions with a patina of legitimacy.

Bivins v. Six Unknown Named Agents of the Federal Bureau of Narcotics was a civil suit for damages. It involved a search but not a seizure. The exclusionary rule did not come into play since nothing incriminating was found. It was a Fourth Amendment violation outrance. Without probable cause six unknown named agents of the

> Federal Bureau of Narcotics acting under claim of federal authority, entered his apartment and arrested him for alleged narcotics violations. The agents manacled petitioner in front of his wife and children, and threatened to arrest the entire family. They searched the apartment from stem to stern. Thereafter, petitioner was taken to the federal courthouse in Brooklyn, where he was interrogated, booked, and subjected to a visual strip search.[10]

---

[9] *Sheppard*, 948.

[10] *Bivins v. Six Unknown Named Agents of Federal Bureau of Narcotics*, 403 U.S. 388, 389 (1971).

The companion case to *Bivins*—decided the same day—was *Coolidge v. New Hampshire*,[11] the 1971 case with which we began this story. It involved a search of a completely different character. Before arresting Coolidge and seizing his car, the police knew that it "matched the description of the car which the two witnesses reported seeing parked where the girl's body had been found."[12] Coolidge had been asked by the police whether he owned any guns and he produced three. Later, "two policemen went to petitioner's home to talk with his wife." In response to the same question she voluntarily offered to the police four guns—"two shotguns and two rifles." A laboratory investigation proved one of the rifles "had fired the bullet found in the murdered girl's brain."[13] The defendant then was arrested and his car seized. A microscopic vacuum inspection subsequently revealed evidence of the girl's presence in the car.

The author of the *Coolidge* opinion is none other than Potter Stewart, our former guide down *The Road to Mapp v. Ohio and Beyond*. The opening words of the opinion make it clear that neither guilt or innocence, nor truth or justice, will sway Mr. Justice Stewart from his sworn duty:

> We are called upon in this case to decide issues under the Fourth and Fourteenth Amendments arising in the context of a state criminal trial for the commission of a particularly brutal murder. As in every case, our single duty is to determine the issues presented in accord with the Constitution and the law.[14]

Decide issues under the *Fourth* Amendment in a *state* criminal trial? Since when? From its ratification in 1791 until June 19, 1961, the day upon which the decision in *Mapp v. Ohio* was handed down, it had been held without deviation that the Fourth Amendment *does not* apply to the states. And as Justice Brennan sternly reminded his brethren in *Stone v. Powell*, the Court's sworn duty is to uphold the

---

[11] *Coolidge v. New Hampshire*, 403 U.S. 443 (1971).
[12] Ibid., 494.
[13] Ibid., 495.
[14] Ibid., 445.

396

Constitution forged by the Framers and not to frame its own. How then did it come about that the Constitution was changed so that the Fourth Amendment became applicable to the states?

It did not happen in *Mapp v. Ohio*. The *Mapp* plurality held that it was in *Wolf v. Colorado* that the Fourth Amendment was held to be "applicable to the States through the Due Process Clause"[15] of the Fourteenth Amendment. But *Wolf* had held precisely the opposite.

> Unlike the specific requirements and restrictions placed by the Bill of Rights (Amendments I to VIII) upon the administration of criminal justice by federal authority, the Fourteenth Amendment did not subject criminal justice in the States to specific limitations. The notion that the "due process of law" guaranteed by the Fourteenth Amendment is shorthand for the first eight amendments of the Constitution and thereby incorporates them has been rejected by this Court again and again, after impressive consideration . . . The issue is closed.[16]

Now *Wolf* did say that the Fourteenth Amendment protects the "security of one's privacy against arbitrary intrusion by the police." So that "were a State affirmatively to sanction such police incursion into privacy it would run counter to the guaranty of the Fourteenth Amendment."[17] But there was nothing new in this. No one had ever contended, for example, that a state could affirmatively sanction arbitrary searches by immunizing its agents from liability. A society that countenanced intrusive searches made without probable cause would be nothing less than despotic. It was as unthinkable that a state would adopt such a policy as it was that the Supreme Court would permit it.

The critical word is *arbitrary*. An intrusive search made without probable cause—like *Bivens*—is not just unreasonable; it is *arbitrary*[18] as well. That such searches would fall within the interdict

---

[15] *Mapp*, 655.

[16] *Wolf*, 26.

[17] *Wolf*, 27-28.

[18] Arbitrary, syn: capricious, tyrannical, peremptory, despotic. *Webster's New Twentieth, Second Edition.*

of the Fourteenth Amendment all would agree. But a search deemed unreasonable simply because of the warrant requirement—like *Coolidge*—is not necessarily *arbitrary*. And it was this distinction that Justice Frankfurter, the author of the *Wolf* opinion, deemed critical.

> It is therefore a complete misconception of the *Wolf* case to assume . . . that every finding by this Court of a technical lack of a search warrant, thereby making a search unreasonable under the Fourth Amendment, constitutes an "arbitrary intrusion" of privacy so as to make the same conduct on the part of state officials a violation of the Fourteenth Amendment. The divisions in this Court over the years regarding what is and what is not to be deemed an unreasonable search within the meaning of the Fourth Amendment and the shifting views of members of the Court in this regard, prove that in evolving the meaning of the Fourth Amendment the decisions of this Court have frequently turned on dialectical niceties and have not reflected those fundamental considerations of civilized conduct on which applications of the Due Process Clause turn.[19]

By the narrowest of margins the Court held the search of Coolidge's car *unreasonable* because the police did not first obtain a warrant—a valid warrant. They were in fact executing a warrant issued by a justice of the peace, who under New Hampshire law was a magistrate authorized to issue search warrants. Given the probable cause, of course, *any* magistrate would have issued the warrant. Unfortunately this magistrate was also the attorney general of New Hampshire in charge of the investigation, so he was not the "neutral and detached magistrate" who, as Justice Stewart reminds us, *Johnson v. United States* had in mind.

> The classic statement of the policy underlying the warrant requirement of the Fourth Amendment is that of Mr. Justice Jackson, writing for the Court in *Johnson v. United States*, 333 U.S. 10, 13-14:

---

[19] *Elkins v. United States*, 364 U.S. 206, 238, 239 (1960).

"The point of the Fourth Amendment, which often is not grasped by zealous officers, is not that it denies law enforcement the support of the usual inferences which reasonable men draw from evidence. Its protection consists in requiring that those inferences be drawn by a neutral and detached magistrate instead of being judged by the officer engaged in the often competitive enterprise of ferreting out crime. Any assumption that evidence sufficient to support a magistrate's disinterested determination to issue a search warrant will justify the officers in making a search without a warrant would reduce the Amendment to a nullity and leave the people's homes secure only in the discretion of police officers . . . ."[20]

The terrible vice of the warrant requirement when used in tandem with the exclusionary rule is that it never weighs or balances the nature and extent of the intrusion on one hand against the gravity of the crime and the exigencies of law enforcement on the other. Cases of bookmaking and murder are on the same footing. A search is a search, be it of a dwelling in the middle of the night or a car in the middle of the afternoon. Rifling through someone's personal papers in his desk is no different from vacuuming an empty car for microscopic evidence of a murdered girl's presence. It equates a *Coolidge* scenario with a *Bivins* scenario when, as Chief Justice Warren Burger pointed out, they are not at all equals.

This Court's decision announced today in *Coolidge v. New Hampshire, post,* p. 443, dramatically illustrates the extent to which the doctrine represents a mechanically inflexible response to widely varying degrees of police error and the resulting high price that society pays. I dissented in *Coolidge* primarily because I do not believe the Fourth Amendment had been violated. Even on the Court's contrary premise, however, whatever violation occurred was surely insufficient in nature and extent to justify the drastic result dictated by the suppression doctrine . . . Freeing either a tiger or a mouse in a schoolroom is an illegal act, but no rational person

---

[20] *Coolidge,* 449.

would suggest that these two acts should be punished in the same way . . . I submit that society has at least as much right to expect rationally graded responses from judges in place of the universal "capital punishment" we inflict on all evidence when police error is shown in its acquisition.[21]

It is now time to close. We have seen the events that led to the American Revolution and the ultimate passage of the Fourth Amendment. To the names of the men who played a part—James Otis, John Wilkes, Judge Charles Pratt, James Madison—we have added the name of Egbert Benson. It is time he was given proper recognition. An exclusionary rule without a warrant requirement would be of no consequence and, but for Benson, the subversion of the Fourth Amendment could never have come to pass. As proposed by James Madison and approved by the House of Representatives, it would have been impossible for even the most creative of judges to infer a warrant requirement from its text.

A study of the language of the Fourth Amendment and the history that led to its adoption makes clear that it was searches and seizures made on the authority of overly broad and unattested warrants that were the concern of the Framers. They chose to meet the danger posed by such "general warrants" by making them void and unconstitutional. Henceforward, the executor of a warrant quashed as unconstitutional would have the same accountability as an officer who acted without a warrant at all. He would be acting at his peril. If the facts that officer thought constituted probable cause proved false, he could be personally liable to those whose privacy he had invaded. And this was the way it was for almost 125 years.

It was not until 1914 . . . that the Court in *Weeks v. United States*, 232 U.S. 383, stated that the Fourth Amendment itself barred the admission of evidence seized in violation of the Fourth Amendment. The *Weeks* opinion made no express confession of a break with the past. But if it was merely a proper reading of the

---

[21] *Bivins*, 418-419.

Fourth Amendment, it seems strange that it took this Court nearly 125 years to discover the true meaning of those words. The truth is that the source of the exclusionary rule simply cannot be found in the Fourth Amendment. That Amendment did not when adopted, and does not now, contain any constitutional rule barring the admission of illegally seized evidence.[22]

It was retired Justice Potter Stewart who took us down the Fourth Amendment road for these 125 years. And along the way we met only a couple of plate glass smugglers named Boyd and New York's "King of Policy" Albert Adams. So if there were, as Justice Brennan assured us, "values embraced by the Framers and cherished throughout our Nation's history," deference to which require that murderers like Edward Coolidge and Darryl James go free, they did not manifest themselves prior to 1914. It was the *Weeks* case that changed everything.

If anyone can be called the "father of the exclusionary rule," it is Felix Frankfurter. Paternity to the warrant requirement can be imputed to him as well. And it is his role in the formulation of our Fourth Amendment jurisprudence which is the nexus of this tale. To Frankfurter, *Weeks v. United States* was not just a case in the United States Reports; it was the watershed of his life. The note Winfred Denison left for him at the House of Truth might as well be appended. "Dear Felix—What can I say to you . . . You were there at the crossing of my Rubicon . . . Faithfully yours. W."

The exclusionary rule *Mapp v. Ohio* applied to the states, stripped to its bare essentials, rests on two cases—*Weeks v. United States* and *Johnson v. United States*. As *Weeks* was a clandestine case connived to protect labor union bombers—the Dynamiters—*Johnson* was a decision made to protect Communists, the term "Bolsheviks" having fallen out of use. FF played the lead in both.

The doctrinal basis for today's warrant requirement, *Johnson* (1948), must be considered in conjunction with *Harris v. United States* (1947), the case it superseded. In *Harris* Justice Frankfurter

---

[22] *Coolidge v. New Hampshire*, 403 U.S. 443, 497 (1971). Black J., dissenting.

attached to his dissenting opinion an exhibit entitled "Analysis of Decisions involving Searches and Seizures, from *Weeks v. United States*, 232 U.S. 383, up to *Davis v. United States*, 328 U.S. 582." This fold-out appendix—now 331 U.S. 175-181—is a nutshell history of the exclusionary rule from its birth in 1914 to post-World War II America.

Reading it, one is amazed at the inordinate degree to which our Fourth Amendment jurisprudence rests on cases arising out of bolshevism and booze. Of the 23 search and seizure cases following *Weeks, Schenck*, and *Silverthorne*, we have seen that one—*Gouled v. United States*—bears all the indicia of a setup brought for the benefit of embattled Bolsheviks caught in the Red Scare. Another, *Burdeau v. McDowell*,[23] may be placed in the same genre. *Agnello v. United States*, the 11th case on the list, we have postulated was a vehicle engineered to permit the Coolidge administration to finesse the political problems posed by Prohibition. Of the remaining 20, 19 were Prohibition cases or involved liquor in one way or another, clearly demonstrating that the beneficiaries of the *Weeks* rule, while it applied to the federal government alone, were bombers, bolsheviks, and bootleggers as opposed to robbers, rapists, and murderers.

It was soon after *Johnson* was decided that the ACLU began their campaign to apply the *Weeks* rule and its warrant corollary to the states. To his credit, FF fended them off for a dozen years. But on that June day of 1961 when the ACLU finally prevailed in *Mapp v. Ohio*, Frankfurter stood mute. Henceforward, he no doubt realized, the beneficiary of the rules of which he was the principal architect would be the violent criminal. And that, of course, is the way it turned out.

It was one thing when the exclusionary rule was applied solely to federal criminal cases. State crime, however, is a completely

---

[23] *Burdeau v. McDowell*, 256 U.S. 465 (1921) appears to have been a fraud that failed. *Silverthorne* gave a Red facing deportation an excuse to object to documentary evidence of Communist Party membership obtained pursuant to legal process such as a warrant or subpoena. *Gouled* covered the situation where an agent of the government obtained such evidence by "espionage." *Burdeau v. McDowell*, had it been successful, would have interdicted the only remaining avenue by which the names of individual Reds might have been obtained. It was a case in which a private citizen, acting on his own, obtained incriminating papers which he later turned over to federal authorities. Like *Silverthorne* and *Gouled*, *Burdeau* was a case which arose in the Second Circuit over which Circuit Justice Brandeis presided.

different matter. Thus, as then Associate Justice Rehnquist observed in *Minjares v. California*, by applying the *Weeks* rule to the states, "*Mapp v. Ohio* brought to bear in favor of accused murderers and armed robbers a rule which had previously largely had an application to bootleggers and purveyors of stolen[24] lottery tickets through the mail." "The societal reaction," observed Rehnquist, "could be expected to be quite different today, when *Weeks* serves to free the perpetrators of crimes affecting life and property, crimes which have traditionally been the principal responsibility of the states to enforce and administer."[25]

The beneficiaries of the exclusionary rule today are not just accused murderers and armed robbers, to paraphrase our Chief Justice, but accused murderers and armed robbers whose right of privacy—in any real sense—has not been invaded at all. Had Americans received the legal representation to which they were entitled, and *Johnson v. United States* properly briefed and argued, *Harris v. United States*, the case it superseded, would be the law:

> This Court has also pointed out that it is only unreasonable searches and seizures which come within the constitutional interdict. The test of reasonableness cannot be stated in rigid and absolute terms. "Each case is to be decided on its own facts and circumstances."
>
> The Fourth Amendment has never been held to require that every valid search and seizure be effected under the authority of a search warrant.[26]

If "reasonableness" in "each case" was to be "decided on its own facts and circumstances," which of the cases we have seen would fail the test? The search of the car of Edward Coolidge, for example, would not be *unreasonable* in the minds of reasonable people, and one would doubt that you could impanel a jury which would think

---

[24] 443 U.S. 927 (1979). There is nothing in the briefs or transcript in the *Weeks* case to indicate that the lottery tickets purveyed were purloined. One can only conclude from this remark that neither of our last two Chief Justices have read them.

[25] 443 U.S. 920, 921.

[26] *Harris*, 331 U.S. 150 (1947) [citation omitted].

Mincey or Hicks the victim of an *unreasonable* search or seizure. Were the right of privacy to be vindicated by the civil suit, as the Framers had originally intended, the gravity of the intrusion would be weighed on the one hand against the exigencies of law enforcement on the other.

And when the verdicts came down, justice would be done; jurors weigh facts and circumstances even if certain judges do not. The vacuuming of an empty car or the moving of a stereo a few inches, if an invasion of privacy at all, is one which the law in any other context would dismiss as *de minimis non curat lex*.[27] It is not to be equated with the abuse and humiliation Bivens suffered at the hands of his tormentors. There is not a jury who would see it otherwise.

Neither Coolidge nor Hicks could get two cents from a jury were they to seek civil damages, but they and their ilk get their convictions for murder and robbery reversed by judges with great regularity. If this means that they go free to prey upon the law-abiding, so be it. After all, to quote Justice Scalia, "there is nothing new in the realization that the Constitution sometimes insulates the criminality of a few in order to protect the privacy of us all."[28]

But what evidence is there that the exclusionary rule is an effective deterrent—or any deterrent at all—to police misconduct? The reason why the majority in *James* reversed his conviction was because they thought that the "expansion of the current impeachment exception would significantly weaken the exclusionary rule's deterrent effect on police misconduct."[29] No authorities were cited for this proposition and one would have to conclude, as did the dissenters, that this was nothing more than "pure speculation."[30] In 1976 former Chief Justice Warren Burger scorned it as "sophisticated nonsense."

> Despite its avowed deterrent objective, proof is lacking
> that the exclusionary rule, a purely judge-created device

---

[27] *De minimis non curat lex.* The law does not care for, or take notice of, very small or trifling matters. *Black's Law Dictionary.*
[28] *Hicks,* 329.
[29] *James,* 317.
[30] Ibid., 329, footnote 3.

based on "hard cases," serves the purpose of deterrence. Notwithstanding Herculean efforts, no empirical study has been able to demonstrate that the rule does in fact have any deterrent effect . . . To vindicate the continued existence of this judge-made rule, it is incumbent upon those who seek its retention . . . to demonstrate that it serves its declared deterrent purpose and to show that the results outweigh the rule's heavy costs to rational enforcement of the criminal law . . . The burden rightly rests upon those who ask society to ignore trustworthy evidence of guilt, at the expense of setting obviously guilty criminals free to ply their trade. In my view, it is an abdication of judicial responsibility to exact such exorbitant costs from society purely on the basis of speculative and unsubstantiated assumptions.[31]

But assuming for the sake of argument that the exclusionary rule is efficacious, what sort of police misconduct does it deter? Obviously the rule will have no effect on officers acting under a mistake of fact or identity. Like the search in *Bivins*, such searches are invariably fruitless anyway. Nor does the rule seem to inhibit searches which are unreasonable because excessive force was used. The federal agents responsible for the 1992 outrage at Ruby Ridge, Idaho, for example, were not daunted by the *Weeks* rule, and the evidence about which they are now most concerned is evidence which might be used against them.[32]

Almost every case in which the exclusionary rule is invoked involves a search which, if judged by the circumstances which attend it, would satisfy the Fourth Amendment's standard of reasonableness. When a search is held to be unlawful, it is invariably held to be unlawful, not because probable cause was lacking, but because the search was not made pursuant to a warrant. In 1976 Justice Byron White spoke to this point in a dissenting opinion:

Whether I would have joined the Court's opinion in *Mapp v. Ohio, supra,* had I then been a Member of the Court, I do not know. But as time went on after coming

---

[31] *Stone v. Powell,* 428 U.S. 499-500, *supra.*
[32] See *Harris v. Roderick, Horiuchi et al,* 126 F. 3d 1189 (9 Circuit 1997).

to this bench, I became convinced that both *Weeks v. United States*, 232 U.S. 383 (1914), and *Mapp v. Ohio* had overshot their mark insofar as they aimed to deter lawless action by law enforcement personnel and that in many of its applications the exclusionary rule was not advancing that aim in the slightest, and that in this respect it was a senseless obstacle to arriving at the truth in many criminal trials.[33]

White noted that in virtually all cases which come before the Court the problem is the warrant requirement despite the fact that "warrantless arrests on probable cause are not forbidden by the Constitution or by state law."

[F]or it is painfully apparent that in each of them the officer is acting as a reasonable officer would and should act in similar circumstances. Excluding the evidence can in no way affect his future conduct unless it is to make him less willing to do his duty . . . Surely when this Court divides five to four on issues of probable cause, it is not tenable to conclude that the officer was at fault or acted unreasonably in making the arrest.[34]

Whether an armed robber like Hicks goes to prison or back to the streets depends not on his guilt or innocence, but on whether the moving of a stereo set a few inches can be labeled a search. That the police officer would have to be a fool not to know that the set was stolen property is disregarded. In a footnote to his dissent, Justice Lewis Powell reduced the majority opinion to its ultimate absurdity.

Numerous articles that frequently are stolen have identifying numbers, including expensive watches and cameras, and also credit cards. Assume for example that an officer reasonably suspects that two identical watches, both in plain view, have been stolen. Under the Court's decision, if one watch is lying face up and the other lying

---

[33] *Stone v. Powell*, 537-538, *supra.*
[34] Ibid., 539-540.

face down, reading the serial number on one of the
watches would not be a search. But turning over the
other watch to read its serial number would be a search.
Moreover, the officer's ability to read a serial number
may depend on its location in a room and light
conditions at a particular time. Would there be a
constitutional difference if an officer, on the basis of a
reasonable suspicion, used a pocket flashlight or turned
on a light to read a number rather than moving the object
to a point where a serial number was clearly visible?[35]

This shows to what level the warrant requirement has reduced
constitutional dialectic. The facts and circumstances which go into
the calculus of what is *unreasonable* and what is not, are never
weighed. A diary or a dishpan or a bloody leotard stand on the same
footing. An intrusion is an intrusion whether an officer moves a
stolen stereo a few inches or breaks down the front door with an axe.
A search is a search, a seizure a seizure, and a crime a crime; all are
equal in the eyes of the law. Reason is bereft.

The results of the exclusionary rule might be mitigated if it
could be shown that the rule actually did deter police misconduct.
This, however, is not the case. As Chief Justice Burger stated, "No
empirical study has been able to demonstrate that the rule does in
fact have any deterrent effect." And bear in mind that for every
James, Coolidge, or *Hicks* there are a thousand murderers and armed
robbers who escape justice by virtue of decisions of state courts
following, as follow they must, the precedents of *Weeks* and *Johnson.*
And we must not forget the most numerous class of all—the guilty
who simply "walk" when it becomes apparent to exasperated police
officers that the evidence they have and need for a successful
prosecution inevitably will be suppressed.

If the *Weeks* rule does not deter and is not compelled by the
language of the Fourth Amendment and the history that led to its
adoption, why do not its proponents either rebut these arguments
or accept them? But reason, it seems, has nothing to do with it; the
exclusionary rule has a political constituency of its own.

---

[35] *Arizona v. Hicks, supra,* 333.

There is a school of thought in this country which misses no opportunity to decry our historic legal process. The belief that a criminal trial ought to be a search for the truth is anathema to them. A crime which is committed bespeaks to this group the culpability of society rather than that of the perpetrator, whose personal guilt they find of little interest. These people wage an incessant campaign to make it as difficult as possible to try, convict, and punish criminals; the idea that this country should have a fair and effective system of criminal justice which will convict the guilty and free the innocent must never be permitted to prevail.

This school of thought and its advocates may with justice be called the *Amicus Criminalis*, the Friend of the Criminal. In the area of public opinion and politics, the constituencies which by virtue of a common bond make up their number are represented by a plethora of groups and organizations. But when it comes to criminal justice, they speak through the mouth of the American Civil Liberties Union.

Essential to the propaganda of the ACLU is the canard that if the criminal goes free, it is only because the Constitution commands that he go free. This permits ACLU supporters to evade accountability for the crimes committed by criminals who thereby go unpunished and by those of similar bent who are no longer deterred. By feigning to find in the Fourth Amendment an exclusionary rule and warrant requirement that are not there, they appropriate the imprimatur of the Founding Fathers to use as a shield against their critics. This, you will remember, was the posture counseled by their founding father, Roger Baldwin:

> We want to also look like patriots in everything we do. We want to get a lot of good flags, talk a good deal about the constitution, and what our forefathers wanted to make of this country, and to show that we are the folks that really stand for the spirit of our institution.[36]

---

[36] Letter from Roger Baldwin to Louis Lochner, August 21, 1917, Lusk Report, *supra*.

By wrapping themselves in the flag and the Constitution the *Amicus Criminalis* wash their hands of the inevitable consequence of their decisions—the explosion in the rate of crime—laying it at the feet of the Framers. Yes, a murderer like Edward Coolidge goes free, they pontificate, but it is the Constitution that sets him free. That is the price the Framers were willing to pay to protect our privacy; who are we to set their command at naught?

The *Amicus Criminalis* would have you believe that it is only the exclusionary rule which keeps overzealous law enforcement officers at bay. But if this were true, why did not such a rule evolve out of genuine cases or controversies involving searches or seizures made by some of the "ham-fisted detectives" or "Keystone Cops" they like to talk about? That it was necessary to collude *Weeks* and *Mapp* to establish the exclusionary rule and apply it to the states is, in itself, a back-handed tribute to the officers, both federal and state, who have enforced the law in this country. What it bespeaks of our judiciary and the legal profession is quite the opposite.

In 1911, the same year as the *Weeks* case began, a fossil was discovered near Piltdown, England, with a human cranium underslung by the jawbone of an ape. The "Piltdown Man," or the "missing link," as it was popularly known, was the subject of much scientific writing. When it was exposed as a hoax in 1953, there was many an anthropologist whose reputation was ruined. *Weeks v. United States* was the most successful hoax ever foisted on a civilized society. More nonsense has been written about *Weeks* than was written about the Piltdown Man by a thousand fold. The stacks in the nation's law libraries sag with the weight of apologia penned by "scholars" whose ignorance of history is exceeded only by their pomposity.

The hard truth is that the Supreme Court created the exclusionary rule and has applied it for more than 85 years without ever hearing argument against it. In *Mapp v. Ohio* not one word was said or written in opposition to the application of the Fourth Amendment and the *Weeks* rule to the states. The last time and the only time those who oppose the exclusionary rule had their day in Court was when they were represented by Winfred Denison in 1913. His 66 word brief stands today as the sum total of the argument made against the exclusionary rule before the Supreme Court of the United States.

One wonders what sort of reaction might be expected when it becomes public knowledge that *Weeks* was a fraud perpetrated on the Court by intriguers whose number included three men who later, as sitting Justices of the Supreme Court, applied and extended its rule. What will be the visceral reaction of law-abiding Americans when they learn that the vicious criminals that *Weeks* now serves to free, go free only because of another sham called *Mapp v. Ohio*? And what will be the reaction of the Court itself when it finds out it has been swindled?

The law of *Weeks* and *Mapp* is without legitimacy; it is the law only in the sense that the coercive power of the national government stands behind it. A monstrous wrong has been done and the Court must set it right. And while the judiciary is putting its house in order, the other two branches of government had better devise a system of checks and balances more suited to accommodate the self-appointed fourth. The exclusionary rule, they will find out, is not the only fraud which has been perpetrated on the Court and the American people. Through "manipulated test cases" our fourth branch of government has planted the poisoned precedents responsible for the crime-ridden society we have today.

SELECTED BIBLIOGRAPHY

MANUSCRIPT COLLECTIONS

American Civil Liberties Union. Papers. Seeley G. Mudd Manuscript Library, Princeton University, Princeton, New Jersey.

American Civil Liberties Union, "FBI Documents About ACLU," American Civil Liberties Union, 132 West 43rd Street, New York, New York.

Baldwin, Roger Nash. Papers. Seeley G. Mudd Manuscript Library, Princeton University, Princeton, New Jersey.

Brandeis, Louis Dembetz. Papers. University of Louisville, Louisville, Kentucky.

Coolidge, Calvin. Papers. Library of Congress.

Donovan, William J. Papers. U.S. Army Military History Institute, Carlisle Barracks, Pennsylvania.

Drew, Walter. Papers. Bentley Historical Library, University of Michigan, Ann Arbor, Michigan.

Frankfurter, Felix. Papers. Library of Congress, Washington, D.C.

Gregory, Thomas Watt. Papers. Library of Congress, Washington, D.C.

House, Edward M. Diary. Yale University Library, New Haven, Connecticut.

O'Brian, John Lord. Papers. Charles B. Sears Law Library, University at Buffalo, State University of New York, Buffalo, New York.

Stimson, Henry Lewis. Papers. Yale University Library, New Haven, Connecticut.

Taft, William Howard. Papers. Library of Congress, Washington, D.C.

Wilson, Woodrow. Papers. Library of Congress, Washington, D.C.

ORAL HISTORIES

Baldwin, Roger Nash. Recollections of a Life in Civil Liberties, 1972, Columbia University, New York, New York.

O'Brian, John Lord. The Reminiscences of John Lord O'Brian, 1953, Columbia University, New York, New York.

U.S. GOVERNMENT SERVICES

Congressional Quarterly's *Guide to Congress*, 4th Ed.

Congressional Record: Hearings before the Committee on the Judiciary (Special Subcommittee No. 7) Sixty Second Congress, Second Session, on H. Res. 488, April 22, 1912, LESLIE J. LYONS JK 1519 l 8A - 5 1912.

Congressional Record: Hearings, Senate Committee on the Judiciary on the Nomination of Louis D. Brandeis to be an Associate Justice of the United States Supreme Court, Senate Doc. No. 409, Sixty Fourth Congress, Second Session, 1916.

Congressional Record: Attorney General A. Mitchell Palmer On Charges Made Against Department of Justice by Louis F. Post and Others. Hearings Before The Committee on Rules, House of Representatives, Sixty Sixth Congress, Second Session, 1920.

Congressional Record: Hearings before a subcommittee of the Judiciary on the Nomination of Felix Frankfurter to be an Associate Justice of the United States Supreme Court, First Session, 1939.

General File of the Counsel General, 1918-1937; U.S. Railway Administration, Record Group 14, National Archives, Washington, D.C.

General Records of the Department of Justice, Record Group 60, National Archives, Washington, D.C.

Records of the District Court of the States, National Archives—
Northeast Region—Bayonne, New Jersey, in re:
United States v. Boyd SDNY 1884
United States v. Silverthorne WDNY 1919
United States v. Agnello EDNY 1922

SELECTED BOOKS AND ARTICLES

Abraham, Henry J. *Justices and Presidents*. New York: Oxford University Press, 1974.

Acheson, Dean. *Morning and Noon*. Boston: Houghton Mifflin Company, 1965.

American Civil Liberties Union. Annual Reports 1920-1969, 7 Vols. New York: Arno Press & The New York Times, 1970.

American Civil Liberties Union and Communist Activity. Law and Labor, February 1931.

Archer, Jules. *Strikes, Bombs & Bullets: Big Bill Haywood and the IWW*. New York: Simon & Schuster, 1972.

Avrich, Paul. *The Haymarket Tragedy*. Princeton: Princeton University Press, 1984.

Baker, Leonard. *Brandeis and Frankfurter: A Dual Biography*. New York: Harper & Row, 1984.

Baker, Liva. *Felix Frankfurter*. New York: Coward-McCann Inc., 1969.

Baldwin, Roger N. *Freedom in the U.S.A. and the U.S.S.R.* Soviet Russia Today, September 1934.

Baldwin, Sara Mullin. *Who's Who in Kansas City 1930*. Hebron, Nebraska: Robert M. Baldwin Corporation, 1931.

Blair, Paxton. *Federal Appellate Procedure as Affected by the Act of February 13, 1925.* 25 Columbia Law Review 393 (1925).

Boot, Max. *Out of Order.* New York: Basic Books, 1998.

Bunn, Charles W. *Review in the Supreme Court of the United States of the District Court and Circuit Court of Appeals.* 35 Harvard Law Review 902 (1922).

Burt, Robert A. *Two Jewish Justices: Outcasts in the Promised Land.* Los Angeles: University of California Press, 1988.

Cave-Brown, Anthony. *The Last Hero: Wild Bill Donovan.* New York: Times Books/Random House, 1982.

Coben, Stanley. *A. Mitchell Palmer: Politician.* New York: Columbia University Press, 1963.

Coffey, Thomas M. *The Long Thirst—Prohibition in America: 1920-1933.* New York: W.W. Norton & Company, Inc., 1975.

Conlin, Joseph R. *Big Bill Haywood and the Radical Union Movement.* Syracuse, New York: Syracuse University Press, 1969.

Cooke, Alisair. *The Vintage Mencken.* New York: Vintage Books, 1955.

Cowan, Geoffrey. *The People v. Clarence Darrow: The Bribery Trial of America's Greatest Lawyer.* New York: Times Books/Random House, 1993.

Craig, Gordon A. *Germany 1866-1945.* New York: Oxford University Press, 1978.

Dawson, Nelson L. *Louis D. Brandeis, Felix Frankfurter and the New Deal.* New York: Archon Books, 1980.

Debates and Proceedings in the Congress of the United States, Vol. 1. Washington, D.C.: Gales and Seaton, 1834.

Donahue, William A. *The Politics of the American Civil Liberties Union*. New Brunswick, New Jersey: Transaction Books, 1985.

Fairman, Charles, and Stanley Morrison, *Does the Fourteenth Amendment Incorporate the Bill of Rights?* 2 Stanford Law Review 5-173 (1949).

Fine, Ralph Adam. *Escape of the Guilty*. New York: Dodd, Mead & Company, 1986.

Flynn, Elizabeth Gurley. *The Rebel Girl: An Autobiography*. New York: International Publishers, 1973.

Fraenkel, Osmond K. *Concerning Searches and Seizures*. 34 Harvard Law Review 361 (1920).

Friendly, Fred, and Martha J.H. Elliott, *The Constitution: That Delicate Balance*. New York: Random House, 1984.

Green, Martin. *The Mount Vernon Street Warrens: A Boston Story 1860-1910*. New York: Charles Scribner's Sons, 1989.

Grover, David H. *Debaters and Dynamiters: The Story of the Haywood Trial*. Corvallis, Oregon: Oregon State University Press, 1964.

Harbaugh, William H. *Lawyer's Lawyer: The Life of John W. Davis*. New York: Oxford University Press, 1973.

Heckscher, August. *Woodrow Wilson*. New York: Charles Scribner's Sons, 1991.

Hirsch, H.N. *The Enigma of Felix Frankfurter*. New York: Basic Books, 1981.

Johnpoll, Bernard K., and Harvey Klehr, *Biographical Dictionary of the American Left*. Westport, Connecticut: Greenwood Press, 1986.

Johnson, Donald. *The Challenge to American Freedoms: World War I and the Rise of the American Civil Liberties Union*. Lexington, Kentucky: University of Kentucky Press, 1963.

Kobler, John. *Ardent Spirits, The Rise and Fall of Prohibition*. New York: G.P. Putnam's Sons, 1973.

Lamson, Peggy. *Roger Baldwin—Founder of the American Civil Liberties Union—A Portrait*. Boston: Houghton Mifflin, 1976.

Lash, Joseph P. editor. *From the Diaries of Felix Frankfurter*. New York: W.W. Norton, 1975.

Lasson, Nelson B. *The History and Development of the Fourth Amendment to the United States Constitution*. Baltimore: Johns Hopkins Press, 1937.

Lazarus, Edward. *Closed Chambers*. New York: Times Book/Random House, 1998.

Levy, David, and Bruce Allen Murphy, *Preserving the Progressive Spirit in a Conservative Time, The Joint Reform Efforts of Justice Brandeis and Professor Felix Frankfurter 1916-1933*. 78 Michigan Law Review 1252 (1986).

Liddell-Hart, Basil H. *Strategy*. New York: Frederich A. Praeger, 1954.

Lief, Alfred. *Brandeis, The Personal History of an American Ideal*. New York: Stackpole Sons, 1936.

Link, Arthur. *Wilson*. Princeton: Princeton University Press, 1947.

Link, Arthur. *Wilson, The New Freedom*. Princeton, New Jersey: Princeton University Press, 1956.

Link, Arthur, ed. *The Papers of Woodrow Wilson*. Princeton, New Jersey: Princeton University Press, 1978-1979.

Lord, Walter. *The Good Years: From 1900 to the First World War*. New York: Harper & Brothers, 1960.

Lusk, Clayton R. [chairman]. Vol. I *Revolutionary Radicalism: Report of the Joint Legislative Committee Investigating Seditious Activities*, filed April 24, 1920, in the Senate of the State of New York. Albany, New York: J.B. Lyon Company, Printers, 1920.

Magill, Frank N. editor. *The American Presidents: The Office and the Men*. Englewood Cliffs, New Jersey: Salem Press, 1986.

Mason, Alpheus Thomas. *Brandeis, A Free Man's Life*. New York: Viking Press, 1946.

Mason, Alpheus Thomas. *William Howard Taft: Chief Justice*. New York: Simon and Schuster, 1965.

McCoy, Donald R., *Calvin Coolidge: The Quiet President*. New York: MacMillan, 1967.

Murphy, Bruce Allen. *The Brandeis/Frankfurter Connection: The Secret Political Activities of Two Supreme Court Justices*. Garden City, New York: Anchor Press/Doubleday & Company, 1983.

Murray, Robert K. *Red Scare: A Study in National Hysteria 1919-1920*. Minneapolis: University of Minnesota Press, 1955.

National Popular Government League. *Report Upon the Illegal Practices of the United States Department of Justices*. Washington, D.C.: National Popular Government League, 1920.

Nicolson, Nigel editor. *Harold Nicholson: The Later Years 1945-1962*. New York: Athenaeum, 1968.

Nicolson, Nigel editor. *Vita and Harold, The Letters of Vita Sackville-West and Harold Nicolson*. New York: G.P. Putnam's Sons, 1992.

Parrish, Michael E. *Felix Frankfurter and His Times: The Reform Years*. New York: The Free Press, 1982.

Payne, Philip M. *The Abolition of Writs of Error in the Federal Courts*. 15 Virginia Law Review 305, 1929.

Percy, Eustace. *Some Memories*. London: Eyre & Spottiswoode, 1958.

Perrett, Geoffrey. *America in the Twenties: A History*. New York: Simon and Schuster, 1982.

Phillips, Harlan B., editor. *Felix Frankfurter Reminisces*. New York: Reynal and Company, 1961.

Pound, Roscoe, and Felix Frankfurter, *Criminal Justice in Cleveland*. Cleveland, Ohio: The Cleveland Foundation, 1922.

Rand School of Social Science. *The Case of the Rand School*. New York: Rand School of Social Science, 1919.

Roosevelt, James. *Affectionately, F.D.R.: A Son's Story of a Lonely Man*. New York: Harcourt, Brace & Company, 1959.

Rothwax, Harold J. *Guilty: The Collapse of Criminal Justice*. New York: Random House, 1996.

Russell, Francis. *The Shadow of Blooming Grove: Warren G. Harding in His Times*. New York: McGraw Hill, 1968.

Schlesinger, Arthur M., Jr. *History of U.S. Political Parties*. New York: Chelsea House Publishers, 1973.

Swartz, Bernard. *Super Chief, Earl Warren and His Supreme Court—A Judicial Biography*. New York: New York University Press, 1983.

Simon, James F. *The Antagonists; Hugo Black, Felix Frankfurter and Civil Liberties in Modern America*. New York: Simon & Schuster, 1989.

Smith, Gene. *Until The Last Trumpet Sounds: The Life of General of the Armies John J. Pershing*. New York: John Wiley & Sons, Inc., 1998.

Stewart, Potter. *The Road to Mapp v. Ohio and Beyond: The Origins, Development and Future of the Exclusionary Rule in Search and Seizure Cases*. 83 Columbia Law Review 1365 (1983).

Stimson, Grace Heilman. *Rise of the Labor Movement in Los Angeles*. Los Angeles: University of California Press, 1955.

Stimson, Henry Lewis. *Memorial of Winfred T. Denison*. 191 New York City Bar 180.

Strum, Philippa. *Louis D. Brandeis: Justice for the People*. New York: Schocken Books, 1984.

Sullivan, Mark. Vol. VI *Our Times; The United States, 1900-1925*. New York: Charles Scribner's Sons, 1935.

Swisher, Carl Brent. *American Constitutional Development*. Boston: Houghton Mifflin, 1943.

Taft, William Howard. *The Jurisdiction of the Supreme Court under the Act of February 13, 1925*. 35 Yale Law Journal (1925).

Toland, John. *No Man's Land: 1918, The Last Year of the Great War*. Garden City, New York: Doubleday & Company, 1980.

Tudor, William. *The Life of James Otis of Massachusetts.* Originally published in 1823, this book was republished in 1970 by DaCapo Press of New York City.

Urofsky, Melvin I., and David W. Levy, editors. *Letters of Louis D. Brandeis*, 5 vols. Albany, New York: State University of New York Press, 1971-1978.

Urofsky, Melvin I., and David W. Levy, editors. *"Half Brother, Half Son": The Letters of Louis D. Brandeis to Felix Frankfurter.* Norman, Oklahoma: University of Oklahoma Press, 1991.

Vexler, R.V., and H.F. Bremer, editors. *Woodrow Wilson 1856-1924, Chronology-Documents-Bibliographic Aids.* Dobbs Ferry, New York: Oceana Publications, Incorporated, 1969.

Walker, Samuel. *In Defense of American Liberties: A History of the ACLU.* New York: Oxford University Press, 1990.

Weinstein, Allen. *Perjury: The Hiss-Chambers Case.* New York: Alfred A. Knopf, 1978.

Weyl, Nathaniel. *The Battle Against Disloyalty.* New York: Thomas Y. Crowell Company, 1951.

Whitney, Carrie Westlake. *Vol. III, Kansas City, Missouri, Its History and its People 1800-1908.* Kansas City: S.J. Clark Publishing Company, 1908.

Woodward, Bob, and Scott Armstrong, *The Brethren: Inside the Supreme Court.* New York: Simon & Schuster, 1979.

Wood, John E.F. *The Scope of the Constitutional Immunity Against Searches and Seizures,* 34 West Virginia Quarterly 137, 138 (1928).

NEWSPAPERS AND PERIODICALS

Boston Globe
Boston Journal
Buffalo Courier
Buffalo Express
Chicago Tribune
Cleveland Plain Dealer
Cleveland Press
Cleveland Press-News
Harper's Weekly
Harvard Lampoon
Indianapolis News
Indianapolis Star
Kansas City Journal
Kansas City Star
Kansas City Times
Labor Defender, The
La Follette's Weekly Magazine
Los Angeles Times
Louisville Courier Journal
Macabees, The
Minneapolis Journal
New York Herald
New York Times
Outlook, The
St. Louis Republic
Soviet Russia Today
Survey, The
Washington Post
Zionist Review

TABLE OF CASES

James v. Illinois, 493 U.S. 307 (1990)

Johnson v. United States, 333 U.S. 10 (1948)

Kaufman v. United States, 394 U.S. 217 (1969)

Linkletter v. Walker, 381 U.S. 618 (1965)

Lord v. Veazie, 49 U.S. 251 (1850)

Mapp v. Ohio, 367 U.S. 643 (1961)

Massachusetts v. Sheppard, 468 U.S. 981 (1984)

Maxwell v. Dow, 176 U.S. 581 (1900)

McBride v. United States, 284 F. 416 (1922)

Mincey v. Arizona, 437 U.S. 385 (1978)

Nardone v. United States, 308 U.S. 438 (1939)

Ohio ex rel Eaton v. Price, 360 U.S. 246 (1959)

Ohio ex rel Eaton v. Price, 364 U.S. 263 (1960)

Olmstead v. United States, 277 U.S. 338 (1928)

People v. Adams, 85 A.D. 390 83 N.Y.S. 481 (1903)

People v. Adams, 176 N.Y. 351, 68 N.E. 636 (1903)

People v. Cahan, 44 Cal. 2d 434, 282 P. 2d 905 (1955)

People v. Foster, 261 Mich., 247, 246 N.W. 60 (1933)

People v. Rochin, 101 Cal. 2d 140, 225 P. 2d 1 (1951)

Roach v. Johnson, 48 F. Supp. 833 (1943)

Robbins v. California, 453 U.S. 420 (1981)

Rochin v. California, 342 U.S. 165 (1952)

People v. Ruthenberg, 229 Mich. 315, 201 N.W. 358 (1924)

Ryan v. United States, 216 F. 13 (7th Cir. 1914)

Schenck v. United States, 249 U.S. 47 (1919)

Scopes v. State, 154 Tenn. 105, 289 S.W. 363 (1927)

Sheppard v. Massachusetts, 468 U.S. 981 (1984)

Silverthorne Lumber Co. v. United States, 251 U.S. 385 (1920)

Simmons v. United States, 390 U.S. 377 (1968)

Skeffington v. Katzeff, 277 F. 129 (1st Cir. 1922)

Spies v. Illinois, 122 Ill. 1, 12 N.E. 865 (1887)

Spies v. Illinois, 123 U.S. 131 (1887)

Smith v. California, 361 U.S. 147 (1959)

Smith v. Maryland, 59 U.S. 71 (1855)

State v. Lindway, 131 Ohio State 166, 2 N.E. 2d 490 (1936)

State v. Mapp, 170 Ohio St. 427, 166 N.E. 2d 387 (1960)

Stone v. Powell, 428 U.S. 465 (1976)

United States v. Boyd (Civil), 24 F. 690 (1885)
United States v. Boyd (Criminal), 24 F. 692 (1885)
United States v. Calandra, 414 U.S. 338 (1974)
United States v. Leon, 468 U.S. 897 (1984)
United States v. Johnson, 319 U.S. 302 (1943)
United States v. Silverthorne, 265 F. 859 (1920)
United States v. St. John, 254 F. 794 (1918)
Walder v. United States, 347 U.S. 62 (1954)
Weeks v. United States, 232 U.S. 383 (1914)
Wilkes v. Wood, 3 Geo. 3, 98 Eng. Rep. 489 (1763)
Wolf v. Colorado, 338 U.S. 25 (1949)

INDEX

A

Acheson, Dean, 124-126
Adams, Albert J., 144-147, 188, 260, 333, 401
Alexander, George, 3, 13
Altgeld, John Peter, 66-69
American Bridge Co., 1
American Central Life Building, 5-6
American Civil Liberties Union (ACLU)
  and *Colyer v. Skeffington*, 212
  and the FBI, 236-237
  and Felix Frankfurter, 269-270
  and *Frank v. Maryland*, 314-316, 354-355
  and *Irvine v. California*, 310
  and *Mapp v. Ohio*, 341-342, 344-346, 349, 350, 352, 359-360
  members of, 216, 349
  mission of, 289-294, 299, 304-306, 402
  and Prohibition, 258
  and *Rochin v. California*, 308
  and the *Weeks* rule, 300
  and *Wolf v. Colorado*, 300, 304
American Federation of Labor (AFL), 6-7, 15, 148, 217
Anderson, Albert B., 171
Anderson, George Weston, 86, 104-105, 151, 170-171, 212-216, 270

Andrews, Lincoln, 259
Anti-Saloon League, 57, 225-227, 239, 259
Atkins, Jesse C., 89, 98

B

Bagley, Arthur T., 41, 49
Bagley Report, 42-43, 51-52, 111
Baker, Frank, 10
Baker, Leonard, 103
Baker, Newton, 162, 166
Baker, Ray Stannard, 61
Baldwin, Roger N., 160-164
  and *Abrams v. United States*, 201-202, 205
  and American Civil Liberties Union, 289-294, 299, 408
  and City Club, 48
  and the FBI, 237-238
  and the IWW, 166-167, 169, 170, 176, 221
  and Workers Liberty Defense Union, 216
Balfour, Arthur, 197
Battle, George Gordon, 254, 258, 260-263
Benson, Egbert, 280-283, 285, 400
Berkman, Alexander, 204
Berkman, Bernard A., 343-345, 352
Bettman, Alfred, 163-165, 169
Bielaski, A. Bruce, 51-53, 112
Billings, Edmund, 86-87

427

C